Death in the New World

D0488102

EARLY AMERICAN STUDIES

SERIES EDITORS
Daniel K. Richter, Kathleen M. Brown, and
David Waldstreicher

Exploring neglected aspects of our colonial,
revolutionary, and early national history and culture,
Early American Studies reinterprets familiar themes
and events in fresh ways. Interdisciplinary in
character, and with a special emphasis on the period
from about 1600 to 1850, the series is published
in partnership with the McNeil Center for Early
American Studies.

A complete list of books in the series is available from
the publisher.

Death in the New World

Cross-Cultural Encounters, 1492–1800

Erik R. Seeman

PENN

UNIVERSITY OF PENNSYLVANIA PRESS

PHILADELPHIA

Copyright © 2010 University of Pennsylvania Press

All rights reserved. Except for brief quotations used for purposes of review or scholarly citation, none of this book may be reproduced in any form by any means without written permission from the publisher.

Published by
University of Pennsylvania Press
Philadelphia, Pennsylvania 19104-4112

Printed in the United States of America on acid-free paper

10 9 8 7 6 5 4 3 2 1

Library of Congress Cataloging-in-Publication Data

Seeman, Erik R.
   Death in the New World : cross-cultural encounters, 1492–1800 / Erik R. Seeman.
   p. cm. — (Early American studies)
   Includes bibliographical references and index.
   ISBN 978-0-8122-4229-4 (hbk. : alk. paper)
   1. Death—America—History. 2. Funeral rites and ceremonies—America—History. 3. Mourning customs—America—History. 4. Cross-cultural studies—America. 5. America—History—To 1810. I. title.
HQ1073.5.A45S44 2010
306.9097—dc22

2009043381

For Victoria,
with love

CONTENTS

ILLUSTRATIONS

Our ways of dying are our ways of living.
Or should I say our ways of living are our ways of dying?

—Toloki the Professional Mourner
Zakes Mda, *Ways of Dying* (1991)

Ways of Dying, Ways of Living

IMAGINE THAT YOU travel to a place you've never been before. Maybe it's not too far off the beaten track, like eastern Kentucky. Maybe it's a once-in-a-lifetime trip to Borneo. What is the first thing you want to know about the locals? For me, it's about food and drink. What do these people eat with friends after a hard day at work? What do they drink when they want to celebrate? For you, perhaps the first thing you want to learn about is their art, or their sports, or their music.

Five hundred years ago, most people would have simply asked, "How do they bury their dead?"

Today we have, with a few exceptions, lost this curiosity about outsiders' ways of dying, or *deathways*, a more expansive term I prefer that includes deathbed scenes, corpse preparation, burial practices, funerals, mourning, and commemoration. But for thousands of years, when people encountered an unfamiliar society they wanted to learn about the strangers' deathways. People recognized that an excellent technique for understanding a society's ways of living was to observe its ways of dying. Through deathways they discerned clues about how unfamiliar peoples conceptualized the afterlife and the supernatural, how they honored elites, what they considered to be the proper relations between parents and children, and many other crucial beliefs and practices.

Because all humans die, but all human societies practice varying deathways, observers of the unfamiliar oscillate between two kinds of reactions: the inclusive ("they're not so different after all") and the exclusive ("now that's strange"). Inclusive reactions embrace a universalistic perspective, recognizing that different societies are united in at least the broadest sense by the imperative to dispose of corpses in a meaningful way. By contrast, exclusive reactions are dismissive of or even hostile toward the different—and, to the observer, sometimes repulsive—practices of the outsiders.

Given what we know about European ethnocentrism in more recent times, it may be surprising that for centuries Western ethnographers and travel writers tended toward the inclusive in their observations of foreign deathways. In what is widely considered the first Western historical writing, the fifth-century B.C.E. *Histories* by Herodotus, the author almost always introduces non-Athenians with their deathways front and center. More than a dozen times in the *Histories*, Herodotus digresses from his narrative to tell the reader about the mortuary customs of peoples from Greece to the Balkans to the edge of the known world. Some of his descriptions provide useful bits of information (the Babylonians embalm their dead with honey). Others introduce practices one might expect to cause revulsion (the Issedonians beyond the Caspian Sea chop up a dead man, mix him with a variety of other meats, and enjoy the mixed grill at a "special meal"). But either way, Herodotus's tone is unruffled and nonjudgmental: inclusive, in the sense of including the foreigners in the medley of practices that defines a common humanity. The effect of the whole, as the historian Anthony Grafton puts it, "made plain that no civilization could claim universal validity."[1]

Likewise, *The Travels of Sir John Mandeville*, one of the most popular books in late medieval and early modern Europe, introduced readers to the (alleged) deathways of peoples across Europe, Asia, and Africa. "Mandeville" was not a real fourteenth-century knight; his words were penned by an unknown author who based his accounts on an amalgam of earlier travel writers, his own observations, and sheer fantasy. But for centuries readers enjoyed *The Travels* for what they took to be an authentic description of encounters with foreigners. In the spirit of Herodotus, Mandeville not only believed that deathways were the key to understanding unfamiliar societies; he also refrained from criticizing other peoples for their mortuary customs. The residents of the isle of Dondun, imagined to be somewhere in the Indian Ocean, were said to suffocate the dying to put them out their misery. Euthanasia accomplished, they feasted on the flesh of the dead. "All those that be of his kin or pretend them to be friends," wrote Mandeville, "and they come not to that feast, they be reproved for evermore and shamed, and make great dole, for never after shall they be holden as friends."[2] Not only did the author avoid negative comment on anthropophagy but he suggested to readers—or at least without comment passed along the suggestion—that those who skipped the cannibalistic feast were the ones deserving criticism.

Not all writers were as unprejudiced as Herodotus and Mandeville, who tended toward the inclusive in their descriptions of all foreign customs, not just deathways. Other European travelers—such as the thirteenth-century friar Johannes de Plano Carpini, who wrote of the "strange or rather miserable" deathways of non-Christians—were not so generous in their assessment of outsiders.[3] Some of the individuals who appear in this book, especially European missionaries, followed Carpini's lead and criticized unfamiliar deathways, an intellectual move that could lead to the belief that the outsiders were inferior in a variety of ways. But even those who had exclusive reactions were at the very least curious about the mortuary practices of those they encountered. If they were repulsed by outsiders' deathways, it was within the context of realizing that the others' ways of dying were central to their ways of living—and thus worth commenting on. They understood the shared humanity of foreigners who, at the bare minimum, also died just as they did and had to do something with corpses.

But what about non-European peoples? They will be central figures in this book, yet their attitudes toward foreign deathways cannot be deduced from the writings of Herodotus and Mandeville. Even though sub-Saharan Africans and North American Indians did not leave written records before the era of European colonization, there is ample archaeological and, later, ethnographic evidence of a similar curiosity about cross-cultural deathways. There are numerous examples of the diffusion of mortuary practices, suggesting mutual interest in deathways when different cultures interacted. For just one illustration of this, consider the Huron Indian Feast of the Dead. This was an Iroquoian ritual of secondary interment: the reburial of bones after they had been allowed to dry on scaffolds. Every decade or so, Hurons—who inhabited the area between Georgian Bay and Lake Simcoe in present-day Ontario—buried hundreds of individuals from many villages in a central ossuary. The Algonquian ancestors of the Ojibwa Indians of present-day Michigan, from an entirely different language and cultural group, were so impressed by the Huron Feast of the Dead that they incorporated the practice into their own culture in the second half of the seventeenth century.[4] The Algonquians must have observed the Feast with curiosity, asked questions about it, recognized the ways in which it was similar to and different from their own mortuary rituals, and then decided to incorporate the practice into their deathways.

Thus, residents of the early modern Atlantic world combined inclusivity and exclusivity—a recognition of similarity and difference—when they interacted with outsiders. They used perceived differences to mark boundaries between themselves and others, and they used perceived similarities to reach beyond those boundaries and communicate across cultures. Sometimes they employed both of these strategies simultaneously; in other contexts one reaction predominated over the other.

This, then, is the complex interplay between similarity and difference across cultures that lies beneath the deceptively simple query "How do they bury their dead?" The question recognizes—indeed depends upon—difference. If all societies observed identical mortuary customs the question would be moot; cultural practices must be different in order to inspire curiosity. But the question also presupposes similarity in two ways. First, interest in unfamiliar deathways assumes that members of other societies have enough respect for the dead and experience enough grief over the deaths of loved ones to generate an elaborate system of mortuary practices. The question is never "Do they bother to do anything with the dead?" Second, this curiosity presumes that unfamiliar practices will be similar enough to those of the observer as to be comprehensible. It would be unsatisfying to watch another society's rituals and have absolutely no idea what was going on. Deep parallels in deathways across cultures allow observers at least to think they understand the motivations behind burials, funeral processions, and memorial feasts.[5]

This intricate dance between perceptions of similarity and difference reached perhaps its greatest intensity in world history in the wake of Christopher Columbus. In the centuries following 1492, peoples from Europe, Africa, and the Americas came together in unprecedented ways and in extraordinary numbers, creating what historians now call the Atlantic world. Early modern peoples participated in a profusion of cross-cultural encounters and observed one another with a combination of curiosity and concern. Placing death at the center of an analysis of those encounters offers one great advantage: it allows us, better perhaps than any other conceptual category, to see the world as the participants themselves viewed it.

There are four reasons why death is virtually unmatched for understanding cross-cultural encounters in the New World. First and foremost, death was ubiquitous. The European project of imperial expansion inadvertently spread diseases and deliberately sowed violence. The virgin soil epidemics that devastated Indian populations, the appalling mortality of slaves during the Middle Passage and on New World plantations, the unfamiliar disease environments that decimated Europeans in the Chesapeake and West Indies, the warfare that raged in every corner of the New World: all of this made death an ever-present reality throughout the Americas.

Second, the religious systems of the groups involved in colonial encounters all centered on explaining death and the afterlife. Using a variety of approaches, Christianity, Judaism, and the many polytheistic religions of American Indians and sub-Saharan Africans all concerned themselves with helping believers understand the meaning of death. These religions offered answers to questions such as What happens to my soul or spirit after I die? What is the relationship between this world and the afterlife? How should I live so as to ensure that I will die well? Moreover, they all attempted to redirect toward spiritual ends the universal human emotions of apprehension regarding death and bereavement in response to the death of loved ones.

Third, because all religious systems shared this fundamental concern with death and the afterlife, when individuals met strangers, they were curious about the outsiders' deathways. People recognized the parallel religious interest in death, and they probed deeply to find exactly what the similarities and differences were. Moreover, literate observers offered written accounts of these practices for audiences they knew would share their interests. This means that there are a greater number of extant descriptions of mortuary rituals than of other cultural practices such as foodways or music, though not always as many sources as one might hope for.

Fourth, deathways leave traces in the material record that many other cultural forms do not. This is especially valuable for individuals—illiterate Europeans among them—who did not leave written records. Archaeologists have long recognized this and have examined deathways exhaustively. Through the study of material culture we can learn how residents of the early modern Atlantic world prepared corpses, what they included in their burials, and, in some cases, how they commemorated an individual's death.

Putting death at the center of the history of the New World reveals the critical role of real and perceived cultural parallels in cross-cultural encounters. When people of different cultures came together in the New World, they were always aware of the differences between their own and the outsiders' mortuary practices; they always had—at least to some extent—an exclusive reaction. But they also usually had an inclusive reaction at the same time, noticing the deep parallels between their own and the others' death rituals. People often recognized that they shared with others an attention to proper corpse preparation, an attitude of respect toward a loved one's remains, a desire to remember the dead with speeches and sacred rituals, the experience of grief at the death of one's friends and family members, and much more. They usually realized that despite important differences in the details, there were deep structural parallels in the emotions, rituals, and spiritual implications of death.

Moreover, at least for Europeans, the intellectual frameworks they brought to the New World inclined them to focus on similarities more than differences. Their belief in monogenism—that there was a single creation from which all humans descended—led them to search for evidence that non-Europeans could be fitted into the biblical chronology. And European efforts to describe the New World using the conceptual categories of the Old World only magnified this tendency. Europeans confronted with the newness of the New World framed their observations in terms comprehensible to themselves and their readers, relying on literary techniques of analogy and simile to draw connections between the familiar and the unfamiliar.[6] Thus when the New England theologian and ethnographer Roger Williams searched for the best way to describe Narragansett mourning practices, he wrote that "the men also (as the English wear black mourning clothes) wear black faces, and lay on soot very thick."[7]

Such real and perceived cultural parallels helped facilitate communication and understanding. When, for example, the English colonist Thomas Harriot wrote sympathetically about Carolina Algonquian treatment of dead chiefs, it was explicitly because he saw in those practices parallels with English funerals for elites. And when people of African descent eventually adopted aspects of European burial practices in the eighteenth century, it was facilitated by West African traditions of earth interments followed by feasts. Death served as a common ground that allowed individuals to reach across cultural boundaries and understand unfamiliar peoples.

But the context of colonial encounters was largely exploitative, so the knowledge and understanding gained through parallel deathways were often, ironically, put to manipulative ends. Europeans initiated the expansion of imperial power into the Atlantic world not out of simple wanderlust but from a desire to gain material riches and religious converts. They forced Indians and Africans to labor on plantations and in mines and to listen to stories of a supernatural being called Jesus Christ. Indians and Africans, for their part, desired the trade goods that Europeans carried with them, but they also wanted to retain control over their labor, land, and religious beliefs. In this adversarial setting, knowledge was a precious commodity, a way to gain an advantage over one's rivals. Deathways often became a means to an end. Missionaries frequently used knowledge about Indian deathways to better understand how to gain converts to Christianity. French Jesuits, for example, studied Indian burials precisely so they could use that knowledge to challenge natives on the "absurd" practice of placing trade goods into their interments. And Europeans occasionally used their knowledge in combination with firepower in order to force changes in non-European deathways, as when Hernando Cortés cleared the sacrificial temples of the Mexica and replaced the bloody representations of gods with an image of the Virgin Mary. In response to such death-related incursions on their sovereignty, Indians throughout the Americas quickly learned that Europeans were horrified by corpse mutilation, so they used that information to terrorize their enemies with scalping and other postmortem humiliations. Africans likewise mobilized this knowledge during their rebellions, large and small, that punctuated the history of slavery in the Americas.

Over time, the possibility for cross-cultural understanding attenuated, as this exploitative legacy increasingly structured most interactions. Yet death-inspired cross-cultural understanding never completely disappeared. In the Seven Years' War (1756–63) British officials used hard-won knowledge about Indian deathways to appeal to their crucial allies, the Iroquois. And toward the end of the eighteenth century many African Americans embraced Christian deathways even as they shaped those practices with their own sensibilities.

In addition to the eventual decrease in opportunities for cross-cultural understanding, change over time emerges in this story through the process of syncretism: the blending of two or more cultures, resulting in the creation of new beliefs and practices. Syncretism, like the question that opens this book, results from the intricate interplay between similarity and difference. Without difference, cultural blending would be meaningless. The creation of new practices through syncretism depends upon the interaction of different cultural forms. Yet syncretism also reveals the importance of cultural parallels, for it was the deep similarities in various peoples' deathways that smoothed the way for the emergence of New World cultural practices. When, for example, New England Algonquians prayed to the Christian god under a tree after a funeral in 1647, they combined pre-contact beliefs about trees connecting this world and the supernatural world with supplication to a new supernatural being.

But just as with cultural parallels, syncretism also demonstrates the importance of power, for it was Indians and Africans whose deathways changed the most in the New World. New England Puritans did not join their Algonquian neighbors in offering postfuneral prayers under trees. Indeed, Christians and Jews in the Americas experienced only minor changes in their deathways. In most ways their mortuary practices continued to resemble those of their co-religionists in Europe. The changes that did occur owed more to the New World environment than to the unfamiliar cultures Europeans encountered there. For example, Euro-Americans were much more likely in the seventeenth century to be buried in coffins than were Europeans, due to the abundance of trees and the resulting low cost of wood in the Americas. By contrast, those with less power in colonial encounters found their deathways eventually changed to a greater degree. Many Indians in eastern North America ultimately became Christianized and thus made important changes in their burial and mourning practices. But despite the best efforts of missionaries, Christian Indian deathways remained a complex hybrid of traditional and innovative practices. Likewise, most Africans in the New World eventually became Christians, though typically later than Indians did. When Africans did embrace Christianity, it was again on their own terms, choosing deathways that blended African and Christian practices.

My arguments about similarity and difference, cultural parallels, and syncretism emerge from an engagement with several fields of historical scholarship. One is the literature on cross-cultural encounters in the early modern period. A generation ago scholars emphasized what they saw as the great cultural differences between Europeans and the Indians and Africans with whom they interacted in the New World. Here is how Neal Salisbury, in his masterful *Manitou and Providence* (1982), described the contrast between Indians and Europeans: "The delicately balanced, self-sufficient, kin-based communities with their ritualized reciprocal exchanges and their Neolithic technologies had been reached by the expanding nation-states of Europe, with all their instability and upheavals as well as their organizational and technological accomplishments."[8] Likewise, in Winthrop Jordan's *White over Black* (1968), English attitudes toward sub-Saharan Africans were shaped primarily by negative English perceptions of difference regarding religion, sexual behaviors, and especially skin color.[9]

More recently, historians have begun to examine the cultural parallels that facilitated communication across cultural boundaries. Scholars of African-European interactions now see numerous correspondences across cultures. John Thornton, for example, argues that deep similarities in Christian and African religions allowed for the creation of a new synthesis. Africans and Europeans, Thornton writes, "had a number of major ideas in common. Had they not shared these ideas, the development of African Christianity would probably not have been possible."[10] Similarly, recent work on Indian-European interactions moves away from older formulations of essential difference. Allan Greer's *Mohawk Saint* (2005) is emblematic of this newer approach. Greer introduces his dual biography of Catherine Tekakwitha and Claude Chauchetière in the following way: "Though difference—the great cultural gulf separating natives and newcomers—will be readily apparent, convergent tendencies are just as notable. In spite of the missionary sources' tendency to exaggerate difference, natives and French had a good deal of common, or at least commensurable, ground in their religious beliefs, medical practices, ceremonies, and customs."[11] Nancy Shoemaker takes this approach one step further. In *A Strange Likeness* (2004), she argues that "Indian and European similarities enabled them to see their differences in sharper relief and, over the course of the eighteenth century, construct new identities that exaggerated the contrasts between them while ignoring what they had in common."[12] For Shoemaker, racial ideologies emerged out of the interplay between similarity and difference. *Death in the New World* builds on the insights of Thornton, Greer, Shoemaker, and others, while insisting that knowledge about cultural parallels was turned toward manipulative ends earlier and more frequently than these authors allow. Given the exploitative context of European colonialism, parallel deathways played a charged role in cross-cultural contests for power.

This book also engages with the rapidly growing field of Atlantic history, which examines the connections among the peoples and products of the four continents bordering that ocean. Much Atlantic scholarship is divided along imperial lines, with separate studies of the English, French, and Spanish Atlantics. Those studies that are comparative have until recently emphasized the differences between various imperial experiences.[13] *Death in the New World* reinforces the newer insights of J. H. Elliott's *Empires of the Atlantic World* (2006) and Jorge Cañizares-Esguerra's *Puritan Conquistadors* (2006) by highlighting the many ways that Spanish and English (and in my case French) experiences in the New World corresponded with one another.[14] With missionaries and traders from all three imperial powers indebted to ideas about death that stretched back long before the Reformation, colonists drew on a common store of conceptual categories, such as the distinction between good and bad deaths and the belief that royal corpses deserved special attention. Although they used these categories in varying ways, individuals from all these European nations attempted to exploit parallel deathways to gain cultural and economic advantages over Indians and Africans, even as Indians and Africans used deathways to resist all three colonizing powers.

Death in the New World, despite its expansive title, focuses only on the eastern third of North America and the Caribbean, and even within that limited range the coverage is not encyclopedic. The narratives are set in places where the sources allow for the most detailed reconstruction of cross-cultural interactions. The chapters proceed roughly chronologically, but there is not a single narrative arc. Rather, the various stories overlap and resonate with one another thematically. They all point to the central role that death played in shaping the encounters among Indians, Africans, and Europeans in the Americas. The stories show that reactions to strangers fell along a spectrum from inclusive to exclusive, pivoting on perceptions of similarity and difference, and how even inclusive reactions could be used to exacerbate the New World's unequal power relations. More broadly, they suggest that in colonial encounters knowledge could facilitate both intercultural cooperation and exploitation, sometimes simultaneously. Together these narratives demonstrate why residents of the early modern Atlantic world saw so much at stake in learning about unfamiliar deathways, and why they so frequently asked about those they encountered, "How do they bury their dead?"

CHAPTER I

Old Worlds of Death

THE EFFIGY OF a dead king is propped up and given three square meals a day. Family members reach into the robe covering their son's months-old corpse and scoop away handfuls of rotting, maggot-infested flesh. The bereaved gather and bury their daughter's body beneath the floor of their bedroom. A woman dies and her children hurry to pour the water out of all the basins in the house. The ghost of a badly behaved schoolboy returns to report that his soul is damned.

These scenes from the dawn of Atlantic encounters—and our reactions of amusement, disgust, and puzzlement—make one thing very clear. When it comes to deathways, residents of far-flung reaches of the early modern Atlantic world shared more with one another than they share with us. In particular, they had an ease and familiarity with death, dying, and the dead that most of us can only barely imagine. Before we can begin our journey into the early modern world of cross-cultural encounters with death, we must don the detached stance of the cultural anthropologist and be prepared for surprises.

In order to understand the cross-cultural encounters that took place in the New World, we must first examine the deathways of the various participants—Indians, Africans, Jews, Catholics, and Protestants—before they came into extensive contact with one another in the Americas. Because all five of these groups encompassed a wide range of diversity in their cultural practices, this chapter will focus on a segment of each: Algonquian Indians of southern New England, Akan-speaking peoples on the Gold Coast of West Africa, Western European Jews, French Catholics, and English Protestants. This narrower focus will not permit a discussion of all the deathways that came into contact in the New World, but it will allow for a fine-grained snapshot of some of the groups that were major players in shaping the history of the hemisphere.

Viewed closely, there were many important differences among the sixteenth- and early seventeenth-century deathways of these five groups. Yet if one steps back and examines these beliefs and practices from a broader perspective, it becomes apparent that the variations were largely in the details. Beneath the surface lay deep structural similarities in the rituals and emotions surrounding death. All the groups examined in this chapter distinguished between good and bad deaths and deathbed scenes. All expressed grief when a loved one died. All carefully prepared the corpse for eventual earth interment. All participated in funeral rites that differentiated between high- and low-status individuals and that ordinarily ended with feasting. All believed that some noncorporeal element—the soul or spirit—eventually entered an afterlife. All believed that the boundary between the afterlife and this world was permeable: communication with the dead and hauntings by ghosts were real possibilities. All mourned the dead with prescribed rituals of remembrance. And because all felt that the dead deserved respectful treatment, corpse desecration marked the highest form of humiliation one could inflict upon one's enemies. Therefore, when the peoples of the early modern Atlantic world came into contact, their first reactions were often inclusive. They spoke in many tongues but shared a common language of mortality and deathways.

*   *   *

It is difficult to discuss "pre-contact" American Indian deathways with much confidence. For the region that we know today as southern New England, the evidence consists of a few pre-Columbian archaeological sites and an abundance of European descriptions, beginning with Giovanni da Verrazzano's brief account of the Narragansetts in 1524. The archaeology is valuable but the sites are too geographically and chronologically scattered to be fully satisfactory. Moreover, the archaeological evidence is mute about important practices such as deathbed scenes and mourning rituals that leave no trace in the material record. The European accounts are quite descriptive, but the bulk of them are from the 1620s to 1640s, after Indians had experienced well over a century of contact with Europeans. Most of this discussion will therefore concern early contact, rather than pre-contact, Indian deathways.

But there are some intriguing hints from the pre-Columbian archaeological record that should not be ignored. During the Late Woodlands period, in the several centuries leading up to the Columbian watershed, burials in southern New England were relatively simple. Bodies were usually buried without any adornment and with few if any grave goods. There were almost no burial grounds as such; most of the burials that archaeologists have discovered are single interments.[1] Indians placed a corpse into the earth in a flexed position (on its side with the knees drawn up toward the chest), but there was no particular directional orientation; that is, it was not deliberately pointed east or west or any other direction.[2] Thus, simplicity of burials seems to have been the rule in southern New England in the several centuries before 1500.

For the sixteenth century we have almost no European descriptions of New England deathways, but archaeological evidence indicates rapidly evolving burial practices at a time when European fishermen and traders began to make contact with Indians along the coast. It seems that these material and biological contacts had impacts well beyond the coastal zone. Throughout southern New England, Indians began to bury their dead in graveyards with as many as several hundred individuals. They still buried their dead in a flexed position, but in the sixteenth century the corpses began to be oriented with the head pointing toward the southwest, in the direction of the land of souls. Most dramatically, Indians now frequently adorned their dead with bracelets and arm bands, and they buried them with numerous goods of native and European manufacture.[3] This, then, was the state of southern New England Indian deathways when Europeans began arriving in greater numbers in the seventeenth century. The early contact deathways Europeans described were not timeless practices but evolving traditions already shaped by over a century of contact with Europeans, their diseases, and their trade goods.

During the early contact period, European observers unanimously reported that southern New England Indians believed deathbed scenes to be very important. As early as 1524, Verrazzano remarked favorably upon the Indians of Narragansett Bay because of their elaborate deathbed scenes. "We judge them to be very affectionate and charitable towards their relatives," Verrazzano wrote. Likewise, a century later Governor Edward Winslow of the Plymouth Colony viewed local Indians' deathbed scenes in a positive light, perceiving in them parallels with English practices. It was, in Winslow's opinion, "a commendable manner of the Indians, when any, especially of note, are dangerously sick, for all that profess friendship to them to visit them in their extremity, either in their persons, or else to send some acceptable persons to them."[4] These practices made great sense to the English colonists, who also felt that deathbed scenes were opportunities to express grief in the company of friends and loved ones.

Linguistic evidence hints that the family members and friends who attended deathbed scenes were exceptionally careful as they monitored the progress of the mortally ill person toward death. Roger Williams reported a fine series of gradations in Narragansett words to describe the dying, including words he translated as "He is not yet departed," "He is drawing on," "He cannot live long," "He is near dead," "He is dead," and finally, "He is gone."[5] It is unclear what distinctions were implied by the last two very different words: *kitonckquêi* and *nipwimaw*. Perhaps they indicate the gradual departure of the spirit from the body.[6]

Furthermore, Williams offered evidence that those who made these painstaking deathbed observations were likely to be women. Williams wrote that when someone first became seriously ill, "all the women and maids black their faces with soot." It was not until the person died, however, that "the father, or husband, and all his neighbors, the men also" would blacken their faces. According to the anthropologist Kathleen Bragdon, blackened faces in this context represented the liminality of the participants.[7] Thus it may have been that not only was the dying person conceived of as being between states (this world and the afterworld) but deathbed observers were so perceived as well (perhaps between an ordinary state and a state of mourning).

The perceived liminality of the dying person and the observers allowed for the relatively easy penetration of the spirit world into this world. All English observers noted that shamans attended the sick and dying: dancing, singing, and performing healing rituals by calling on powerful spirits.[8] The spirit world penetrated into the world of the dying in other ways as well: Williams reported being with a dying man who repeatedly called upon the spirit Muckquachuckquand (defined by Williams as "the Children's God"), who "had appeared to the dying young man, many years before, and bid him whenever he was in distress call upon him."[9] English observers of Indian deathbed scenes in early New England thus focused on the importance and solemnity of deathbed visitations and the grief and careful observations of the dying person's family and friends, both of which had parallels in their own culture. They also noticed the easy slippage between the natural and supernatural for both the dying and the observers.

When English writers turned to burial practices, they found some things that reminded them of their own rituals, and others that were quite foreign.

According to Winslow, the Indians around Plymouth Colony "sew up the corpse in a mat" made of fibers from grasses and reeds before burial. Roger Williams even reported that the Narragansetts had a special verb for this, *wesquaubenan*, "to wrap up, in winding mats or coats, as we say, winding sheets." As soon as Indians had wrapped the corpse they brought it to the graveside to commit it to the earth. Here too Williams was reminded of English practices. In particular, he was touched by the lamentations of the living in remembrance of the dead. "When they come to the grave, they lay the dead by the grave's mouth and then all sit down and lament, that I have seen tears run down the cheeks of stoutest Captains, as well as little children in abundance." [10]

As the Indians of southern New England wept over the death of a loved one, they likely began to think about the afterlife that awaited the deceased individual. The evidence about the Indian afterlife is conflicting. William Wood wrote that Indians believed their "enemies and loose livers" went to an afterlife where they were tortured. According to Roger Williams, however, Narragansetts believed that the souls of "murderers, thieves, and liars . . . wander restless abroad," with no mention of an afterlife resembling hell. Edward Winslow agreed with Williams that the souls of "bad men . . . wander in restless want and penury." [11] Whatever the exact shape of the New England Indian afterlife, the testimony of Wood, Williams, and Winslow suggests that Algonquians had a concept of differing fates for the souls of good and bad individuals.

For those individuals who went to the afterlife for the good, their experience was decidedly idyllic. According to Wood, New England Indians believed that upon death the spirits of the dead traveled to the southwest, where they lived forever, "solacing themselves in odoriferous gardens, fruitful corn fields, green meadows," and "bathing their tawny hides in the cool streams of pleasant rivers." [12] This was "Cautantowwit's House," the abode of the benign and munificent god who had taught the Indians of New England the secrets of maize agriculture and who ensured plentiful harvests.

For this reason, as soon as the lamentations beside the deceased's deathbed began to ease, the Indians turned to burying the corpse in the proper southwest orientation. The precise details of that burial, however, depended on the status of the deceased. According to Thomas Morton, "the more noble" were buried in a sort of unjoined coffin: "they put a plank in the bottom for the corpse to be laid upon, and on each side a plank, and a plank upon the top in form of a chest, before they cover the place with earth." "Chest" was a seventeenth-century synonym for "coffin"; Morton was calling attention to a parallel with coffin burial, a practice that was becoming increasingly common in England at the time. Most Indian burials, however, were not "chested" in this way, and the corpse was instead placed directly in the earth. In addition, most burials received grave goods of Indian and European origin, sometimes placed directly onto the corpse as a form of ornamentation.[13]

Perhaps because the use of abundant grave goods had begun relatively recently in southern New England, the quantity of goods was not as closely linked to status as was the case in many other societies, where those of highest status received the most valuable and numerous grave goods. In fact, archaeological and observational evidence indicates that children received the most grave goods. One anthropologist suggests that grave goods may have been especially abundant for children whose death was unexpected, the result of a sudden case of influenza or smallpox, compared with a child who had suffered chronic illness throughout his or her life. If so, these goods may not have been for the deceased to use in the afterlife but to help appease the gods who had shown themselves unhappy by taking the child's life.[14]

Unlike pre-Columbian graves, which seem to have been scattered around the landscape, early contact graves were gathered into sizable graveyards. As the Pilgrims were stumbling around Plymouth in 1620, trying to understand the lay of the land, they "found a great burying-place, one part whereof was encompassed with a large palisado, like a churchyard, with young spires, [twisted boughs] four or five yards long, set as close one by another as they could, two or three foot in the ground." Set apart from the surrounding landscape and surrounded by a formidable fence, the burial ground reminded the Pilgrims of nothing so much as an English churchyard. Here the similarity ended, for some of the graves had built over them a structure like an unthatched Algonquian wigwam.[15] The Indians of southern New England clearly were interested in remembering the dead. Not only were burial grounds set apart with twelve-foot-high palisades, and not only were some graves marked with miniature wigwams, but most were decorated with other items as well.

After burial, a period of mourning commenced. English observers were deeply affected when they witnessed the grief Indians showed for the deceased. William Wood, who lived in New England for four years before writing his account, asserted that "to behold and hear their throbbing sobs and deep-fetcht sighs . . . would draw tears from adamantine eyes."[16] These lamentations were most commonly described as "howlings," with at least two observers writing that the cries reminded them of "the howlings of the Irish," who in this period were known for the practice of keening over the corpse, which took place both at wakes and at funerals.[17] Though the term "howling" strikes us today as having bestial connotations, the fact that the English were moved by these expressions of grief suggests that they were trying to use the word in a more neutral sense.

Mourning Indians marked themselves in several ways, blackening their faces with soot and cutting their hair in an unstylish manner. It is unclear for how long grieving Indians maintained these external tokens of sorrow. Roger Williams asserted that the face blackening could persist for weeks and months—or even a year if the deceased was a great leader.[18] Several English writers also noted that New England Indians observed a yearly commemoration of their most notable leaders' deaths.[19] When Indians marked these anniversaries—and in general when they were remembering the dead, even those who were not leaders—they were careful not to mention the name of the deceased. The significance of this prohibition is not entirely clear. Williams said it was evidence of how "terrible is the King of Terrors, Death, to all natural men," and left it at that.[20] It seems more likely that this taboo was meant to prevent the spirit of the deceased from being disturbed by being named by the living. Whatever the exact meaning, New England Indians lived in a world where the boundaries between the living and the dead were permeable, and the memory of the dead lingered on in the minds of the living.

*   *   *

Unlike North American Indians, for whom a fair amount of archaeological scholarship exists, West Africans in the early modern period have been the subjects of very few archaeological investigations. This leaves historians with a body of sources that has numerous limitations—shortcomings to which scholars have not paid careful enough attention in their accounts of West African deathways. Some historians have drawn examples from all over a homogenized West Africa, from Kongo to Senegambia, when looking for the antecedents to New World slave burial practices.[21] This approach sometimes neglects cultural differences among the many peoples who lived in a 2,500–mile-long swath of Africa. Similarly problematic, some historians rely far too much on upstreaming, the technique of extrapolating the distant past from more recent informants.[22] These later sources include nineteenth-century travelers' accounts and twentieth-century ethnographies. The obvious problem with upstreaming is that it assumes that West African deathways did not change appreciably over the course of four centuries.

With these concerns in mind, I will describe the deathways of one relatively small stretch of Africa in one century: the region Europeans dubbed the Gold Coast, including the Akan-speaking peoples of what is today Ghana, in the seventeenth century. The Gold Coast supplied a huge number of individuals bound for slavery in the New World: 1.04 million by the end of the transatlantic trade.[23] In addition, the Gold Coast attracted a number of competing European nations and traders eager to obtain slaves and gold. More so than for any other region of West Africa, a large number of European descriptions of African cultural practices survive.[24]

Africans of the seventeenth-century Gold Coast embraced a polytheistic belief system marked by frequent interaction between the natural world and the supernatural world. In particular, many individuals reported communicating—often in dreams—with the spirits of their deceased ancestors. William Bosman, a Dutchman who lived for fourteen years on the Gold Coast, reported that "they talk very much concerning the apparition of the ghosts of their deceased ancestors or relations; which yet happens only to them in their sleep, when they come and warn them to make this or that offering."[25] The offerings to which Bosman referred were directed to the individual's "fetishes," representations of spirits made out of straw, grass, leaves, earth, and other materials. Every Gold Coast adult had at least one fetish, and there were also communal fetishes to which entire villages made offerings. Europeans were fascinated with Gold Coast fetishes, variously offering descriptions, drawings, and condemnations of these sacred objects.[26]

Fetishes played an important role in Gold Coast deathways. It is unclear whether they were used during deathbed scenes, for no European recorded the dying moments of a West African on the Gold Coast in the seventeenth century. It is possible that this is because Akan speakers did not see the deathbed scene as a crucial moment in the transition from life to death. Much more likely, this reflects a limitation of the sources: European observers were probably not intimate enough with Africans to witness their deathbed scenes.

Europeans did, however, observe and even occasionally participate in the rituals that took place after an African died. Pieter de Marees recorded a detailed account of a fetish being used to aid the spirit of a recently deceased man into the afterlife. We know little about de Marees except that he was Dutch, spent a great deal of time on the Gold Coast, and in 1602 published the best early modern ethnography of the Gold Coast. De Marees wrote that when a resident of the Gold Coast died, the deceased's friends and relatives, along with a priest, fashioned what we might call a mortuary fetish and prayed to it "that it may bring the corpse to the other world." To help secure the dead person's safe passage to the afterlife, those gathered killed a hen and dripped its blood onto the mortuary fetish. The priest then fashioned a necklace out of "green herbs." Plucking two or three leaves from his necklace and rolling them into a ball, the priest passed the leaves between his legs and spoke to the fetish, squeezing the juice from the leaves onto the fetish. Anointed by blood and the juice of the leaves, the sacred object now ensured that "the corpse will be at peace." [27]

To further ensure that the deceased would have a peaceful transition to the afterlife, the priest and those assembled then questioned the corpse about why he or she died and who (if anyone) caused the death. This practice, which one historian calls a "supernatural inquest" for the way the deceased seemed to impel the bearers to move toward the person responsible for the death, was the subject of frequent, often mocking commentary by Europeans, as it would be later when slaves brought it to the New World.[28] Europeans referred to this aspect of the Gold Coast mortuary ritual as "ridiculous" and resembling "childplay." [29] But questioning the corpse had a serious purpose, as can be seen from even the most dismissive European accounts. The men and women of the Gold Coast sought answers to the most fundamental human questions—What causes death? Why do we have to die?—as they mourned their loss.[30]

With some insight gained into the supernatural world, it was now time to prepare the corpse for burial. First, as in so many cultures, the body was washed. Next the corpse was wrapped in cloth. Finally, with symbolism that would have been readily apparent to Christian observers, the assembled family members and friends sprinkled ashes on the washed and shrouded corpse.[31] The deceased was ready for burial.

The aspect of Gold Coast funeral processions that most struck European observers was the noise: singing, weeping, wailing, beating on metal basins, and, later in the century, firing muskets all accompanied the corpse to the grave. According to de Marees, after the corpse was bound to a board, men carried it to the grave, with women joining alongside (Figure 1). Wilhelm Müller, a German Lutheran pastor who lived for seven years on the Gold Coast, remarked that in the procession the closest relatives displayed their grief "with much shouting, wailing, and lamenting." [32]

Figure 1. Akan funeral procession. This engraving, which accompanied Pieter de Marees's *Description and Historical Account of the Gold Kingdom of Guinea* (1602), represents three stages of a single Akan funeral. In the foreground (A and B), the procession heads toward the covered grave, banging cymbals and copper basins. In the middle distance (C), mourning women crawl under the grave covering, weeping and wailing. In the background (D), mourners emerge from the sea, having bathed themselves after the funeral. Image shelfmark 566.K.15.(9),17. © The British Library Board. All rights reserved 2009.

When this noisy procession reached the gravesite, it was time to inter the corpse. There were two types of burial sites on the Gold Coast. Some individuals were buried in cemeteries, while others were interred beneath the floor of their homes, a practice referred to by archaeologists as subfloor burial. Several Europeans commented—sometimes negatively—on subfloor burial, and indeed the elimination of this practice due to hygienic concerns would become the goal of British colonial officials in the nineteenth century.[33] Fortunately, at least one European bothered to ask about the significance of subfloor burial. Andreas Ulsheimer was a German who, as a shipboard barber and surgeon, spent a year in West Africa. Like other Europeans, Ulsheimer noticed that on the Gold Coast "they bury [the deceased] in his bedroom, where he slept." Unlike other Europeans, Ulsheimer inquired into the meaning of this practice. His informants explained that the deceased's eldest son "has his bed very close to his father, who lies buried there; and when he eats or drinks something, he gives his father the first mouthful. When one asks them what they mean by this, they say that if they eat and do not also give their deceased father some of it, their father ensures that they will have neither happiness nor prosperity." [34] Those Gold Coast residents who had family members buried within their houses—and archaeologists have found as many as ten skeletons in one house—maintained a daily connection with the spirit world through offerings of food and drink. [35] What remains unclear is why some individuals were buried in cemeteries and others within their homes. [36]

To provide for the deceased in the afterlife, Gold Coast residents offered a variety of grave goods. But unlike North American Indians, Akan speakers placed goods *on top* of the grave in addition to inside it. The deceased's fetishes and some of his "household stuff (as his kettles and clothes)" were placed inside the grave. But even more of the grave goods remained atop the burial site, yet another tradition that would be carried to the New World. The items were placed beneath a "small straw hut . . . like a sepulchre" and were allowed to remain atop the grave "till they disintegrate of their own accord." [37] Thus did the deceased's corporeal remains return to earth beneath the ground while his possessions returned to earth above ground.

After the burial, the mourners headed back to the home of the deceased and began what all European observers agreed was a festive, even rowdy, funeral. Johann Peter Oettinger, a German ship's surgeon who lived for a year on the Gold Coast, was more judgmental than most Europeans, but still his account gives a sense of the vibrant liveliness of Akan funerals. Having just described the African dances marking the new year, Oettinger remarked that "similar and even crazier things take place among them at what are called the *costümos* (funeral festivities), which often last three days or longer. On such occasions the whole village is drunk; and men and women, howling and singing to the beating of drums, perform the most indecent dances." [38] Without the fear that their loved one's spirit might be heading for hell or some other place of terror and torture, residents of the Gold Coast saw no reason not to celebrate the departure of their friend's spirit for the afterlife.

This is not to imply, however, that Akan peoples did not miss the deceased. Rather, like all residents of the early modern Atlantic world, they remembered the deceased through a variety of memorialization practices. In the case of subfloor burial, the presence of the dead was quite literally unavoidable, as the very earth beneath one's home became a sacred space of remembrance. In the case of burial in a cemetery, those who wished to remember the dead brought food and drink to the grave, sometimes for an extended period of time.[39]

In the foregoing description of Gold Coast deathways in the seventeenth century, the focus has been on continuity: those practices that occurred throughout the period. But, images of changeless primitive societies aside, Akan deathways were not preserved in amber in this period. This should be obvious, given that contact with European slavers brought contact with European religion, material culture, and diseases. But historians have not, in general, paid attention to the ways that African deathways changed in the era of the transatlantic slave trade. On the Gold Coast, change was apparent in two ways. At the start of the seventeenth century, Akan funerals were marked by the noise of wailing and cymbals, but not of musket fire.[40] Later in the century, however, numerous observers reported that muskets were central to Gold Coast funerals. This newly abundant artifact of European material culture, imported through the trade for slaves and gold, was quickly incorporated into the noisemaking aspects of Gold Coast funerals. For example, Müller's account from the 1660s indicated that funerals were accompanied by "many musket-shots," while Bosman's late seventeenth-century account described muskets being fired both immediately after a person died and during the funeral procession. Higher-status Africans were even sometimes honored with the booming of European cannon.[41] In light of the European role in supplying the arms that led to gunfire at funerals, it is ironic that Christian missionaries in nineteenth-century Ghana would try to prohibit the practice.[42] But while the custom persisted, it likely did not alter Gold Coast spiritual beliefs; rather, Akan speakers comfortably incorporated this practice into their funerals.

The case of grave goods and other material expressions of deathways may have represented more fundamental change in the meaning of Akan burials. Like many North American Indians, residents of the Gold Coast seem to have experienced a rapid expansion in the use of grave goods—especially of European origin—after commencing trade with Europeans. Archaeologists working around the Portuguese (later Dutch) fort of Elmina found more imported items than local goods in African graves. European pipes, jewelry, glass beads, and trade ceramics became increasingly plentiful in Akan graves. Even locally made terracotta figurines—not precisely grave goods but rather mortuary statues—seem to have come into use only after trade with Europeans began.[43] There is no archaeological or documentary evidence for the use of terracottas before 1600. The figurines, over a foot tall and sporting a

Figure 2. Akan mortuary terracotta. This figure is 14½ inches high and dates to approximately 1700. It was unearthed in the Twifo area of central Ghana. When originally made, it likely portrayed the entire body, either standing or sitting. Such figures were used in cemeteries outside the town and seem to have represented either the deceased or, in the case of a nobleman, members of his retinue. They were set in a portion of the cemetery known as the "place of the pots." Courtesy of James O. Bellis.

human face (Figure 2), were placed in a special part of the cemetery known as the "place of the pots." These finely crafted statues represented either the deceased or, in the case of a nobleman, his servants. It is unknown whether the greater material abundance of mortuary goods shaped Akan spiritual beliefs in the era of the slave trade. But it is possible that the desire for more death-related goods fueled trade with Europeans, and even perhaps the slave trade. The desire for such items may help explain the extraordinary demand on the Gold Coast for Portuguese brass basins, which, in addition to their function as containers, were used both to bang on during funerals and to bury with the deceased. In the period 1504–31, the Portuguese traded over 30,000 basins *per year* on the Gold Coast.[44]

Gold Coast mortuary practices differed in some details from those customs found in other regions of West Africa. But deathways across West Africa shared numerous fundamental commonalities. Virtually all groups washed the body, prepared it for earth burial by wrapping it in cloth, and included grave goods in and atop the grave, and many performed supernatural inquests and subfloor burials.[45] Although slaves recently carried to the New World were able to maintain the practices of their specific village or region, as time went on and slaves from all parts of West Africa and their descendants were mixed together on plantations, regional differences became muted and deep parallels came to the fore. Some of the commonalities in African practices resembled the beliefs and practices of the Europeans who enslaved them—a fact that would facilitate the death-based communication between these peoples.

*　*　*

Western European Jews likewise embraced a religion that tried to answer basic questions about death and the afterlife. For Jews, however, centuries of written texts interacted with folk customs and the influence of a Christian majority to shape deathways. Sixteenth- and seventeenth-century European Jews were divided into two broad groupings: the Sephardic Jews of the Iberian Peninsula and the Ashkenazic Jews of Eastern Europe and the German states. Although their mortuary customs differed in certain details, their broad outlines were similar, as they were based on most of the same textual sources. This discussion will therefore focus on the commonalities.

The original source of Jewish attitudes toward death and the afterlife was the Hebrew Bible (what Christians call the Old Testament). The Hebrew Bible's perspective on the dead body was seemingly paradoxical: it insisted on the impurity of the corpse while implying that the corpse deserved reverent treatment. In the Pentateuch, the first (and oldest) five books of the Hebrew Bible, the corpse's power to defile is stated unequivocally: "He that toucheth the dead body of any man shall be unclean seven days" (Numbers 19:11). This insistence on the impurity of the dead body was in productive tension with the doctrine of bodily resurrection, an idea that appears only obliquely in the early books of the Bible but which receives concrete expression in the books of the later prophets. This can be seen most clearly in the book of Daniel, which scholars date to roughly 165 B.C.E. Daniel stated, "Many of them that sleep in the dust of the earth shall awake, some to everlasting life, and some to shame and everlasting contempt" (Daniel 12:2). Even though the corpse itself was unclean, the doctrine of bodily resurrection suggested that the living should do their best to maintain the integrity of the corpse, in order to facilitate resurrection of the body.[46]

These attitudes were elaborated in postbiblical Jewish commentary. The third-century *Semahot* (literally "Rejoicings," ordinarily translated as the tractate *"Mourning"*) was the first compilation of Jewish regulations regarding death and burial.[47] While these regulations inspired a great deal of discussion in subsequent centuries, it was not until the thirteenth century that another compilation of laws regarding death appeared, the *Torat ha-Adam*. This was the major source for the sections on death in Rabbi Joseph Caro's influential sixteenth-century Code of Hebrew Law, the *Shulhan 'Aruk*. The code's "nearly universal acceptance," as one scholar puts it, helped ensure a degree of uniformity in early modern European Jewish deathways.[48]

Among European Jews in the sixteenth and seventeenth centuries, the deathbed scene was not improvised but carefully scripted. It was considered a *mitzvah* (good deed or religious duty) to attend a deathbed scene, so the dying person was typically surrounded by friends and relatives offering prayers and support. Indeed, the community did all in its power to make sure that an individual did not die unattended.[49]

If at all possible the dying person was to offer a "confession" before ten Jews—not a recounting of specific sins but a prayer with a set text that began, "I confess before Thee O Lord, my God and the God of my fathers, that my healing and my death are in your hand." This confession was so important that its omission could cause a person to be denied elements of a proper burial. But most Jews were able to offer the confession, and before they did so, women and young children were supposed to be sent away so their weeping would not disturb the dying person.[50] But then they regathered, for following the example of the biblical patriarch Jacob (Israel), the dying person was supposed to offer blessings to family members. When the individual died, those present rent their garments from the neck downward about a handsbreadth as a symbol of their grief.

Now the corpse demanded immediate attention, for Jews were expected to bury their dead as soon as possible, ideally before the following morning, and certainly within twenty-four hours. Because of the corpse's impurity its preparation for the grave was often performed by members of a local charitable group dedicated to providing comfort to the dead. These specialists washed the corpse with warm water, which might be infused with chamomile and dried roses. All of the corpse's orifices were stopped with clean linen and then the whole body was wrapped in a linen shroud, as a result of the belief that the dead would arise clothed on the day of resurrection.[51] Finally, the shrouded body was eased on its back into a simple wooden coffin.

Soon after the body was washed and coffined the procession began. The journey from the home to the *beth haim* (cemetery, literally "home of the living") was likely to be circuitous, for this was an opportunity for as many Jews as possible to join the procession. It was considered a "very meritorious work" to attend someone to the grave, so numerous people tried to get their shoulder under the coffin for part of the procession. The length of the journey to the *beth haim* can also be explained by the impurity of the corpse: Jewish cemeteries were ordinarily outside the most populated portions of a town to protect residents from defilement.[52]

At the graveside people were obliged to praise the deceased (while being careful to avoid exaggerating the dead person's virtues).[53] Even someone who in life had been unpleasant was supposed to receive some lamentations. It had become customary in parts of early modern Europe, even though nothing in Jewish law required it, for ten of the "most considerable relations and friends of the deceased" to walk around the coffin seven times while reciting a prayer, the number seven having a variety of mystical associations (Figure 3).[54] At last the coffin was lowered into the ground, and all present helped shovel earth into the hole. The mourners then said *Kaddish* (often called an *escaba* by Sephardim), an ancient prayer glorifying God that has surprisingly little direct connection to death or mourning: "May His great Name be magnified and sanctified," it begins. This prayer seems to have emerged in the Middle Ages in response to the depredations of the Christian Crusades.[55] Finally, the mourners washed their hands, both to cleanse themselves of impurities and also to signal the end of the burial ritual.

But not everyone qualified for these burial rites. According to Jewish law going back at least to the third century, no one rent garments or mourned for someone who committed suicide. A person who had been formally excommunicated during his or her lifetime received the same treatment as the suicide, with the additional indignity of being buried with a large stone on top of the coffin.[56]

Whereas the suicide and the excommunicant were not mourned, once the deceased who died an ordinary death had been ritually prepared and buried, the work of mourning began. There were very specific requirements for those who had lost a near relation: a spouse, parent, sibling, or child. These individuals returned to the house where their kin had died for a seven-day pe-

Les ACAFOTH ou les sept tours, autour du CERCUEIL.

Figure 3. Seven circuits around the coffin. In early modern Europe a tradition emerged among Sephardim to have ten men walk around the coffin seven times before burial. Each time around the coffin the men said a blessing and made an offering. This image of *hakkafot* (literally "circuits") was engraved by Bernard Picart in the early eighteenth century for his *Cérémonies et coutumes religieuses de tous les peuples du monde.* Reproduction by permission of the Buffalo and Erie County Public Library, Buffalo, N.Y.

riod of deep mourning called *shivah*. During this period the mourners wore no shoes, did not bathe or shave, and did not even prepare food for themselves. Sustenance was provided by members of the community, a symbol of how the mourners were not left alone during their time of grief. After the seven days of *shivah* mourners could leave the home, but for the first thirty days after the death mourners were supposed to continue their avoidance of bathing, shaving, and changing their clothes; according to one Christian commentator, after thirty days the Jewish mourner looked "as a man just risen from the grave."[57]

Indeed, in Europe Jewish deathways evolved at least partially with the Christian gaze in mind. Based on a Talmudic passage in which God was reported to say, "I had placed my image among you, and for your sins I upset it;

upset now your beds," mourning Jews in ancient times had overturned their couch or bed (which would have been used for sitting as well as sleeping) and sat upon the floor for the seven days of *shivah*.[58] In the early modern period the requirement to sit on the floor or a low stool persisted, but according to the sixteenth-century compiler of the *Shulhan 'Aruk*, "Now it is not the common practice to overturn the couch because the Gentiles will say that it is [a kind] of sorcery."[59] Likewise, even though in much of Europe it was customary for a large gathering of Jews to accompany the bereaved back to the house of mourning after Sabbath services, Amsterdam's Jewish leaders forbade this tradition in 1639: "There shall be no accompaniments either to a bridegroom or to those in mourning, in order to avoid occurrences prone to such large gatherings, and to avoid our being singled out among the inhabitants of the land."[60] Even in relatively tolerant Amsterdam, Jews shaped their mourning practices to avoid Christian scorn.

These were not groundless suspicions on the part of Europe's Jews; bitter experience had taught them of Christian hostility to their religion in general and their burial rites in particular. In Rome, for example, popular comic theatrical productions called *giudiate* satirized Jewish burial customs. Elsewhere, Christians were known to disrupt Jewish funerals with mocking commentary and catcalls. At times, things got so bad that a police escort was needed to ensure the safety of those participating in a funeral procession.[61]

Memorialization practices were likewise shaped by the presence of hostile Christians. The Jewish cemetery itself is a relatively recent historical development. Exclusively Jewish cemeteries apparently date only from the eleventh century; before that Jews were likely buried among their Christian or Muslim neighbors, without headstones. But increasingly fervent Christian attachment to funerary space seems to have necessitated that Jews create their own separate burial grounds.[62] Within these cemeteries, those wealthy enough to afford them used gravestones to remember the dead. In addition to standard information such as name, birth and death dates, and perhaps parents' names, epitaphs could include a favorite scriptural text or more elaborate details about the deceased. Some of the most popular Hebrew phrases on Jewish gravestones included "May the memory of this righteous person be a blessing," "His rest shall be in honor," and "May her soul be bound up in the bond of eternal life."[63]

But epitaphs were not the only way deceased Jews were remembered: a complex range of mourning prayers ensured that the memory of the dead lingered among the living. Though formal mourning ended on the one-year anniversary of the person's death, Jews were supposed to fast and say Kaddish on every anniversary of a parent's death.[64] In addition, some people's wills included bequests to the local synagogue to pay for memorial prayers, sometimes in perpetuity. Thus could a person be sure that his memory outlived him, and that the dead could therefore continue to influence the living.

*   *   *

"Wake up, wake up, you who sleep, and pray God for the souls of the dead, whom he wants to forgive!" So called out the town crier in sixteenth-century Troyes, a small city some 150 kilometers southeast of Paris, as he patrolled the streets from midnight until two each morning.[65] Residents were therefore reminded on a nightly basis—if they needed reminding at all—of their duty to pray for the souls residing in purgatory so God might more quickly allow them to go to heaven. For early modern European Catholics, perhaps even more so than for Jews, the dead were very much a part of everyday life. Belief in purgatory permeated all levels of society and informed a variety of distinctive deathways aimed at speeding the souls of the dead toward their hoped-for final destination in heaven. The dead were so omnipresent in the physical and mental worlds of early modern Catholics that they formed, as the historian Natalie Zemon Davis phrases it, "a kind of 'age group' to put alongside the children, the youth, the married, and the old."[66]

Catholic emphasis on purgatory was both ancient and a relatively recent innovation. Intimations of an intermediate state between heaven and hell are found in the writings of Augustine and others in late antiquity. At the end of the sixth century Pope Gregory the Great formalized the previously inchoate belief that the souls of those who were not absolutely bad and not absolutely good were subject to purifying fires. But it was not until the second half of the twelfth century that purgatory *as a place* gained currency among theologians. Most souls resided there until they had been purified by fire, after which God released them to heaven. And it was not until the sixteenth century that belief in purgatory became truly widespread and not merely the province of theologians. The popularity of this belief had a profound impact on Catholic deathways because the living could help souls escape purgatory through earthly actions: prayers, payments for Masses, and acts of charity. As a result, the living and the dead remained joined by memory and ritual practice.[67]

Ordinary Catholics' devotion to the souls of the dead intensified during the Catholic Reformation, the changes and clarifications of Church doctrine spurred by the emergence of Protestantism in the early sixteenth century. The Council of Trent (1545–63) was the Church's formal response to the challenges of Protestantism, and in its decrees Catholic leaders did not back away from their teachings on purgatory. Rather, they reaffirmed purgatory's importance, proclaiming that the concept should be "everywhere preached and expounded," even as the Church sought to rein in the abuses of those who believed they could pay for the release of souls from purgatory through the purchase of indulgences.[68]

If one key component of the Catholic Reformation was to get people to think more about the souls of the dead, a related goal was to get people to think more about the fate of their own soul. The devout used thoughts of death to focus on the hereafter rather than the here and now. Others joined one (or more) of the many confraternities associated with deathways. In the seventeenth century, death-focused associational life only intensified, as the wildly popular Confraternity of the Good Death spread throughout Italy, France, and Catholic portions of the German states. In some towns, more than one-third of residents belonged to the Good Death society.[69]

These innovations inspired by the Catholic Reformation complemented ancient practices joining the living and dead. Unlike Jews, who believed in the impurity of dead bodies, Catholics attributed great power to some corpses. Indeed, the veneration of relics—the belongings and body parts of the "very special dead"—was a central component of Catholicism stretching back to late antiquity.[70] Relics also received a boost from the Council of Trent, even as the Church tried to reform some practices that had crept into popular Catholicism. As the Council put it bluntly, "People are not to abuse the celebration of the saints and visits to their relics for the purpose of drunken feasting."[71] Aside from that caution, the Church endorsed the use of relics to help focus the prayers of the laity, as they asked for the intercession of the saints whose bones they caressed. In the proliferation of relics we once again see the omnipresence of the dead. Throughout sixteenth-century Catholic Europe laypeople continued to make pilgrimages to holy sites in order to touch relics—in Paris the finger of St. Ouen cured the deaf, for example—and pray to the saints for healing and for the souls of the deceased.[72]

Even with the intercession of saints and the healing power of holy bones, Catholics inevitably sickened and died. As they lay upon their deathbeds, they became the centerpiece of a communal drama in which onlookers witnessed the dying person struggle to choose between good and evil. Fortunately for the dying person, she did not face this trial alone and unsupported.

She was surrounded not only by neighbors, friends, and family members—not to mention the priest with his ritual accouterments—but also by centuries of writings about how to perform a good death. Again this tradition bore the marks of ancient origins and recent developments. Theologians had been writing about the good death for centuries when, in the early fifteenth century, an anonymous author penned the brief *Tractatus artis bene moriendi* (Tract on the Art of Dying Well). This might not sound like a bestseller, and in its original incarnation it wasn't, but then someone converted it into a block book, a publishing format in which each page was carved from a single block of wood. This one featured eleven large illustrations with brief captions. Here was a book—now referred to as the *Ars moriendi*, or art of dying well, a term that would come to be applied to the whole genre of advice about dying—that could be appreciated by the masses, for one did not need to be able to read in order to understand the story. This was easily the most popular block book of its time: of some three hundred extant block books, sixty-one are the *Ars moriendi*.[73]

This book was so popular because it gave Catholics a model to follow, something to *do* to help alleviate the inevitable terror of dying. Reading about dying therefore was not a macabre or horrifying exercise. Rather, it could be surprisingly empowering.[74] Catholics learned that a good death entailed a number of actions within their power: praying to the saints and to Jesus and Mary, resigning oneself to God's will and accepting that death was inevitable, offering blessings and forgiveness to one's family and friends, settling one's worldly accounts, avoiding despair and impatience, and rejecting the entreaties of Satan. But the *Ars moriendi* never suggested that all this would be easy. In fact, the book resonated with Catholics because Moriens (literally "the dying man") is depicted as an ordinary person, subject to the same anguish most people experienced on their deathbeds. In one illustration, "Temptation to Impatience," Moriens is frustrated by his pain and the slow pace with which the release of death arrives. He is tempted by an evil little demon portrayed with bat-like wings and an oversized tongue. In his impatience Moriens overturns his bedside table, sending his bowl and glass flying, and he kicks out in the direction of the physician attending him (Figure 4).

If that had been the end of Moriens's deathbed scene, it would have been considered a bad death. But through the power of prayer, Moriens was able to overcome his impatience. Thus, Catholics were taught that they should reject the temptations of the demons that would accost them as they lay dying. This last point was a key aspect of the Catholic deathbed scene (and something

Figure 4. *Ars moriendi.* This woodcut, "Temptation to Impatience," is from a German *Ars moriendi* published in roughly 1466. The dying man, urged on by the demon beneath his bed, lashes out at the physician and nurses attending him. As explained in the English *Crafte and Knowledge For to Dye Well* (c. 1490), the dying frequently experienced impatience "for they that be in sickness in their deathbed suffer passingly great pain and sorrow and woe." Courtesy of Octavo Corporation and the Library of Congress Rosenwald Collection.

Protestants would later reject): the dying person was able to choose between good and evil on the deathbed. Turning away from evil would not necessarily ensure that a person went to heaven or had only a brief stay in purgatory, but it surely helped. With the aid of prayers by friends and family members the dying person could hope to reject the Devil's entreaties.

Another guard against evil was the local priest, and specifically the sacrament of extreme unction, or last anointing, that he performed. When it was clear that recovery was impossible, the dying person's family summoned the priest. He made his way as quickly as possible, for the deathbed was the site of an epic battle between good and evil, and the priest carried a powerful weapon. As the Council of Trent put it, "By the sacrament of last anointing [Christ] has guarded the end of life by a very strong defense."[75] This was valuable because the Devil was at his most wily as a person lay dying. To combat this devious adversary, the priest hurried to the bedside and asked the dying person to confess her sins, after which he offered her the body of Christ as a viaticum (literally "traveling provisions"). Thus cleansed, the dying person was ready for last anointing. The priest dipped his right thumb into holy oil and anointed the dying person's eyelids, ear lobes, and lips, representing body parts that had been the agents of sin.

It was not a problem if a person who received extreme unction somehow survived; she could receive anointing again the next time she was dangerously ill. But most people died after last anointing, at which point the priest had the church bells rung to elicit prayers from the living for the soul of the deceased. Family members then began to make arrangements for the funeral. As in so many cultures, the first step in preparing the body was to have the female relatives—or hired women if the family could afford it—wash and shroud the body. Catholic leaders would have liked to have the shrouded body moved immediately to the local church, but dictum after dictum could not prevent the bereaved from holding a wake inside the home of the deceased. Although this community gathering may have originated as a way to watch for signs of life from the person presumed dead, by the sixteenth century the wake was an occasion to lament, mourn, joke about, and even insult the dead.[76]

The wake over, the body was now ready for the procession from the home to the church. In sixteenth-century France, coffin burial remained the exception rather than the rule due to the great expense of wood, so the shrouded corpse was placed either directly upon a bier or into a coffin that would be used for the procession but not for the burial. Both the bier and the coffin were typically owned by the parish and rented to users at a low cost.[77] Catholics often had very precise ideas about their funeral processions, and many outlined their desires in great detail in their wills. When Jeanne Passavent dictated her will in 1582, she made provisions to ensure that her procession would be glorious. This wife of a Parisian merchant requested that the curé and priests of her parish attend, along with members of four mendicant orders, nuns from two different convents, and children from three hospitals. Each of the convents and hospitals received cash for their efforts in exchange for saying prayers for her soul. This sizable cortege followed Passavent's body from her house to the fourteenth-century cathedral of Saint-Jean-en-Grève.[78]

When Passavent's body reached Saint-Jean, the bearers placed the corpse before the altar, which was magnificently illuminated by forty-eight two-pound candles provided for in her will. Others, of course, could not be so lavish. Thiebault Cambron of Reims could afford only six three-quarter-pound candles when he died in 1577, and others could not pay for any.[79] Whether the church was filled with candles or not, the burial liturgy now commenced with a series of sung or chanted psalms, antiphons (responses), and prayers (including the Lord's Prayer). It is likely that the full office of the dead was sometimes abbreviated due to time constraints. But never omitted was the funeral Mass itself, with the consecration of the host marking the holiest moment. When the priest sprinkled the bier with holy water and used his thurible to waft incense over the body, this signaled that it was time to carry the dead to the place of burial.[80]

Glorious though a funeral for a member of the Parisian bourgeoisie might be, it could not compare with the bizarre pageantry of a French royal funeral.[81] Consider the events following the death of Francis I on March 31, 1547. The day after the king died surgeons performed a crude embalming: they placed the royal heart and entrails into separate caskets and then encased the disemboweled corpse in lead and put it into a wooden coffin. The heart and entrails were soon interred in a monastery vault but the corpse remained unburied. On April 24, more than three weeks after the king's death, the proceedings took a dramatic turn: a lifelike wooden effigy of Francis—complete with wax hands and head, human hair for locks and beard, and realistically painted face—appeared on a "bed of state" in the royal palace. Faux Francis sported a crimson waistcoat, blue tunic, red satin slippers, and ermine-trimmed robe, all topped by the jewel-studded imperial crown. For eleven days the effigy reclined upon the bed of state. To make sure the effigy did not grow hungry during the long wait for the funeral, he was presented with three meals a day, including wine, and a napkin to tidy up with. Finally, on May 4 the effigy was given his last meal, and the coffin holding Francis's embalmed body replaced the effigy in the palace's hall of honor. Still, Francis's son, Henri II, was not considered king. The shout of "The king is dead! Long live the king!" would not ring out until Francis was buried inside the church of Saint-Denis on May 23.

Although almost everything about the French royal funeral served to differentiate the king from his subjects, in one respect Francis was just like an ordinary citizen: something had to be done with his remains. There were basically two options in early modern France. The wealthy and the noble usually chose to be buried inside a church, just as King Francis did. Some were buried in catacombs below the church, but more were simply buried in the church floor. The original logic behind church interment was that people desired burial *ad sanctos*, near the saints, or more specifically near the relics that most churches held. People believed that having their corpse in close proximity to relics would speed their entrance to heaven. But because there was limited space within churches, burial *ad sanctos* took on a second desirable quality, at least from the perspective of the wealthy: it became very expensive. By the sixteenth century, only elites such as Jeanne Passavent could afford church burial. She specified a location within Saint-Jean: "facing and below the crucifix . . . nearby where her late mother was buried." [82] In yet another way were the dead omnipresent in Catholic Europe, beneath the very feet of worshippers.

The vast majority of early modern Catholics could not afford to maintain such physical reminders of kinship ties. For those below Passavent's station, burial in an unmarked grave in the churchyard was the norm. At some point in the seventeenth or eighteenth century, large parishes in cities and towns began using mass graves due to a lack of space. In the sixteenth century, most French parishes probably still dug individual graves, except in large burial grounds for the poor, such as the Cemetery of the Innocents in Paris. Still, the modern North American conception of burial in perpetuity, where graves are supposed to remain undisturbed forever, had no place in early modern Europe. When gravediggers opened the earth for a newly arrived corpse, they routinely encountered skulls and longbones from previous burials, which they cleaned and placed in a *charnier* or charnel house. Thus secondary burial—the relocation of previously buried remains—was common in early modern France. [83]

Ordinary Catholics were concerned that burials be performed properly, because a bad burial could lead to hauntings. Early modern belief in ghosts demonstrates that the Catholic Church did not have a monopoly on the supernatural. Rather, sixteenth-century men and women held a range of beliefs about ghosts that could not be quashed by church leaders, despite their best attempts. In the ghostlore of early modern France, the unquiet dead returned not to scare the living, as we imagine ghosts today, but to take care of unfinished business. Parents frequently returned to haunt their children, usually demanding that their children take care of unfulfilled obligations, such as praying for the ghost's soul, executing a portion of the will that had been neglected, or fixing something that had gone wrong at the burial.[84] In sixteenth-century Brittany, a man's specter returned after his wife murdered him and hid his corpse in the family's salted-meat cellar. The ghost pointed the victim's brother toward the corpse and with this evidence the woman was not just executed but decapitated and quartered.[85]

The treatment of the homicidal wife's body suggests that the very worst thing that could happen to a corpse was for it to be deliberately desecrated. Outside of legal proceedings this did not happen often, but during the Wars of Religion between Huguenots (French Protestants) and Catholics in sixteenth-century France it occurred frequently enough to become the centerpiece of propaganda efforts on both sides of the conflict. The logic behind corpse desecration is not as obvious as it seems at first glance. On the one hand, both Protestants and Catholics cared deeply about respectful treatment for the dead, and thus to desecrate the corpses of one's religious antagonists was to show the greatest contempt for their beliefs. On the other hand, it had been orthodox Christian belief since Augustine that upon resurrection, the soul would be united with the body and rise from the grave. The body that ascended would be a perfect version of the individual's body—even if it had been chopped into a hundred pieces.[86] Thus it is not entirely clear what corpse dismemberment was meant to accomplish. Whatever the exact motivation, both Huguenots and Catholics desecrated corpses with abandon during the Wars of Religion.[87]

But it would be a mistake to end a discussion of Catholic deathways on such a violent note. Even though the Catholics who ventured to the New World would bring with them the idea that corpse desecration was a powerful weapon in their struggle for religious supremacy, the image of mutilated corpses hardly captures the essence of their faith. A much better representation of the spirit of sixteenth-century Catholicism is the *danse macabre*, or dance of the dead (Figure 5). First appearing in the fifteenth century, *danse*

Figure 5. *Danse macabre*. This anonymous sixteenth-century German *danse macabre* is unusual in that it appears on paper rather than on the walls of a cemetery or charnel house. It shows noblemen, bishops, and other notables dancing with skeletons, unsubtly demonstrating that when the rich and powerful die they will look the same as any peasant. As Death taunts the King in a mid-fifteenth-century English *danse macabre* poem, "For who-so aboundeth in great riches / Shall bear with him but a single sheet." The painting measures only 7½ by 5¼ inches and was rendered in ink, watercolor, and gouache. Image © The Metropolitan Museum of Art.

macabre paintings portrayed the dead alternating with the living, hand in hand in a great circle, as they danced among the graves in a churchyard. The dead were naked and eager to dance; their living companions were dressed in the costumes appropriate to their stations, and not at all in the mood to dance. These images were painted on the walls of numerous burial grounds and usually included monitory verse, such as the following:

> By Divine sentence
> No matter what your estate
> Whether good or evil, you will be
> Eaten by worms. Alas, look at us,
> Dead, stinking, and rotten.
> You will be like this too. [88]

The explicit messages of the *danse macabre*, which remained popular through the sixteenth century, were that the viewer should prepare for death to strike at any moment and that in death all are equals. But in its subtext the *danse macabre* stands as an apt metaphor for sixteenth-century Catholic Europe: the dead are everywhere, they are joined by the hand to the living, and it is this connection that animates the circle of life.

*   *   *

In contrast with France, where only a small minority of the population embraced the new doctrines of the Reformation, England became a solidly Protestant nation by the end of the sixteenth century. As a result, England witnessed a dramatic break in the relationship between the living and the dead. No longer were the dead everywhere: Martin Luther, John Calvin, and numerous English reformers decreed that purgatory was a papist fiction with no basis in scripture. They therefore reasoned that the actions of the living could not affect the souls of the dead. Lay Protestants radically altered their deathways to reflect the new separation between the living and the dead.

Or so we had been told by the narrative of the Protestant Reformation that was dominant through the middle of the 1980s. Since then, historians have come to understand that the reality was more complex.[89] Yes, the denial of purgatory by Protestant theologians had a powerful impact on the deathways of lay men and women in England and elsewhere. But there were numerous continuities between traditional practices and the new regime. Not only did some Catholic deathways persist for several decades after they had been officially repudiated by religious authorities but even when most lay-people had become thoroughly Protestant—by the end of the sixteenth century in England—numerous similarities remained. Because many mortuary practices had no theological or liturgical foundation (post-funeral feasting, for example), they survived the Reformation. Others with some theological import also endured, as the people reinterpreted old practices in light of new doctrines. The Protestant migrants to the New World, like their Catholic counterparts, carried a belief system in which death and the dead stood at the very center. As a result, the interactions between both groups and non-Christians would revolve around similar themes.

The Reformation's reevaluation of Catholic eschatology began tentatively. Martin Luther himself believed in purgatory when he posted his ninety-five theses in 1517 and he did not deny its existence until 1530.[90] By the 1530s, though, a consensus had emerged among Protestant theologians that there was no scriptural basis for purgatory, that the soul went directly either to heaven or hell upon death, and that Masses and prayers for the dead could therefore not affect the fate of the soul. Moreover, the Protestant insistence that there were only two sacraments (baptism and the Lord's Supper) instead of the seven of the Catholic Church meant that extreme unction lost its status as a sacrament.[91]

By the middle of the sixteenth century, some radical reformers pushed these changes about as far as they could go and attempted a sweeping overhaul of deathways. When the Scottish reformer John Knox was exiled in Geneva in the 1550s during the reign of the Catholic Queen Mary, he whittled the burial liturgy almost to the vanishing point.[92] The vast majority of Protestants, however, did not see the need for such a dramatic break with tradition. Especially in England, change came relatively slowly, in small steps rather than great leaps. When Henry VIII broke with Rome and founded the Church of England in 1533, little changed theologically. Henry had no zeal for reform and, like most of his subjects, was comfortable with traditional deathways. Indeed, when Henry died in 1547 he followed Catholic tradition and left a substantial sum to the poor to pray for his soul.[93]

Henry's succession by the boy-king Edward VI marked the beginning of substantial changes. Edward's advisors included a number of reformers who seized the opportunity to push the nation in a more Protestant direction. The crown endorsed a new prayer book in 1549, which included moderate Protestant revisions to the Catholic burial liturgy, and a second prayer book in 1552 that represented a much sharper departure from tradition. Edward did not live to implement the work of his advisors, however, and was succeeded in 1553 by his Catholic half-sister, Mary, nicknamed Bloody Mary by the Protestants she persecuted. Not until Elizabeth's long reign (1558–1603) did Protestant deathways gradually become the norm for most English men and women, as the Elizabethan Book of Common Prayer of 1559—based closely on the 1552 version—became the foundation for the liturgical portions of deathbed scenes and burials.[94] The Book of Common Prayer included many important departures from Catholic practices, but also a surprising number of continuities. Other nonliturgical aspects of deathways showed even greater resilience.

Deathbed scenes are a good example of the complex interplay between innovation and tradition in English Protestantism. The Protestant emphasis on predestination—that God had chosen before time who would go to heaven and who would go to hell—had important implications for deathbed behavior.[95] Whereas Catholics saw one's final hours as a battle between good and evil, with the dying person able to choose between the angels and devils that surrounded the deathbed, Protestant ministers argued that such a choice was not possible. Because God had already determined the final estate of a person's soul, one's dying actions could not secure a place in heaven. This might have generated a great deal of deathbed anxiety, except that Protestants asserted that assurance of one's salvation was indeed possible. A believer could know whether he was one of the lucky ones upon whom God had freely bestowed his grace. Still, ministers cautioned that such knowledge was hard to come by and that people easily fooled themselves into thinking they were saved, thereby taking away much of the comfort the doctrine of assurance seemed to offer. All of this meant that by the strict logic of Protestantism observers and the dying person himself could not know whether he was saved based on his deathbed behavior. As William Perkins wrote in *Salve for a Sicke Man*, his bestselling 1595 guide to dying well, "a man may die like a lamb, and yet go to hell." [96]

But if Protestant theology implied an attitude toward one's dying moments very different from that held by Catholics, in practice it was not so simple. Indeed, Protestant deathbed scenes retained numerous elements from the widely popular Catholic *Ars moriendi* tradition. Despite what Protestant ministers urged, people paid a great deal of attention to a person's deathbed behavior and drew conclusions about whether the person went to heaven. As Perkins complained, it was a "common opinion" that a person who died easily went "straight to heaven." [97] Like Catholics, Protestant deathbed observers watched the dying carefully for signs that they were going to heaven.

Ministers likewise negotiated between changes and continuities in the prescribed ritual activities at the deathbed. On the one hand, there were important changes to the deathbed ritual. For example, in the prayer books of 1552 and 1559, anointing the sick was removed altogether.[98] On the other hand, many similarities remained. When a minister entered the house of a dying person, the Elizabethan prayer book directed him to say, "Peace be in this house, and to all that dwell in it." This was an English translation of the Latin benediction uttered for centuries by Catholic priests, as outlined in the Sarum rite (the liturgy of Salisbury, the rite most widely used in late medieval England).[99]

When turning to the nonliturgical aspects of the deathbed, continuities with Catholic practices are even more apparent. Parish bells continued to alert local residents that someone was dying. Those who heeded the call and went to the dying person's home partook of a Protestant deathbed scene that was just as much a social event as Catholic deathbeds had been. Friends and family members gathered around the deathbed in order to pray, weep, and reminisce. They hoped to receive exhortations and good wishes from the dying, and perhaps even forgiveness for earlier conflicts. They maintained a vigil around the bed so that when the person finally died the moment would not go unnoticed.

Now the deathbed was transformed into a site for corpse preparation, and in this there were numerous continuities with pre-Reformation practices, as virtually everything about corpse preparation was nonliturgical. Female family members (or servants if the family had the money) washed and shrouded the corpse. The elite might be crudely embalmed so the corpse would not become offensive in the long period it took to organize an appropriately sumptuous funeral.[100] Once the corpse had been washed and shrouded, it was placed onto a bier or into an open coffin. The coffin either belonged to the parish or, increasingly in the sixteenth and especially the seventeenth century, was purchased by the deceased's family. This latter option worked its way further down the social scale as time went on, so that by the end of the seventeenth century most middling families felt it was imperative to purchase a coffin so the deceased might have a "decent" burial.[101]

Whether the body was coffined or simply on a bier, now began the period of watching the corpse, as in Catholic Europe, when people did their best to make sure the body was never left unattended. Friends and neighbors would gather around the corpse in the deceased's house in order to cry, laugh, and tell stories. Protestant ministers frequently reminded their parishioners that during the wake they were allowed to pray in the presence of the dead, but they were not supposed to pray for the soul of the deceased. One imagines that many Elizabethan men and women did not make such fine theological distinctions. Many certainly did not listen to their ministers about keeping the wakes solemn affairs. People at wakes drank alcohol, told jokes, and even played bawdy games. One informant from seventeenth-century Yorkshire told the antiquarian John Aubrey about a game common at wakes in his part of the country: "hot cockles," which Aubrey translated as "hot arse." Apparently the good men and women of Yorkshire took turns spanking blindfolded members of the party, in what one historian calls "a sexual variation on blind man's buff." [102]

Perhaps groggy (and sore!) from the previous evening's festivities, townspeople assembled for the funeral procession. When the procession reached the church, a number of Protestant departures from Catholic practices immediately became apparent. The Book of Common Prayer dictated that the office of the dead begin with the same reading from John 11:25–26 called for by the Catholic Sarum rite, beginning "I am the resurrection and the life," but this and the rest of the office were performed in English, not Latin. More fundamental, the Protestant liturgy did not include the requiem Mass and the consecration of the host. And in a Protestant funeral the corpse played a much less central role than in a Catholic funeral. Whereas Catholic practice revolved around praying for the soul of the deceased, that rationale was absent from Protestant funerals. [103]

The Reformation, however, altered little in the physical dimensions of interment practices. This was not an obvious outcome, given the new theology. Luther famously wrote that one could bury his body in the forest or in a river for all he cared; the geographical location of a burial had no impact whatsoever on its estate in the afterlife. And indeed in Germany the Reformation dramatically increased the practice of extramural burial, with corpses interred outside city walls. [104] But only a handful of radical English Protestants followed this logic and argued that burial in consecrated ground was superstitious. [105] As a result, English Protestants continued to bury their dead in the same churchyards their Catholic predecessors had used. Historians have not adequately explained this difference in outcome between Germany and England, yet the fact remains: in England the dead and living continued to cohabit as they had before the Reformation, with human remains at the very center of the geographic and metaphorical community.[106]

Moreover, wealthy English people continued to be buried within churches, even though this too was rejected by reformed Protestants elsewhere.[107] For those who could afford it, burial within the church continued to be a source of status: conspicuous decomposition, as it were. The practice was now shorn of its pre-Reformation rationale—that burial *ad sanctos* would help speed one's soul to heaven—not least because relics had been removed from nearly all churches by Elizabeth's reign. Yet due to the high cost of church burial, most English Protestants settled for burial in the churchyard. Stone markers remained rare through the seventeenth century, except within the wealthiest stratum of society.[108] The vast majority of English men and women expected to be interred anonymously and eventually have their dry bones dug up and removed to make room for new burials.

But dry bones were far from the minds of those who had recently committed their neighbor or loved one to the earth—dry mouths were more like it. After the funeral the thirsty crowd headed back to the deceased's house and, just like their Catholic predecessors, enjoyed a funeral feast. Those who attended a funeral were grateful for the generous spirit of people like John Coult of Heydon, who specified in his 1561 will, "I ordain at my burial a solemn drinking to be made by my executors, i.e. three fat sheep, three barrels of beer, and six dozen of bread, to be provided for my poor and rich neighbors that will come to it." [109] Coult's neighbors undoubtedly indulged the "drinking" part of his request; whether they honored his wish that it be "solemn" is an open question.

Either way, after the townspeople staggered away from Coult's funeral feast, bellies full of beer and mutton, Coult's family members were left behind to contemplate their loss. In this they had fewer resources than they would have had before the Reformation. With purgatory now derided as "the pope's boiling furnace," in Thomas Becon's vivid phrase, English Protestants were no longer supposed to remember their loved ones by praying for their souls.[110] They could not celebrate a month's mind, a Mass to commemorate the one-month anniversary of a person's death. Coult's family members also were not supposed to observe All Souls' Day, though once again reformers found traditions regarding the dead slow to change.[111]

But even without purgatory, prayers for the dead, month's minds, and All Souls' Day, English Protestants still had a variety of ways to remember the dead. First came the grief and mourning that followed the death of a loved one. All could grieve, but only those of some means could mourn: that is, put on the demeanor and the expensive mourning costume considered fashionable.[112] Although some radical Protestants mocked mourning attire as unnecessary, most people seem to have been comfortable with the tradition, and this is reflected in the wills of many members of the gentry.[113]

The bereaved could begin to assuage their grief by participating in a variety of practices that memorialized the dead. Because the churchyard was typically located in the center of town, visiting the gravesite was easy. And when graveyard visitors returned home, they might read the funeral elegies and sermons that became increasingly available in the sixteenth and especially seventeenth century. In the immediate aftermath of the Reformation, funeral sermons were highly suspect, as they smacked too much of the requiem Mass and praying for the souls of the dead. But soon most Protestant ministers came to see the funeral sermon—delivered after the burial and sometimes published—as an opportunity to instruct the living in the new theology and practice of death.[114]

A less comfortable fit with orthodox Protestant notions of memorialization were the ghostly visitations that continued in spite of a new theology that worked against them. Because souls now went directly to heaven or hell, apparitions could not be the spirits of the dead returned from purgatory. As Keith Thomas put it in *Religion and the Decline of Magic*, belief in ghosts "was in the sixteenth century a shibboleth which distinguished Protestant from Catholic almost as effectively as belief in the Mass or the Papal Supremacy." [115] But more recent historians have shown that this formulation is too simplistic. First of all, even Protestant theologians allowed that apparitions did exist, though they were the work of the Devil rather than the returned dead. But even more important, popular belief in the returned dead remained powerful in the century after the Reformation. As with Catholics—and with all other groups examined in this chapter, for that matter—English Protestants believed the boundary between this world and the next was permeable.[116] The memory of the dead was too powerful to be contained by orthodox Protestant teachings.

*   *   *

It is true that some of the English Protestants who made their way to the New World in the seventeenth century were the zealous sort that would come to be known as Puritans. The most pious of these men and women would work hard to suppress ghostlore and some of the other continuities with Catholic deathways that survived the Reformation. New England Puritans, for example, would maintain a greater hostility toward funeral sermons than members of the Church of England; the first funeral sermon would not be published in New England until 1679.[117] But after that, funeral sermons, elaborate burials, and gravestones would all follow English fashions, with their connections to the Catholic past. Moreover, Puritans made up only a minority of English migrants to the New World. Even in New England their hold on the culture was not complete, and elsewhere they were greatly outnumbered by more mainstream Protestants.

In the New World, English Protestants would share with their Catholic and non-Christian counterparts numerous powerful ideas about death and the afterlife. Most fundamentally, the religious systems of all those who interacted in the New World centered on trying to answer the most basic eschatological questions: What is the relationship between the living and the dead? How should we live so that we may die well? Where do we go when we die? How should we prepare the dead to ensure their happy arrival in the afterlife? As they tried to make sense of the extraordinary frequency of death in the New World, all participants in the encounter asked these questions and were curious about the answers that others gave. Their reactions to others were, depending on the context of the encounter, sometimes inclusive, sometimes exclusive—though more frequently inclusive than one might expect. Now we turn to the beginnings of those interactions.

CHAPTER 2

First Encounters

EVEN THOUGH CROSS-CULTURAL interactions have been an aspect of the human condition for millennia, arguably the most intense era of such encounters was ushered in by Christopher Columbus. The century following 1492 was marked by the unprecedented interactions of Europeans, American Indians, and Africans. On a scale previously unimaginable, peoples separated by vast distances came together—voluntarily and forcibly—and slowly began to form the cultural and economic connections that constituted the Atlantic world.

European Catholics and, later, Protestants came to the Americas in search of riches and converts to their religions. They brought different theologies and different deathways, but their goals were more similar than they might have cared to admit. As J. H. Elliott has recently written, "The English saw their mission in America in the same terms as the Spaniards."[1] Both viewed Indians as needing—even wanting—to be converted to Christianity. Both saw deathways as central to their mission, as the "reform" of Indian deathways would be crucial to the success of Christianization, and the Christian afterlife would be one of the Europeans' greatest selling points.

The very first Europeans to encounter the New World were too awestruck by its "marvelous" qualities to pay much attention to the deathways of its indigenous inhabitants, and the reverse is probably likewise true. But soon, as death tolls on both sides of the encounter climbed due to disease and warfare, Indians and Europeans began to take close measure of each other's deathways. They found surprising similarities and chilling perversions of what both groups believed to be the proper way to deal with dying and the dead, oscillating between inclusive and exclusive reactions. Sixteenth-century Spanish conquistadors tended to be more exclusive in their assessments of native deathways, largely because they were more interested in military conquest than in the kind of cross-cultural communication later Spanish missionaries would need to accomplish their goals. Some late sixteenth-century English colonists, by contrast, offered more inclusive interpretations of Indian deathways. This was especially true for those such as Thomas Harriot who hoped to convert natives to Christianity.

Soon after their first encounters, as Europeans and Indians learned about the deathways of the other, they used their newfound knowledge to their own best advantage: sometimes to build bridges and work with the other group, more often to try to change the other's deathways or even to use the other's cultural practices against them. Communication, cooperation, and exploitation marked the interactions among the peoples of the Atlantic world. This is how a New World of death began to emerge from the Old.

*   *   *

The story begins in 1492 with Columbus's voyage across a sea only dimly understood. Columbus believed he was sailing toward Cipangu (Japan) and in a way he was right, except that he didn't count on being nine thousand miles short of his destination and having two continents in his way. Columbus expected to find people awash in gold, silks, and spices, and even though he tried to remain upbeat in his dispatches to Ferdinand and Isabella, he could not hide his disappointment that those who greeted him were "a very poor people in all respects."[2] Columbus went to his death thinking that the people he met were residents of the East Indies—*los Indios*, later Anglicized to "Indians"—rather than the Tainos of what Europeans would call the Bahamas, Hispaniola, and Puerto Rico.

Indeed, Columbus was so overwhelmed by the novelty of what he saw—the native canoes were "marvelously carved," the native trees were "quite marvelous"—that he had little capacity for observing indigenous cultural practices.[3] Several times on his first voyage he was content to note that "the people have no religion" and leave it at that.[4] On subsequent voyages Columbus paid a little more attention to native culture, but only a little. The one aspect of Indian culture on which he did comment at length was religion, especially deathways, because the Indians' belief in the afterlife signaled to Columbus that these people could be successfully converted to Christianity. Columbus and his contemporaries believed that it was easier to get non-Christians to switch from one afterlife to another than to have to start from scratch with the whole concept of an afterlife. For this reason Columbus and his chief missionary Ramón Pané, a Hieronymite friar, eagerly searched for parallels between European and Taino beliefs in immortality of the soul.

After his second voyage Columbus still asserted that "I have not been able to discover any idolatry or other religious beliefs" among the Tainos of Hispaniola, but then he went on to describe the *zemis* used in a variety of religious practices. These large figures were carved from wood or fashioned from other natural materials in the shape of humans; they represented deceased ancestors. *Zemis* were sometimes made out of human bone: x-rays of one extant example show an entire human skull hidden beneath the woven cotton.[5] As described by Pané, *zemis* such as this "contain the bones of [its owner's] father and mother and relatives and ancestors."[6] Columbus reported that every settlement in Hispaniola—where scholars believe as many as 500,000 Tainos lived—had a "special house apart from the village" that contained at least one *zemi* and as many as ten.[7] Columbus had only the vaguest notion about how Tainos used their *zemis*. Subsequent ethnohistorical and archaeological evidence indicates that the Tainos ritually purified themselves by inducing vomiting (using a "vomiting spatula") and snorting a hallucinogenic substance called *cohoba* before deploying their *zemis* to communicate with deceased ancestors.[8]

Columbus and Pané paid more attention to Taino funeral customs than other religious practices, even if they did not fully understand the deathways. According to Columbus, "They prepare their caciques [headmen] for the tomb by cutting open the body and drying it over a fire so as to preserve it entire. Of some common people they preserve only the head; others they bury in a grave, placing above the head bread and a gourd of water; and yet others they burn in the houses where they die."[9] Columbus could not figure out why commoners' corpses were treated variously, but he was nonetheless interested in the details because he knew that deathways would have to be one of the first things changed if the Tainos were to accept Christianity.

Columbus also worked hard to discover whether the Tainos had a concept of the immortality of the soul. Therefore, according to Columbus, "I have made strenuous efforts to discover what they know and believe about the place to which they go at death." He learned that after death "they go to a certain valley which each principal cacique imagines to lie in his own country. They state that here the dead meet their fathers and ancestors, eat, have wives, and take their pleasure and consolation with them." [10] Pané indicated that the line between the world of the living and the afterlife was not impermeable for the Tainos. He wrote that the spirits of the dead "converse with the living, and take the form of men." [11] In accounts that contain scant information about Taino cultural practices—nothing about their music, art (aside from *zemis*), political organization, or family relations—it is significant that Columbus and Pané believed deathways to be the key to unlocking the mystery of Taino society. Ultimately, though, Columbus was too bewildered by the novelty of his surroundings and too distracted by his hunt for gold and spices to engage fully with native deathways.

Subsequent Spanish explorers and adventurers, however, picked up on Columbus's inchoate sense of the importance of Indian deathways and placed even more emphasis on them. To be sure, Hernando Cortés and the men who accompanied him on his quest to conquer Mexico were not partaking in an ethnographic jaunt. They were even more single-minded in their desire for gold than Columbus and his men. As the Mexica famously wrote several decades after the conquest, "Like monkeys they [the Spanish] grabbed the gold. It was as though their hearts were put to rest, brightened, freshened. For gold was what they greatly thirsted for; they were gluttonous for it, starved for it, piggishly wanting it." [12] Still, Cortés, out of some combination of sincere belief and the knowledge that this was what the Spanish emperor Charles V wanted to hear, made his campaign into a religious crusade with one of its goals being the radical reformation of Nahua deathways.[13]

When Cortés and the 550 men under his command arrived in central Mexico in 1519, they found much to admire. Cities, markets, status differentiation: in a word, civilization. The city of Tlaxcala left Cortés nearly breathless with enthusiasm. As he wrote to Charles V, "The city is indeed so great and marvelous that though I abstain from describing many things about it, yet the little that I shall recount is, I think, almost incredible." [14] If Tlaxcala was marvelous, the imperial city of Tenochtitlan was dazzling beyond compare. The island city even outshined most Spanish cities. It had a market square "twice as big as that of Salamanca" with a breathtaking variety of luxury goods for sale, including "colors for painting of as good quality as any in Spain." [15] Fruits and vegetables, game birds and fish, ornaments of gold and silver: all were presented in seductive displays. And like the cities of Spain with their soaring cathedrals, Tenochtitlan was dominated by its religious architecture. As the Mexica would later recall, the city was graced with seventy-one towering temples.[16] Cortés could not make the same mistake as Columbus that these were people without religion: he observed that "there are a very large number of mosques or dwelling places for their idols throughout the various districts of this great city." These sacred temples were not only enormous but magnificently decorated. "The workmanship both in wood and stone," Cortés enthused, "could not be bettered anywhere." [17]

With the aid of his invaluable translators, the Spaniard Jerónimo de Aguilar and the native woman he called Doña Marina, Cortés quickly discerned the purpose of the temples. "The towers all serve as burying places for their nobles," Cortés explained to the undoubtedly curious Charles V.[18] This made perfect sense to Cortés and his royal correspondent, because Spain had a long tradition of architecture that combined politics, religion, and death. Although what the historian Carlos M. N. Eire calls the "dynastic necropolis and temple" of El Escorial was still seventy years in the future, Cortés was certainly familiar with a number of Spanish palaces that included combined monasteries and burial grounds for the nobility. These—such as the palaces at Santa Creus (1280), Poblet (1380), and San Juan de Toledo (fifteenth century)—provided the inspiration for the later and better-known El Escorial of Philip II.[19] Cortés thus had a clear conception of the function—if not the exact sacred meanings—of Tenochtitlan's temples. Parallel deathways allowed Cortés to understand the Mexica in ways he otherwise would have been unable to do.

Because of this, Cortés declared holy war on the temples and all they stood for. "The greatest of these idols and those in which they placed the most faith and trust I ordered to be dragged from their places and flung down the stairs." With the religious symbols removed, Cortés "had the temples which they occupy cleansed for they were full of the blood of human victims who had been sacrificed, and placed in them the image of Our Lady and other saints." [20] Cortés came, he saw, and he *understood* that the temples represented the conjunction of political and religious power as expressed through death, just as Spanish palaces with the nobility buried within represented the same intersection of earthly and otherworldly power.

There were, of course, numerous differences between Spain's palaces and Tenochtitlan's temples, the most glaring of which was the Nahua practice of human sacrifice. Here is how the Mexica coolly described the fate awaiting a typical captive: "Four men stretched him out, grasping his arms and legs. And already in the hand of the fire priest lay the sacrificial knife, with which he was to slash open the breast of the ceremonially bathed captive. And then, when he had split open his breast, he at once seized his heart. And he whose breast he laid open was quite alive. And when the priest had seized his heart, he dedicated it to the sun."[21] It is impossible for us to fully understand the multiple resonances of Nahua human sacrifice, given the great distance in time and worldview between today and sixteenth-century Tenochtitlan. One scholar's ambitious yet controversial attempt to unravel the meanings of this practice centers on the suggestion that humans and the vegetable world (especially maize) represented a continuum of life. On the temples, human sacrifices confirmed the connection between the human and the natural worlds, and between the human and the sacred worlds. As present-day Nahuatl speakers put it in song, "We eat of the earth / then the earth eats us."[22]

But there is no question that we are unable to grasp the full significance of this practice. Likewise, Cortés and his men stood bewildered and disgusted before the blood-soaked scenes they witnessed: they had powerfully exclusive reactions to human sacrifice. Indeed, Cortés interpreted the Mexica fascination with human blood to be a satanic perversion of his own faith's holiest ritual of drinking the blood of Christ.[23] The parallels between the two traditions seem to have hit too close to home for Cortés, according to the Nahuatl "Annals of Tlatelolco": "Sacrifices were made before the Captain [Cortés], at which he was angered. They gave the Captain blood in an eagle vessel, and because of it he killed the person giving him blood, striking him with a sword."[24] The blood of Christ in a silver chalice was one thing, the blood of a recently pulsing heart in an eagle vessel was quite another.

Thus did Cortés and his men have great respect for the Mexica way of life, but not their way of death. Because of this, the attempted conquest of Mexico took on the character of a holy war. According to Bernal Díaz del Castillo, the proud old soldier who began writing his eyewitness account in the 1550s, the Spaniards set up the accouterments of their religion within the great temple. "Our altars and an image of Our Lady and a Cross were set up, apart from their cursed Idols, with great reverence and with thanks to God from all of us, and the Padre de la Merced chanted Mass." Thus fortified by their religion, the Spanish commenced their attack on the Mexica and their sacrifices, for as Cortés put it without a trace of irony, "he who kills shall be killed."[25]

This aphorism was nearly turned on its author, as the Mexica responded in kind to the attacks on their religious system. In fact, the Mexica decided that if the Spanish were so concerned about human sacrifice, they would show them just how fearsome a weapon of intimidation it could be. Numerous times the Mexica captured Spaniards and taught them to fear the obsidian blade. After one battle the Mexica "carried all the Spaniards they had captured, both living and dead, naked, up to certain lofty towers near the market place, and there sacrificed them, cutting open their breasts and tearing out their hearts to offer them to their gods. This the Spaniards under [Pedro de] Alvarado could plainly see from where they were fighting." The tactic had its desired effect: the Spaniards "were seized with great sadness and dismay and retreated to their camp." Another time, the soldiers under Gonzalvo de Sandoval did not witness the sacrifice of their comrades but discovered the grisly aftermath. The men entered a temple and found "two faces which had been flayed, and the skin tanned like skin for gloves, the beards were left on, and they had been placed as offerings upon one of the altars." Again the assault on the Catholic belief in the sanctity of the corpse shook the Spaniards: "Sandoval and all his soldiers were moved to pity by all this and it grieved them greatly." [26]

But despite their best efforts the Mexica had two things working against them as they tried to hold on to their empire. First was what they called "the great rash" or the "illness of pustules": smallpox. The disease struck even before the Spaniards made their way to Tenochtitlan, the pathogens likely introduced by earlier, abortive Spanish efforts to reach central Mexico. The Mexica described the devastation wrought by the disease: "Large bumps spread on people; some were entirely covered. They spread everywhere, on the face, the head, the chest, etc. . . . [The people] could no longer walk about, but lay in their dwellings and sleeping places, no longer able to move or stir. . . . The pustules that covered people caused great desolation; very many people died of them, and many just starved to death; starvation reigned, and no one took care of others any longer." [27] Thus the effects of the disease were multiplied. Not only did smallpox kill a significant portion of the population; it also worked to short-circuit ritual life, especially those rituals surrounding deathways, as there were too many corpses to handle by ordinary means. In some places the Mexica dealt with the surfeit of smallpox corpses by simply bringing down houses on top of the bodies contained within. [28] This is what the Mexica likely meant by "no one took care of others any longer," as the inability to practice traditional mortuary rituals—which ordinarily included cremation and the burial of ashes in order to feed the earth gods—caused serious demoralization. [29]

The second and even more decisive factor undermining the power of the Mexica was the deep enmity of numerous nearby Indian groups toward them. The Mexica Empire was a relatively recent creation, less than a century old when the Spanish arrived. Those natives subject to the Mexica chafed under their tribute requirements, and other Nahua groups, in particular the residents of Tlaxcala and Cholula, never were part of the empire and despised the prideful Mexica. Cortés quickly came to understand just how precarious the empire was, and he exploited that knowledge by recruiting thousands of Indian allies.[30]

In 1520, as the battle for Tenochtitlan reached a fever pitch, Cortés demonstrated how much his Indian allies meant to him through a display that mobilized Spanish deathways to communicate with the Tlaxcalans. Fleeing from Tenochtitlan, Cortés and his men headed for Tlaxcala, where they hoped to gain reinforcements under the direction of their "great friend," the "great chief" Maxixcatzin, who had earlier raised 10,000 warriors for the Spanish. The Spanish were distraught to learn that Maxixcatzin had recently died of smallpox. According to Bernal Díaz, "We all grieved over his death very much and Cortés said he felt as though it were the death of his own father." Cortés's statement about his father was not an exaggeration. Cortés "put on mourning of black cloth, and so did many of our Captains and soldiers."[31]

While this might not sound like much, for sixteenth-century Spaniards it was an extraordinary gesture: in Spain at this time it was illegal to wear mourning for anyone outside of one's immediate family. In 1502 Ferdinand and Isabella had undertaken to reform what they perceived as "mourning abuses" in Spain. They argued that wearing black cloth and other outward signs of mourning were, in their words, "only invented as signs of grief by people who did not believe in the resurrection, but instead believed the soul died with the body." Seeing everywhere the threat of Jews, Muslims, and other non-Christians, Ferdinand and Isabella insisted the bereaved invest their money and energies into more Catholic alms and Masses. It is therefore remarkable that Cortés chose to demonstrate his regard for Maxixcatzin by putting on mourning, given that this action was illegal. Then again, perhaps Cortés did not break the law. There was an exception to Ferdinand and Isabella's 1502 decree: "in case of a royal death, all citizens were allowed to wear mourning garb." Was Cortés implying that Maxixcatzin deserved the same tokens of respect as a Spanish monarch?[32] Whatever the case, Cortés donned mourning not only because he was grieved but also to demonstrate to his men and to his Indian allies how important the Tlaxcalans were to him. Thus did Cortés use deathways to build some cross-cultural bridges even as he used deathways to burn others.

With the help of the Tlaxcalans and numerous other Indians, the Spaniards were able to conquer Tenochtitlan in 1521. Even though Cortés framed the conquest in his letters to the emperor as a struggle to replace satanic human sacrifice with godly Catholic rites, the fall of Tenochtitlan did not lead to the rapid Christianization of Mexico's indigenous deathways. For many Nahuas, the most obvious change as they went from being part of the Mexica Empire to part of the Spanish Empire was simply the identity of the person collecting their tribute. Only slowly would some Nahuas embrace the faith—and the deathways—of the Spaniards.[33]

For the Spanish Empire, the impact of the Cortés expedition was profound. The conquest of Mexico reaped extraordinary riches for the crown and led to a scramble to find the next Tenochtitlan, the next El Dorado. Adventurers such as Hernando de Soto, who had come to the New World in 1514 barely in his teens, were inspired to seek gold and glory in the unexplored reaches of the New World. In the 1520s de Soto gained a reputation for ruthlessness enslaving Indians in Nicaragua, so in 1531 Francisco Pizarro invited the young tough to join his expedition to Peru.[34] There de Soto learned to associate Indian burials with riches, as most of the best caches of gold and silver were found in Inca tombs, and he learned to be exceedingly brutal with uncooperative Indians.[35] There de Soto also gained enough wealth to finance his own expedition to La Florida, the Spanish name for southeastern North America and the site of several failed Spanish attempts to find cities the equal of Cuzco or Tenochtitlan. The plundering tenor of the expedition was set with Charles V's declaration that one half of looted grave goods belonged to the crown.[36]

De Soto sailed into Tampa Bay in May 1539 with nine ships and six hundred men. He would spend the next three years trudging through the swamps and over the mountains from present-day Florida to North Carolina, Alabama, and Arkansas, seeking but never finding a city of gold. What he did find were numerous Indian chiefdoms descended from the Mississippian cultures famous for the burial and ceremonial mounds they built from Wisconsin to Mississippi. The Mississippian centers of Cahokia and Moundville had fragmented before de Soto's arrival, but the southeastern chiefdoms were still powerful societies when the Spaniards arrived. As in Mexico, the violent encounter between these cultures would play out in part within the burial temples of the native peoples—with some Indians joining de Soto in sacking their enemies' temples.

By the spring of 1540, de Soto was getting frustrated. He had been slogging through the southeast for nearly a year and the natives he encountered had nothing resembling great wealth. But he had been hearing rumors from captured Indians that the town of Cofitachequi in present-day South Carolina might satisfy his lust for riches, so he was glad when his army finally made it there. The *cacica* (female chief) of the town made a dramatic entrance. The Lady of Cofitachequi, as the Spanish called her, was brought by her attendants "with much prestige on a litter covered in white (with thin linen) and on their shoulders." This seemed to foretell the possibility of unseen wealth. To complete her royal bearing, she was "young and of fine appearance" and she "spoke to the Governor [de Soto] with much grace and self-assurance." Even better, she took off a strand of pearls and put it around de Soto's neck "in order to ingratiate herself and win his good will."[37] The *cacica* of Cofitachequi could not have picked a better way to appeal to de Soto.

What happened after this auspicious meeting is the subject of some dispute in the sources. Garcilaso de la Vega, known at the time as "El Inca" because he was a Peruvian mestizo, claimed that the *cacica* pointed to a building and said, "That structure is the burial place of the nobility of this town. Within it you will find large and small pearls and in addition many seed pearls. Take what you want."[38] But Garcilaso was not part of the expedition; two men who were actually there suggest that the Spanish did not have permission to raid the tomb. Luys Hernández de Biedma wrote in 1544 that "the Governor sent people to look for her [the *cacica*], and when she could not be found, he opened a temple that was there, where the important people of that land were buried."[39] Likewise, de Soto's secretary Rodrigo Rangel wrote simply that he and de Soto "entered in the temple or oratory of these idolatrous people," with nothing about gaining permission to do so.[40]

Like many native people of the southeast (and like the Spanish, for that matter), the residents of Cofitachequi treated the corpses of their leaders differently from those of commoners. Elites were adorned with pearls, wrapped in skins, and placed on platforms within a burial temple. It is possible that the deceased Cofitachequi nobles had pearls not only strung on their body but placed within their body cavities, in which case the Spanish must have wreaked havoc on the venerated corpses in their lust for pearls. According to Rangel, the Spaniards, "having unwrapped some interments" found "the breasts and openings and necks and arms and legs covered in pearls." By "openings" did Rangel mean body cavities? Hernández's account suggests that this was so. Hernández was happy to find pearls weighing six and a half or seven *arrobas*—at roughly 25 pounds per *arroba*, that meant an astonishing 160 to 175 pounds of pearls. But he was disappointed that "they were not good because they were damaged through being below the ground and placed amidst the adipose tissue of the Indians."[41] Not only did the Spanish enter the sacred burial tombs, and not only did they remove the adornment from the corpses, but they seem to have reached inside the very body cavities of the corpses in their quest for riches.

The Spaniards had no doubt about how the residents of Cofitachequi felt about this kind of grave robbing. If Garcilaso prevaricated when he claimed the *cacica* told the Spanish to take what they wanted from the burial temple, he was closer to the mark later in his account when he described the importance placed on these sacred structures by the local Indians. "The temples and sepulchres . . . are the most venerated and esteemed sites among the natives of Florida," by which he meant the entire southeast. Moreover, Garcilaso and his Spanish readers could easily understand the Indian veneration of burial sites: "I believe that the same is true in all nations, and not without good cause, for these places are monuments, I would not say of saints, but of those who have passed on, and such monuments recall the dead to us as they were while living."[42] Indeed, Spanish law discouraged the burial of the dead with valuables precisely because it might lead to the despoliation of the grave by treasure hunters.[43] Certainly the Spanish, with their vibrant tradition of venerating the relics of the esteemed dead, understood the role that the burial temples played within Indian communities.[44] Here was an area of understanding shared by the two societies.

Because of this convergence between Spanish and Indian ideas about the burial sites of especially holy and powerful individuals, the Spanish were not the only ones to desecrate burial temples in the southeast. Indians also entered their enemies' tombs, but their goals were more about psychological and spiritual intimidation than material gain. When de Soto crossed the Mississippi in 1541 into present-day Arkansas, he found two groups at war with one another: the chiefdoms of Casqui and Pacaha.[45] De Soto decided to employ the divide-and-conquer strategy that had worked so well for Cortés in Mexico. He convinced the paramount chief of Casqui to mobilize warriors against their enemies in Pacaha. The Casqui fighting men knew just what to attack in order to inflict the most pain on Pacaha: "the temple in the large public plaza, which was the burial place of all who had ever ruled that land." According to Garcilaso, the Casquis entered the temple and threw to the floor the chests that held the corpses, scattering the bones all around. They stepped on and kicked the remains "with utter contempt and scorn." Later, after the desecration of the temple had ceased and the victorious Casqui Indians returned to their homeland, the paramount chief of Pacaha surveyed the damage: "lifting from the floor with his own hands the bones and bodies of his ancestors which the Casquis had thrown there, he kissed them and returned them to the wooden chests which served as sepulchres." This was the greatest affront the Casquis could have perpetrated, and the chief of Pacaha vowed to get revenge.[46] Here the Spanish needed no interpreter to understand the Indians' actions. All parties involved knew how to speak the language of corpse desecration.

As a result, when de Soto's own mortal end arrived his burial was shaped by the Spanish fear that his corpse might be similarly mistreated. After the events in Casqui and Pacaha, de Soto and his men continued to wander the region, spending the next year in Arkansas hunting fruitlessly for a city of gold, with de Soto becoming increasingly irrational as his desperation grew. In April 1542 de Soto took ill near the Indian town of Guachoya on the Mississippi River. Within a few weeks he was dead. Some Spaniards "rejoiced" that their cruel and single-minded leader was no more.[47] Others, more respectful, wanted to give de Soto a proper burial, but they feared that the Indians "might commit upon his body such outrages and dishonors as they had inflicted upon other Spaniards."[48] Corpse desecration was an important part of southeastern Indians' arsenal: not only scalping but other forms of mutilation. So the Spaniards kept de Soto's stinking corpse in a house for three days until the coast was clear and then buried him under cover of darkness. The Indians began to ask questions: What has happened to your ill leader? And why is the ground disturbed over there? So the Spaniards once again snuck out at night and disinterred their former commander. They carried the corpse to a canoe, filled the shroud with sand, and paddled out to the middle of the Mississippi, where they dumped de Soto into the water.[49] No coffin, no procession, no candles, no Masses: this is not how de Soto would have imagined his funeral.

At the bottom of the river de Soto was safe from Indians who might want to commit "outrages" upon his corpse to pay him back for three years of murder and plunder throughout the southeast. But he was not safe from the judgments of history. And he would not have wanted to be: in early modern Spain, a soldier's death was defined as good or bad in part by the *fama* (fame or reputation) he gained in the memory of his exploits. *Fama*, according to the historian Laura Vivanco, "persisted only as long as memory" and therefore "it was thought necessary for the deeds of the famous dead to be recorded."[50]

In the chronicles of the de Soto expedition some have found a brave explorer, others a murderous thug. But the encounter between de Soto and the Indians of the southeast was more complex than that dichotomy allows, as revealed in the ways that both groups used deathways to pursue their own ends.

*   *   *

Even though de Soto's expedition was a failure in that it did not conquer a great city like Tenochtitlan, it did succeed in securing Spain's claims to La Florida. As the Spanish extended their dominance throughout Mexico, Peru, and La Florida in the sixteenth century, they began to look northward for economic and religious gains, and their eyes turned to Ajacán, the Spanish name for what the English would later call Virginia. On sixteenth-century maps, Ajacán lay intriguingly near the Strait of Anian, reputed to be a sea route to Asia.[51] In theory, the Spanish claim to La Florida extended from the Florida peninsula to Newfoundland and thus included the Bahia de Santa Maria (Chesapeake Bay) and the alleged Strait. But to solidify those claims Spain would need to send soldiers and missionaries to an unfamiliar region, believed to be as far north as one could survive in La Florida.[52]

The ensuing encounter between the Spanish and the Ajacán Indians would leave eight Jesuits hacked by axes and pierced by arrows, eight Indians hanged by their necks from a Spanish ship's yardarms, and persistent tales of murderous Indians killed by gazing upon a crucifix that had belonged to their victims. Historians who have narrated these events have glossed over the baroque and magical elements of the story, understandably sticking to the more earthly details of murder and revenge.[53] Yet the story's seemingly bizarre aspects—all relating to Spanish and Indian deathways—help shed light on the religious sensibilities that came into contact over four hundred years ago in Ajacán.

When the Spanish arrived in Ajacán aboard the caravel *Santa Catalina* in 1561, they knew they needed an interpreter. Ever since Cortés's stunning success with Doña Marina and Jerónimo de Aguilar, Spaniards in the New World had made it a priority to find young natives who could learn Castilian and serve as intermediaries between the two cultures. Thus on one of their first voyages to explore the Bahia de Santa Maria they tried to find a potential interpreter among the Paspaheghs, who lived on the shores of what the English would call the James River and who would later join the Powhatan confederacy. The Spanish managed to convince two Indians, a high-status

Paspahegh adolescent named Paquiquineo and his "servant," to come away with them. Though Spaniards (and other Europeans, to be sure) were not above kidnapping potential interpreters, it seems that Paquiquineo went with his people's consent, though they probably did not know precisely what he was getting into. Because the youth was the son of a chief, the Paspaheghs apparently considered him an appropriate choice to serve as an envoy to the potential trading partners in their impressive ships. The boy was taken to Spain and renamed Don Luís de Velasco, after the viceroy of Mexico. There he spent about six months before sailing to Mexico in May 1562. In Mexico City Don Luís and his servant became so ill that, according to the Spanish, they requested baptism "many times" before finally receiving the sacrament.[54] Don Luís recovered, perhaps believing that baptism saved him, and he spent the next four years learning the language and religion of his hosts.

The Spanish treated Don Luís well, befitting his royal lineage. He was educated at royal expense and moved in the circles of the elite and powerful. He eventually relocated to Havana. Finally, Pedro Menéndez de Avilés, the governor of Cuba, outfitted an expedition back to the Bahía in August 1566. Menéndez asked Don Luís, now a young man, to accompany the voyage as an interpreter and to help the crew find his people. Curiously, though, when the ship sailed into the Bahía, Don Luís professed to be unable to find his homeland and the captain decided to sail to Spain. Could it have been the thirty-seven Spanish soldiers aboard the ship that caused Don Luís's amnesia? Was Don Luís protecting his people from the arquebuses and mastiffs that undergirded Spanish colonialism, which the young man knew all to well from his years in Mexico City? Perhaps: four years later, on a 1570 voyage with eight Jesuits and without any soldiers, Don Luís had no trouble at all finding the land of his birth, which he called Ajacán.[55]

As soon as the Spanish Jesuits set up their mission on the peninsula between today's York and James rivers—less than ten miles from where the English would establish Jamestown thirty-seven years later—their interactions with the Paspahegh Indians revolved around death and the supernatural. One day after his arrival, Father Luís de Quirós wrote to his superior that Don Luís's people were surprised to see the person they knew as Paquiquineo return after a nine-year absence: "They seemed to think that Don Luís had risen from the dead and come down from heaven."[56] Though the Paspaheghs would not have used the term "heaven" (nor the direction of "down"), it is perfectly plausible that they believed Don Luís to have returned from the afterlife. As we will see elsewhere, eastern Indians not infrequently relied on individuals apparently back from the dead—sometimes even after they had been buried—to confirm details about the afterlife.[57] Nor was this Indian belief entirely scorned by Christians, who sometimes used cases of apparent death to gain insight into the details of heaven and hell.

Moreover, the Paspaheghs were primed for an act of divine intervention because they had been suffering six years of famine and drought.[58] Many Indians had moved away in search of less parched conditions; those who remained "say that they wish to die where their fathers have died." For the Indians of the eastern woodlands, the graves of their ancestors served to sanctify the landscape. Though some Paspaheghs chose to leave the area, at least temporarily, ancestral bones served as a magnet to keep others from departing. Those who remained seem to have hoped that Don Luís and his curiously clothed companions brought with them the spiritual power to end the famine—and the dying.[59]

Indeed, the very first request the Indians made was to have the Jesuits baptize a dying child. According to Quirós, the chief—Don Luís's father— had a three-year-old son (and thus a brother of Don Luís) who "now seems certain to die." The chief, speaking through Don Luís and perhaps at Don Luís's urging, asked the Jesuits to send someone the roughly twenty miles to where the boy lay so he could be baptized. Given the terrible conditions of drought and the prevalence of death, the Indians hoped to harness any spiritual power that might help them. Though less than twenty-four hours in Ajacán and still without even a makeshift camp, the Jesuits eagerly complied with this request. Their first soul saved for Christ![60]

It had been an eventful day for the Jesuits. They had arrived safe from a long sea journey and had been greeted warmly by the local Indians. With the help of their trusted intermediary, they already had baptized one Indian; who knew how many more might be in the offing? Father Quirós practically glowed with contentment: "Don Luís has turned out well as was hoped, he is most obedient to the wishes of Father [Juan Baptista de Segura] and shows deep respect for him, as also to the rest of us here."[61]

Things began to unravel the very next day. After a night in the Jesuits' hut, Don Luís refused to sleep beside his Spanish companions. Three days later Don Luís was gone, living now in his brothers' village some twenty miles away. Don Luís began to take on the trappings of a princely Paspahegh Indian, including (most distressingly to the Jesuits) plural wives. Meanwhile, the Jesuits slowly starved during the surprisingly cold Ajacán winter. Twice a young novice Jesuit was sent to retrieve Don Luís; twice Don Luís rejected the Spaniard's overtures. Finally, in February 1571, after five months in the region, three Jesuits were dispatched to try to bring Don Luís back to his erstwhile sponsors. Could he have forgotten ten years of kind treatment?

Despite their entreaties, the Jesuits could not convince Don Luís to leave his village. But this time Don Luís made sure he would not be bothered again. Helped by several companions, the former star pupil murdered the three Jesuits as they returned to their mission. Don Luís then led the Indians to the Jesuits' humble encampment and killed the five remaining Black Robes.[62]

At this point we must pause to consider the sources of this information, for the surviving accounts diverge on important points. There seems no reason to doubt the veracity of Quirós's letter of September 1570, which was an unexceptional description of the mission's prospects. The accounts of the Jesuits' deaths, however, are more problematic. All ultimately rely on the testimony of Alonso de Olmos, a Spanish boy who accompanied the expedition as a catechist: a Jesuit-in-training who assisted the Fathers in celebrating Mass. Olmos was spared the Indians' wrath, perhaps because he was not yet a full-fledged Jesuit, or perhaps because they hoped to adopt him into their community. When found by the Spaniards in August 1572, Olmos narrated the events that occurred after Quirós's letter. Father Juan Rogel of the return expedition recorded Olmos's words in a letter to Rogel's superior. Olmos put his own actions into the most heroic light possible, claiming, for example, that he asked the Indians to kill him rather than take him captive, "for it seemed better to him to die with Christians than live alone with Indians."[63]

Despite the problems with Olmos's testimony, Rogel's August letter is the most reliable account of the Jesuits' deaths: it was written soon after Olmos—an eyewitness (or at least an earwitness)—recounted his story. However, subsequent retellings of the events in Jesuit histories of missionary efforts in La Florida embellish details in increasingly baroque renditions. In these later accounts, the deaths become classic martyrdoms. The narratives conform to the Catholic hagiographic tradition that death, in the words of the historian Allan Greer, was "the central event in the subject's life."[64] The retellings are nonetheless valuable, as they demonstrate how death was mobilized to create a spiritually satisfying tale for future generations.

Take, for example, the manner in which the Jesuits were murdered. In Rogel's August letter the details are relatively straightforward. Don Luís killed Quirós with an arrow and then murdered the other two Jesuits. He brought "a large group" of Indians to the Jesuits' village, killed Father Segura with an axe, and his companions "finished off the others." As this description was not sufficiently heroic (or detailed) enough to conform to the Catholic hagiographic tradition, subsequent renditions became much more graphic. In a relation written in 1600, Don Luís used his axe to give Father Segura "many blows on the head, the arms, the legs, and his whole body, which lay gravely wounded and maltreated." By the time the Indians finished, the bodies lay "all naked and cut to pieces." Yet more grotesque imagery appeared in a 1610 account. The Indians killed the priests only after they were made to bless themselves, and the Indians fiendishly desecrated the Jesuits' corpses: "Fashioning their skulls into cups, [the Indians] waved them about in their drunken feasts." [65] Corpse desecration was a sine qua non of martyrdom; for this reason the author could say that the Black Robes died "blessed happy deaths." [66]

After the murders there was a surprising development. Don Luís, according to Olmos, buried the slain priests. Here is how Rogel put it in his August letter: "This boy [Olmos] then told Don Luís to bury them since he had killed them, and at least in their burial, he [Don Luís] was kind to them." [67] Allowing for the potential that Olmos self-aggrandizingly presented himself as the impetus for the burial, it seems quite possible that Don Luís did in fact bury the Jesuits. This was not a typical part of a martyrdom narrative (more conventional would have been that their desecrated corpses rotted in the sun), and so Olmos had little incentive to fabricate this detail for posterity.

The question remains: why might Don Luís have been "kind" to the corpses of those he had just murdered? This is especially vexing since the burial of slain enemies does not seem to have been typical behavior for the Indians of Ajacán, who were more likely to take trophies from enemies' corpses (scalp, ears, fingers) than to bury them. Burial after battle or murder, if it was done at all, was generally performed by the deceased's own people. [68] This makes it likely that Don Luís's burial of the Jesuits stemmed from his Catholic education. Historians generally portray Don Luís as chafing under his Spanish bondage, eagerly awaiting the day when he could trade his black robe for buckskin. Certainly his actions in August 1571 suggest a strong desire to live among his ancestral community, to live by their rules. But could he have forgotten all he was exposed to in ten years—nearly half his life—among the Spanish? More to the point, would he have even wanted to forget? After all, this was a person who may well have believed that Christian baptism saved his life in 1562. It seems very possible that Don Luís, seeking spiritual power from two different religious systems, tried to appease the Christian god with the decent burial of those who tried to spread that god's word.

Memory of Catholic teachings may also have informed Don Luís's next move. The Indians scattered after killing the Jesuits, but soon they returned to gather the spoils. One of Don Luís's brothers was attracted by the Mass vestments and the altar cloth; he was later seen wearing these novel items.[69] For his own part, Don Luís threw away several images, apparently not of interest to him, and focused on two things: the chalice and the paten. Perhaps he singled out these items because they were silver. But another possibility suggests itself: during the Mass the chalice holds the blood and the paten carries the body of the Christian savior. And not metaphorically, but literally, for Catholics believe that wine and bread are transformed during the Mass into the actual blood and body of Christ. What could be more powerful than to possess these magical tokens, talismans that had been in physical contact with another god?

But Don Luís did not hoard these items. In classic Amerindian fashion, he used the supernatural silver to foster alliances. Anthropologists and ethno-historians have long demonstrated how Indians gave gifts in order to create reciprocal obligations, and this is just what Don Luís seems to have done.[70] A captured chief told Father Rogel in August 1672 that "Don Luís gave the silver chalice to an important chief in the interior." Likewise, Rogel recorded, "the paten was given to one of the Indians we captured."[71] Don Luís didn't even trade the items, he *gave* them away, the most effective way to demonstrate one's power and generosity. In a society that stressed reciprocity, the Indians who received Don Luís's otherworldly gifts now would feel indebted to him.

After describing the division of spoils, Rogel's letter includes one hard-to-explain detail. "Some Indians told" Olmos that once they had divided up the vestments, chalice, and paten, only one item remained: a locked chest. Curious to discover what the chest held, three Indians pried open the lock and found a large devotional crucifix. They did not enjoy their discovery for long. According to the Indians, the three men "fell down dead on the spot."[72]

In the next chapter we will see how the English, mere miles from this spot, heard an anecdote that resonates with the tale of the deadly crucifix. In the later story, Indians died after viewing real corpses, whereas in 1571 Indians allegedly died after viewing the *representation* of a corpse: the tortured body of the Christian savior. But for the Jesuits, perhaps even more so than for other Catholics, the power of the crucifix was very real. The Jesuits in Ajacán were infused with the mystical zeal of their order's founder, Ignatius of Loyola, who had died only fifteen years earlier. As Ignatius urged in his

Spiritual Exercises, "Imagine Christ our Lord suspended on the cross before you, and converse with him in a colloquy."[73] The Jesuits in Ajacán had no doubt conversed often with their savior as he hung from the cross.

The story of the deadly crucifix may simply have been an invention, in line with the trope, common in Spanish literature about the New World, of the Cross destroying demons/Indians.[74] But if the story had a basis in fact, it may have been that the unlucky Indians died shortly after the division of spoils, perhaps as the result of pathogens introduced by the Spanish. In this case, the story has a powerful metaphoric component: the crucifix serves as a synecdoche not for beliefs but the people who carry them, fallen humans infected with earthly diseases. Whether the story was invented from whole cloth or not, the Spanish found it irresistible. It was recounted in every subsequent retelling of the events, serving to represent the mysterious power of the god whose son lay dead on the cross. As one Jesuit put it in 1610, "The Crucified One was offended by the cruel death worked on these blessed Fathers and wanted to strike them [the murderers] down suddenly."[75]

If the Spanish god meted out vengeance immediately, the Spanish themselves had to wait eighteen months to do likewise. They sent a relief ship later in 1571 and captured several Indians, one of whom told them that Olmos and Don Luís were still alive. But the Spanish feared they were not well armed enough to handle the hostile Indians of Ajacán, so they returned to Cuba. Finally, in August 1572, the governor of Cuba himself led an expedition to find Olmos and Don Luís and bring the Jesuits' murderers to justice. Again the Spanish captured a group of Indians. Now the governor, Pedro Menéndez, knew he was on the right track, for one of the unlucky fellows wore the Jesuits' silver paten around his neck. Menéndez demanded that Olmos and Don Luís be brought back to the ship. The Indians returned Olmos but Don Luís would never again be seen by Europeans. To make the Indians pay for their lack of cooperation, and in line with the biblical injunction of an eye for an eye, Menéndez ordered eight of the hostages to be hanged from the ship's rigging. But not before Father Rogel, with Olmos acting as an interpreter, "catechized and baptized them." Thus were saved the souls of eight Indians, the last converts the Spanish gained in Ajacán.[76]

*   *   *

The Spanish were very much on the minds of the next Europeans to try to plant colonies in southeastern North America: the English, who brought a different theology but followed a similar pattern of using deathways to communicate with Indians even as they tried to change native deathways. England watched with envy as Spain became ever wealthier over the course of the sixteenth century from the gold and silver extracted from the New World. The English followed these developments with dismay as well, for Spain was not simply a rival power but the chief defender of Catholicism in the Old World and promoter of Catholicism in the New World. So in the 1580s a small group of well-connected Englishmen led by Sir Walter Ralegh convinced Queen Elizabeth that the best way to sap the strength of the Spanish Crown was to embark on a privateering campaign against the Spanish treasure fleet. Privateering differed from simple piracy in that it required a license from the government. Queen Elizabeth thus issued licenses and, true to their word, the privateers quickly found success against the less maneuverable Spanish galleons.[77]

English privateers initially harassed Spanish ships in European waters, but Ralegh had bigger game in his sights. Set up a colony in North America, he argued, and privateers could use this as a base to attack the Spanish flotilla as it sailed along the Atlantic coast of Florida before heading out into the open sea. Elizabeth found the argument compelling and in March 1584 issued Ralegh a patent to establish colonies in the "heathen and barbarous lands" of North America.[78] The very next month Ralegh outfitted an expedition to America to find a suitable site. Arthur Barlowe and Philip Amadas captained the two English ships and decided that Roanoke Island on the coast of present-day North Carolina was the ideal location for a privateering base: close enough to the West Indies to provide access to the treasure fleet, far enough away from the small Spanish outpost at Saint Augustine to remain safe, and sheltered by the string of barrier islands known as the Outer Banks.

Auspiciously, the natives of Roanoke greeted the English warmly. The wife of a local *werowance* (headman) commanded her retinue to carry the English on their backs from the water's edge to dry ground. Barlowe and his men were placed around a crackling fire and their feet were washed in warm water. And then they were feasted: men weary of ship's biscuit savored stewed venison, roasted fish, and boiled maize. No wonder that Barlowe rhapsodized, "We were entertained with all love, and kindness, and with as much bounty, after their manner, as they could possibly devise."[79] And like Paquiquineo/ Don Luís before them, two Indians stepped forward to accompany the expedition back to England.

As the historian Michael Oberg reminds us, these high-status men—

Manteo and Wanchese—were not duped into joining the English. Rather, they went on a mission, determined to learn as much as possible about these powerful and possibly dangerous strangers.[80] They boarded Barlowe's ship and after an uneventful journey arrived in England. There they lodged with Thomas Harriot, the mathematician and scientist who would join the 1585 expedition to Roanoke and who would later become fascinated with Indian deathways. Manteo and Wanchese learned some English and taught Harriot the basics of the Carolina Algonquian language.

The 1585 expedition was an impressive undertaking. In April seven ships set sail from Plymouth, England, with about six hundred people aboard: sailors, soldiers, and colonists. After some time in the Spanish West Indies, the fleet made contact with the Indians of Roanoke Island in July. Wanchese quickly abandoned the English, but Manteo helped make overtures to the region's *werowance*, Wingina. This powerful leader gave the English permission to establish a settlement on Roanoke Island, probably because there was a nearby Indian village from which the natives could keep an eye on the newcomers.[81] The English quickly set about building a fort. In this they were successful but they soon realized that supplies were running low, so most of the colonists went back to England, while about one hundred others remained under the command of Ralph Lane. One of those remaining in Roanoke was Harriot, who, with the help of Manteo, began gathering information for scientific purposes.

After Harriot spent about a year in Roanoke, he wrote a natural history and ethnography of the region, *A Briefe and True Report of the New Found Land of Virginia*, first published in 1588. This tract became enormously influential in Europe, especially after it was reprinted in a four-language edition (English, French, German, and Latin) by Theodore de Bry in 1590. The 1590 edition included engravings, done by de Bry, based on the detailed watercolors painted by a member of the Roanoke expedition, John White. Because of Harriot's relationship with Manteo and his grasp of at least the rudiments of the local language, he could move beyond a description of Indian behaviors to discuss Indian beliefs, aided by his "special familiarity with some of their priests." [82] Together, Harriot and White made a serious attempt to understand Carolina Algonquian culture. As part of this endeavor, both were interested in Indian deathways, which they portrayed as central to Roanoke religion. Their generally sympathetic perspective on Indian deathways was aided, in part, by some of the congruences they perceived between Indian and English practices. Because so many Indian beliefs about death and the afterlife made sense to Harriot and White, they were able to describe them without scorn or ridicule: in the inclusive style of Herodotus and other earlier European travel writers.

Take, for example, the Carolina Indians' reported belief in the immortality of the English. Harriot could understand the rationale behind such a view. As several Roanoke colonists attested, the new colony was relatively healthful, at least for the English; Harriot reported that only four out of 108 colonists died the first year. The local Indians were not so fortunate, as Old World diseases swept through their ranks. As a result, according to Harriot, "Some people could not tell whether to think us gods or men." Harriot was likewise careful to say that only "some" therefore believed "that we were not born of women, and therefore not mortal, but that we were men of an old generation many years past then risen again to immortality." [83] Some Indians may have briefly believed that the English among them were immortal due to their seeming imperviousness to disease. But such ideas could not have been held by Manteo and Wanchese, who had almost certainly witnessed funeral processions in their months in England. This belief also would not have persisted long among the rest of the Roanoke Indians, who learned soon enough that the English could die—and be killed—just like any people. But the important point is that Harriot felt the Indians' purported belief made sense. Might not "some" Europeans, confronted by an alien people who seemed not to die, think likewise?

Even closer to European beliefs was Harriot's portrayal of the Roanoke afterlife:

> as soon as the soul is departed from the body, according to the works it hath done, it is either carried to heaven the habitation of gods, there to enjoy perpetual bliss and happiness, or else to a great pit or hole, which they think to be in the furthest parts of their part of the world toward the sunset, there to burn continually: the place they call *Popogusso*. [84]

This passage, with its resemblance to the Christian heaven and hell, may represent the recent influence of Christian missionaries among the Roanoke Indians, perhaps the Spanish Jesuits who met their end in 1571 a hundred miles to the north of Roanoke. Or the Christian gloss may have been introduced by Harriot, who put the words of his informants into terms he and his readers could understand. [85] Or it is possible that the Carolina Algonquians had long believed in a pleasant place for the souls of the good and a place where the souls of the evil roasted. But the larger point is this: Harriot believed there was a similarity between native and English beliefs in the afterlife, and this helped him portray the Indians as fully human and comprehensible.

Harriot even related without mockery two stories of extraordinary disinterments, when individuals thought to be dead were unearthed to tell of the afterlife. The first incident happened "but few years before our coming into the country." In this case a "wicked" man died and his fellow Indians buried him. Nothing seemed out of the ordinary until the following day, when a few Indians saw the earth above his grave move. The villagers dug up the man and found him, amazingly, alive. He told a harrowing tale: he nearly entered Popogusso, but at the last minute the gods told him to return to his people to tell them what they should do "to avoid that terrible place of torment."[86]

The second incident occurred in a town about sixty miles from Roanoke sometime in 1585. Harriot noted that "it was told me for strange news," and the story is, like the first, strange indeed. Again a man died, was buried, and was disinterred. This resuscitated man reported that his soul had witnessed things far more pleasant than the first returnee: he saw beautiful trees laden with fruit, he saw comfortable houses, and he saw his father, long dead. This was the habitation of gods! His father told him to return to their town and tell his friends and neighbors what they should do to ensure that they would wind up in this pleasant afterlife.[87]

Harriot seems to have accepted these tales as perfectly reasonable, and when he described the effects these stories had on the Indians, he made their beliefs sound much like those in England. According to Harriot, the result of these two disinterments was that "the common and simple sort of people" among the Indians "have great respect to their Governors, and also great care what they do, to avoid torment after death, and to enjoy bliss."[88] This was similar to the belief of most English Protestants regarding the relationship between earthly behavior and one's eternal estate.[89] And Harriot's point about status differentiation—that "common" Indians had "great respect to their Governors"—played into contemporary English debates. As Karen Kupperman has shown, if English ethnographers could demonstrate that Indians recognized status distinctions like those found in England, this would be evidence in favor of hierarchy being a natural and thus immutable element of human society.[90]

Moreover, aiding Harriot's comprehension of these stories was the fact that the returning "dead" were not unknown among English Protestants: early modern England was filled with stories of returning ghosts.[91] Plus, England possessed a vibrant literature describing individuals purported to have been buried alive and disinterred, or hanged and revived.[92] When Richard Watkins published *Newes from the Dead* in 1651, his title was not meant to be facetious. Anne Green, hanged for infanticide but revived on the dissection table, was—like the disinterred Carolina Algonquians—a messenger from the other side.[93]

In yet another way did the Roanoke Indians make a distinction between "the common and simple sort of people" and "their Governors." Some common people among the Carolina Algonquians, such as the two men who were eventually disinterred, were buried in simple pits in the earth; others were placed on scaffolds where they awaited secondary burial. But a much more complicated procedure awaited Roanoke Indian leaders. Although the archaeology of coastal Carolina is not as extensive as that of tidewater Virginia, it nonetheless offers suggestive evidence about ordinary burials. This is especially important because Harriot and White wore cultural blinders: they described in great detail the burial of chiefs and *werowances*, but they were not interested in common burials. For these English elites, the elaborate burial of one's leaders was a mark of civilization, and thus noteworthy in this New World setting.

Archaeological evidence suggests that there were two types of burial that awaited nonelite Indians of the northern Carolina coast. In some places, individuals (like the men who came back from the dead) were placed into pits just outside their village in a designated burial ground. In these pit burials, the individuals were usually placed on their sides in a semiflexed position. Grave goods were not common. Harriot's only description of this process is part of an unrelated discussion of the Indians' lack of metal goods: "neither use they any digging, but only for graves about three foot deep." [94]

Elsewhere in the region, individuals seem to have been placed on scaffolds, where they decomposed relatively quickly as a result of their exposure to the elements. After a certain period of time, probably several years, all the bones on a village's scaffolds were gathered up. Each individual's bones were disarticulated, that is, taken apart and rearranged into a bundle. These bundles were then carried to an ossuary near the village for a secondary burial. If someone had died only recently, and flesh remained on the bones and the ligaments still kept the bones together, this corpse was carried to the ossuary without disarticulating the skeleton. Finally, all the bundles (and the complete corpses) were placed tightly into the ossuary together: men and women, young and old, usually between thirty and sixty individuals altogether. The

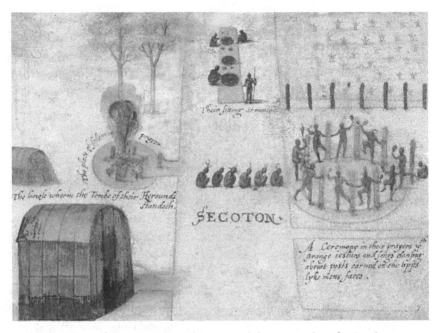

Figure 6. Village of Secotan. John White painted this watercolor of a Carolina Algonquian village in 1585. In the lower left is a *Machicómuck*, "the house wherein the tomb of their herounds [*werowances*] standeth." The fire just beyond the tomb is labeled "their place of solemn prayer," and to the right nine Indians dance in "a ceremony in their prayers." Evidently Secotan's tomb was located in a part of the village reserved for religious rituals. Image © Trustees of the British Museum.

only grave goods found by archaeologists in these ossuaries are the phalanges ("fingers") of big cats like lynx and mountain lions, a few conch columella beads, and one panther mask.[95] Based on Harriot's brief mention of three-foot-deep graves, in addition to the stories of the resuscitated men, pit burials seem to have predominated around Roanoke Island, with scaffold burials elsewhere in the nearby coastal region. But Harriot's lack of detailed reportage means that we do not know this for sure, nor do we understand the significance of things like the cat claws or the orientation of the pit burials.

Harriot and White did, however, leave a great deal of information about elite burials, in the form of White's watercolors and Harriot's captions. White's drawing of the Indian village of Secotan, located about sixty miles southwest of Roanoke Island on the south bank of the Pamlico River, shows a small open village consisting of several longhouses, cornfields, and ceremonial sites (Figure 6). In the picture's left foreground, next to "the place of solemn prayer," is a charnel house, what the Indians called a *Machicómuck*, "the house wherein the tomb of their herounds [*werowances*] standeth." [96] This structure was not unlike the burial temples de Soto found throughout the southeast.

Another drawing shows a "tomb" in greater detail, though because the close-up image depicts the building standing on poles, it appears to be a different *Machicómuck* from the one in Secotan (Figure 7). White's drawing depicts a cross-legged wooden statue of the god called Kiwasa watching over ten princely corpses prepared in a time-consuming process. First, according to Harriot, a *werowance*'s corpse was disemboweled, then flayed. After the skin was removed, the flesh was cut from the bones and dried in the sun. Once fully dried, this flesh was kept wrapped in mats, which one can see in the back of the tomb, near the corpses' feet. Then the bones, "still fastened together with the ligaments whole and uncorrupted," were covered with deerskins and finally with the *werowance*'s own skin. This helped make the corpse look as natural as possible, "as if their flesh were not taken away," even down to the hair that remained on top of the head. Finally, the corpse took its place in the tomb, next to the *werowances* who had died before. The Indians believed that once the corpses were in this position, guarded by Kiwasa, "nothing may hurt them." [97]

It might be thought that Harriot and White would have found this procedure repulsive and macabre, evidence of Indian barbarity. Quite the contrary. For the English, the *Machicómuck* stood as physical evidence of the complexity of Indian society. That the Roanoke Indians made a sharp distinction between the treatment of dead commoners and *werowances* demonstrated that this was a society sophisticated enough to recognize the inherent distinctions of rank among men. As Barlowe enthused after his 1584 reconnaissance, "No people in the world carry more respect to their King, Nobility, and Governors, than these do." [98]

Moreover, Harriot and White drew on their own cultural inheritance to help understand the Indians' desire to preserve their kings' bodies. In Harriot's and White's native land of England, royal corpses had been afforded special attention for hundreds of years, similar to the French practices described in the previous chapter. Starting in the twelfth century, the custom of English royal funerals was to bury the heart and entrails separately from the king's body. This way, the corpse could more easily be embalmed and displayed during the entire funeral, which lasted a few days. By the fourteenth century,

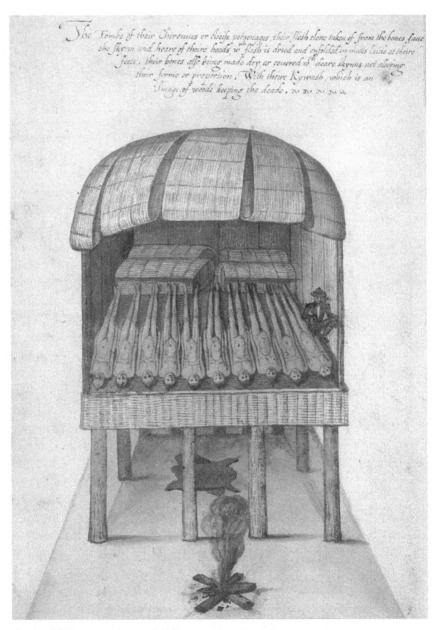

The Tombe of their Cherounes or cheife personages, their flesh clene taken of from the bones saue the skynn and heare of theire heads, wch flesh is dried and enfolded in mats laide at theire feete, their bones also being made dry or couered wth deare skynns not alterinc their forme or proportion. With theire Kywash, which is an Image of woode keeping the deade.

Figure 7. Carolina Algonquian burial temple. This appears to be a different
Machicómuck from the one John White portrayed in Secotan, as it is on stilts.
Ordinarily the mats hung down, but White rendered them lifted up in order to show
the ten mummified corpses and the wooden statue of Kiwasa to the right. In the
back of the tomb stand four chests, which held the *werowances'* dried flesh. Image ©
Trustees of the British Museum.

funeral ceremonies had become so elaborate that the crude embalming techniques of the day could not keep the corpse looking fresh for a long enough time. Beginning in 1327 and continuing through the funeral of James I in 1625, the English substituted effigies for embalmed corpses in funeral processions. These effigies were noteworthy for their lifelike appearance—down to the hair on the head (though in England the hair was not the king's own).[99]

The treatment of Queen Elizabeth's corpse after her death in 1603 is instructive. When Elizabeth died she was probably disemboweled, embalmed, and placed within a coffin.[100] Her corpse was moved to Whitehall, where it lay in state within its coffin for over a month while funeral preparations took place. During that time her attendants waited on the encoffined queen almost as if she were alive, with the same ceremony and expenditure as usual, "down to the household and table service," according to one witness. This observer, the Venetian ambassador Giovanni Carlo Scaramelli, mocked the respects paid to the dead queen, "as though she were not wrapped in many a fold of cere-cloth, and hid in such a heap of lead, of coffin, of pall, but walking as she used to do at this season."[101]

Then, during the funeral procession, attention turned from the corpse to the effigy of the Queen that lay atop her coffin (Figure 8). The effigy was made of wood, with wax hands and face to appear more lifelike. To heighten the resemblance to the queen, the wax face was cast from a death mask. This was no idealized image of the aged queen; indeed, a later observer noted that the face appeared "a little wrinkly." With bright red hair, rouged cheeks, and open eyes, wearing a robe of crimson satin trimmed with white fustian, the effigy was meant to appear alive. Contemporary observers generally agreed that it was a most splendid representation of the queen. One man who watched the funeral procession called it "the lively picture of her highness['s] whole body." Another stated that the effigy was carved and colored "so faithfully that she seems alive." A third reported that when onlookers "beheld her statue" there was "such a general sighing and groaning, and weeping, and the like has not been seen or known in the memory of man."[102] With all this interest in verisimilitude, the question becomes: if the English had possessed Carolina Algonquian technology, would they have mummified their monarchs' remains for the funeral procession?

It would do violence to the complex cultural rationales that undergirded English royal funerals and the Carolina Algonquian *Machicómuck* to overdraw their similarities. Yet the larger point is that the Roanoke colonists were part of a culture in which a dead queen required personal servants and a

Figure 8. Queen Elizabeth's funeral effigy. Below the gaily colored bannerols (square flags) lies the effigy, or "representation" as the artist delicately put it, made for Queen Elizabeth's funeral in 1603. The hearse was drawn by four horses draped in black velvet. The effigy queen, dressed in crimson robes, wore the imperial crown and held the royal orb and scepter. The wooden effigy's hands and face were made of wax to appear more lifelike. Cast from a death mask, the face appeared "a little wrinkly." Image shelfmark Add. 35324, f.37v. © The British Library Board. All Rights Reserved 2009.

wax-and-wood effigy could bring crowds to tears. The Indian treatment of royal corpses that Harriot and White reported was thus closer to their own worldview than to ours.

Yet despite points of contact between English and Indian beliefs, relations between the two groups deteriorated during the first year of the Roanoke colony. This was because the colonists, including Harriot, embedded their observations about Indians within an exploitative framework, just as the Spanish had done decades earlier. At the beginning of his *Briefe and True Report*, Harriot addressed prospective migrants to Roanoke, assuring them that his book would help "you . . . know and learn what the country is," so that a voyage there "may return you profit and gain." Not only did Harriot fill the bulk of his tract with detailed descriptions of potentially profitable plants, minerals, and dyestuffs; he portrayed the Roanoke Indians as yet another crop to be harvested, this one for Jesus Christ. Harriot crafted his sensitive and valuable ethnography of the Carolina Algonquians, then, to aid in their ultimate conversion. "Some religion they have already," Harriot pointed out, "which although it be far from the truth, yet being as it is, there is hope it may be the easier and sooner reformed." [103]

In the autumn of 1585, after most of the colonists had returned to England, Harriot and the others who remained set about trying to "reform" the Indians and their faulty religion. In every town he went to, Harriot preached about the "true and only God" whose words were found in the Scriptures. That some of Harriot's message was lost in the translation was suggested by the Indians' reaction to the physical Bible. Harriot tried to tell them that the book itself had no magical powers, "yet would many be glad to touch it, to embrace it, to kiss it, to hold it to their breasts and heads, and stroke over all their body with it." So impressive seemed the English religion that when Wingina twice fell ill and seemed to be upon his deathbed, he requested that the English pray for him.[104]

But as winter turned into spring, Wingina and many other Indians began to tire of the English and their god. The one hundred Roanoke colonists were badly undersupplied and heavily dependent on their Indian hosts for food. Without Indian corn and fish, the colonists would have starved. As a result, most of the Indians "began to blaspheme," lamented governor Ralph Lane, "and flatly to say, that our Lord God was not God, since he suffered us to sustain much hunger." English weakness, these Indians reasoned, reflected the weakness of the English god.[105]

Into this deteriorating situation stepped Ensenore, a "savage father" to Wingina and "the only friend" the English had at this time among the Indian leaders. Ensenore, like Harriot, paid a great deal of attention to his new neighbors' deathways; Ensenore's speeches to his fellow Indians emphasized the special relation the English seemed to have with death. Ensenore argued that the English "were the servants of God," and thus even if the Indians could kill them, the English "being dead men were able to do them more hurt, than now [they] could do being alive." Ensenore also pointed out to his fellow leaders that it was the Indians, not the English, who were dying of the mysterious diseases afflicting the region. Wasn't this a sign of the English god's strength? And again, according to Lane, Ensenore reminded his listeners of his view that the English were "dead men returned into the world again, and that we [Englishmen] do not remain dead but for a certain time, and that then we return again." [106] Killing the English would not be a successful strategy of removal.

These speeches bought the colonists some valuable time. Wingina and others heeded their elder's words and continued to aid the English. But then disaster: Ensenore died on April 20. Ensenore's death, combined with the earlier death of another pro-English leader named Granganimeo, discredited their accommodationist stance.[107] As Wingina began to see it, Ensenore's and Granganimeo's support for the English had gotten them nothing but an early trip to the *Machicómuck*. The time had come to rid the island of these parasites.

Wingina's plan—like the great uprising of the Powhatan Indians in 1622, and like numerous slave revolts throughout the Americas—was to use the cover of a funeral ceremony. A large gathering of Indians from various tribes would not seem suspicious, Wingina concluded, if the purpose was to commemorate Ensenore's death. Wingina decided, Lane later learned, that about 1,500 bowmen "should be invited to a certain kind of month's mind which they do use to solemnize in their savage manner for any great personage dead."[108] A "month's mind" was no longer commonly practiced in Protestant England, but in Lane's boyhood (he was born ca. 1530) he would have likely been familiar with this Catholic practice of marking the one-month anniversary of a person's death with a Mass.[109] Requests for month's minds were "not uncommon" in wills through the 1560s, and even though the practice had virtually ceased by the 1580s, the phrase "to have a month's mind" remained current, meaning "to have a great longing."[110] So if Wingina had been able to keep his attack plans secret, the colonists likely would have been caught off guard, as an Indian month's mind—especially for an esteemed leader—seemed to the English like a perfectly reasonable explanation for an assemblage of 1,500 men.

Wingina's plan called for the men gathered at the June 10 ceremony honoring Ensenore to attack the English "in the dead time of the night." Their first targets were to be Lane and his "werowances (as they call all our principal officers)." Lane's thatched hut would be set on fire, and when he ran out in his nightshirt the Indians "would have knocked out my brains." Then they would have done the same to Harriot's hut, the huts of the other leaders, the fort, and the town. In one carefully timed attack, the English would have been destroyed.[111]

But Lane learned of the plan. The governor held a young Indian named Skiko prisoner, but made sure that this son of a chief was "well used at my hand." Lane's uncharacteristic "good cop" role was rewarded when Skiko revealed Wingina's plot. Lane responded with a preemptive attack on May

31. During the ensuing engagement Wingina feigned death after receiving a flesh wound and then bounded up and ran off into the woods. Lane worried that his nemesis had escaped, but his fears vanished when he saw an Irishman named Edward Nugent "returning out of the woods with [Wingina's] head in his hand." [112] Imposing the traditional English postmortem humiliation for treason, Lane had Wingina's head placed on a pole.

*   *   *

Wingina's impaled head symbolizes the disintegration of English-Indian relations at Roanoke. Between Barlowe's men having their feet washed by Indian women in 1584 and Nugent beheading Wingina's corpse in 1586, there had been moments of cross-cultural cooperation and understanding. Thomas Harriot, with his knowledge of the local language, questioned his hosts about their most sacred beliefs and told them about his own. He and other Englishmen were impressed by the similarities they perceived between their own and Indian deathways—especially the Indian respect for rank, and their belief in separate destinations for the souls of good and evil individuals. But these affinities and moments of understanding could not overcome the ultimately exploitative foundations of the colonization efforts. The colonists were aiming to gain profits for themselves and for their queen. As a result, the Indians withdrew their earlier support for the English, leaving the colonists in an untenable position.

So the English—like the Spanish in Ajacán before them—left. At least most of them did: fifteen Englishmen remained behind to guard the fort. All too predictably, when the English fleet returned in 1587, all they found were the bones of one of the men. The colonists had been victims of a carefully planned Indian attack. The bones should have been a warning to the new batch of colonists that their prospects were not good. Even with the continued help of Manteo—who, according to the governor of the 1587 colony, "behaved himself toward us as a most faithful English man"—the colonists could not survive on their own.[113] When war with Spain prevented the English from resupplying the colony until 1590, the colonists disappeared into the woods, perhaps to starve, perhaps to be killed, perhaps to blend in with the local Indian population. This last possibility, supported by Indian oral histories,[114] spurs some intriguing questions about deathways. Imagine one of these Lost Colonists, an ordinary soldier, marrying an Indian woman. They have a daughter who dies in infancy. How do they bury her?

CHAPTER 3

Burial and Disinterment
in the Chesapeake

JOHN SMITH WAS keenly interested in the Roanoke expeditions. Smith, the stocky soldier of fortune who became the leader of the Jamestown colony, read Thomas Harriot's *Briefe and True Report* carefully. When Smith later wrote his own histories and ethnographies of the New World, he quoted liberally from Harriot. Among other descriptions he borrowed from Roanoke's scientific observer, Smith used all of Harriot's examples of Indian-English interactions regarding deathways: the men who returned from the dead to tell of the afterlife, the Roanoke Indians' belief that the English were immortal, and Wingina's use of Ensenore's funeral as a cover for his planned rebellion.[1] Though Smith shared Harriot's interest in using deathways to facilitate cross-cultural communication, even more than Harriot he sought to parlay his knowledge of Indian religion and culture into domination of the local natives.

Although Smith spent only two years in Virginia, he is today credited (or blamed) for setting the tone of the Jamestown colony's early years. Americans closely associate Smith and Jamestown, not merely because Smith was, as one of his rivals put it, "an ambitious unworthy vainglorious fellow," who in his accounts of Virginia always put himself at the center of the action.[2] Rather, Smith survives in historical memory because the lessons he drew from Roanoke informed his—and the colony's—approach to relations with the Indians, and this knowledge allowed the colony to survive. Smith felt that Roanoke demonstrated that the Indians had to be treated sternly in order to be of greatest benefit to the English. As in the sixteenth century, the deathways of their new neighbors continued to be a source of fascination and contention for both Indians and the English. Both sides perceived in the others parallel mortuary practices, which allowed for a degree of mutual understanding. But in Jamestown more so than in Roanoke, knowledge of foreign deathways was often mobilized to attack or gain advantage over the other group. This pattern started first with Smith and continued later with Powhatan, the elderly paramount chief of eastern Virginia's Algonquian Indians. The English and the Indians frequently grasped the underlying rationales of the other group's deathways, and each sought to use this knowledge to its own advantage.[3] Later in the century, some of these same deep parallels facilitated syncretism, as Indians combined their traditional beliefs with selected aspects of Anglo-Virginian material and religious culture.

*   *   *

The English announced their arrival in the Chesapeake on April 29, 1607, by planting a large cross on a point of land they called Cape Henry.[4] A cross was arguably not the most fitting symbol of the expedition, for this group of colonists did not include someone like Thomas Harriot, who used his knowledge of Algonquian to preach to the natives. Perhaps a more apt symbol of the group would have been a matchlock, the state-of-the-art English firearm, as this was a well-armed group anticipating hostile Indians.

The colonists need not have worried so much, at least at first. Most of the Indians they met treated them well, including the very first group the colonists sat down with, in the village of Kecoughtan. Here the English were "entertained by them very kindly." After some initial ceremonies and chanting that the colonists could not fathom, the Indians brought their guests "such dainties as they had," including "their bread which they make of their maize."[5] With only a few exceptions, the natives welcomed the colonists in 1607.

Heartened by this reception, the English looked for a place to settle, deciding on an uninhabited site fifty miles upriver that they christened Jamestown Island. The English liked the depth of the river that surrounded the "island" (actually a peninsula connected to the riverbank by a narrow spit of land), which allowed their ships to approach safely. But the island was uninhabited for a reason: during the summer the newly named James River flowed less forcefully, allowing salty bay water to back up, and causing the river to become a cesspool of pathogen-bearing human waste.

But in the spring the location looked promising, so the colonists set out building a fort. This they completed successfully, though their food supplies soon ran low. To the colonists' aid came the local Indians, who "did daily relieve us with corn and flesh," as Edward Maria Wingfield wrote.[6] One reason for this generosity is that Powhatan, the area's paramount chief, hoped to use the English as allies against his enemies. Powhatan controlled an area of eastern Virginia with about two dozen villages. He impressed the English with both his physical presence and leadership abilities. William Strachey described the seventy-year-old leader as "of a tall stature, and clean limbs." Powhatan's size was undiminished despite his age: he was "not yet shrinking, though well beaten with many cold and stormy winters." The paramount chief was, according to Strachey, "of a daring spirit, vigilant, ambitious, subtle to enlarge his dominions."[7] It is unclear whether this last point was true; Powhatan may not have wished to expand his chiefdom but merely hoped to fend off attacks from hostile Siouans and Iroquoians to the west and north. In either case, his and his people's aid to the colonists was shaped by considerations of realpolitik.

Despite this help, the colonists were laid low by a situation that caught them off guard. Unlike Roanoke, Jamestown proved deadly for the English. Whereas only four of 108 Roanoke colonists died in 1585–86, the English in Jamestown dropped like flies. Forty-six of 105 colonists were dead within four months of landfall. This seems to have been the result of Jamestown's unhealthful, swampy location at the fresh-salt boundary of the James. Colonists died in the summer of 1607 from "bloody flux" (dysentery), "swelling" (edema, possibly from salt poisoning caused by drinking out of the brackish James River), and typhoid. In characteristically egocentric fashion, John Smith interpreted these deaths as a sign that God was "angry with us" because Smith was "so disgraced through others' malice," a reference to the infighting and dissension that plagued the colony's first months.[8]

The summer's staggering mortality meant that "the living were scarce able to bury the dead," according to Smith's 1608 narrative.[9] By this Smith may have meant that English corpses went unburied, or that they almost went unburied but were interred with heroic effort. In either case, Smith mobilized a trope of extreme disorder. English writers used unburied corpses as evidence of the most chaotic times: bloody battles, plague years, and the like.[10] But just as the English were not all equal in life, neither were they equal in death. During the very worst stretch of the summer epidemic, Captain Bartholomew Gosnold died. Gosnold was a well-respected explorer—he had named both Cape Cod and Martha's Vineyard—and a member of a distinguished English family. His corpse, unsurprisingly, did not remain unburied. Instead, "he was honorably buried, having all the ordnance in the fort shot off with many volleys of small shot." [11] Indeed, the special treatment accorded this esteemed corpse has allowed archaeologists to identify Gosnold's skeleton "with something approaching probability." A skeleton unearthed in 2003 was found buried with a half pike, nearly six feet long and with a cruciform iron spike at the tip. The half pike is the key piece of forensic evidence indicating that this was probably Gosnold: only individuals of high military status were buried with this symbol of martial leadership, usually placed on top of the coffin. [12] By burying Gosnold with gunfire and a half pike—classic elements of European displays of military honor—the colonists sought to recreate an aspect of home in the disorienting New World environment.

The Powhatan Indians watched the colonists during these first months with increasing concern. It was worrying to see how little attention the newcomers gave to basic matters of survival. The English simply were not planting enough corn, and the Indians ultimately paid for this lack of foresight, as Smith had no qualms about bullying the Indians into supplying the colonists with food. At the same time the Indians were dealing with the ravenous colonists, they (like their English counterparts) were dying in terrifying numbers. Their deaths were not caused by dysentery and salt poisoning; they knew enough not to drink from the James River. Rather the Powhatans were dying of European diseases. As Powhatan lamented, "I have seen the death of all my people thrice." [13]

Against this backdrop of high mortality all around, several colonists crossed the Chesapeake to Virginia's Eastern Shore in June 1608, where they met the "king" of the village of Accomac. This *werowance*, with his "comely" visage and "civil" deportment, greatly impressed the English. The *werowance*'s descriptions of the fertility of his lands excited the colonists, who were scouting for places to expand their settlement. But then the "king" told a story that gave the English pause. Like the "strange news" of disinterments in Roanoke that Harriot heard, the colonists learned of a "strange accident" involving disinterment on the Eastern Shore.

The *werowance* told them that two children had recently died and been buried. Their parents, against all conventions, disinterred the small corpses. The "king" could not explain this transgression of ordinary practices. Perhaps it was due to the bereaved parents' "extreme passions," or perhaps "some dreaming visions, fantasy, or affection." The disinterment of recently buried children was unusual, but what awaited the parents was even more surpris-

ing: the "benumbed bodies reflected to the eyes of the beholders such pleasant delightful countenances, as though they had regained their vital spirits."
The children were dead yet looked alive. The amazed parents quickly spread
word of the "miracle," and many of their fellow villagers came to behold the
bodies. All those who viewed the corpses, however, soon died, "and not any
one escaped." [14]

It is possible that those who came to see the miraculous corpses died from
exposure to some infectious agent carried by the bodies. But this is improb-
able. In fact, corpses are less likely than living humans to spread infectious
disease: the dead do not exhale, cough, expectorate, or do much of anything
that readily transmits disease. Instead, the connection between disinterment
and death was probably a narrative that helped the *werowance* explain some
puzzling recent developments in Accomac: why were so many people dying?
and why were there so many children among the dead? The high mortality
caused by Old World diseases led the *werowance* to seek an explanation in the
transgression of ordinary burial practices. The bereaved parents' act of disinterring their children's corpses was so unusual that the *werowance* believed
the gods were punishing his people for this act—not unlike the way Smith
thought his own god was punishing his people for their backbiting ways.

To understand how transgressive disinterment was, it is first necessary to
understand typical burial practices among the Powhatans. Like the Carolina
Algonquians to their south, the Powhatans (who were Algonquians as well)
sharply distinguished elite and commoner burials, though archaeological and
historical evidence suggests a fair degree of variability regarding burial practices in the region. Archaeological excavations in the James River and York
River drainages indicate that ossuary burials had once been common in the
region. These were probably used for nonelites, as there is little evidence of
status differentiation in the ossuaries, with one important exception that will
be discussed below. At ten sites with radiocarbon dates from the thirteenth to
the fifteenth centuries, scholars have unearthed about twenty-five ossuaries.
These were relatively small ossuaries, usually with ten to twenty individuals
buried in each.[15] As was the case farther south, Indians used these pits for
secondary burials, that is, for burials after the skeletons had decomposed on
scaffolds.

But how do we know that the corpses had been placed on scaffolds? Isn't
it possible that the corpses had been buried in the earth, allowed to decompose, and then dug up and reburied in ossuaries? If this were the case, then
disinterment would not have been at all transgressive among the Virginia Al-

gonquians. But an insect—specifically the mud dauber wasp—comes to the aid of archaeologists. Mud dauber wasps aren't very picky about their nesting sites. They will build their small mud nests in all sorts of protected spaces: under the eaves of a house, hidden beneath a rocky ledge, or, it turns out, inside a decomposed human head. When archaeologists look inside skulls from an ossuary and find nests resembling tiny clay pots—the telltale sign of the mud dauber—it is strong evidence that the individuals decomposed on scaffolds long enough to allow the wasps to call the cranial cavity home. This is exactly what archaeologists have found in some of the Virginia ossuaries.[16]

By the time the English established Jamestown, however, ossuary burials for commoners seem to have been on the wane. At least we have no description of them in the James and York rivers area, and unlike Thomas Harriot, several Virginian writers paid attention to the burial of commoners. "For their ordinary burials," John Smith wrote in 1612, "they dig a deep hole in the earth with sharp stakes and the corpse being lapped [wrapped] in skins and mats with their jewels, they lay them upon sticks in the ground, and so cover them with earth."[17] Thus, by the contact period individual pit burials seem to have predominated for commoners, replacing the earlier ossuaries.[18]

Powhatan Indians preserved their elites in temples, though the process differed somewhat from that of the Carolina Algonquians. Our primary informants are Smith and William Strachey—who lived in Virginia from May 1610 to September 1611 and who had long interviews with two Indians—with some details added by an anonymous writer from the 1680s (perhaps Reverend John Clayton).[19] When a leader died, the body was first disemboweled and then laid upon a scaffold to dry. The survivors placed near the corpse "tobacco and pipes, turkey and deer and other victuals and pocoon, which is a root they paint themselves withal."[20] When the bones had completely dried they were placed with "bracelets or chains of copper, pearl, and such like, as they used to wear" into skins or mats.[21] Then these bundles were sewed up and placed into a temple, where they were guarded by an idol. Unlike the Carolina Algonquians, then, the Powhatan Indians did not mummify their leaders but preserved their bones in disarticulated bundles inside their temples.[22] As a result the Powhatans did not need to employ any methods to keep the corpses lifelike. Strachey wrote, "We hear of no sweet oils or ointments that they use to dress or chest [to coffin] their dead bodies with, albeit they want not of the precious rosin running out of the great cedar, wherewith in the old time they used to embalm dead bodies."[23]

One question remains: after the bones of elites had been kept in bundles for a period of time, were the bones ever buried? English observers do not offer any clues, but one intriguing archaeological site very near Jamestown holds a possible answer. In the area inhabited by the Quiyoughcohannock, a tribe within the Powhatan confederacy that lived about ten miles west of Jamestown, archaeologists have uncovered ten ossuaries that held a total of 107 individuals. An Early Colonial–style pipe stem, with designs impressed by a metal tool, suggests a post-1607 date for at least one of the ossuaries. This site's central ossuary is unique, as it contains eleven skulls "placed 'cheek-to-cheek' in two semicircles facing each other." [24] Without any supporting documentary evidence we must be cautious about interpreting this finding, but its rarity and difference from the rest of the ossuaries suggest that Powhatans reserved this practice for their leaders. Is this what they did with the bones of their leaders after a certain length of time in the temple?

In sum, the Powhatan Indians buried their commoners in individual pits (a practice that seems to have mostly replaced earlier ossuary burials for commoners) and preserved their leaders' disarticulated remains in bundles within their temples. Perhaps the leaders' bones were later buried in an ossuary. In the descriptions of the Algonquians in North Carolina and Virginia, then, there is no evidence—documentary or archaeological—for disinterment of earth inhumations as an ordinary part of mortuary practices. Getting back to the "king" of Accomac on Virginia's Eastern Shore, this helps explain why he was so horrified by the disinterment of two children by their parents. This was such a breach of ordinary behavior that he believed it resulted in the death of all those who witnessed the strange sight—and he felt that it was worth telling his new English neighbors.

The Englishmen who first heard this story recorded it without registering any disbelief; in the style of Herodotus or Mandeville they simply presented the *werowance*'s words and offered no commentary. This attitude likely resulted from sympathy with the *werowance*'s revulsion. Englishmen also came from a culture that viewed disinterment in a harshly negative light. Before the Protestant Reformation, the English dealt with the problem of crowded urban graveyards by occasionally disinterring dry bones and placing them into a charnel house. With the Reformation's attack on purgatory, Protestants began to feel that charnel houses were unseemly, as they encouraged the banned practice of praying for the souls of the deceased. By the early seventeenth century, disinterment smelled to the English nose dangerously of Catholicism. [25]

The English associated disinterment not only with Catholicism but also with the humiliation of the infamous. In the early modern period—when spectacles of violence helped demonstrate state power—maiming, torturing, and killing miscreants was often not enough.[26] Corpses were subject to state-sanctioned violence. Heads were lopped off and placed on poles, genitals cut off and thrown to the pigs, limbs severed. But what if someone died and was not subject to the posthumous humiliation he or she deserved? The solution was simple: disinter the corpse and let the desecration begin. English Catholics occasionally did this to notable Protestants during the reign of the Catholic Queen Mary (1553–58). Catholic officials, for example, unwittingly helped make the Protestant reformer Martin Bucer into a martyr by digging up his bones—which had lain in the grave for nearly two years—and burning his remains.[27] But Catholics had no monopoly on disinterment in England. One of the best-known Protestant performances of disinterment occurred at the end of the English Civil War. After the Restoration of the monarchy, the bodies of Oliver Cromwell and other regicides were exhumed from Westminster Abbey, hanged at Tyburn from sunup to sundown, beheaded, and finally buried under the gallows.[28] Later, in 1670s Virginia, some residents wanted to do much the same to the unsuccessful rebel Nathaniel Bacon. Bacon's opponents hunted for his grave, "with design to expose his bones to public infamy," but they never could find it.[29]

As was the case among the Powhatan Indians, disinterment was not a part of ordinary English burial practices. For Protestants disinterment represented a terrible fate reserved for only the most notorious, and for the Powhatans disinterment represented a breach of ordinary practices that could bring punishment from the gods.

After Accomac's *werowance* told the English about his people's disinterment of children, colonists continued to use death as a means of communicating with their Indian neighbors. At least twice in the first year of the colony Smith presented himself as a healer in order to impress the Powhatans with his powers to halt or even reverse death. In the first example, Smith was being held captive by Powhatan and was asked by the Indians to revive a man believed to be "breathing his last."[30]

In the second instance, the tables were turned and this time Smith held an Indian captive. Smith had thrown the unlucky fellow into the fort's dungeon and threatened to hang him unless his brother returned a stolen pistol. In an uncharacteristically generous moment, Smith sent some charcoal down to the dungeon so the man could warm himself. Soon the brother showed up at the fort with the pistol, but when he and Smith went to the dungeon to free the prisoner, they found him "so smothered with the smoke he had made, and so piteously burnt," that he appeared dead. The brother broke down wailing and weeping, typical of the Powhatans' mourning practices. Smith sensed an opportunity. Using a little brandy and vinegar, he revived the smothered Indian, but not before exacting a promise from his brother that he would never steal again if Smith brought the man back from the dead. Writing about himself in the third person, Smith noted the effects of this performance: "This was spread amongst all the savages for a miracle, that Captain Smith could make a man alive that is dead." [31]

While the miracle may have awed the Powhatans for a while, the English magic soon ran out: it seemed to the Indians that the newcomers also excelled at making living men dead. Unable to follow up on Smith's healing performances with parallel supernatural control over growing food, the English quickly lost any advantage their miracles may have given them. The summer of 1609 was especially dry, and several times a nearby *werowance* asked Smith to pray to the Christian god "for rain, or his corn would perish, for his gods were angry." [32] Not only was Smith's god unable to deliver the desired rain but the local *werowances* learned that the English needed more corn than ever, as their ineptitude at raising maize continued.

In this volatile situation of English desperation and Indian impatience, even trivial offenses could spark violence. The English made the mistake of committing a serious offense. To ease his people's continued hunger, Smith ordered several groups to leave Jamestown and try to live off the land. This, of course, quickly turned into living off of the Indians. One band, under the command of Captain John Martin, left Jamestown in September 1609 and tried to settle among the Nansemond Indians, wary members of the Powhatan confederacy. Martin and his men could not get the Nansemonds to agree to give them the island on which they lived near the falls of the James, so the English simply took possession of it. But the Indians were not so easily displaced. Their island contained not only their houses but also their "monuments," or burial temples. Upset by the occupation of their island, and perhaps fearing what might happen to their sacred bones, the Indians attacked. In retaliation for this—and in response to the news that two English messengers had been brutally killed, their brains "cut and scraped out of their heads with mussel shells"—the English exceeded the Indians' worst fears and desecrated the temples. As George Percy later proudly recounted, "We beat the Savages out of the island, burned their houses, ransacked their temples, took down the corpses of their dead kings from off their tombs, and carried away their pearls, copper, and bracelets, wherewith they do decore their kings' funerals." [33]

Pillaging the temples turned out to be a terrible miscalculation. As one historian puts it, this act of desecration caused the Powhatans to declare "holy war" against the English. This low-intensity war would result in the deaths of at least two hundred Indians and three hundred colonists—between one-fifth and one-fourth of the English population—before it was over in 1614. [34] One indication that holy war had begun was the symbolically meaningful ways in which the Indians desecrated English corpses in retaliation. Soon after the temples were ransacked, Lieutenant John Sicklemore "and divers others were found also slain with their mouths stopped full of bread." Like the New England Indians who would later mock European agriculture during King Philip's War by burying Englishmen alive up to their necks and wondering if they would grow when planted, the Powhatan Indians used unmistakable symbols when they stuffed their victims' mouths with cornbread. So unmistakable were the symbols that even a poor ethnographer such as Percy could unravel their meanings: it was "done as it seemeth in contempt and scorn that others might expect the like when they should come to seek bread and relief amongst them." [35]

If symbolically charged killings were the first sign of a holy war, the second was a new reluctance of most Powhatan Indians to trade their corn with the English. At about this time, in October 1609, John Smith was burned terribly in a gunpowder accident. To aid his recovery he sailed for England—never to come back to Virginia, as it turned out. So now Indian relations rested with the diplomatically challenged Percy. Percy could not convince the Powhatans to resume trading corn, so his people simply died of hunger. The English referred to the winter of 1609–10 as the Starving Time, and with good reason: by springtime only 100 of some 220 colonists remained alive. [36]

The English survived as long as they could on whatever they could find that cruel winter. One group of colonists was found later by a relief party to have "fed upon nothing but oysters eight weeks' space." And these were the lucky ones. Those remaining in Jamestown subsisted on "dogs, cats, rats, and mice." When no more small mammals could be found, the English chewed on shoe leather and made porridge from laundry starch. These meager supplies exhausted, the colonists foraged in the woods for "serpents and snakes." [37]

And ironically (in light of long-standing European revulsion toward alleged Amerindian cannibalism), some Jamestown colonists violated their culture's strictest taboo and feasted on human flesh. They began "to dig up dead corpses out of graves and to eat them." [38] The English even indulged in cross-cultural cannibalism: according to John Smith, "so great was our famine, that a Savage we slew, and buried, the poorer sort took him up again and eat him." And one can only imagine the hunger-induced insanity that caused one man to kill his pregnant wife, chop her into pieces, and salt her to preserve the flesh. Percy drew the line of civilization here: disinterring corpses to eat was disgusting yet permissible; he executed the murderous husband for his heinous acts. But this did not prevent John Smith from making light of the situation. In what passes for humor in his writings, Smith facetiously wondered "whether she was better roasted, boiled, or carbonadoed [grilled], I know not, but of such a dish as powdered [salted] wife I never heard of." [39]

A less outrageous response than humor was the English attempt to find religious significance in the Starving Time, much like the way the "king" of Accomac drew religious meaning from transgressive disinterments. In the slayings of two colonists George Percy found a divine allegory. Once there were two men: a fat butcher and a skinny blasphemer. Hugh Price, "pinched with extreme famine," questioned God's existence. Price went even further than did the Roanoke Indians, who felt that English starvation proved the weakness of the English god. Price ran into Jamestown's marketplace "exclaiming and crying out that there was no God." During his harangue, Price argued that "if there were a God he would not suffer his creatures whom he had made and framed to endure those miseries and to perish for want of foods and sustenance."

Unlike Price, the fat butcher was not sacrilegious. One day the butcher and the blasphemer went for a walk, looking perhaps for roots and snakes to ease their hunger. Like many unlucky colonists that winter, they were felled by arrows, as the Powhatans continued to wage their holy war. For Percy, the amazing part of the story was this: the butcher's corpulent corpse was untouched except by the arrows that killed him, while Price's skinny body "was rent in pieces [by] wolves or other wild beasts." Miraculously, the ravenous animals had overlooked the butcher's body, merely twenty feet away. Thus, "God's indignation was showed upon Price's corpse." [40] For Percy and the rest of the colonists, a mutilated corpse was the ultimate sign of God's displeasure. Finally, the spring of 1610 brought berries and birds in abundance and starvation loosened its grip.

But to the colonists' horror, the mutilated corpses continued to pile up during the holy war. The English responded with additional attacks on the dead, torching the burial temples of the Chickahominies in 1610. [41] This holy war lasted until 1614, when John Rolfe married Powhatan's favorite daughter, Pocahontas. Several years of uneasy peace ensued, a long enough time for the English to grow complacent. To English eyes, it seemed a modus vivendi had been reached: colonists would continue to expand their landholdings and grow tobacco, their newly profitable commodity, and the Indians would provide them with trade items, craft goods, and labor. On March 22, 1622, however, the English were aroused from their complacence by the grisly spectacle of hundreds of mutilated corpses.

The Powhatan uprising of 1622 was a one-day spasm of violence fifteen years in the making. At its heart, the issue was land. Ever since the colonists had arrived in 1607 and shown themselves more than willing to appropriate "vacant" areas, the Powhatans had recognized that their relationship with the land was in danger. What appeared to the colonists to be "unused" land was often hunting and fishing grounds crucially important to the Indians' survival. And the colonists did not merely limit themselves to occupying hunting grounds, as Captain Martin's forcible takeover of the Nansemonds' island during the Starving Time demonstrates.

After the first Anglo-Powhatan War ended in 1614, the English used the goodwill generated by the marriage between John Rolfe and Powhatan's daughter Pocahontas to expand their settlements ever further inland. In 1616 the colony began a generous program of granting land to old and new inhabitants alike, aiming to make the colony more attractive to potential migrants. Residents who arrived before 1616 received one hundred acres each, while those who arrived after were entitled to fifty acres. Plus, anyone who paid the way of another person to Virginia was granted a "headright" of fifty acres. By 1622, the banks of the James were almost entirely claimed by English planters. The James River Indians had lost their access to an important source of food and transportation.[42]

At the same time, leadership among the Indians was in flux. Powhatan died in 1618 and was succeeded by his brother, Opechancanough, who was warier about allying with the English than his older sibling.[43] Moreover, a charismatic warrior named Nemattanew gained increasing prominence among his people. The English dubbed this impressive adversary "Jack of the Feather" for his eye-catching battle garb "strangely adorned" with plumage. According to Percy, Nemattanew "used to come into the field all covered over with feathers and swans' wings fastened unto his shoulders as though he meant to fly."[44] There is perhaps no better symbol of the post-1614 English belief that the Powhatans were their firm and enduring allies than the military training Nemattanew received: colonists schooled the Indian warrior in the proper use of English firearms.[45]

Now that peace seemed so deeply entrenched—so "sure and unviolable," as Governor Francis Wyatt wrote to England—the English finally began to make good on their earlier professions of interest in converting the Powhatans to Christianity.[46] The missionary impulse had languished for the first twelve years of Virginia's existence, as simple survival was enough to keep the colonists' hands full. But by 1619 the colonists were ready to proselytize, and they declared their intentions of Christianizing Indian children. That same year the Virginia Company set aside ten thousand acres, the profits from which were to endow a college where Indian youths would learn the finer points of Protestantism and English civilization. George Thorp, a former member of Parliament, arrived in May 1620 to oversee the land and make the college a reality.[47]

Thorp was passionately committed to the project of Christianizing the Powhatans. He felt that Indians needed only to be treated kindly before they would see the truths of Christ's teachings. Thorp soon realized that Anglo-Virginians had not treated their Indian neighbors as well as the Bible instructed them to. The colonists were quick to blame the Indians for various offenses, but if there was blame on any side, Thorp asserted, "It is on ours who are not so charitable to them as Christians ought to be, they being (especially the better sort of them) of a peaceable and virtuous disposition."[48] Thorp did not want to relegate his support for Indians to words alone, so he took concrete steps to demonstrate his regard for the Indians. When some Indians complained of the colonists' mastiffs, arguing that the terrifying beasts of war belied a policy of peaceful coexistence, Thorp ordered several dogs killed in the Indians' presence, "to the great displeasure of the owners."[49] Such actions earned Thorp the contempt of some colonists; one later groused that Thorp was guilty of "letting the Indians have their head and none must control them."[50]

Yet this was a post-facto complaint. The first inkling the colonists had that the Powhatans were not as contented as they seemed came in the summer of 1621. Virginia's leaders learned from "the King of the Eastern Shore" (perhaps the same *werowance* who told them of the extraordinary disinterments of 1608) that Opechancanough had scheduled an attack "at the taking up of Powhatan's bones, at which ceremony great numbers of the savages were to be assembled to set upon every plantation of the Colony."[51] Though the colonists seem not to have made the connection, this resembled the Roanoke Indians' planned use of Ensenore's funeral as cover to gather numerous warriors in preparation for an attack. The difference is that the ceremony for Ensenore was likened to a month's mind, because Roanoke Indian leaders were mummified soon after their death. By contrast, the Powhatans apparently waited nearly three years, until their former leader's flesh had completely decomposed, before gathering the bones together and placing them into a burial temple. In both cases, the connection between funerals and pan-tribal resistance was not coincidental. Carolina and Virginia Algonquians used their death rituals not only to provide cover for the gathering of warriors but also to inspire their fighting men with a sense of spiritual mission.

But Opechancanough's attempt to use deathways to gain military advantage came to naught; his plan was betrayed by the Eastern Shore *werowance*, a fringe member of the Powhatan confederacy. "Earnestly denying the plot," Opechancanough managed to convince the English that their intelligence was suspect, so the colonists "fell again to their ordinary watch" and assumed that Anglo-Indian relations remained untroubled.[52] Soon enough the English had reason to worry, for in early March 1622 a colonist shot Nemattanew for his suspected role in the murder of a man named Morgan.[53] As Nemattanew lay dying, he made two significant requests: "the one was, that they would not make it known he was slain with a bullet; the other, to bury him amongst the English."[54] Unlike other New World natives, who occasionally requested Christian burial as a token of their (whole or partial) acceptance of Christianity, Nemattanew's request was to be buried "amongst the English," not, as the governor's father George Wyatt would later have it, "to be buried in Christian burial."[55] There is no evidence that Nemattanew was Christianized. His dying requests seem motivated, instead, by an attempt to maintain morale among his fellow warriors. He apparently claimed to be invulnerable to English bullets and he probably did not want others to know the truth of the matter.

Again Opechancanough dissembled, feigning unconcern about Nemattanew's slaying. He put the colonists at ease by sending a message in the middle of March that he regarded the warrior's death as a tragic but isolated incident. Opechancanough "held the peace concluded so firm, as the sky should sooner fall than it dissolve."[56] But in fact Nemattanew's death put the spark to fifteen years of kindling, the accumulated grievances of the Powhatan Indians.

The conflagration of killing started the morning of March 22, and before the day was over some 330 colonists—more than one-fourth of Virginia's residents—lay dead.[57] Eyewitnesses and historians have long noted that the

Indians used their familiarity with English lifeways to perpetrate the killings.[58] Because the Indians had interacted with the English on an intimate
basis for a decade and a half, they knew just how to surprise the colonists.
In some cases the Indians sat down to breakfast with the colonists and,
when finished, coolly picked up their hosts' tools and weapons and began
the slaughter. And when they went looking for more victims, the Indians
knew just where to find the colonists: in their gardens, fields, and workshops.
Evidence that colonists were killed by their own tools exists in the archaeological record. A victim of the uprising unearthed by researchers at Martin's
Hundred plantation seems to have been killed by a blow to the forehead with
an iron garden spade.[59]

But commentators have not remarked that Indians also used their knowledge of English deathways to give their killings maximum impact. The attack
of 1622 represents the culmination of a decade and a half of cross-cultural
communication about death. The Indians had learned that the English held
corpses in high regard. It was one thing to kill an enemy, it was quite another
to mutilate the corpse—this, as we have seen, was treatment reserved by the
English for the most heinous criminals. The Indians discovered this English
cultural sensibility during numerous violent interactions, including Captain
John Martin's immoderate response to the Nansemonds' postmortem mutilation of two English messengers.

So, to drive home their message that the English must leave Virginia, the
Powhatans ripped apart their victims' corpses. Archaeologists believe that the
Martin's Hundred victim, killed by an iron garden spade and lying face down
in the dirt, had the back of his head crushed by a club. Indians then scalped
him by cutting a hairlock from the left side of his head.[60] Others lost more
than a scalp. Describing the grisly scene at Captain Nathaniel Powell's plantation, John Smith wrote that the Indians "not only slew him and his family,
but butcher-like haggled their bodies, and cut off his head, to express their
uttermost height of cruelty."[61] Comparing the Indians to butchers, Smith
expressed the English belief that only animal corpses deserved to be treated
with such disrespect. Likewise, as Edward Waterhouse vividly put it, "Not
being content with taking away life alone, they fell after again upon the dead,
making as well as they could, a fresh murder, defacing, dragging, and mangling the dead carcasses into many pieces, and carrying some parts away in
derision, with base and brutish triumph."[62] This was hyperbole, of course—it
is not possible to commit a "fresh murder" upon the dead. But the disgust of

Smith and Waterhouse shows that the Powhatans had assessed their adversaries accurately. Corpse mutilation had sent the desired message.

And thus it was not at all a coincidence that George Thorp's corpse received the most brutal treatment. The godly man who had reached out to the Powhatans by killing the dogs they feared could not believe it when he learned that the Indians were coming to kill him. Thorp's servant ran for his life but Thorp stayed in his house. Thorp's trust did him no good; the Indians arrived and killed him. We do not know if Thorp's death came quickly or after painful torture. In either case, according to Waterhouse, "They not only willfully murdered him, but cruelly and felly, out of devilish malice, did so many barbarous despites and foul scorns after to his dead corpse, as are unbefitting to be heard by any civil ear." [63] Although Waterhouse left the details of the corpse mutilation to the reader's imagination, the Indians' motivation seems clear enough. As the symbol of the colony's efforts to replace the Powhatan gods with the Christian god, Thorp generated special rage among his former charges. The Indians knew that the English would pay careful attention to the "foul scorns" heaped upon Thorp's lifeless body.

Given that this was the age of Shakespeare and Donne, and given the deliberately provocative ways in which English corpses were treated, it is no surprise that the English rose to remarkable rhetorical heights when they described the uprising. Indeed, the colonists' outrage and betrayal are still palpable nearly four centuries later. Sir Francis Wyatt, Virginia's governor at the time of the uprising, described the colonists' sense of helplessness as the attack progressed: "We were forced to stand and gaze at our distressed brethren, frying in the fury of our enemies, and could not relieve them." Predictably, Wyatt's immobility received harsh criticism. As one colonist put it, "The Governor stood at that time for a cipher whilst they stood ripping open our guts." In an earlier letter this same colonist demonstrated why he was casting about for someone to blame: Virginia's very existence was threatened by the uprising. "God forgive me," he begged, "I think the last massacre killed all our country, beside them they killed, they burst the heart of all the rest." [64] Images of bodily violation—ripped guts, burst hearts—filled the descriptions of the uprising.

In the wake of these bodily violations, victims suffered one final indignity. To the horror of survivors, the English were forced to bury most of the dead without any ceremony, if they were buried at all. The uprising victim described earlier, who had been murdered with a garden spade, left archaeological traces of a peremptory burial. According to the researcher who found this man's remains, "The person had been buried in haste. No winding sheet had held the arms in place; instead, the body had been swung into the hole from the west side by two people, one holding it by the shoulders and the other by the feet. The left arm had swung loose, hitting the side of the grave and falling behind the left buttock . . . This had been no slow and reverent interment, no gentle lowering into the ground while mourners watched and wept." [65] And the indignities continued for a full year after the uprising. Reeling from the attack and abandoning their most far-flung plantations, the colonists could not grow enough food to last them through the winter. Hundreds more died, and "unregarded and unburied" bodies could even be found lying in the hedgerows.[66] Lack of attention to proper burials signaled that this was a society in terrible distress.

With so many victims of violence unable to be properly buried, March 22 proved to be Virginia's September 11. And just as Americans today commemorate each September 11 as "Patriot Day," Virginians passed a law soon after the attack mandating "that the 22nd of March be yearly solemnized as [a] holiday." [67]

The parallel runs even deeper: just as many Americans responded to September 11 with calls for revenge against a religious Other, Virginians reacted to March 22 with calls to shed Indian blood. This was necessary, in a biblical eye-for-an-eye framework, because the colonists themselves had been victims of "a flood, a flood of blood." [68] As Governor Wyatt proclaimed, revenge was necessary "for the glory of God, and love toward our brethren (whose blood, no doubt, cryeth to heaven for vengeance)." [69] Echoing Wyatt's sanguinary imagery—and the words of Genesis 4:10, where the blood of the slain Abel cries out to God—the Virginia Company declared, "Since the innocent blood of so many Christians, doth in justice cry out for revenge, . . . we must advise you to root out from being any longer a people, so cursed a nation." In order to adequately punish the Indians, the company recommended, among other things, "demolishing their temples." [70] In the English campaign of revenge even the bones of deceased Powhatan leaders were not safe. Thus the holy war that began with John Martin's desecration of Indian temples in 1609 continued with further destruction of burial temples.

Today we generally associate with Indians the idea that the bones of ancestors sanctify the landscape. We saw this when the Spanish landed in Ajacán in 1570 and learned that some local Indians refused to flee a terrible drought because they did not want to leave the land where their ancestors' bones lay buried. The English demolition of Powhatan temples makes sense in this context: to "root out" the Indians, to rip them from the land as one would do to a weedy shrub, required severing the connection between Powhatan bones and Powhatan land. In fifteen years of coexistence the English had learned this of their Powhatan neighbors.

But the English also believed that the remains of the dead sometimes sanctified the landscape. For the English, this belief was more situational than it was for the Indians; the English generally held this view only about those killed in an important cause, such as a war. That this belief persists among many Americans should come as no surprise to anyone who has heard places like the Manassas Civil War battlefield or Ground Zero in lower Manhattan referred to as "hallowed ground."

This view—that the remains of the dead can sanctify the landscape—was expressed most vividly by Samuel Purchas, the great propagandist for English colonization. Writing only a few years after the uprising, Purchas used the Bible to show the connection between the bones of the ancestors and possession of the land. Purchas wrote, "The Holy Patriarchs had a promise of Canaan, yet held no possession but with their dead bodies." [71] Here Purchas referred to the stories of Jacob (Israel) and his son Joseph. As Jacob lay dying in Egypt, he commanded his sons, "I am to be gathered unto my people: bury me with my fathers in the cave that is in the field of Ephron the Hittite" in Canaan (Genesis 49:29). And so it was done. Likewise, as Moses led his people out of Egypt and toward the Promised Land, he was careful to bring along the remains of Joseph. "Moses took the bones of Joseph with him: for he [Joseph] had straitly sworn the children of Israel, saying, God will surely visit you; and ye shall carry up my bones away hence with you" (Exodus 13:19). After decades of being carried through the desert, Joseph's bones were finally buried in the Promised Land (Joshua 24:32).

For Purchas, the crux of this story was that the bones of Jacob and Joseph gave the Israelites title to Canaan. The Israelites had every right to evict the Canaanites from the Promised Land. In parallel fashion, the bones of the English men and women slaughtered by the Powhatans in 1622 gave the English the right to possess Virginia and to dispossess the Powhatans. Here is how Purchas's argument deployed the victims: "Their carcasses, the dispersed bones of their and their countrymen's since-murdered carcasses, have taken a mortal immortal possession, and being dead, speak, proclaim, and cry, 'This

our earth is truly English, and therefore this Land is justly yours O English.'"
Thus did the victims of March 22 cry from their graves, at least in Purchas's
imagination, for the dispossession of the Indians.

*   *   *

So the English went about making the land theirs. Their first step in actual-
izing the "mortal immortal possession" offered by the victims of March 22
was to declare open season on the Powhatans. In campaigns large and small,
the English killed countless Indians in eastern Virginia. As the historian
Edmund Morgan has written, "Within two or three years of the massacre
the English had avenged the deaths of that day many times over."[72] Consequently Powhatan territory shrunk considerably. Before long the Indians of
eastern Virginia were "isolated on ever-shrinking islands of tribal territory."[73]
This caused the English to feel safer, so they reversed the earlier contraction
of their settlements that occurred after 1622 and began again to spread out
across the landscape. English plantations pushed ever farther inland.

At the same time that the English were trying to domesticate the landscape, the colony's leaders proceeded on several paths to try to tame their
unruly Anglo-Virginian society. They promoted policies that helped diversify
Virginia's economy, moving away from the earlier dependence upon tobacco.
They divided counties into parishes and built churches so people's spiritual
needs could be attended to—and so the colonists' activities could be better
monitored.

One aspect of colonists' behavior that needed better regulation, at least
in the eyes of Virginia's leaders, was their deathways. The aftermath of the
1622 uprising, with some corpses buried unceremoniously and others buried
not at all, highlighted the fact that Virginia's deathways had diverged somewhat from English practices. Even outside the exceptional circumstances of
1622, Jamestown burials show evidence of being less careful than English
norms required. Archaeologists have uncovered a burial ground just outside
Jamestown that dates to 1610–30. In sixty-three grave shafts researchers found
seventy-two individuals, and many show evidence of having been buried in
haste. Some of the graves were unusually shallow and haphazardly aligned.
Several individuals were interred in their clothes instead of a shroud, which
was highly unusual at the time in light of the high cost of clothing. One man
was buried so quickly that his friends forgot to check his pockets, which
held a spoon and a pipe. Most of these burials (90 percent) were without cof-

fins, but even those in coffins seem not to have always received a great deal of respect: one woman was jammed into a narrow, reused wooden shipping crate.[74]

In response to the helter-skelter burial practices that had become characteristic of Jamestown, the recently formed House of Burgesses (1619) and church courts tried to get Anglo-Virginian deathways back into line with comforting English traditions. This would help keep at bay the specter of savagery raised in 1622. The very first act of the first legislative assembly after the uprising mandated two things in every locality: a church (or at least a room reserved for worship), and a burial ground, which was to be "a place empaled in [fenced], sequestered only to the burial of the dead." The language of this act indicates that legislators were also reacting against the local practice of burying people in private fields. The almost universal practice in England was churchyard burial, but Virginia had such a dispersed settlement pattern—and such an abundance of formerly Indian land—that many people outside Jamestown chose to bury their dead on their own land. Landowners had the space, and besides, for many it was a chore to get to the nearest churchyard. Private burial grounds would later become the most common final resting place in other plantation-based English colonies. That Virginia's dispersed settlement pattern made it difficult to require churchyard burial is suggested by the fact that revised versions of this law had to be passed three times in the next fifteen years.[75]

Because private burials so starkly departed from English norms, and because this practice was the result of Virginia's "wilderness" setting, legislators sought to restrict burials to the more civilized-seeming churchyards. Is it possible that Virginia's burgesses were also unnerved by the close resemblance between the burial of Powhatan commoners—in unmarked (at least to English eyes) cemeteries—and the humble burials of Anglo-Virginian Christians in shallow graves within unfenced private burial grounds?

If this concern lurked in the back of the legislators' minds shortly after 1622, it likely receded in the 1630s, as colonists interacted less frequently with the shrinking Powhatan bands. Nonetheless, leaders still wanted to regulate burial practices, as deathways remained central to the society's image of itself as civilized. By the 1630s it became clear that private burials were not going to be legislated away, so the colony's leaders tried to make the best of a less than ideal situation. A vestry meeting at Accomac on the Eastern Shore in 1636 is emblematic of this shift toward a "control what you can't prevent" mentality. At this vestry—an Anglican institution consisting of a minister and "twelve of the most substantial and intelligent persons in each parish" who dealt with disciplinary and regulatory matters—the Eastern Shore's most highly respected men determined that some residents were freed from the obligation to bury their dead in the churchyard.[76] Because of the "remote living of the [members] of this parish from the church," those farthest away were given an alternate location for burial: "on part of the land of William Blower where William Berriman liveth." This policy simply ratified the existing local practice. But the key point for the vestry was to try to bring these non-churchyard burials into the parish's regulatory orbit, not just by singling out a particular site for a burial ground but also by mandating the minister's presence. Anyone who wanted to bury a body had to "give notice unto the minister and provide convenient means for his coming there to bury the dead which whosoever shall refuse such decent and christianlike burial that then they are to stand to the censure of this vestry."[77] Perhaps this policy was connected to the English feeling that they were living in the wilderness and hence especially vulnerable to straying from "decent and christianlike" practices. In any case, the members of the vestry worried that without sufficient oversight private burials might veer from standard Christian practices, and they sought to make private burials resemble their churchyard counterparts.

There was another concern that caused leaders in the southern mainland British colonies to worry about non-churchyard burials: the potential for secretly burying victims of violence. Because of their plantation-based economy, Virginian landholders had an insatiable desire for labor. This translated into an intense demand for indentured servants and, later, slaves. Masters who tried to get the most labor from their reluctant charges occasionally resorted to violence. Some Virginians worried that servants and slaves killed by their masters might be buried privately without anyone realizing the true cause of death. As a result, the House of Burgesses passed this law in 1661: "Whereas the private burial of servants and others gives occasion of much scandal against divers persons and sometimes not undeservedly of being guilty of their deaths, be it enacted that there be in every parish three or more places set apart for places of public burial, and before the corpse be buried there, three or four neighbors be called who may view the corpse."[78] Thus did the violent context of life in Virginia shape attitudes toward burial.

Overall, however, by the middle of the seventeenth century Virginian funerals were more similar to than different from English funerals. Though evidence is sparse, Virginian funerals seem to have been conducted along familiar English lines, allowing for differences due to Virginia's less elaborate material culture, a result of the colony's small number of wealthy families. As in England, ministers were supposed to preside at funerals; there is every indication that they usually did so. Ministers' fees for presiding at a burial were low enough that virtually everyone could afford them: the burgesses set the rate at merely one shilling in 1632. In 1643 the burgesses changed the rate to ten pounds of tobacco, presumably making it even easier to pay than the previous requirement for hard currency.[79]

In another carryover of English practices, elites were sometimes buried within the church, with a fee schedule set for "breaking ground in the church" and "breaking ground in the chancel."[80] The chancel is the eastern part of the church, usually set off by a screen, where the altar stands and where communicants receive the Lord's Supper. At the Bruton Parish Church in Williamsburg, it cost twice as much to be buried in the chancel as elsewhere in the church.[81] Elite burial in the chancel—and in less prestigious areas within the church—had deep pre-Reformation roots throughout Europe, as discussed in Chapter 1. Puritans and other reform-minded Protestants did not like church burial's connections with Catholicism, particularly the implication that burial near the altar could help the soul of the deceased get into heaven. But mainstream Anglicans in England and Virginia remained comfortable with church and chancel burial, arguing that it was merely a symbol of rank and not an aid to heavenly admission.[82] Indeed, this practice was so deeply ingrained that the Anglican William Strachey wrote that the bones of Powhatan kings were preserved "within the chancel of the temple."[83]

There is also considerable evidence that the traditional English post-funeral feast was transferred to Virginia. As in England, a degree of merriment was sanctioned after the somber funeral proceedings.[84] In fact, some sources suggest that post-funeral revelry may have been valued more highly than piety in Virginia. In the 1630s and 1640s the going rate for a minister to preach a funeral sermon (rather than to simply preside) was 100 pounds of tobacco. In the same period Robert Lawson (or more precisely, his estate) was not unusual in running up funeral charges of 360 pounds of tobacco, likely spent on food and drink. The surgeon John Severne's funeral featured even more lavish hospitality: the cost of the "steer killed at the funeral" alone was 800 pounds of tobacco.[85]

One aspect of a funeral feast that seems to have been more prevalent in Virginia's frontier setting than in England was the firing of guns. Given their greater need for hunting and the perceived threat of Indian attack, Virginians possessed more guns than their English counterparts—and delighted in firing them at any and all celebrations.[86] In 1656, however, the House of Burgesses decided that this practice had gone too far. Because Indians might "suddenly invade this colony to a total subversion of the same," colonists had to be at the ready to sound the alarm if such an attack occurred. With church bells fairly rare, the quickest way to raise a ruckus was to fire guns repeatedly into the air as a sign of distress. But if this happened every time a few men with guns gathered over cider and ale, it would soon become a case of the boy who cried wolf. So the burgesses forbade the colonists to "shoot any guns at drinking (marriages and funerals only excepted)."[87] Even 350 years ago politics was the art of the possible; the legislators must have realized that prohibiting gunfire at funerals would have raised the ire of their well-armed constituents.

In yet one more way did burials in Virginia (and elsewhere in British North America) depart from English norms: coffins became much more common in the New World than the Old. In medieval England, parishes usually owned a wooden coffin that was used to transport corpses to the grave, at which point the shrouded body was removed from its receptacle and buried uncoffined. Starting in the sixteenth century and increasing throughout the seventeenth and eighteenth centuries, coffined burials became more widespread. Unsurprisingly, coffined burial—as a display of conspicuous consumption—was initially an elite practice that slowly worked its way down the social scale.[88] In Virginia, however, the abundance of trees allowed for the nearly universal use of coffins by the middle of the seventeenth century. Archaeologists in Virginia have shown that coffins were used in almost all burials in the second half of the century, except during times of epidemic disease or Indian violence.[89] This is because coffins were so inexpensive. One inventory from 1640 shows that a man's coffin cost only as much as his shroud: 100 pounds of tobacco.[90]

Due to the dearth of surviving letters and diaries from the seventeenth century, there is little evidence about Anglo-Virginian deathbed scenes, though it is likely they followed English norms. In one important respect, however, Virginian deathbeds departed from English practices. With shallower networks of kin and community, and with great distance between dwellings, Virginians seem to have been more likely to receive cursory attention as they lay dying. (This generalization would not hold true, of course, in situations like the terrible London plague of 1665.) One early observer complained that in Virginia "many depart the world in their own dung for want of help in their sickness."[91] To be fair, this graphic comment was written in 1623 as the colony struggled to recover from the Powhatan uprising of the previous year. But the perception continued that dying Virginians too often lacked familial and spiritual comfort on their deathbeds. In 1632 the burgesses even felt it necessary to legislate ministerial deathbed visits. The new law stated, "When any person is dangerously sick in any parish, the minister having knowledge thereof shall resort unto him or her to instruct and comfort them in their distress." [92] Legislators in England and New England certainly never felt the need to mandate such an obvious component of a pastor's duties. And the problem was not confined to the seventeenth century: as late as 1724, Hugh Jones, the Anglican minister of Jamestown, felt the need to urge his ministerial colleagues to do a better job visiting the dying.[93]

As the seventeenth century turned into the eighteenth, Virginia's increasingly robust economy allowed planters to follow English fashions in mourning attire, coffin hardware, and other aspects of material culture. In one way, however, Anglo-Virginians hewed to their own traditions: non-churchyard burials not only proliferated but gained cachet as they were increasingly associated with the wealthy. All of Virginia's Anglicans had the right to be buried in an Anglican churchyard, but such an all-embracing policy made the churchyards seem terribly plebeian. By this time churchyards were used primarily by the poor; planters set aside a portion of their abundant land for burials. An early eighteenth-century description of Virginia's private burial grounds gives a sense of their ordered gentility: "It is customary to bury in gardens or orchards, where whole families lie interred together, in a spot generally handsomely enclosed, planted with evergreens, and the graves kept decently." [94] By 1724, when most Anglo-Virginians wrote about Indians in the past tense, planters no longer feared that their private burial grounds might be mistaken for Indian cemeteries.

*   *   *

But the Indians of eastern Virginia did not disappear. Nor did they (with the exception of the small number who had been Christianized) simply adopt the deathways of the numerically predominant English who surrounded them. Instead, the non-Christian Indians of eastern Virginia retained many of their earlier beliefs and practices, supplemented with elements gleaned from the material and spiritual culture of their English neighbors. One glimpse of this process comes from the 1660s. The Weyanocks had been a member of the Powhatan confederacy living on the south shore of the James River, but they left their homeland in the 1640s as their relationship with the English became increasingly conflictual. They moved south of the James, but unfortunately for the Weyanocks, there they came into conflict with other Indian bands. This was a very fluid situation in mid-seventeenth-century Virginia, with many former members of the Powhatan confederacy seeking safer places to live, and these groups sometimes came into conflict over territorial issues. When the Weyanocks' *werowance* was killed in intertribal warfare in 1663, the group requested asylum from the English. By this time there were clear signs of Anglicization among the Weyanocks: the slain leader's name was Geoffrey, and the Weyanocks' town included a small fort, an English-style house, and an apple orchard. Yet the English reported that (at least to their eyes) Geoffrey's corpse received traditional treatment: his body had been taken outside the fort and "laid on a scaffold and covered with skins and mats." [95] Indian deathways proved slower to change than other aspects of their culture, such as housing styles and food production.

Yet this does not mean that Indian deathways persisted unchanged in seventeenth-century Virginia. The best source on the non-Christian Indians of eastern Virginia in roughly 1700 is Robert Beverley's *History and Present State of Virginia*, published in 1705. This was the first history of the colony written by a native Virginian. Beverley famously opened his book with a breathtaking gambit: "I am an *Indian*," he declared. [96] In defiance of European fashions, Beverley rhetorically adopted the (imagined) plain dress and plain-spokenness of his colony's native people to convince his readers of his honesty. In his literary persona, however, Beverley did not forget about the real native inhabitants of his colony, writing about them with greater sensitivity than most of his contemporaries. If Beverley's techniques are grotesque by modern anthropological standards—rooting around in a burial temple while the local Indians were otherwise occupied, getting an Indian leader drunk so he would spill religious secrets—his observations are nonetheless valuable.

Beverley had long been interested in Indian religion but had been frustrated in his attempts to learn much about it. He had talked to several Indian leaders, "but I could learn little from them, it being reckoned a sacrilege, to divulge the principles of their religion." Virginia's Indians had learned the hard way that discretion about their beliefs helped them avoid undue attention, rather unlike Anglo-Virginian Christians, who always seemed eager to talk about their beliefs. So when Beverley and a few companions found themselves in an Indian town—deserted for a few hours while the residents were away discussing land issues with the English—the temptation to enter the forbidden burial temple proved too great to resist. Beverley and his small band of tomb-raiders removed fourteen logs that had been used to barricade the door and entered the darkness within. After their eyes adjusted to the gloom, they could see elements of Algonquian temple burials with continuities going back to the descriptions and drawings of Harriot and White. They saw a small fireplace, posts with faces carved and painted on them, and a mysterious chamber behind a partition.[97]

Reaching behind the screen, the curious men discovered three mats rolled up and sewn shut. Using a knife, they cut the laces and found "some vast bones": the remains of the Indians' leaders. Along with the bones they found a combination of Indian and European items: "some Indian tomahawks," wild turkey feathers, and "red and blue pieces of cotton cloth," almost certainly European in origin. Thus did the Indians in this town retain their traditional practices for burying their leaders, while incorporating elements of European material culture seamlessly into those practices. Beverley and his friends might have continued their investigations longer, but, based on a presumed similarity between Indian and Anglo-American concerns about corpse desecration, they feared what they were doing would anger the Indians. Worried that "we might be caught offering an affront to their superstition," the group put things back together the best they could and made for home.

An example that parallels Beverley's findings of European goods being incorporated into traditional burials can be seen among the Indians of eastern North Carolina. As described by the promotional writer John Lawson in 1709, these Indians wrapped corpses in "blankets or match coats," the latter a native garment produced by the English. The term "match coat" comes from John Smith's rendering of the Virginian Algonquian term "matchcore," an Indian outergarment made of skins. Soon after Smith noted the term in 1612, English traders began to supply Indians with "match coats" made out of coarse woolen cloth, often dyed red or blue.[98] The match coats Indians used to wrap their dead were, by the early eighteenth century, very likely made of wool and obtained in trade from Anglo-Carolinians. Lawson reported that after the bodies were wrapped in European textiles, they were then covered "with two or three Mats, which the Indians make of rushes or cane" in pre-contact style. Lawson was pleased with the overall effect of this Indian "coffin," as he called it, writing that it "looks very decent and well."[99] Lawson seems to have felt that this similarity between Indian and European "coffins" served as evidence of Indian civility.

Indians were likewise incorporating some English elements into their beliefs regarding death and the afterlife by 1700. Regarding the afterlife, however, the changes seem to have been more profound than was the case with
burial practices. Apparently Beverley's interest in Indian beliefs was piqued
by his afternoon in the burial temple, so when he chanced upon an Indian
known for his "ingenuity and understanding" in an Englishman's house,
Beverley's ethnographic impulse once again could not be restrained. He plied
the man with strong cider to loosen his tongue and began asking him questions about his religion. Among other things, Beverley learned that at least
some of the non-Christian Indians of eastern Virginia had incorporated a
version of the Christian heaven/hell dichotomy. But this was a version with
a distinctly Indian twist. The afterlife for "those who have done well here,"
the tipsy informant explained, was filled with "plenty of all sorts of game,
for hunting, fishing, and fowling." Moreover, it was "blessed with the most
charming women, which enjoy an eternal bloom, and have a universal desire
to please." The modern reader wonders how an Indian woman would have
described the afterlife, but Beverley had no such concerns. He was delighted
by this image of a sexualized paradise, with lovely young women offering
themselves to men, and so it is no surprise that Beverley focused on the antithesis of this image in the Indian's description of the afterlife for the wicked.
Here, those who had lived scandalously were not only roasted by flames but
also "persecuted and tormented day and night, with furies in the shape of old
women." [100]

It will be remembered that English writers in the early seventeenth century maintained that the Powhatans' afterlife did not have different destinations for the good and for the wicked. The one distinction was that the
afterlife was reserved for priests and *werowances*; commoners had no afterlife
at all. This seems to have changed after a century of contact with the English.
In this case, syncretism may have been facilitated by deep parallels between
English and Powhatan ideas about the existence of an afterlife. Thus did the
Indians of eastern Virginia, at least according to Beverley's informant, adopt
and transform the Christian afterlife.

*   *   *

Robert Beverley differed from most of his Anglo-Virginian contemporaries in
his interest in Indian beliefs and religious practices. By 1705, when Beverley
wrote, Indians had been replaced in most Anglo-Virginians' minds with an-

other symbol of difference, another source of anxiety. These were, of course, the African slaves that made up an increasingly large proportion of Virginia's population. The first "20 and odd" Africans arrived in Jamestown in 1619, but for nearly a half-century people of African descent remained few in number. As late as 1670, Africans and African Americans made up only 5 percent of the colony's residents. By 1700, however, that figure had leapt to 28 percent and it would only grow in the eighteenth century.[101]

In the midst of this influx of Africans, Virginia's burgesses decided that African deathways represented a threat to the colony's safety. The legislature declared in 1680 that because "the frequent meetings of considerable numbers of Negro slaves under pretense of feasts and burials is judged of dangerous consequences," slaves could no longer carry arms or leave their plantation without a certificate from their owner.[102] Westmoreland County, Virginia, went even further and in 1687 banned nighttime slave funerals outright. The slaveholding elite in this county feared that funerals could provide cover for slaves plotting rebellions.[103] In Chapter 6 we will see how the interactions between African and Euro-American deathways played out in Britain's colonies in North America and the West Indies. But now we will turn to the Europeans who followed the English at Jamestown as the next successful colonizers of North America: the French.

CHAPTER 4

Holy Bones and Beautiful Deaths in New France

LIKE THE ENGLISH, the French became interested in exploring North America in the sixteenth century. Also like their Protestant rivals, the French would have to wait until the early seventeenth century to establish a permanent colony. But when they finally did so, they embraced the missionary project with much greater zeal than did the Chesapeake colonists. The Jesuits responsible for this missionary passion had very different goals in their interactions with Indians than did John Smith and others in Virginia, who were much more concerned with securing political alliances and procuring food. Given the Jesuits' desires to convert the Indians of New France to Christianity, deathways were even more central to the communication between Indians and Europeans than they were in the Chesapeake.

As in the Chesapeake, Europeans and Indians in New France each quickly perceived deep parallels between their own and the other's deathways. Jesuits recognized the centrality of deathways to Indian religious practices, and because their own religion placed great weight on purgatory, Masses for the dead, and elaborate funerals, they soon developed a conversion strategy that focused on deathways. Jesuits and the Indians of New France shared certain attitudes toward human remains—"holy bones"—and they shared ideas about the importance of deathbed scenes for making a successful transition to the afterlife, what the Jesuits referred to as "beautiful deaths." [1] The Jesuits' reactions to some of these parallels could be exclusive: they mocked native healers' uses of human bones in their rituals, and they did not like the way the Indians' deathbed visions always seemed to focus on obtaining material goods. But more frequently their assessments were inclusive, aware of the similarities between their own and native practices. Indeed, they held up for emulation by European Christians the native stoicism in the face of death and the great care the Indians of Canada lavished upon human remains.

Parallels between Indian and Catholic deathways thus fostered communication, for good and ill, between the two groups in New France. Jesuits used this communication to understand Indians but also to try to convert them to Christianity, as Indian deathbeds became a crucial site of missionary activity. Some Indians embraced Christianity, in particular its vision of the afterlife and its death rituals, demonstrating an inclusive reaction to these new deathways. Others, by contrast, used what they learned from the Jesuits about Christian deathways to resist the newcomers' teachings. Still others used their new knowledge of Catholic deathways against their would-be teachers, desecrating French corpses in ways meant to exact the most intense psychological pain. Death was thus both a means of cross-cultural understanding and an arena for contestation in Canada. The success or failure of France's imperial project depended on the outcome of these negotiations.

*   *   *

Before the Indians of New France could die good Catholic deaths they needed, the French believed, to be introduced to the basic rituals and beliefs of Christianity. This is what brought Father Pierre Biard to Acadia in 1611. Biard was forty-three years old and had been a Jesuit for over twenty-five years when he arrived in Acadia. Instead of heading to Quebec, the trading post that Samuel de Champlain had established in 1608, Biard and his fellow Jesuit Enemond Massé sailed to Port Royal. This small settlement was on the Bay of Fundy coast of what is today Nova Scotia and what the French called Acadia. Here lived the Micmac Indians, who had long experience with Europeans. As far back as 1534, on Jacques Cartier's initial voyage, the first Indians he encountered were Micmacs, and they already had been trading with Europeans for years. Indeed, the Micmacs called out to Cartier something he transcribed as *Napou tou daman asurtat*, which he assumed was "in their language," but which one ethnohistorian asserts was a pidgin trade language with Portuguese and Micmac elements. In this interpretation, the Micmacs actually called out *Napew tu dameu a cierto*, which means, "Man, give me something."[2]

Whether or not this is correct, the Micmacs had been trading with

Portuguese, Norman, and Basque fisherman since at least the early sixteenth century, and perhaps as far back as the late fifteenth century. Reports of their friendliness and openness to European material culture made them seem to Biard and Massé perfect candidates for Christianization. And Port Royal seemed a promising spot from which to launch a mission. Port Royal had been founded in 1605 by Pierre Du Gua, the Sieur de Monts, a Calvinist with connections to the Protestant-turned-Catholic King Henri IV. Shortly after establishing this small settlement, the French befriended Membertou, a local chieftain whose villagers had their summer fishing encampment set up nearby. Membertou was very old, allegedly over one hundred, but he cut a striking physical appearance nonetheless. Marc Lescarbot, a young lawyer who arrived in 1606, gave a sense of Membertou's physical vigor: "He is at least a hundred years old, and may in the course of nature live more than fifty years longer." [3] Membertou was, according to Biard, "of splendid physique, taller and larger-limbed than is usual among them; bearded like a Frenchman, although scarcely any of the others have hair upon the chin." [4]

Undoubtedly this imposing figure would have been described in much more foreboding terms—a hulking giant, a savage Goliath—had he not been so friendly to the French. Membertou addressed the French using paternal imagery they could readily understand. As Champlain remembered, Membertou "promised to look after them [the French], and that they should be no more unhappy than if they were his own children." [5] Encouraged by Membertou's support, de Monts built an impressive Norman-style stronghold but was forced to abandon the site in 1607 when the king of France revoked his trading privileges. The French left the buildings under Membertou's care and sailed for France.

This was too auspicious a site to lay fallow for long. In 1610 Jean de Biencourt, Sieur de Poutrincourt, returned to reclaim the land grant he had received from de Monts. Poutrincourt found everything as he had left it and Membertou remained eager as ever to ally with the French in order to gain access to their trade goods. Poutrincourt and his twenty-year-old son Charles de Biencourt, who spoke passable Micmac (an Algonquian language), began to instruct the Indians in the basic outlines of Catholicism. In order to seal the alliance—spiritual and temporal—between the Indians and the French, Poutrincourt had Membertou and twenty other Indians baptized on June 24. Membertou was named Henri in honor of the recently assassinated king, his wife took the name Marie to remember the late king's wife, and so on down the line, with the members of Membertou's extended family taking the names of various French noble men and women.

Membertou was now nominally a Christian, but he did not yet know enough about Catholic deathways to justify the label. Later that winter he sickened and turned to his shamans for help. He knew well the shamans' methods; he had been a "celebrated" shaman earlier in his life.[6] Given his advanced age, however, the shamans reasonably enough deduced that he would not recover. Membertou performed his *naenie*, a "death-song" or "funeral chant" during which the dying person addressed his family and fellow villagers. He then stopped eating and awaited death, as was the Micmac custom. But, as Biard recalled later that year, "one thing still troubled him, that he did not know how to die like a Christian." When Poutrincourt heard this he rushed to the old man's side and, instead of teaching him how to die, tried to keep him alive. Poutrincourt urged Membertou to eat something. Membertou eventually recovered and Poutrincourt's intervention further cemented the bonds between the aged chief and his allies. According to Biard, "Today he tells this story with great satisfaction, and very aptly points out how God has thereby mercifully exposed the malice and deceit" of the shamans.[7]

European healing strategies had thus been proven superior to those of the Micmacs, the French liked to believe. But even more crucial to successful Christianization, the French felt, would be the demonstration of superior deathways. And this would be demonstrated by force, if necessary. Later in the winter of 1610–11, after Membertou's recovery but still before the arrival of Jesuits, an unnamed "Christian" Indian died. He was one of the twenty-one Indians baptized the previous summer, and as he lay dying he requested the prayers of the French. But after he died, his mourning friends and relatives sought to bury him in the traditional Micmac way and not in the French Catholic fashion. Poutrincourt could not stand idly by. "Firmly resolved to oppose these ceremonies," he "armed all his men" and went to the Indians "in force."[8] He demanded that the Micmacs hand over the corpse. In this case deathways mirrored power relations between the two groups: faced with the overwhelming firepower of the French, the Indians complied and the man was buried as a Christian. "It could not be prevented by the Indians," Biard later gloated.

Less persuasively, Biard also claimed that this act "was and still is, greatly praised by them." It is more likely that most Micmacs resented this interference, even as some of them were beginning to explore Christianity and the power it promised. Later, in another context, Biard explained the Micmacs' attachment to their own healing methods despite being offered "proof" that they did not work. The Micmacs offered an aphorism, *Aoti Chabaya*, which Biard translated as, "That is the Indian way of doing it. You can have your way and we will have ours; every one values his own wares."[9] But for the French the stakes were too high to embrace such a "live and let live" philosophy. A Catholic burial clearly demarcated the line between heathen savagery and Christian civilization.

But how different, in fact, were Christian and traditional Micmac burials? To the participants on both sides of Poutrincourt's armed showdown, the differences probably loomed large. Biard paid a great deal of attention to the dissimilarities in his 1616 description of Micmac burial practices. The Micmacs shrouded their dead "not lengthwise, but with the knees against the stomach and the head on the knees." Likewise, the Micmacs buried their deceased "not upon the back or lying down as we do, but sitting."[10]

From a greater distance, however, some similarities stand out. Biard's description makes clear that both the French and the Micmacs shrouded their corpses, the former in linen, the latter in skins. Both buried their dead in the earth. And both paid attention to status differentiation in their burial markers. In France, burials ranged in status from the unmarked mass graves for the poor in Paris's Cemetery of the Innocents to elaborate tombs for the nobility. Among the Micmacs similar distinctions existed, and the parallels were not lost even on Biard. He reported that if the deceased was "some illustrious personage they build a Pyramid or monument of interlacing poles; as eager in that for glory as we are in our marble and porphyry [feldspar]."[11]

Sadly, the Micmacs would have ample opportunity in the coming years to explore the similarities and differences between Catholic and Micmac burials. Epidemics had been stalking the Micmacs throughout their century of contact with Europeans. According to Membertou, in his youth his people were "as thickly planted . . . as the hairs upon his head"; now they were greatly thinned. During the winter of 1610–11 disease struck the region with a power previously unknown, but providentially (in French eyes) its effects were not evenly distributed. In one Indian village sixty people died, "the greater part of those who lived there." But among the French, no one was even sick, which showed the Indians, according to Biard, that "God protects and defends us as his favorite and well-beloved people."[12] The French well understood the terror that epidemic diseases brought. In sixteenth-century Paris bubonic plague was the most horrifying example, with major epidemics in 1529–33, 1553–55, 1560–62, 1580, and "the terrible years" of 1595–97.[13] In Christian France, the plague made it almost impossible to die a good death. According to the historians Laurence Brockliss and Colin Jones, a plague death was the very antithesis of a good Christian death: "The plague victim died suddenly, alone, bereft of family and friends and was buried without a proper funeral and cast into an unconsecrated pit."[14]

In non-Christian Acadia, by contrast, epidemics presented missionaries with an opportunity to teach about good Christian deaths. Jesuits hoped that the Micmacs might be more open to Christianity—and the comfort it held out to those who feared illness—during periods of increased mortality. This dynamic could be seen in the summer of 1611. Biard and Massé had now arrived in Port Royal and so the mission had begun in earnest. The Micmacs had dubbed the peculiarly clad Jesuits *maqtawe'kji'j*, "little black ones," after their conspicuously non-Indian black robes.[15] Despite their unusual appearance, the Jesuits were accepted as holy men by at least some of the Micmacs. This was the case when Membertou's second son, Actodin, appeared to be dying, perhaps from the epidemic diseases that Biard mentioned. Actodin had been baptized, and so was a Christian in Biard's eyes, but clearly he retained a deep attachment to Micmac deathways. Biard learned that Actodin was gravely ill and so he made the fifteen-mile trek to Actodin's village. To his surprise, Biard found this nominally Christian Indian participating in the entirely Micmac *naenie* (funeral oration) and *tabagie* (farewell feast). Several kettles filled with boiling water perched above a roaring fire in preparation for the ritual slaughter of dogs. Actodin sat upon the beautiful fur robe that would serve as his burial shroud. Normally a dying man would have worn his burial robe, but it was summer and that would have been uncomfortably hot. Just as Actodin was about to give his speech, Biard burst onto the scene and declared the proceedings to be an impermissible breach of Christian standards. Membertou, always eager to please his French allies, stepped forward and explained "that they were but neophytes" and did not fully understand the problem.[16] All Biard had to do was teach them the proper way to deal with the dying.

Biard's response is a classic example of the Jesuit missionary philosophy. Biard could have responded that everything was wrong, and everything must go: dogs, fur robes, kettles, all of it. He could have prescribed a burial straight out of France. But Jesuits drew a distinction between indigenous practices that directly contradicted Christian practices and "matters of indifference," local practices that did not interfere with the spirit of Catholic belief. Alessandro Valignano, an Italian Jesuit missionary to Asia, called this *il modo soave*, the "gentle way" of conversion. As Valignano instructed the Jesuit missionaries to China and Japan in 1579, "Do not attempt in any way to persuade these people to change their customs, their habits, and their behavior, as long as they are not evidently contrary to religion and morality. What could be more absurd, indeed, than to transport France, Italy, or some other European country to the Chinese? Do not bring them our countries but the faith." [17] Although Biard had probably not read Valignano's instructions, he too had been schooled in this approach to conversion.

Therefore Biard responded to Membertou's request with clear instructions about what was acceptable and what was unacceptable among the practices of the *naenie* and *tabagie*. Biard stated that several practices were permissible: "the farewells and a moderate display of mourning, and even the tabagie." At the same time he declared that "the slaughter of the dogs, and the songs and dances over a dying person, and what was much worse, leaving him to die alone, displeased me very much." [18] His reactions oscillated between the inclusive and the exclusive.

What was the logic behind these distinctions? Why allow the *tabagie*, a purely Micmac ritual, but make a fuss about leaving Actodin to die alone after the *tabagie*? Part of the answer lies in the status of what the historian Susan Karant-Nunn calls "pararituals," elements not required by the liturgy of Christian burial but not condemned by it either.[19] For example, it was widespread European practice for a corpse never to be left alone between death and burial. So-called watchers would remain with the corpse, day and night, sometimes praying, sometimes just watching for signs of life. Feasting after the funeral was another European pararitual. The Catholic burial liturgy did not specify that the family of the deceased should provide food and drink for friends and family after the burial, but, as discussed in Chapter 1, this was a tradition of long standing in France and elsewhere.[20] Thus the *tabagie*—even though it took place before the death of the honored individual—was similar enough to French pararituals as to seem permissible.

The elements that Biard forbade more clearly contradicted Catholic belief. The Micmacs sacrificed dogs at the *tabagie,* according to Biard, so that "the dying man may have forerunners in the other world." [21] According to Catholics, animals do not have souls, and thus the sacrifice of dogs clearly served no legitimate religious purpose. It must be remembered that even though the Jesuits had a tradition of respecting indigenous traditions, they took this only so far. The Jesuits were also on the vanguard of the Catholic

Reformation, the Church reforms undertaken in the wake of the Protestant Reformation. In a 1563 decree on purgatory, the Council of Trent summed up much of the thrust of the Catholic Reformation when it demanded that priests "prohibit all that panders to curiosity and superstition." [22] For Biard, the dog sacrifice clearly pandered to superstition.

Likewise, leaving Actodin to die alone after the *tabagie* would not only have been a breach of the Catholic model of the good death, which will be described at length later in this chapter. This alone might have been permissible. But Biard understood the logic that underlay the Micmac tradition of dying alone, and it did not please him. According to Biard, after the *tabagie* "it is no longer lawful for the sick man to eat or to ask any help, but he must already consider himself one of the 'manes,' or citizens of the other world." [23] Here Biard struggled to put a Micmac concept into terms a European reader—his superior in Paris—could understand. He used as a metaphor the Manes, spirits of deceased ancestors worshipped in pre-Christian Rome. Though the analogy was inexact, the point was clear: Actodin was going to be left alone to die because after the *tabagie* he was believed already to have crossed, in some respect, to the other side.

Membertou assured Biard that they would follow his dictates. No dogs, and Actodin would not be left alone. But Biard was not finished. He asked that Membertou carry his son the fifteen miles to Port Royal so the French could try their hand at healing him. Membertou complied with this extraordinary request, perhaps more out of hope that the Jesuits could work their healing magic on his beloved son than out of blind obedience to Biard. And, amazingly, within a few days Actodin was walking again and on his way to a full recovery. The Jesuits had turned to one of the most powerful healing agents in their arsenal, something the Micmacs fully understood: holy bones. [24]

When Actodin arrived in Port Royal he was in terrible shape. During his first few days in the French settlement his condition actually worsened to the point that his wife and children were certain that he was about to die. But then Biard unveiled the holy bone, specifically "a bone taken from the precious relics of the glorified Saint Lawrence, archbishop of Dublin in Ireland." [25] St. Lawrence O'Toole had died in 1180 after a life spent ridding Ireland of pagan errors and excesses. The parallels with the Christian missionaries in the New World were certainly not lost on Biard.

Monsieur Hébert, an apothecary who also attended to the patient, declared that the efficacy of St. Lawrence's bone was nothing less than "a genuine miracle." Biard modestly wrote to his superior, "For my part, I scarcely know what to say; inasmuch as I do not care either to affirm or deny a thing of which I have no proof." [26] Biard would not try to claim that it was a genuine miracle, leaving it to his reader to decide. But he was pleased with Actodin's unlikely recovery, not least because he knew it would impress the Micmacs.

This might seem to support the argument of the medievalist Patrick Geary, that Roman Catholicism is a religion uniquely devoted to the veneration of human remains. Although Catholicism, Geary admits, "has no monopoly on relics," he nonetheless insists that "a comparison of traditions reveals their far greater importance in [Roman Catholicism] than in any other culture." [27] Yet it was the parallel between Catholic and Micmac use of human remains in healing that rendered the holy bone so effective.

The overlap between Micmac and Jesuit healing can be seen in a dismissive account of native shamans that Biard penned in 1616. Biard wrote that the "charlatan" healer jumps around and "froths like a horse." At a key moment in the ceremony the shaman produces several objects, including "decayed and moldy bones." Biard could not disguise his contempt for the native healer and his bones. But several years earlier, Biard had no problem using a four-hundred-year-old bone of St. Lawrence to heal Actodin. In this way Biard partook of a Catholic tradition of using healing relics that stretched back over a millennium to late antiquity. [28] Biard must have followed the Council of Trent's lead in how to interpret relics like the holy bone. The council decreed that relics, like images of the saints, were reverenced "not because some divinity or power is believed to lie in them" but because they represented individual saints, who, "reigning together with Christ" in heaven, "offer their prayers to God for people." [29] The Micmacs undoubtedly did not understand this theological distinction; the Jesuits were still struggling to convey the most basic tenets of Christianity in their fractured Micmac. Instead, the Micmacs almost certainly interpreted the power of the relic through their long experience with the role of bones in their own healers' rituals; they seem to have had an inclusive reaction to St. Lawrence's bone. The Jesuits' magic, it turned out, wasn't as unfamiliar as it first seemed.

As we have seen, Jesuit burial likewise had some parallels with Micmac burial. Nonetheless, the differences that did exist would cause tensions in the early months of the Jesuit mission. These differences in burial practices raised the stakes when Membertou sickened shortly after Actodin's recovery. It turned out that Membertou would not live fifty more years, as Lescarbot had predicted in 1606. Membertou came down with a bad case of dysentery in September 1611.[30] Having witnessed Actodin's remarkable recovery, the ailing man made his way to Port Royal for treatment by the Jesuits. Biard and Massé were happy to have this opportunity to offer charity to Membertou, the first Indian in the region to be baptized. As they had been directed by the writings of St. Ignatius, Jesuit missionaries should "occupy themselves in undertakings . . . directed toward benefits for the body through the practice of mercy and charity."[31] Thus they welcomed the sick man into their tiny cabin and hauled wood to keep a fire burning for the next few days. The fire took the edge off the chilly night air as fall approached and combated the odor in the cabin, as the dysentery caused Membertou to lose control of his bowels.

As Membertou's end drew near he was joined by his wife, his daughter, and his daughter-in-law. Because Biard was mostly blind to issues of gender among the Micmacs, he wrote nothing about whether women had a special role in taking care of the dying, preparing the corpse, or mourning the dead. But Membertou's all-female entourage—when he had several healthy sons—suggests that Micmac women were considered central to the deathbed scene. This accords with what we know about some other Algonquian Indian groups. So with the women assembled, Biard took the dying man's confession "as well as I could," a reference to the Jesuits' continued difficulties with the finer points of the Micmac tongue.[32]

Membertou then delivered the traditional Micmac funeral oration and dropped a bombshell: he wanted to be buried in the Indian burial ground, not the Christian cemetery. Membertou explained his reasoning as simply as he could. He "wished to be buried with his wife and children, and among the ancient tombs of his family." Biard was shocked. The "first fruit" of his missionary labors, their steadfast ally, choosing heathen over Christian burial! This would be a terrible setback to the mission: "the French and Indians would suspect that he had not died a good Christian." It is important to note that Biard's responsibilities included the French of Port Royal as well as the local Micmacs. In fact, most of Biard's time in Acadia was taken up ministering to French sailors, a notoriously ungodly lot. As Biard put it, these sailors had "no sign of religion except in their oaths and blasphemies, nor any knowledge of God beyond the simplest conceptions which they bring with them from France."[33] Biard was faced with two equally skeptical audiences, French sailors and Micmacs, and both would take Membertou's desire to be buried with the Indians as a sign of Biard's failure. The politics of competing deathways were in this moment starkly on display.

But Biard was in for an even greater shock, for the younger Biencourt sided with Membertou. Biencourt was also present at the deathbed scene, helping with translation. In fact, Biencourt's father, the Sieur de Poutrincourt, had promised Membertou even before he was baptized that his traditional burial ground could be consecrated and that he could then be buried there. Poutrincourt had also vowed to "have a chapel built on the spot where he was buried . . . and that we were to pray for his soul." Now Biard was placed in the awkward position of having his fellow Frenchman take the side of his erring neophyte. Biard stuck to his guns, however, explaining that in order to consecrate the Indian burial ground he would have to "disinter the Pagans who were buried there," that is, all the Indians in the burial ground. Non-Christians were simply not allowed in consecrated ground.[34] Biard had been in Port Royal long enough to realize that the Micmacs would be horrified to see their ancestors systematically disinterred so that the Jesuits could perform their own magic on the site.

It seemed that an impasse had been reached. Biard walked out, according to Biencourt, "in a rage."[35] But, trying to rise above the fray, Biard soon returned in order to perform the sacrament of extreme unction. Although this was just before the Church would issue guidelines on all rituals and sacraments in the Roman Ritual of 1614, it is likely that Biard proceeded as the Ritual would soon dictate, as it mostly standardized existing practices. If so, Biard dipped his right thumb in holy oil and anointed Membertou in the form of a cross on his eyelids, his ear lobes, both nostrils, his closed lips, his palms, and finally the soles of both feet. Biard would have intoned in Latin, "Through this holy anointing and through His tender mercy may the Lord forgive thee whatever sins thou hast committed by the sense of sight," and by the sense of hearing, and so on through "the power of walking."[36]

This was undoubtedly a powerful scene for the Indians who witnessed it, with the French holy man offering his solemn incantations while touching the dying man tenderly and intimately. And indeed, according to Biard the sacrament had its desired effect. The next morning Membertou surprised Biard and Biencourt by declaring that he had "of his own free will, changed his mind."[37] He now desired burial in the Christian cemetery. "I want my burial place to be large and honorable, just as my brother [Poutrincourt] promised me."[38] Membertou's change of heart required changes of those who survived him as well. He instructed the Indian women observing his deathbed scene that "they should not avoid the place [the cemetery] in accordance with their old and erroneous notion, but rather, with the wisdom of a Christian people, should love and frequent it, in order to utter pious prayers for him." [39] Among the Micmacs the custom had been to avoid burial grounds and, as with numerous other Indian groups in northeastern North America, to avoid speaking the deceased's name. This latter tradition was maintained in Membertou's case; after his death his people would not utter his name but instead referred to him as "the great Captain." [40] There is no mention about whether his wife and daughter obeyed his wishes and, against their people's long tradition, visited his grave in the Christian burial ground.

Membertou was dead, having died, according to Biard, "in my arms." Now all that remained was to bury the chief's body in the Christian cemetery. A simple burial would not do. "We deemed it well to celebrate his funeral with great pomp." [41] For themselves, Jesuits preferred unpretentious burials. When, for example, a beloved Jesuit died in Billom, France, and the townspeople wanted to honor him with a torchlight procession and other marks of devotion, a Jesuit sternly told them that "we conduct our services with simplicity." [42] Biard would likely have agreed had his own funeral been in question, but for Membertou he wanted to harness the symbolic power of a magnificent funeral. By this Biard hoped to make a statement about the greater grandeur of the Catholic religion. Accordingly, Biencourt was put in charge of the funeral. With his noble upbringing the young man was the perfect choice: among seventeenth-century French elites funerals were, in the words of the historian Michel Vovelle, a "grandiose social ceremony." [43] Biencourt thus organized the burial to include a great deal of pomp, "imitating as far as possible the honors which are shown to great Captains and Noblemen in France." [44] The phrase "as far as possible" is key for imagining what transpired at Membertou's funeral, for without the elaborate material culture of France, the funeral almost certainly paled in comparison to those of noblemen in France. It certainly did not resemble the French noble funeral in which the corpse was carried on a hearse covered in black velvet and silver ornaments and drawn by six horses draped in ermine, the whole affair lighted by the flames of three hundred torches. [45]

But the funeral did have some impressive touches. First, Biencourt organized a wake, displaying Membertou's corpse from the afternoon he died until the following morning, "as is customary for captains' corteges." Then the French brought the body to the church, "with the children and relatives taking part in the procession." It was important to include the Micmacs and not simply have them as passive observers. Then the procession followed Membertou's coffined body from the church to the grave that had been dug in the Christian cemetery. At the graveside the proceedings undoubtedly had some of the sensual appeal of contemporary French funerals, with the smell of incense, the sound of chanting and singing, and the sight of the priests in their elaborate funeral garb.[46] There was also an impressive monument to Membertou. As Biencourt described it, "I erected a large cross over his grave; his weapons were hung from this cross." This latter gesture was yet another attempt to raise the status of the burial, for arms and armor were associated with aristocratic graves in France.[47] Finally, Biencourt hosted a feast for Membertou's children and relatives. The Indians seemed impressed with all the solemnity and pageantry: according to Biencourt, they "thanked me for the respect I had shown to their late father."[48]

Biencourt and Biard were pleased with themselves for mustering the symbolic power of a Christian funeral in the cause of converting the Micmacs and cementing ties of friendship. And some of the Micmacs were impressed—or at least politely thankful—for the French respect for their deceased leader. But did Membertou's family and villagers miss the trappings of a traditional funeral? Did they secretly perform part of the Micmac funeral ritual? If they did, perhaps it looked something like the 1606 funeral of Panoniac, described by Champlain and Lescarbot.[49] Panoniac was killed in a dispute with Indians some 150 miles from Port Royal. After his body was brought back to his village, his friends and relatives began a period of ritualized lamentations and weeping that lasted eight days, "taking some intermission during the day."[50] When this period finished, the villagers burnt Panoniac's belongings, including bows, arrows, tobacco, and a few dogs. The next day, wrote Champlain, "They took the body and wrapped it in a red coverlet which Membertou . . . had much importuned me to give him, inasmuch as it was large and handsome." Before Panoniac was wrapped, however, his relatives painted his face and decorated his body with "beads and bracelets of several colors."[51] Finally, the deceased warrior was buried.

We know that the Micmacs were not able to wrap Membertou's body or paint his face, but we do not know whether they performed ritualized lamentations for him, out of earshot of the French. One fact, however, suggests that Membertou's friends and relatives may have performed some traditional rituals for him, or at least wished they could: Membertou's death and funeral proved to be the high water mark of Biard's mission among the Micmacs, rather than the beginning of a glorious period of conversions as he hoped. The Jesuits were able to gain a few more converts, but none with Membertou's zeal. Try as they might, the Jesuits never found another Membertou, so willing to embrace their religion and deathways. Moreover, the feud between

Biencourt and Biard that had showed itself as Membertou lay dying intensified to the point where Biard began to look for a new place to set up a mission. He found what he was looking for on Mount Desert Island, near present-day Bar Harbor, Maine, where in 1613 he set up the mission he called St. Sauveur. The mission lasted only a few months, however. As part of the continued struggle between England and France over northeastern North America, an English ship from Virginia raided the coast from Maine to Cape Breton Island. St. Sauveur was destroyed and Biard taken prisoner. He was carried to Jamestown, then to England, and finally allowed to go to France. He never returned to the New World and died in 1622.

For the Micmac Indians of Kespukwitk, as they called this part of Acadia, their brief encounter with the "little black ones" from 1611 to 1613 was but one phase in a centuries-long dance with Christian missionaries. Each group of missionaries would bring its own strategies for altering Micmac deathways. Next would come the *sesaki'kewey*, the "Bare Feet" Franciscans, to be followed by Capuchins, more Jesuits, and eventually even Protestants. The Micmac name given to this last group would have pleased Biard: their comparative lack of rituals—including those pertaining to death—earned them the appellation *mu alasutmaq*, "those who do not pray." [52]

*   *   *

After Biard's capture in 1613, it would be twelve years before Jesuits returned to New France with the full array of Catholic death rituals and beliefs they hoped to instill among the Indians. In 1625 three Jesuits disembarked in Quebec, a fur-trading post not even two decades old. This small cadre of Black Robes included Enemond Massé, Biard's partner in Port Royal, and Jean de Brébeuf, an indefatigable thirty-three-year-old missionary who would play an important role in the history of the Huron people for over two decades. In 1626 Brébeuf and another Jesuit made the month-long canoe journey to Huronia, the land between present-day Georgian Bay and Lake Simcoe, an area occupied by the 21,000 or so individuals in the Huron confederacy. [53] After their strenuous trek, the Jesuits settled on the outskirts of the village of Toanché. The Jesuits thought the Hurons, or *Wendats* as they called themselves, would be a good target for Christianization because they were sedentary agriculturalists. Living in villages and growing corn, squash, and beans, the Hurons seemed more "civilized" to the urbanized Jesuits—and thus more likely to embrace Christianity—than nomadic or semi-nomadic Indians. But because the missionaries' linguistic skills were still poor and the Hurons were not eager to embrace these men's unfamiliar practices, the Jesuits made little headway at first. In their three years at Toanché, they baptized only one Indian.

The Jesuits did not have the opportunity to continue their labors long in Toanché, for in 1629 Quebec officials demanded that all French people return to the town due to worsening relations between France and England. A war had broken out between the two rivals in 1627 and now it threatened France's North American colonies. Indeed, the English took control of Quebec in 1629 and did not return it to the French until 1632. During that period the missionaries had to return to France, but in 1633 Brébeuf and three other Jesuits sailed back to Quebec. The following year Brébeuf restarted his mission among the Hurons, this time in the modest village of Ihonatiria, a town with ten longhouses and roughly three hundred residents fitted inside the typical Huron log palisade. Here Brébeuf was named *Echon* by the Hurons, a word meaning "beautiful tree" that was both close to the French "Jean" and an apt reflection of Brébeuf's impressive physical stature.[54] Brébeuf's language skills slowly improved in Ihonatiria, but he continued to make mistakes. Trying to translate the phrase "guardian angel," he used the ungrammatical Huron construction *aesken de iskiacarratas*, literally "I am the dead, who, you take care of me." The Hurons must have been simultaneously amused by and leery of this magical outsider who confidently intoned, "I am the dead!"[55]

Cheerfully ignorant of the occasional linguistic misstep, Brébeuf, upon returning to Huronia, placed death practices at the center of his attempts to bring Christianity to these people. Like Biard, he and his fellow missionaries used solemn Catholic burials to impress the Hurons. Brébeuf and the other Jesuits had numerous opportunities to do so, because their arrival in Huronia coincided with a series of deadly epidemics. These periods of high mortality disproportionately affected the very young and the very old. During one epidemic, for example, Brébeuf baptized and oversaw the burial of an eighty-year-old man named Tsindacaiendoua. Brébeuf made sure to bury him "solemnly," which for Brébeuf meant not in the Huron cemetery with its above-ground scaffolds, but in a separate place reserved for Christians. Brébeuf's use of death rituals paid off: "This ceremony attracted upon us the eyes of the whole village, and caused several to desire that we should honor their burial in the same way."[56]

One dying man was especially impressed by the way the Jesuits dressed for Tsindacaiendoua's funeral. It is not known what Brébeuf and the others brought with them to New France, but the Roman Ritual of 1614 clearly specified what priests presiding over funerals should wear. In addition to the cassock, or black robe that Jesuits wore daily in New France (and after which they were nicknamed), for a funeral they were supposed to be vested in a white linen robe over the cassock, a "purple chasuble" or sleeveless vestment over that, and another piece of linen around the neck and shoulders. They were also to wear the belt called a "cincture," a silk band around the wrist, and the silk or linen scarf called a "stole" over the shoulders.[57] The Hurons, like virtually all peoples, understood the powers of ceremonial dress, and this departure from ordinary priestly garb made quite an impact.[58] Witness the case of Joutaia, who lay dying and could not make it to the funeral. He heard about how the Jesuits looked and asked to have them brought in their funereal splendor to his longhouse. Suitably impressed, Joutaia asked Brébeuf to bury him in the Christian fashion.[59]

At the same time that Brébeuf sought to awe the Hurons with Catholic burial rituals, he had an opportunity to be impressed by one of the most elaborate burial rituals native to North America: the Huron Feast of the Dead. Although the Feast was an indigenous ritual, it should not be imagined that it was some kind of a "pure" pre-contact practice stretching back from before Columbus. The Feast of the Dead that dazzled Brébeuf in 1636 was shaped by European goods that began arriving in Huronia by the 1570s at the latest.[60] It was likewise the ritual expression of the slow formation of the Huron confederacy out of the scattered Iroquoian bands between Lake Ontario and Georgian Bay.

In the thirteenth century there was no Huron confederacy. Instead there were Iroquoian groups along the northern shore of Lake Ontario that shared a common culture that archaeologists call the Pickering culture. Whereas the Feast of the Dead involved an ossuary with bones from hundreds of individuals, Pickering burials were much less elaborate. They were either single primary interments (unlike the ossuaries, which contained secondary burials), or burial pits containing between one and thirteen secondary burials. In the fourteenth century, some Iroquoians began to migrate from Lake Ontario to the previously uninhabited region to the north that would come to be known as Huronia. Along Lake Ontario and in Huronia, as villages grew ever larger, secondary ossuary burials became the norm. These ossuaries grew in size from the small Pickering burials, and now held anywhere from one hundred to five hundred individuals.

At this point it is fair to call this process of secondary burial a Feast of the

Dead, as it resembles the ceremonies of the historic period in that it was held whenever a sizable village changed location. Yet even in these large ossuaries very few grave goods have been found. The burial pit known to archaeologists as the Moatfield ossuary, located some seven miles from the shore of Lake Ontario in what is now Toronto, dates to roughly 1300 and held eighty-seven individuals. It contained almost no grave goods other than a turtle effigy pipe. Another fourteenth-century burial pit, the Fairty ossuary, held over five hundred bodies. Nonetheless, even this enormous ossuary contained almost no grave goods: archaeologists unearthed only one stone scraper and a shell bead.[61]

In the fifteenth and sixteenth centuries the villages on the shores of Georgian Bay continued to grow and eventually (in a process not fully understood) they coalesced into the four nations of the Huron confederacy.[62] Starting in roughly the 1570s, European goods began to trickle into Huronia via Algonquians who lived to the northeast. After 1609 the Hurons began to participate directly in the fur trade with the French. As agriculturalists located about as far north as was possible in North America, they were perfectly positioned to serve as middlemen between Europeans eager to trade for beaver and northern hunter-gatherers eager to trade their beaver pelts to the Hurons for dried corn.[63] Quite rapidly Huronia was flooded with material goods: furs from the north, tobacco from the south, and French trade items like copper kettles, iron hatchets, and glass beads.

All these things found their way into Huron burial practices, because for the Hurons the primary impetus to acquire goods was to give them away, and people were especially eager to give gifts to the dead. As Brébeuf observed, "We have seen several stripped, or almost so, of all their goods, because several of their friends were dead, to whose souls they had made presents."[64] The reason for all this gift giving was that the souls of the dead needed these goods in the afterlife. After the Feast of the Dead, the souls of all those interred in the pit journeyed to the west, to the village of souls. According to Brébeuf, "They [the souls] go away in company, covered as they are with robes and collars which have been put into the grave for them."[65] The souls needed these items because the afterlife resembled Huronia and the souls hunted and fished much the way they did while living. For this reason, "axes, robes, and collars are as much esteemed [by souls] as among the living."[66] Thus, as Hurons acquired more goods through the fur trade their grave offerings increased exponentially.

At the same time that Huron burial rituals were involving more and more material goods, the Feast of the Dead took on greater regional significance. Instead of involving members of only one village, an entire nation took part. According to the Franciscan Recollet Gabriel Sagard, who spent a year and a half in Huronia in the 1620s, the Hurons explained to him that "just as the bones of their deceased relatives and friends are gathered together and united in one place, so also they themselves ought during their lives to live all together in the same unity and harmony."[67] Not only that, but non-Iroquoian allies were invited to participate to demonstrate the friendship among the various groups. Algonquian peoples of the Upper Great Lakes—such as the ancestors of Michigan's Ojibwa—were so impressed by the Feasts they attended that they imported the custom into their own societies in the middle of the seventeenth century.[68] One aspect of the Feast that must have impressed the Algonquians was the sheer volume of presents distributed, a result of the Hurons' newfound material wealth.

Jesuits knew about the Feast but had never attended one when Brébeuf and two other Jesuits were invited to the Bear nation Feast in May 1636. By this point Brébeuf's grasp of the Huron language was quite good, so he was well positioned to observe the Feast and understand the proceedings. Brébeuf was also culturally well positioned to understand this ritual of secondary burial, as he hailed from a society where the disinterment of bones was routine. As discussed in Chapter 1, since the fourteenth century French gravediggers in crowded urban cemeteries collected the dry bones from old graves as they made way for new ones. They placed these bones in *charniers*, similar but not identical to the charnel houses of the English.[69] Thus in Brébeuf's homeland there was nothing inherently bizarre or repellent about moving the remains of the dead from one resting place to another.

At least partly for this reason Brébeuf's description of the Feast was sympathetic. Nor was Brébeuf's inclusive reaction unique. Fellow Frenchman Sagard addressed his readers: "Christians, let us reflect a little and see if our zeal for the souls of our relations . . . is as great as that of the poor Indians for the souls of their dead in like circumstances, and we shall find that their zeal is more intense than ours, and that they have more love for one another, both in life and after death, than we who call ourselves better."[70] Likewise, Brébeuf sought to impress upon his European readers how they could learn a thing or two about compassion for the dead from the Hurons. Brébeuf began his observation of the ritual by watching the residents of Ihonatiria prepare their corpses for the Feast. As the Feast was held only once in ten or twelve years, the villagers went out to their rather full cemetery to collect the remains of the deceased. The cemetery was located a short distance from the dwellings—"usually an arquebus-shot distant from the town," according to Sagard—where corpses wrapped in beaver robes had been placed in bark tombs eight to ten feet above the ground.[71] The caretakers of the graves entered the cemetery and brought forth the corpses that belonged to each family of the village. Fresh tears fell as family members embraced the bones of their departed loved ones.

This moving scene did not fail to stir Brébeuf, who connected on a deeply human level to the Huron expressions of grief. But Brébeuf's admiration of this moment went beyond shared emotions. As he put it, "I do not think one could see in the world a more vivid picture or more perfect representation of what man is." That is, Huron deathways were a model for grappling with human mortality. True, French cemeteries with the mingled bones of the rich and poor were graphic reminders that one ought to prepare for the afterlife. "But it seems to me that what our Indians do on this occasion touches us still more, and makes us see more closely and apprehend more sensibly our wretched state."[72] For these corpses were brought forth for the whole village to see. The condition of a particular corpse depended on the length of time it had remained on its scaffold. "The flesh of some is quite gone, and there is only parchment on their bones; in other cases, the bodies look as if they had been dried and smoked, and show scarcely any signs of putrefaction; and in still other cases they are still swarming with worms."[73] The living then set about cleaning the bones, scraping any remaining flesh and throwing it into a fire. The family members took apart each skeleton and bundled the disarticulated bones in a beaver robe.

But if a corpse was too recently deceased to be scraped properly, the family members simply wrapped the corpse in a new beaver robe. Brébeuf was amazed by the Huron comfort with human remains. He witnessed one corpse of a man who had recently died. The body was swollen and stinking, writhing with worms and oozing corruption. Yet the man's surviving family members were not disgusted. They reached into the fouled robe in which the man had been buried, scooped away the decaying flesh as best they could, and wrapped the body in a fresh robe. "Is not that a noble example to inspire Christians," Brébeuf asked his readers, "who ought to have thoughts much more elevated to acts of charity and works of mercy towards their neighbor?"[74] In the opinion of many Jesuits, the piety of ordinary French men and women was sorely wanting. When Jesuits traveled the French countryside on domestic missions, they were repeatedly discouraged by the low level of knowledge and observance they found.[75] Granted, the Hurons were not Christians, Brébeuf was telling his audience, but Christians could learn from them about an appropriate focus on the afterlife.

For Hurons this ritual preparation of bones had profound meaning because of their beliefs about the souls of the dead. They believed that each person had two souls. One stayed with the body even after death, the other hovered above the village cemetery until the Feast. At that point the second soul was able to fly away to the afterlife, the village of souls. So the participants in the Feast were preparing to set free the souls of their deceased family members.[76]

Despite the profound implications of allowing one's relatives to enter the village of souls, we should not imagine that the Feast was all solemnity and gravity. The Jesuit term for this ritual, *Fête des Morts*, might more accurately be translated into modern English as Festival of the Dead, which better suggests the festivities that accompanied the gathering. As the residents from across Huronia carried their bundles and assembled in Ossossané, the village chosen for the 1636 Feast, the atmosphere of a country fair prevailed. Over here a group of women competed using bows and arrows to win a string of porcelain beads or a belt decorated with porcupine quills. Over there a group of men tried to shoot a narrow stick with their arrows. Everywhere food was shared, stories were told, and the cathartic "cry of souls" resounded, *haéé haé*.

When it came time to place the bundles in the ossuary, however, participants became more solemn. About noon on the appointed day everyone brought their bundles to the enormous pit that had been dug in preparation. Brébeuf tells us that the pit was thirty feet across, which is very close to the actual diameter of twenty-four feet ascertained by archaeologists in the 1940s.[77] Around the pit families gathered to say a final tearful farewell to their loved ones. Brébeuf was especially taken with the tenderness that one woman displayed toward the bones of her father and children. First she caressed her father's bones. "She combed his hair and handled his bones, one after the other, with as much affection as if she would have desired to restore life to him." Then, even more emotionally, she took her children's bones out of their robes. "She put on their arms bracelets of porcelain and glass beads, and bathed their bones with her tears." The ceremonial leaders could "scarcely tear her away" from the bones, but they did for the ritual had to continue.[78]

Using the European trade goods that had become ubiquitous in Huronia, this woman shared a physical intimacy with her family members' bones that some modern readers find surprising, yet which Brébeuf "admired."

Brébeuf's admiration stemmed from Catholicism's long veneration of holy bones. Brébeuf would not have put the bones of the nameless Huron woman's family on the same plane as the saint's bone with which Pierre Biard cured Actodin—or of the bones of the seventeen other saints whose relics made their way to New France—but he certainly understood the woman's impulse.[79] To get a sense of the attitudes toward bones that French priests and nuns brought with them to New France, witness the intense engagement of the Ursuline nun Marie de l'Incarnation with the bones of her fellow nun and missionary, Marie de Saint-Joseph. In 1663 Marie de l'Incarnation wrote from her convent in Quebec to a nun in France to describe the ecstasy she experienced when opening the coffin of her dear friend. The coffin had to be moved in order to make way for a chapel they were building, so the nuns of the Ursuline Convent took the opportunity "to see in what state her body then was." Fearing corruption and decay—the young woman had been dead eleven years—they instead "found all her flesh consumed and changed into a milk-white paste of about a finger's depth." The heart, brains, and bones were all in their proper place, "the whole without any ill odor." This was a delightful sight. "The moment we opened the coffin we were filled with a joy and sweetness so great that I cannot express it to you." Before reburying their deceased companion, the women decided to wash the bones. "The hands of those who touched them smelled of an odor like irises. The bones were as if oily, and when they had been washed and dried, our hands and the linens had the same odor." Touching these bones did not fill these women with fear and dread, but, similar to the Huron woman's experience, "they filled us rather with feelings of union and love for the deceased." [80]

But the Feast of the Dead was about more than just love for the deceased; it was an expression of love and amity among the villages of Huronia and their allies. So after the tearful Huron woman was pulled away from the bones of her father and children, the ceremony commenced. The roughly two thousand participants gathered according to village, but then, in a symbol of unity, all came together bearing their bundles to mingle their bones in the pit. First the pit was lined with forty-eight beaver robes, each containing ten beaver pelts. Then the bone bundles were arranged in the pit, along with three copper kettles of French manufacture. Brébeuf did not know how many bone bundles were interred in the pit, but osteoarchaeologists have determined a minimum number of individuals of 681, based on a count of right ilia (a part of the pelvis).[81] In addition, presents were placed in the ossuary for the dead to use in the afterlife. Some of the presents were native to North America but many more were European in origin: a wealth of glass beads; a variety of iron knives including table knives, butcher knives, and jackknives; several copper kettles; and novelties like a wineglass stem and a magnifying glass.[82] As Sagard put it, the Hurons evinced "great joy and satisfaction at having provided the souls of their relatives and friends with something . . . wherewith to become rich in the other life."[83] Once all the bundles and presents were safely arranged, the remaining space in the pit was filled with mats, bark, and finally sand.

This ritual included not only elements of European material culture but also aspects of European religious culture. Because there were fifteen or twenty Christian Indians buried in the pit, Brébeuf and his two Jesuit companions said a *De profundis* for the Indians' souls. It is unclear whether they did this surreptitiously or as a sanctioned coda to the Feast. In either case, they offered the words of the Psalmist, "Out of the depths have I cried unto thee, O Lord." They did so with "a strong hope that . . . this feast will cease, or will only be for Christians, and will take place with ceremonies as sacred as the ones we saw are foolish and useless."[84] At the end of his lengthy and largely sympathetic description of the Feast, Brébeuf let his true colors shine through as he cried to his god. He was not a modern anthropologist, describing deathways to serve value-neutral ends, but a missionary convinced that Huron deathways were wrong, "foolish and useless," and needed to be changed.

Back in Ihonatiria Brébeuf set about trying to change Huron deathways by focusing on deathbed scenes. The Jesuits believed that proper Indian deathbed scenes were absolutely crucial to Jesuit missionary success.[85] As one historian has summed up the Catholic attitude in this period, "the most important act of a lifetime is the act of dying."[86] This was especially true for adult converts to Christianity, whose seemingly sincere efforts could be undone by a poor deathbed performance. Catholics believed that Satan was especially likely to victimize believers as they lay dying. For this reason Ignatius of Loyola urged Jesuits to care for one another in their final hours. Because of "the vehement attacks of the devil and the great importance of not succumbing to him, the passing away is itself such that the sick man needs help from fraternal charity." If such was the case in Europe, imagine how much more of a threat Satan posed in a New World setting with few Christians and fewer priests.[87]

So the Jesuits paid a great deal of attention to Indian deathbed scenes and had good reason to believe that French readers of their *Relations* hungered for the details of these crucial moments. A significant proportion of books published in seventeenth-century France—reaching as high as 5 percent of all titles by the last quarter of the century—dealt with deathbed scenes and preparing to die well.[88] In response to this demand, Jesuits recorded at least 134 Indian deathbed scenes in the *Relations*. But despite the volume of these records, scholars have been reluctant to analyze deathbed scenes recounted by Jesuits and other North American missionaries.[89] The choice to ignore missionaries' descriptions of deathbed scenes is certainly understandable. In missionary sources that already provide scholars with difficult challenges of bias and ethnocentrism, deathbed scenes seem to be among the least reliable passages. Clergymen had numerous incentives to exaggerate how pious dying Indians were. The trial of dying, missionaries believed, tempted converts to revert to old ways. A glorious death, therefore, was the best proof of missionary success. Dying speeches also had the advantage, from the missionaries' standpoint, of being irrefutable. Once dead, an Indian could not complain that his or her words had been misquoted. Furthermore, many deathbed descriptions simply lack the ring of authenticity. Indians often speak in these accounts in a stilted and formal fashion that modern readers find unrealistic. This tendency toward stock speeches partly resulted from the genre conventions of hagiography, which influenced both Catholic and Protestant descriptions.[90] And, finally, it does not inspire confidence that missionaries recorded long speeches—sometimes many years after the fact—as direct quotations.

But paying attention to the distinctions between model and unorthodox deathbed scenes allows one to use these sources more carefully and critically than has been possible previously.[91] I argue that *model* deathbed scenes— those that adhered to the conventions for a good death—lend themselves to a representational style of analysis. This kind of analysis, favored by literary scholars, is premised on the belief that because European representations of Indians are deeply colored by ethnocentrism, they tell us much more about European attitudes toward Indians than about actual Indian practices. Because model deaths draw so much inspiration from centuries of Christian writings on good deaths, and because the heavy hand of these tropes flattened individual experiences into didactic lessons that supported the missionaries' agendas, they are better suited to revealing what missionaries wanted Indians to believe than how Indians actually died. This should not be taken to mean that Indians could not, in fact, become orthodox Christians and die model Christian deaths. I am persuaded that many native people did both. Nonetheless, European descriptions of model deathbed scenes are simply not reliable sources for learning about these orthodox individuals' beliefs and practices.

On the other hand, descriptions of *unorthodox* deaths—those that departed from the model in ways that missionaries found problematic—often worked against the missionaries' manifest interests. Clergymen who wished to demonstrate their success sometimes narrated deathbed scenes that could be read as undermining that goal. Moreover, because there were not scripts of unorthodox deaths, such accounts do not appear to be squeezed into pre-existing narratives. Unorthodox deathbed scenes, therefore, represent fissures through which something closer to the actual experience of dying Indians may be glimpsed; as a result they may be used in what can be termed an ethnohistorical fashion.[92]

Before examining Jesuit accounts of Christian Indians' deathbed scenes, it is important to get a sense of how dying Hurons may have conducted themselves before the arrival of the Jesuits, so we can understand the practices the Jesuits were trying to change. Uncovering pre-contact deathbed rituals is a difficult task. In contrast with burial customs, Indians' deathbed customs have not left traces in the archaeological record. As a result, there is nothing to corroborate or contradict the sources that exist: European descriptions from the early contact period. At best, then, these Jesuit sources can only hint at the pre-contact deathbed practices of the Hurons.

Missionaries asserted that Hurons placed a great emphasis on a person's deathbed scene. According to the Jesuits, family and friends surrounded the dying person. Paul Le Jeune wrote that the Hurons were noteworthy, compared to other native groups of the northeast, for how seriously they took deathbed visitations. "The Hurons," he wrote in 1638, "inconvenience themselves to assist a person who is sick unto death." Moreover, the Hurons expected the mortally ill to die bravely. As Brébeuf phrased it, dying people "sometimes sing without showing any dread of death."[93] This trait was especially valued in warriors—and every man was a warrior—who might be tortured to death by their enemies. Hurons were expected to die stoically, even (or perhaps especially) under torture.[94]

Among those Hurons who did not die under torture, some participated in a farewell feast (*astataion* or *athataion*), not unlike the *naenie* of the Micmacs. It is unclear whether women ever offered farewell feasts; the Jesuits did not explicitly state that this was a sex-specific ritual, but all the examples they described were the farewell feasts of adult and infant males.[95] During the *astataion*, the dying person was often dressed in his burial robe, in which garb he would offer those assembled fine food, make a farewell speech to his friends and relatives, and lead them in songs. If the dying person was an infant, his parents would make the speeches and sing. Thus, formalized deathbed speeches had a long history among the Hurons, which probably rendered the Christian tradition of dying speeches easily understandable.

It appears that the Hurons' complex deathbed proceedings were, in part, enacted to recognize the liminal status of the dying person, who straddled this world and the next. This liminality made the dying person especially receptive to supernatural intervention, hence the frequent presence of shamans, who served to interpret visions. Not only did Hurons apparently consider the dying more likely to have supernatural visions; they seem to have believed that these visions were especially trustworthy. According to the Jesuits, Hurons gave deathbed visions a great deal of credence.[96]

Even though the Jesuits were interested in these early-contact Indian deathbed scenes, their curiosity arose primarily from a desire to change these practices. So when they arrived in the New World, Jesuits quickly set about fashioning a model deathbed scene for their Christian converts to follow. This model drew heavily on European antecedents but was also influenced by the peculiarities of the New World setting and by the Indians themselves. Although individual descriptions of model Indian deathbed scenes varied somewhat from case to case, these texts were highly formulaic, with standard plots and stock phrases.

The deathbed scene began when an Indian realized he or she was dying. This could be as the result of a sickness that took a turn for the worse, a severe accident or injury, or the commencement of torture. If the Indian had previously embraced Christianity, he or she would begin to pray to God. A wide range of subjects was appropriate for deathbed supplications: the dying person might pray for the health of friends and family, for mercy, or for the continued success of the missionaries in converting non-Christian Indians. Dying Christian Indians often asked to receive communion, take confession and perform penance, or receive extreme unction.

As the model death continued, the dying Indian expressed a variety of pious sentiments. Because of this, the ability to speak was very important. A deathbed scene in which the dying person could not manage to utter at least a few words, due to delirium or physical incapacity, was considered highly problematic. Model dying words often included an exhortation to family and friends, urging them to continue in the faith and to avoid sins, especially drunkenness. In addition, these statements often evinced hope for mercy, rendered in highly stylized fashion. Belief in God's mercy through Christ led to a willingness or even desire to die and go to heaven. Again, Jesuits represented Indians as expressing these sentiments in formulaic terms: a girl declared, "Mother, I am glad to die; I am going to Heaven," and a man describing the transition from life to death stated, "I do not fear the passage, for . . . I am going to heaven." The model deathbed scene concluded, of course, with the Indian's death, but not before some final pious statement or gesture. As with much else in the model deathbed scene, these dying actions drew on a small repertoire of stock behaviors. The Indian might look longingly toward heaven, or raise his or her hands in prayer, or gasp an appropriate sentiment like "Jesus have pity on me" or "Jesus, take me!" [97]

This model death was derived from the European *Ars moriendi* tradition, but there were some elements distinctive to the New World.[98] First of all, the Jesuits reserved especially high praise for dying Indians who expressed a desire for Christian burial. Simply not an issue in European and Euro-American scripts for good deaths, desire for Christian burial, as in Membertou's deathbed scene, was a sign of missionary triumph in the New World. Another departure from the European model was the possibility that a non-Christian might be converted on the deathbed. Similar occurrences were not a part of the European and Euro-American Catholic model of a good death, as these took place within a Christian context. The closest a priest might come to such a case would be a dying person who was ignorant of some of Catholicism's fundamental tenets. Likewise, in the Indian model of a good death the dying person often urged family members and friends to maintain their adherence to Christianity. This too was not relevant in a European context.

Unfortunately for Brébeuf and the other Jesuits, model deaths were few and far between in their early years in Huronia. Epidemics in 1636 and 1637 led many Indians to believe that the Jesuits were the source of their problems. As a Jesuit later wrote, the Hurons had "no doubt we carried the trouble with us, since, wherever we set foot, either death or disease followed us." A rumor began to spread that the Jesuits "had brought a corpse from France" and hidden it in the tabernacle of their chapel. The alleged corpse, some believed, was the cause of the epidemics. It seems that this rumor was based on the Huron understanding of the apparent cannibalism of the Jesuits' communion ritual, in which the outsiders devoured the body and blood of their god.[99] Because of this rumor the Jesuits faced unprecedented difficulties in convincing the Hurons of their good intentions.

Given how hard it was to get healthy adult Hurons to embrace Christianity, unorthodox deaths were more common than model ones in the early years of the Jesuit mission. In 1636 and 1637, numerous Huron men and women died in ways the Jesuits found problematic. Many that the Jesuits thought were candidates for baptism due to their seeming interest in Christianity refused baptism on their deathbeds. One woman, for example, seemed like a perfect candidate for baptism: not only had several of her children been baptized but "she seemed very docile, and had declared herself to be well satisfied with the baptism of those children." Moreover, the Jesuits had rendered her the valuable service of caring for her and healing her after she had injured her leg, and while they cared for her they made sure to instruct her as often as they could about "our holy mysteries." But her death did not go as the Jesuits hoped. Brébeuf "could never induce her to consent to baptism" as she lay dying. Her reason? "She desired only to go where one of her little sons was, who had died without baptism." [100] This proved quite a stumbling block for the Jesuits in the early years of their work in Huronia. It was all well and good to extol the glories of the Christian heaven and the torments of the Christian hell. But most Hurons worried that accepting baptism would mean they would be separated from their loved ones and ancestors who resided in the traditional village of souls.

Another type of unorthodox deathbed scene that occurred during this period was one in which the dying Indian had a vision or dream that troubled the Jesuits. As we saw earlier, Hurons placed a great deal of stock in the visions of the dying. Not unlike European and Euro-American laypeople, they viewed a dying person as poised between this world and the next, sometimes able to bring communications or information from the afterworld to those still living.[101] In November 1636 a woman had a deathbed vision that the Jesuits dismissed as "amusing" and "imaginary" but which nonetheless reveals Huron ideas about the permeability of the boundary between this world and the next. A recently baptized woman was dying. Her condition worsened and she appeared dead. Then she revived and related a surprising vision to her father. She had traveled "to the Heaven where the French went" where she had seen "a vast number of Frenchmen, wonderfully beautiful." In addition, she had met a few Indians who had died Christians, including one of her uncles and her sister. The sister showed her the bead bracelet Brébeuf had given before her death. The visionary woman decided to return to Huronia to ask Brébeuf for her own bracelet, at which her corporeal self briefly awakened and told her father of the vision. But before she could summon Brébeuf she died, this time for good. When the father told Brébeuf about the vision the Jesuit dismissed the account out of hand as a transparent ploy for beads, but we should not be so sure. The vision fits with what we know about the deathbed practices of the Hurons and other Indian groups of northeastern North America.[102]

Likewise, at about the same time, another unorthodox deathbed scene involved a vision that the Jesuits mocked as containing nothing but "fancies." This was an unorthodox scene that went from bad to worse, in the eyes of the Jesuits. In this case, a woman was dying but refused to be baptized. The presiding Jesuit tried to scare her with descriptions of the hell that awaited her if she continued in her obstinacy, but to no avail. She cheekily replied that "she did not mind going to hell and being burned there forever." Soon she was, by all appearances, dead. But then she awoke with news from the other side. "'I was dead,' said she, 'and had already passed through the cemetery to go directly to the village of souls, when I came upon one of my dead relatives.'" The deceased relation urged her to return to her village. Who else would prepare food to place in graves for souls to take to the afterlife? The woman took her relative's advice and returned to her village, resolving to live. The Jesuits ridiculed this and other visions, but their derision did not blind them to the realization that such occurrences "serve as a foundation and support for the belief they have regarding the state of souls after death." [103]

Throughout the terrible years of 1636 and 1637 death was rampant in Huronia. The frequency of unorthodox deathbed scenes reflected the difficulties that the Jesuits were having in presenting their religion as the answer to the region's problems. Instead, most Hurons turned to their own time-tested strategies for dealing with sickness and death. A blind shaman named Tsondacouané from the village of Onnentisati sought to induce visions by fasting for seven days. During this period he was visited by spirits (called "demons" by the Jesuits) who told him that the Hurons needed to appease the evil spirit who lived on the nearby island of Ondichaouan and who "feeds upon the corpses of those who are drowned in the great lake." Tsondacouané learned during his communication with spirits that Hurons needed first to slaughter a dog and hold a feast. This accomplished, the shaman's fellow villagers awaited his next instructions. Tsondacouané informed them that the spirits "ordered that those who would be delivered entirely from this disease should hang at their doorways large masks, and above their cabins figures of men" made out of straw. The residents of Onnentisati performed these tasks with alacrity: "in less than 48 hours all the cabins of Onnentisati and the places around were almost covered with images, a certain man having 4 or 6 of these straw archers hung to the poles of his fireside." [104]

Whereas a shaman performing a vision quest and obeying the instructions of spirits were traditional Huron practices, other responses to the epidemics involved innovations in deathways. Tsondacouané's vision had burnished his reputation across Huronia, and as a result he led a council in February 1637 that issued further instructions on how to combat the high mortality. The blind shaman made two recommendations. First, "that they should henceforth put the dead in the ground, and that in the spring they should take them out to place them in bark tombs raised upon four posts, as usual." And second, "that they should give them [the dead] no more mats, at least no new ones." The precise significance of these measures is unclear, but there can be no doubt that these were drastic and perhaps unprecedented alterations in Huron deathways. Hurons traditionally performed earth inhumation only for those who drowned or froze to death, as these bad deaths indicated the sky spirit's anger.[105] Thus, burying in the earth all who died may have been borrowed from or influenced by Catholic practice. Whether it was or not, by recommending earth burial followed by disinterment several months later, Tsondacouané demonstrated to the council's participants that radical actions were necessary to curb the epidemics.

Of course, the most radical step of all was to accept all or part of the Jesuits' magic as a solution to the epidemics. Brébeuf continued to do his best to use deathways to demonstrate the superiority of his supernatural powers, communicating with Hurons in terms they could understand. In October 1637 Brébeuf drew up his will in light of the increased danger he felt of being killed by traditionalists. Brébeuf combined this quintessentially European act with a classically Huron ritual: he held an *astataion,* or Farewell Feast. He sought to demonstrate "the little value we placed upon this miserable life." If *Echon* himself was willing to face death with equanimity, surely that would be a powerful statement about the glories of the Christian afterlife. The Hurons were impressed, because Brébeuf's actions resonated with their own beliefs. As Brébeuf noted in another context, Hurons at their Farewell Feast did not show "any dread of death" because they considered death "only as the passage to a life differing very little from this." As a result, according to Brébeuf, his cabin "overflowed with people" who came to witness the *astataion*. Brébeuf took the opportunity "to speak to them of the other life." [106] By these and similar gestures the Jesuits made slow headway. As the dying eased somewhat in 1638, more and more Hurons embraced aspects of Catholicism in order to protect themselves and their families. By 1639 there were almost one hundred professing Christians in Huronia.[107]

The Jesuits' progress in the early 1640s—at least by their own standards —can be measured by the increasing number of model deathbed scenes they recorded. Whereas 37 percent (ten of twenty-seven) of the scenes they described in 1637 were unorthodox, only 11 percent (four of thirty-six) in the 1640s were. Even though Brébeuf spent 1641 to 1644 in Quebec, numerous other Jesuits continued the missionary efforts in Huronia. The model deaths they recorded in the *Relations* were testament to the ever greater numbers of adult Christian Indians who had learned how to die well. These model deathbed scenes were so heavily influenced by the European *Ars moriendi* tradition that they are problematic sources for discovering what actually transpired as the Hurons lay dying. But they are very valuable sources for determining how the Jesuits sought to represent their efforts among the Hurons.

In 1642, for example, an eighty-year-old Christian Huron woman was dying. She had been baptized some time before and had continued her Christian behavior from that point forward. Now, in her final illness, she "begged to be raised in a sitting posture in order to pray to God with more respect." Her words were reported to be straight from the European model for good deaths: "Jesus, have pity on me; take me into your paradise. I am content to die; I aspire but to Heaven. Jesus, have pity on me." [108] With these few and simple words, the Jesuit who recorded this deathbed scene hoped to make several points. First, that the promise of the Christian afterlife, "your paradise," was one of the key elements in successfully converting Indians to Catholicism. Second, that an acceptance of Christianity allowed Indians to avoid fear of death, "I am content to die." And finally, that some Hurons had successfully mastered the basic language of Christianity in their own language, *Jesous Taïtenr*, "Jesus, have pity on me."

But it was not only long-time Christian Indians like the eighty-year-old woman who could have model deaths. In the 1640s the *Jesuit Relations* abounded with examples of non-Christians converted as the result of last-minute argumentation with indefatigable Black Robes. Jerome Lalemant described one such scene in 1646 at the Mission of Saint Ignace among the Hurons. A dying man named Saentarendi was not only a non-Christian; he was "one of the greatest enemies of the faith." But on his deathbed, Saentar-endi had a remarkable change of heart. In the kind of speech that has made historians wary of how accurately missionaries represented Indians' words, Lalemant wrote that Saentarendi proclaimed to the attending priest, "How good is God, even to the impious, since he brings you hither in order to grant me at death a favor of which I had rendered myself unworthy! I ask him for pardon with all my heart, and of you I ask Baptism." The good fa-ther complied with the dying wish, administered the sacrament of baptism, and gave Saentarendi the Christian name François.[109] As with the case of the eighty-year-old woman, the important point for this discussion is not whether Saentarendi uttered those exact words in the Huron language as he lay dying. Rather, statements such as these are significant because Jesuits felt they were important components of the model death. Deathbed conversions of non-Christians were among the most dramatic evidence of Jesuit success and divine power.

And indeed, by their own standards, the Jesuits were remarkably success-ful in Huronia during the 1640s. As their command of the Huron language improved, and as years of cultivating personal relationships began to bear fruit, they gained increasing numbers of converts. And not just deathbed converts, like Saentarendi, but more and more converts like the eighty-year-old woman, individuals who received baptism long before their deathbeds. In 1639 the Jesuits began construction of the stockaded mission town that would come to be known as Sainte-Marie among the Hurons. During the 1640s the population of Sainte-Marie grew to fifty-eight French men—nearly a quarter of the European population of New France—and by the end of the decade hundreds of Hurons sought temporary refuge there.[110] The mission site in-cluded numerous buildings, including several European-style dwellings, two longhouses, a barracks, a barn, and the two areas where Hurons would be ministered to in life and in death: the church of St. Joseph—deliberately con-structed with the high ceilings and overall dimensions of a longhouse (Figure 9) —and a consecrated Christian cemetery.

This cemetery was the site of much activity, as the increasing number of converts and continued high mortality led to numerous Christian buri-als (Figure 10). By the early 1640s the population of Huronia had dropped precipitously, from 21,000 before direct French contact to 8,600—a reduc-tion of almost 60 percent.[111] The Jesuits reported that Christian Indians from throughout Huronia—many of whom suffered from European infectious diseases—made their way to Sainte-Marie in order to be buried in the Chris-

Figure 9. Reconstructed Church of St. Joseph. Deliberately built with the high ceilings and overall dimensions of a longhouse, the Church of St. Joseph became increasingly busy as Iroquois attacks intensified during the 1640s. This reconstruction is based on the archaeological work of Wilfrid Jury in 1950 and must be considered only a best guess about the materials the French used to build the church. Sainte-Marie among the Hurons, Midland, Ontario. Photograph by the author.

tian cemetery. A woman named Tsorihia, baptized Christine, had been a Christian for seven years when she died in her village. After her death, her family followed her last wishes and carried her corpse the eighteen miles to Sainte-Marie so she could be buried there.[112] Another Christian woman embarked on an extraordinary journey to reach Sainte-Marie before her death. She was visiting relatives in a far-off part of Huronia when she began to feel sick. She worried that this might be her final illness. So she got into a canoe and paddled twenty-seven miles to her village, then got out of the canoe and walked the final nine miles to Sainte-Marie. She explained her reasoning, according to the Jesuits, in a way that shows that deathways were central to her experience of her new faith: "I wish to die among the faithful, and near my brothers who bring the words of eternal life. They will assist me at death, and I desire that they attend to my burial. I shall rise again with them, and I

Figure 10. Reconstructed Christian cemetery. This is where Christians were buried at Sainte-Marie. The stone marker represents the lone European burial, donné Jacques Douart, who was killed by traditionalists in 1648. The wooden crosses indicate the burials of Christian Indians. All the markers are conjectural; there is no evidence of how or indeed whether the graves were marked. Sainte-Marie among the Hurons, Midland, Ontario. Photograph by the author.

do not wish my bones to be mingled with those of my deceased relatives, who will be nothing to me in eternity." [113] She died at Sainte-Marie and received the Christian burial she desired.

The way the Jesuits reported her words—with her distaste at the thought of mingling her bones with her heathen ancestors—suggested a clear dichotomy between Christian and non-Christian deathways. And indeed some Christian Hurons renounced traditional practices in the 1640s, including even the Feast of the Dead. [114] But what the Jesuits did not report, perhaps because they were unaware of it, was that Huron burial practices at Sainte-Marie were, for many individuals, a syncretic blend of Christian and non-Christian Huron practices. Archaeological excavations performed in the late 1940s found seven bodies (out of twenty-one) buried with rosaries. Three of the rosaries were made of large wooden beads stained black, two were glass, and two were light blue porcelain. The presence of rosaries in these graves fits comfortably with contemporary French practice: burial with prayer beads became widespread after the Council of Trent inspired efforts to educate the laity using the rosary.[115] On the other hand, almost every grave contained Huron grave goods that Jesuits derided for being of no use to the deceased. Pipe stems, wampum, seeds, and potsherds were evidence of gifts for use in the afterlife. One body was buried with the teeth and jawbone of a dog, the significance of which remains unclear.[116]

One coffin contained an extraordinary example of syncretism. The coffin held two skeletons: a man buried on his side, knees flexed, with rosary beads, an iron knife, and a fourteen-inch-long French pewter pipe beautifully decorated with fleurs-de-lis. With him was a smaller skeleton, probably of a woman, disarticulated and deposited as a Huron burial bundle would have been for the Feast of the Dead. The archaeologists speculate that the bundle burial was the man's wife, who had died as a non-Christian and had been buried upon a scaffold in typical Huron fashion. Later, the man became a Christian, and when he died he had his wife's skeleton removed from the scaffold, cleaned and bundled, and placed within his coffin.[117] In their *Relations* the Jesuits mention nothing of non-Christian burial practices as Sainte-Marie, so it is unclear whether these practices occurred with their blessings or not. In either case it is a reminder of the value of archaeology in complementing written sources when trying to reconstruct the past.

Not only did non-Christian practices continue to mix with Christian practices at Sainte-Marie but non-Christian practices also continued among the majority of Hurons who remained unbaptized. In the Jesuits' narrative of Christian triumph in 1640s Huronia it is possible to overlook the persistence of so-called traditionalists, those who continued and even increased their hostility toward the Jesuits in this period. Deathways remained a locus of contention between traditionalists on the one hand and Jesuits and Christian Indians on the other. In some cases this contention was expressed in relatively ineffectual symbolic terms, as when a group of traditionalist children went up to "a great cross" in a Christian Indian cemetery and threw "stones and filth" at it. This action "somewhat injured" the cross, but it was not the most effective way to counter the Jesuits.[118]

Much more threatening to Jesuit success in the mid-1640s was what the historian Bruce Trigger calls a "nativist movement," ideological resistance to Christianity that was expressed through deathways, similar to the underpinnings of the 1622 Powhatan uprising.[119] One story circulating among Huron traditionalists asserted that some Algonquins had returned from the land of souls and had learned that Jesuit teachings about heaven and hell "are fables." Even more widely believed, perhaps because it emerged from Huronia and not the neighboring territory of the Algonquins, was the startling tale of a Christian Huron woman returned from the dead. This woman had been buried in the Christian cemetery at Sainte-Marie—could it have been Tsorihia?—but she had returned from the afterlife with an awful warning for her people. She related that after she had died she had gone to the Christian heaven. There the French welcomed her soul, "but in the manner in which an Iroquois captive is received at the entrance to their villages: with firebrands and burning torches, with cruelties and torments inconceivable." Heaven was nothing but fire, and the French took diabolical delight in capturing and burning Indian souls. This, it turned out, was the true motive of the French mission in Huronia. After being tormented by the fires of the French heaven for a day, "which seemed to her longer than our years," she was able to return to Huronia to bring her people the terrible news. According to the Jesuits, "this news was soon spread everywhere; it was believed in the country without gainsaying." [120]

This was a new sort of resistance to the Jesuits' teachings. Not simply indifference, this was an ideological counterattack aimed straight at the heart of what the Jesuits felt was most appealing about Christianity: its vision of a glorious afterlife for the saved. The battle for souls in native North America was largely a contest over competing visions of the afterlife, and the Huron traditionalists—aided by their communication with the dead—argued that the Jesuits' heaven was a hellish inversion of all they claimed it to be.

The Jesuits characteristically redoubled their efforts when the appeal of the nativist movement became clear. More manpower was brought into Huronia, and well-established mission sites like Sainte-Marie allowed the Jesuits to provide shelter to those who needed it. In the second half of the 1640s Hurons became Christians in unprecedented numbers, the nativist movement notwithstanding. By 1646 there were approximately five hundred professing Huron Christians. The following year five hundred more were baptized, the next year eight hundred more. By 1648 about one in five Hurons was Christian. The next year the figure rose to nearly one in two.[121]

In all this the Jesuits were aided by a crisis several decades in the making: Iroquois attacks on Huronia threatened the very existence of the confederacy. In the years since the Dutch had established Fort Orange (later Albany) in 1624, the Iroquois had increased their power and wealth by participating in the fur trade. When the fur supply began to diminish in territory controlled by the Iroquois, they looked to other areas for supply. Huronia, long an entrepôt in the fur trade, naturally attracted their attention. Although there were occasional Iroquois attacks on the Hurons in the 1630s, intensified attacks aimed at Huron villages rather than hunting parties began in 1642. In 1643 hundreds of Hurons were killed and taken captive by Iroquois warriors. The Hurons responded by invading Iroquois country in order to avenge their dead, which only increased the spiral of violence.[122] By 1648 Huronia was on the verge of collapse. Deaths from Iroquois attacks and European diseases were piled upon deaths from starvation, as crops went untended. The world the Hurons had known before the arrival of the Black Robes was but a distant memory. In this state of despair they turned to the Jesuits in increasing numbers, accounting for the surge of baptisms in the late 1640s.

The winter of 1648–49 saw the Iroquois make one final push to control Huronia. They attacked ruthlessly, destroying four villages. In the spring of 1649 the Hurons made the decision to abandon and burn their remaining villages so the Iroquois could not benefit from them. The Huron confederacy had been destroyed; the Huron diaspora was now created. Some refugees sought shelter with the Jesuits on the island of Gahoendoe, where the missionaries built Sainte-Marie II. Others went to Quebec for French support. Still others were incorporated by the Iroquois as replacements for those who had died during this decade of warfare.

It was some of these Hurons, "former captives of the Iroquois, naturalized among them," who would have one final opportunity to seek vengeance for the destruction of their homeland. Tellingly, they did not direct their ire toward the Iroquois who captured them but toward the Jesuits who had ushered in a period of mind-numbing change. In March 1649, 1,200 Iroquois warriors attacked the Huron village of St. Louis as part of their campaign to destroy the confederacy. They found two Jesuits in the village: Jean de Brébeuf and Gabriel Lalemant. According to several Christian Hurons who witnessed the scene, the Iroquois stripped the priests naked, tore out their fingernails, and marched them to the village of St. Ignace (Taenhatentaron) to await further torture. A few Hurons stepped forward to make sure that Brébeuf suffered the most painful tortures they could imagine. One, in a perverse inversion of baptism, poured boiling water on Brébeuf. Three times the Huron man took a kettle of boiling water and dumped it on the helpless priest, reportedly saying, "Go to Heaven, for you are well baptized." Other Hurons tortured Brébeuf with red-hot awls and hatchets, still others set fire to a belt of pitch around his waist, perhaps in imitation of the fires of hell. Throughout the ordeal Brébeuf remained stoic. When he tried to speak of Christ's mercy, the Indians cut out his tongue and cut off his lips. Finally, *Echon* died. Having spent over two decades trying to teach the Hurons how to die a good Christian death, Brébeuf died a good Huron death, brave in the face of unimaginable tortures. Impressed by his fortitude, the Iroquois roasted and ate his heart and drank his blood, hoping to gain his courage by doing so.[123]

The next day, hearing of the deaths of Brébeuf and Lalement, a shoemaker, Christophe Regnaut, went to St. Ignace and found the corpses. According to the "Veritable Account" he subsequently composed, he saw on their bodies the physical evidence of the tortures: horrible blisters from the unholy baptism, legs and arms stripped of flesh. Not satisfied merely to look, Regnaut also reported that he touched Brébeuf's corpse. "I saw and touched" his blisters, "I saw and touched" his burns, "I saw and touched his two lips, which they had cut off because he constantly spoke of God while they made him suffer." Regnaut buried Brébeuf and Lalemant, but as conditions in Huronia worsened he realized he was going to have to flee to Quebec. He did not want to leave the Jesuits' bodies vulnerable to depredations. So in an unwitting mirror of the Feast of the Dead, Regnaut prepared the corpses for transport. He disinterred the bodies, boiled them in lye, and scraped the bones clean. Then he set about drying the bones. "I put them every day into a little oven which we had, made of clay, after having heated it slightly; and, when in a state to be packed, they were separately enveloped in silk stuff." His bone bundles ready, Regnaut headed for Quebec. There, transformed into relics, Brébeuf's holy bones were "held in great veneration." [124] The bones even performed miracles, for which Brébeuf would be sainted by the Roman Catholic Church in 1930. In death Brébeuf gave Christians life; in life he had taught the Hurons more than they wanted to know about death.

CHAPTER 5

Grave Missions: Christianizing Death in New England

IF THE STORY of missionary work in New France is replete with miracles, such as the remarkable healing powers of Jean de Brébeuf's holy bones, there are fewer such wondrous tales in the history of New England's missionaries. This is the result not only of Protestants' distaste for miracle stories but also of the different political and demographic circumstances of each colony's founding, which in turn shaped relations between Europeans and Indians. New France was primarily a colony of traders, so alliances with Indians were crucial. New England, by contrast, was populated almost entirely by settlers, whose numerical advantage allowed them to pay less attention to the fine points of Indian diplomacy. As a result, the French became more adept than the English at negotiating the gift-based alliances that gained strength from pre-contact Indian ideas of mutuality between groups. Moreover, French Jesuits gained more converts than did English Protestants, not least because Jesuits allowed Indians to retain aspects of their culture that did not directly contradict Catholic doctrine. In their histories of New France and New England, scholars have emphasized these differences.[1]

But in terms of missionary *tactics* the English and the French were not as different as we have been led to believe. After all, even the most tolerant, canoe-paddling Jesuits still wanted Indians to abandon their traditional beliefs in favor of Christianity. And like their Jesuit rivals, most English missionaries—with the important exception of John Eliot—were deeply curious about Indian deathways precisely so they could use that knowledge to gain converts. Even Eliot, who was less of an ethnographer than most missionaries in the New World, shared with others the conviction that death provided the best entry point for discussions of Christianity with Indians. Missionaries and colonists thus had inclusive reactions to some native practices, especially Indian expressions of grief and deathbed rituals. Moreover, the Algonquians of southern New England—primarily Massachusett, Wampanoag, and Narragansett peoples—responded to the missionaries in their midst much like the Hurons and Micmacs of New France did. They interpreted the missionaries' message through the prism of perceived parallels between their pre-contact beliefs and Christianity, especially regarding the afterlife and the relationship between religion and healing. And as frustrations mounted among some of the Indians of southern New England, they used their hard-won knowledge of English deathways to terrify the colonists during King Philip's War, desecrating corpses in ways packed with religious significance.

As in New France, New England's missionaries found parallels between Christian and Indian ideas about death—the dying should be visited, corpses deserved solemn burials in well-marked cemeteries, the soul traveled to the afterlife upon death—that they used to communicate their messages about the spiritual power that could be gained from praying to the Christian god. This communication using the language of death gained increased urgency from the staggering death toll Indians faced in the wake of several epidemics. Over time, some New England Indians altered their deathways to reflect their changing belief system, a syncretic hybrid of old and new.

*   *   *

The dying was foreshadowed by an unholy buzzing in the forests. In 1616 the cicadas commonly known as seventeen-year locusts emerged from their underground burrows and made their way to the forest canopy, where their mating calls, multiplied by the millions, generated an anxiety-producing racket throughout New England.[2] That same summer an epidemic, or series of epidemics, began that lasted through 1618 and reduced the indigenous population of southern New England by perhaps 90 percent.[3] Because there were very few European observers to recount details of the epidemic, historians are not sure whether the dying was caused by bubonic plague or smallpox or some other pathogen. In any case, the effects on native societies were horrible.

Just before the epidemic began, a shipwrecked Frenchman who had been enslaved by coastal Indians threatened his captors with divine vengeance. In response the natives, "boasting of their strength," claimed that "they were so many that God [the Christian god] could not kill them." But this proved not to be the case, in the eyes of the English. As one colonist, Thomas Morton, wrote, "Contrary wise, in short time after, the hand of God fell heavily upon them, with such a mortal stroke that they died on heaps as they lay in their houses." From 1616 to 1618 the Indian societies of southern New England descended into mortality-induced chaos to such a degree that the survivors could not—or would not—bury the dead. Perhaps the Indians, fearing contagion, left those near death to die alone and remain unburied, as Morton reported. Or perhaps the epidemic killed so many spiritual specialists that it became impossible to pay proper ritual respect to the dead. What happened when a village's *Mockuttáun*, the keeper of graves, and all his assistants perished? Thus did Morton famously describe New England upon the arrival of the English as a "new found Golgotha," referring to the hill of Calvary where Jesus was crucified, a place littered with human bones.[4]

This was the morbid scene that greeted the bedraggled band of English colonists who in November 1620 came ashore in Patuxet, the place that the English later dubbed Plymouth. Known to posterity as Pilgrims, the colonists consisted of thirty Separatists, dissenters from the Church of England, and seventy "strangers" who hoped to better their material conditions in the New World. This proved to be an elusive goal, at least for several years. First off, the English began to die at a rate that roughly matched that of Indians during the worst epidemic years. About half of the colonists died during that first terrible winter. Short of food, arriving too late to plant anything before winter set in, the English hunkered down and slowly died of scurvy and other diseases exacerbated by near-starvation conditions. "Fearing the savages should know" of their weakened state, they "set up their sick men with their muskets upon their rests" and "their backs leaning against trees."[5] Thus was the colony precariously propped up against potential threats.

Some of these threats emerged because the Plymouth colonists embarked on at least two expeditions during which they plundered Indian graves. To be fair, grave desecration was not the primary goal of these exploring parties; that's just the way they turned out. The first expedition set out to explore Cape Cod on November 15, four days after making landfall in the New World but before settling on the Patuxet site. Led by Miles Standish, who was hardened by years of experience in wars with the Dutch, sixteen men wearing armor and bearing arms marched through the tangled brush in single file. They hoped to find towns, trading partners, and most urgently, food. Finally they came across some land that looked as if it had been recently cultivated. The men followed a path away from the field and toward curious heaps of sand, one of which was covered with old mats. The men began to dig; they found not the food they desired but a bow and rotten arrows. Grave goods, the men surmised. "We supposed there were many other things, but because we deemed them graves, we put in the bow again and made it up as it was, and left the rest untouched." Plymouth governor William Bradford explained their caution: "We thought it would be odious unto them to ransack their sepulchers."[6] Significantly, even before they had encountered any native people, the English attributed to Indians attitudes toward the dead similar to their own. The English would not want strangers digging around in their graveyards, so it stood to reason that Indians would feel likewise.

Two weeks later, however, the English allowed their curiosity and desperate hunger to get the better of them when they came upon another grave, this more spectacular than the first. They got down on their knees and started digging. First they removed some "boards" that covered the whole assemblage. Removing the boards revealed a mat, presumably a woven mat of reeds and grasses of the sort used by the Indians of southern New England in their burial rites.[7] Under this they found a bow, and then another board, this one about two-and-a-half feet long, "finely carved and painted, with three tines or broaches on the top, like a crown." Could the crown signal a royal burial? What might they find in the grave of a sachem? They dug deeper and found "bowls, trays, dishes, and such like trinkets." Surely this presaged yet greater treasure. Further down they went until they found two bundles, one large, one small. They opened the larger bundle. It was filled with red powder, likely ochre, a mineral substance containing iron oxide that the Indians of southern New England used to impart a rusty hue to corpses. Mixed with the ochre were the bones and skull of a man. But not the sachem the English had anticipated: the skull still had yellow hair attached to it. It seems that the English had unearthed the remains of a European.[8]

Additional evidence that this was a sailor comes from the items buried with the bones in the bundle. Tied up in "a sailor's canvass cassock and a pair of cloth breeches" were "a knife, a packneedle, and two or three old iron things," likely the belongings of a European seaman.[9] Could this have been one of the shipwrecked French sailors enslaved by the Indians a few years earlier? Several decades later Phineas Pratt remembered the Massachusett leader Pecksuot telling him about the Frenchmen. In 1622 Pecksuot said the Frenchmen "lived but a little while. One of them lived longer than the rest, for he had a good master [who] gave him a wife. He is now dead, but hath a son alive." [10] The burial is consistent with this report of a European who lived for several years among the Indians and had at least one child by an Indian woman.

The contents of the other bundle suggest just such an intermingling of European and native cultures. When the English peered inside, they found more ochre and the bones and skull of a young child. The child's arms and legs were adorned with strings of fine white wampum and he was accompanied by a pint-sized bow, just over two feet long. Having been disappointed in their search for corn, the English covered the corpses back up, "brought sundry of the prettiest things away" with them, and resumed their search for food. The English, seemingly untroubled by the implications of their grave desecration, debated the significance of their find. They argued about whether the man in the larger bundle was an Indian or a "Christian." But they did not concern themselves with the identity of the child.

The child, however, may be the most remarkable aspect of this extraordinary burial. If the Frenchman had a living son by his Indian wife, it is certainly possible that these bones were those of another son by the same woman. At the end of Chapter 2 I wondered how the offspring of a Roanoke colonist and an Indian woman would be buried. What blend of European and Indian burial rites would be appropriate for a bicultural child? If indeed the Plymouth burial represents a European sailor who lived some years with the Indians and his half-Indian offspring, the answer to that question, at least for this one case in southern New England, is this: the burial has no obvious European elements, other than a few items of European material culture incorporated into an indigenous-style burial. It is possible that the sailor's burial departed in important ways from the burials ordinarily conducted by his hosts. The bone bundles suggest secondary interment and seem to differ from the typical local practice of primary interment. But there was no cross, no coffin, nothing to suggest the European origins of the boy's father, other than the father's yellow hair and sailor's accouterments. The burial hints that although the surviving evidence forces us to focus on Indian adoption of European burial practices, there are unexplored—and perhaps unexplorable— moments when Europeans were buried according to indigenous logic.

One week after looting the sailor's grave, the colonists were still on the lookout for a favorable site to establish their settlement. Once again they came upon a "great burying-place." These graves were even "more sumptuous" than the sailor's grave and the others they had seen the previous week. Despite the temptation to look for buried food or treasure, "we digged none of them up, but only viewed them and went our way."[11] So the Plymouth colonists' record on grave desecration stood as follows: three gravesites found, one disturbed and returned to its original condition, one looted and reburied, and one left alone. It is impossible to say what accounts for these different outcomes. The most persuasive guess is that the English felt that disturbing graves was wrong, but in two cases their curiosity and hunger overcame their better judgment.

That the colonists had a degree of respect for Indian deathways, based on their belief that Indians were indeed human and shared with the English some fundamental attitudes toward the dead and dying, can be seen in an incident just over two years after the grave disturbances. By this time the Plymouth colonists had gotten through their worst period of mortality and had settled into a routine of uneasy interactions with the local Indians. Massasoit, the paramount Wampanoag sachem who lived in the village of Pokanoket, southwest of Plymouth, played a key role. Massasoit's people wanted access to the trade goods available through Plymouth, in part because European goods were considered desirable for burial with the dead. The Massachusett Indians to the north of Plymouth also wanted European goods, and this led to a rivalry between the Massachusetts and the Wampanoags. To ensure that Wampanoags would be able to trade with Plymouth, Massasoit signed a treaty formalizing an alliance between his people and the English.

The incident that shows English respect for Indian deathways is Edward Winslow's well-known sojourn to the apparent deathbed of Massasoit. This moment demonstrates that English encounters with Indian deathways were more complicated than stereotypes of the English as callous grave robbers will allow. Though less frequently than the French, the English did have inclusive reactions to Indian deathways. In this case the English perceived commonalities in deathbed practices and in the human expression of grief.

In March 1623 the Plymouth colonists learned that Massasoit was "like to die." The Wampanoag sachem had been a useful ally, so Winslow, a leading member and later governor of the Plymouth colony, was no fool to pay his respects to the man who remained powerful even as he lay dying. But Winslow's reasoning went beyond mere power politics. As Winslow later explained, it was "a commendable manner of the Indians, when any, especially of note, are dangerously sick, for all that profess friendship to them to visit them in their extremity, either in their persons, or else to send some acceptable persons to them." Winslow decided against sending someone in his stead, as his interpretation of Indian practices suggested he might, and rather made the long journey himself. "It was thought meet," he wrote, "being a good and warrantable action, that as we had ever professed friendship, so we should now maintain the same, by observing this their laudable custom." [12]

Why was Winslow so effusive in his praise of Indian deathbed scenes? Why insist that the practice was not just *commendable*, but also *good, warrantable*, and *laudable*? One reason is that Winslow was responding to what he regarded as a parallel between Indian and English practices. In such tracts as William Perkins's *Salve for a Sicke Man* (1595), English Protestants stressed the social nature of the deathbed scene. The "helpers," as Perkins called them, ought to play a central role in the deathbed scene, assisting the dying while simultaneously reinforcing the bonds of the religious community.[13] Like Perkins, Winslow was demonstrating for his readers the importance of attending to the dying. If non-Christian Indians do this, he implied, surely we who are good Christians should do as Perkins and other authorities urge.

Thus Winslow desired to heed the Indians' laudable custom and so he set out to the village of Pokanoket with an English companion and his Indian guide, Hobomok. En route they received unhappy news: they were too late, Massasoit was dead. For a moment Winslow considered turning back, but he urged the party on, saying that they could attend the burial and thereby curry favor with Massasoit's successor. As they trudged down the path to Pokanoket, Hobomok bewailed the loss of Massasoit. *Neen wamisu sagimus*, "My loving sachem!" No one has ever ruled with such reason, with such respect for the opinions of all, Hobomok lamented. Winslow was touched by the outpouring of emotion: "it would have made the hardest heart relent." [14] Winslow knew grief; he had lost his wife during the terrible first winter at Plymouth. He also hailed from a culture that valorized mourning for a deceased monarch, as in the royal funeral for Queen Elizabeth discussed in Chapter 2. In the shared understanding of loss, Winslow connected with his Indian guide.

But Hobomok's grief was premature. A messenger arrived, breathlessly bearing the news that Massasoit still lived, though just barely. The three men hurried to Pokanoket and found the aged sachem surrounded by helpers and ritual specialists. The dying man was so weak he could not see and he could barely speak. Someone told Massasoit who had arrived. The dying man reached out his hand and whispered, "Oh Winslow I shall never see thee again." Winslow decided to ignore such maudlin speculation and get right to work as a healer. First he put some jam, a rare delicacy, on the tip of a knife. He slid the knife between Massasoit's clenched teeth and got him to swallow some, to the great delight of the bystanders, who said he had not eaten anything for two days. Winslow then inspected Massasoit's mouth and found his tongue so "exceedingly furred" and swollen that it prevented him from swallowing. So Winslow scraped his tongue, removing an "abundance of corruption" and reducing the swelling.[15]

Winslow's intimate attentions continued. He asked Massasoit whether he had been sleeping well, and when he had last moved his bowels. Massasoit replied that he had not slept in two days, had not moved his bowels in five. Winslow's prescription: broth. He searched the area outside Massasoit's wigwam and found strawberry leaves and a sassafras root and made a tea. The concoction helped revive Massasoit, so Winslow made a stronger broth out of a duck. There were some setbacks—at one point Massasoit vomited violently after eating too much of the rich duck broth, which caused his nose to bleed profusely and led the Indian observers to worry that he was again near death—but Winslow stayed by the old man's side and nursed him back to health, gently wiping the vomit and blood from his face with a linen cloth. It is no wonder that Massasoit proclaimed, "Now I see the English are my friends and love me, and whilst I live I will never forget this kindness they have showed me." [16] There were few other moments of cross-cultural interaction in this period that allowed for greater intimacy between two men, men who were still learning about one another's cultures but who realized they shared certain fundamental attitudes toward sickness and dying: that the dying should be visited, and that sickbed ministrations were among the most tangible signs of friendship.

Shortly after Massasoit's recovery, however, events demonstrated that shared ideas about deathways could also be a source of conflict between the English and the Indians. To show his thanks for helping him recover, Massasoit revealed that Massachusett Indians were plotting against the English. Historians have been skeptical about whether this plot actually existed; Massasoit likely had his own self-interest in mind when he gave the English information that would lead them to attack his rivals. But Massachusett Indians may well have been very angry at the Plymouth colonists for a reason directly related to deathways.

This at least is the version of events narrated by Thomas Morton, whose *New English Canaan* (1637) attempted to show how the Plymouth colonists treated Indians more harshly than necessary. Despite its anti-Plymouth bias, Morton's account is plausible regarding deathways. His close observations of native beliefs over several years gave him a sensitivity to death practices that many of the Plymouth colonists lacked.

Morton asserted that several months before Massasoit revealed the plot, the Plymouth colonists had infuriated the Massachusetts by wantonly desecrating a grave in November 1622. Obtakiest (later called Chickataubut), a Massachusett sachem, had recently buried his mother in the traditional manner. He and his fellow villagers first placed her body into the earth. Then, after covering her corpse with mats, sand, and soil, they had taken "two great bears' skins sewed together at full length" and propped them up over the woman's grave, probably upon a small scaffolding made of branches. Twice Morton wrote that this bearskin marker reminded him of an English "hearse cloth." The hearse cloth or pall covered English coffins—especially those of the wealthy—as they were carried from the home to the graveyard. The hearse cloth did not always lay flat on the coffin, as we might imagine. Instead, some coffins of the early seventeenth century were peaked so the heraldic shields on the pall might be more visible during the solemn procession to the graveyard. Similarly, the grave of Obtakiest's mother was decorated by a large bearskin marker that was propped up so it could be more easily seen.[17]

This seems to have been a relatively common practice among the Indians of southern New England, though it may have been reserved for high-status individuals. Certainly two great bearskins would have represented a major investment of time and effort in capturing the bears, skinning them, preparing the hides, and sewing them together. Roger Williams observed similar grave coverings among the Narragansetts. He wrote that "a fair coat of skin" was "hung upon the next tree to the grave," but he indicated that this happened only "sometimes," likely only for those of high status. Even more to the point, Williams asserted that "none will touch" the skin after it had been placed on the grave; instead the Indians "suffer it there to rot with the dead."[18]

This was the terrible miscalculation of the Plymouth colonists: when they visited the village of Passonagessit in November 1622, they not only touched the bearskin hearse cloth on Obtakiest's mother's grave but they removed it as well. They "defaced" the grave, according to Morton, "because they accounted it [placing a bearskin atop a grave] an act of superstition." This act of grave desecration reveals the Plymouth colonists at their most arrogant. When Winslow stayed by Massasoit's bedside for days, scraping the sick man's tongue and wiping his soiled face, he did not (at least in his telling) overtly proselytize. He did not make Massasoit repeat prayers to the English god to help him avoid death. But Winslow let few other teachable moments pass him by. On his return from curing Massasoit, for example, he spent the night with Corbitant, sachem of Nemasket. As the English and their Indian hosts sat down to eat, Winslow prayed to his god to thank him for the food. Curious, Corbitant asked the meaning of the custom. This polite question led to a lecture on the biblical creation, God's "laws and ordinances," and the Ten Commandments. Although the Plymouth colonists were too weak and underfunded to mount a well-organized missionary campaign in the 1620s, they were not content to let the paganism in their midst go unchallenged.[19]

Arrogance, however, was not the only reason the English stripped an aged woman's grave of its bearskin covering. It must be remembered that the Separatist Plymouth colonists were among the most radical Protestants when it came to simplifying their burials so they in no way seemed to partake of Catholic practices. Even accouterments such as hearse cloths, widely used by well-off Anglicans in England, were anathema to reformed Protestants like the Separatists. This attitude could be seen in the 1640s, when reformed Protestants came briefly to power during the English Civil War and quickly acted to simplify English burials. In the *Directory for the Publique Worship of God* (1645), a compendium of new religious regulations, reformed Protestants demanded that the dead be buried "without any ceremony." Not even a minister was necessary! Kneeling down and praying to the corpse and other seemingly Catholic practices were banned as "superstitious."[20] The Plymouth colonists likewise buried their own dead simply. Their burials were so plain that the local Indians at first assumed that none of the English were of high status. According to Morton, "They marvel to see no monuments over our dead, and therefore think no great sachem is yet come into those parts, or not as yet dead." As part of their radical reformation of Catholic burial practices, the Separatists did not even mark their dead with gravestones in the colony's early years. Therefore, a bearskin grave covering was objectionable on so many levels that the Plymouth colonists removed it. In this way did the English witness Indian deathways, understand them—and seek to change them. This brazen act served, as Morton put it, to "breed a brawl."[21]

Obtakiest was enraged by the high-handed grave desecration but did not respond immediately. Soon, however, a vision of his mother's spirit convinced him to act. One night as Obtakiest was just drifting off to sleep, his mother's spirit appeared to him and cried out, "Behold, my son, whom I have cherished . . . canst thou forget to take revenge of those wild people that hath my monument defaced in despiteful manner, disdaining our ancient antiquities and honorable customs?" According to the spirit, her grave had been not merely defaced but made common. Like English elites, Indian leaders guarded their special burial prerogatives jealously: "See now the sachem's grave lies like unto the common people of ignoble race, defaced." The spirit seemed to threaten hauntings and bad tidings from the land of souls if the matter was not rectified. "If this be suffered," the spirit warned, "I shall not rest quiet within my everlasting habitation." [22] Obtakiest awoke in a sweat and told his kinsmen of his vision. The unanimous reaction was that they should attack the English to make them pay for the grave desecration.

But the Indians never had a chance to exact vengeance. Massasoit apparently got wind of the planned attack and shared the information with Winslow to repay his sickbed kindness. Winslow thanked Massasoit for the intelligence and the Plymouth colonists began planning a preemptive strike against the Massachusetts. Miles Standish lured two *pnieses* (powerful politico-religious specialists) and two other Massachusett men into a house; Standish and his English henchmen then killed all four Indians. One of the slain *pnieses* was Wituwamet, "of whom [the Indians] boasted no gun would kill." [23] Like Nemattanew, the supposedly immortal Powhatan Indian who was killed by the English in 1622, Wituwamet had enhanced his reputation by claiming to be impervious to European weaponry but had been proved disastrously wrong. Obtakiest and his men still made a charge at Standish and his troops, but without their *pnieses* the Indians were demoralized. After a few arrows and bullets flew back and forth, the Indians fled into the forest.

This was not the last armed confrontation between Plymouth colonists and Indians, but it marked an important transition in the colony's history. Standish and his men had shown themselves to be quite willing to resort to violence in their dealings with Indians they perceived to be hostile. Given the demographically weakened state of the Indian groups that surrounded the colony, and the Indians' continued desire for trade items that had spiritual power as grave offerings, even acts of arrogance such as the removal of the bearskin hearse cloth would go largely unpunished.

*   *   *

Compared with the Plymouth colonists, Roger Williams has a relatively positive reputation among scholars for his dealings with Indians. [24] But the reality is complex. Williams was a diligent ethnographer and linguist whose fieldwork, as it were, remains valuable to this day. Yet his ethnography contains numerous blind spots; in particular, Williams was blithely unconcerned with Narragansett women and children. There seems to have been genuine mutual affection between Williams and several Indians, most notably the Narragansett sachem Canonicus, but these relationships were mediated by Williams's unshakable belief in the superiority of Christianity. Throughout his years of dealings with the Narragansetts, Williams paid careful attention to deathways, both as a recorder and defender of native practices and as an unofficial missionary who sought to reform native burials.

Williams was born in England around 1603; in 1630 he and his wife were among the vanguard of English Puritans who embarked for a new life in the New World. This was a migration stream unlike any other the hemisphere had seen. During the Great Migration of the 1630s, some twenty thousand English men, women, and children sailed for New England to fashion a community among like-minded reform Protestants. Never before had such a large, self-sustaining population of European families transplanted themselves in the New World. The impact on the indigenous residents of southern New England was dramatic. Before long they were outnumbered by the land-hungry newcomers; by 1670 there were perhaps five Europeans for each Indian in New England.[25]

Williams's scholarly reputation as a friend of the Indians is based partly upon his ideas regarding land. In 1632, Williams wrote a treatise that criticized the practice of seizing Indian lands based on the legal device of the royal patent, arguing that this amounted to the "sin of unjust usurpation upon others' possessions."[26] The leaders of Massachusetts Bay were so infuriated with Williams's treatise that they burned it. As a result we know of Williams's incendiary arguments only from the angry responses to them. Although the legal and theological intricacies of the debate over royal patents is beyond the scope of this discussion, the controversy has two important implications. First, Williams had early shown himself willing to side with Indians against New England's leading men. And second, the royal patent debate helped get Williams banished from Massachusetts Bay in 1635.

As a result, in 1636 Williams and a few followers founded the small settlement of Providence in the middle of Narragansett territory. The Narragansetts remembered Williams from his time spent in Plymouth, when, unlike most colonists, he worked hard to learn Indian languages. Therefore Canonicus, the "great sachem of Narragansett" who was about seventy years old, was willing to allow the planting of the Providence colony.[27] Canonicus seems to have hoped that Williams and the Providence colonists would bring with them access to English trade goods. In this Canonicus was not disappointed, as Williams opened a trading post in the late 1630s.[28]

In later decades Williams would remember his relationship with Canonicus as warm and affectionate, but in the 1630s the two men had their share of disagreements. The first time Williams wrote about Canonicus, in a 1637 letter to Massachusetts Bay authorities, he referred to the sachem as "an old man, alike fretful and rude."[29] Williams accused Canonicus of rudeness because the Indian leader "accused the English and myself for sending the plague amongst them, and threatening to kill him especially."[30] Canonicus was referring to the devastating smallpox epidemic of 1633 that decimated Indian populations from present-day Maine to Rhode Island. The Narragansetts escaped this epidemic with relatively light mortality, but still they suffered hundreds of deaths.[31] Canonicus was, reasonably enough, upset about these deaths and he rightly suspected that the epidemic had something to do with the recent arrival of English families in the region. Thus Canonicus was, according to Williams, "very sour."

But Williams "sweetened his spirit" and even, in his own telling, convinced Canonicus that "the plague and other sicknesses were alone in the hand of the one God, who made him and us."[32] Williams explained to Canonicus that the English god, "being displeased with the English for lying, stealing, idleness, and uncleanness . . . smote many thousands of us ourselves with general and late mortalities." Here the "many thousands of us" killed by disease referred not to New Englanders but to residents of England, where a smallpox epidemic struck in the spring of 1636. Williams claimed that Canonicus was convinced by this explanation, but that seems questionable. The sachem might well have wondered whether Williams was accusing the Indians of deserving the English god's vengeance for "lying, stealing, idleness, and uncleanness." Indeed, that is precisely what Williams meant to imply. In his letter to Massachusetts Bay, Williams wrote that these were "the natives' epidemical sins."[33] An epidemic of sin warranted an epidemic of disease, according to Williams, hardly an argument destined to win the hearts of the Narragansetts.

Unless, that is, Williams could convince them that faith in the Christian god might help them avoid future displays of divine wrath. This is what Williams attempted in the years following the establishment of his trading post. When Narragansetts came to exchange their furs and wampum for English cloaks and looking glasses, Williams used the opportunity to teach his trading partners about Christianity.[34] But Williams did not expect the mass conversion of Indians to Christianity, as Spaniards claimed for their New World holdings. As Patricia Rubertone has observed, Williams was a "tentative and hesitant missionary."[35] He worried that in light of the corrupt state of most earthly churches, the widespread conversion of Indians was unlikely.[36] So Williams worked instead to introduce the Narragansetts to Christianity in order to prepare the way for future missionary work.

To this end he sought to improve his facility in the Narragansett language and to observe the Indians' religious practices, including deathways. As part of this ethnographic project, Williams witnessed the extraordinary funeral rites held for Canonicus's son. Williams was impressed by what he saw. In contrast with European practices, where death entailed the descent of property from one generation to the next and the occasional ugly spectacle of contested wills, Williams observed a much less materialistic, almost antimaterialistic celebration of death. Canonicus, "having buried his son, burned his own palace, and all his goods in it (amongst them to a great value)." Canonicus performed this destruction of property, according to Williams, "in a kind of humble expiation to the gods, who (as they believe) had taken his son from him."[37] There are no other accounts of similar practices among the natives of New England, so this may have been an isolated occurrence, brought on by a confluence of Canonicus's high status and great grief. Whether typical of his people's deathways or not, it is likely that among the items Canonicus burned were goods he had bought at Williams's trading post, the closest place to get European items that Williams would have considered of "great value." If that was the case, it is possible that Canonicus's "expiation" was inspired by his concerns that too great a love of English goods had somehow contributed to his son's death. Williams did not consider this latter possibility; instead he focused on how impressive Narragansett deathways were. Thus he described his inclusive reaction to their deathways a quarter-century later: although "most" of their "laws and customs . . . are (like themselves) barbarous, yet in the case of their mournings they are more humane."[38]

This sympathetic tone regarding Narragansett deathways pervades Williams's great work of ethnography and linguistics, *A Key into the Language of America* (1643). Williams conceptualized his *Key* as a kind of phrasebook with commentary, organized topically ("Of Their Government," "Of Parts of Body"), for Europeans who might wish to interact with New England Indians. Williams went to great lengths to emphasize his belief that Indians and English were equals in God's eyes:

Two worlds of men shall rise and stand
'Fore Christ's most dreadful bar;
Indians and English, naked too,
That now most gallant are.

This was a powerful image of Europeans and Indians raised from their graves at the Last Judgment, naked as the day they were born, stripped of the clothing of which they were so proud. Even on earth, Williams argued, a common creation made Indians and English equals:

Boast not, proud English, of thy birth and blood,
Thy brother Indian is by birth as good.
Of one blood God made him and thee and all,
As wise, as fair, as strong, as personal.

Although "personal" may sound to our ears like a rather lackluster compliment, in Williams's time one of the word's meanings was "characteristic of a person or conscious being." Williams was saying that Indians were sentient humans just like the English.[39]

Williams paid a great deal of attention to deathways in his ethnography. Indeed, his *Key* culminates in two dramatic chapters, "Of Sickness" and "Of Death and Burial." In Chapter 1 I used these sections to help sketch early-contact Indian deathways in southern New England. Without recapitulating that discussion, two points are relevant here. First, Williams highlighted parallels between English and Narragansett deathways. For example, when explaining how Narragansetts in mourning blackened their faces with soot, Williams wrote that "the men also (as the English wear black mourning clothes) wear black faces, and lay on soot very thick." Elsewhere, Williams offered the Narragansett word meaning "to wrap up, in winding mats or coats, as we say, winding sheets." Second, Williams was respectful of Narragansett deathways throughout his ethnography. Like Herodotus and Mandeville, he avoided negative commentary in his discussions of mortuary practices. For example, he concluded his discussion of Narragansett deathways with this "general observation," the moral of his story: "O, how terrible is the look [of] the speedy and serious thought of death to *all* the sons of men?"[40] In deathways—more so than in any other aspect of Indian culture—Williams uncovered a common link of humanity that bound Narragansetts and the English together.

Nonetheless, Williams remained convinced of the superiority of Christianity to Narragansett religion. Therefore he used his knowledge of Indian deathways to show the Narragansetts the errors of their ways. Williams gave an example of a discourse "which from myself many hundreds of times great numbers of them have heard with great delight."[41] Even allowing for exaggeration on Williams's part, his claim that he preached about the Christian afterlife "many hundreds of times" suggests that Indians found discussions of competing deathways nearly inescapable in this period.

Williams began his discourse crisply. "Hearken to me," he demanded. "English men, Dutch men, and you and all the world," he addressed his Narragansett listeners, "when they die, their souls go not to the Southwest. All that know that one God, that love and fear Him, they go up to Heaven. They ever live in joy in God's own house." By contrast, "they that know not this God, that love and fear him not . . . go to Hell or the Deep. They shall ever lament."[42] Although Williams spoke these words over and over again to the Narragansetts who visited his trading post, it seems that the Indians were more interested in Williams's material wares than his spiritual ones, for he reported virtually no successful conversions.

The one exception was Wequash, a Pequot "Captain" whose conversion Williams took credit for. Williams's claim was not undisputed; Massachusetts Bay officials claimed that Wequash was converted by the devastating power of the English god as revealed in the Pequot War of 1637. According to Thomas Weld, Hugh Peter, and Henry Dunster, the presumed authors of the anonymous *New Englands First Fruits* (1643), Wequash embraced Christianity after "beholding the mighty power of God in our English forces, how they fell upon the pagans, where divers hundreds of them were slain in an hour."[43] Here the Massachusetts Bay authors referred to the terrible massacre of Pequots, mostly women and children, at Mystic River by the English and their Narragansett allies.

Williams, by contrast, citing a deathbed conversation with the Pequot leader, dated Wequash's conversion to a visit the Indian paid to Williams's home in 1639 or 1640. According to Williams, his sermons about "the wrath of God" and the afterlife made a lasting impression on Wequash. On his deathbed the Pequot told Williams, "Your words were never out of my heart to this present."[44] As he lay dying, poisoned by non-Christian Indians (allegedly for his attachment to the word of Christ), Wequash reportedly lamented in broken English, "Me so big naughty heart, me heart all one stone!" Ultimately, Wequash "died very comfortably," according to John Winthrop.[45]

Based on the evidence of Wequash's seemingly sincere repentance and comfortable death, a "godly minister" in Massachusetts (Thomas Shepard) declared that Wequash was "certainly in heaven." Williams was not so sure: "I dare not be so confident as others."[46] Given the agendas of those who recounted Wequash's death—the authors of *New Englands First Fruits* sought to justify the violence of the Pequot War, while Williams attempted to set himself up as the only New Englander teaching Indians about Christianity—it would be a mistake to place too much faith in the exact details of this model deathbed scene. The important point is that, for all his admiration of Indian deathways, Williams tirelessly worked to convince Indians that the Christian afterlife was superior to the Indian afterlife. Yet in the end, all Williams had to show for his efforts was one deathbed confession.

Perhaps Williams's lack of success in getting the Narragansetts interested in Christianity resulted from his unwillingness to research his ethnography as carefully as he might have. There is no doubt that his chapter "Of Their Religion" is a valuable description of Narragansett spirituality based on a great deal of time spent with Indians. But the chapter has numerous blind spots. As Patricia Rubertone has pointed out, Williams's informants were almost all men, and relatively powerful men at that. Williams paid little attention to the spirituality of Narragansett women and children.[47] Moreover, Williams could not get beyond his belief that Narragansett rituals were, at bottom, satanically inspired. Concluding an otherwise dispassionate account of a Narragansett feast, Williams editorialized, "By this feasting and gifts, the Devil drives on their worships pleasantly, as he doth all false worships." Because of this, Williams did not actually observe as many rituals as a reader might at first assume. "I confess," he wrote, "to have most of these customs by their own relation, for after once being in their houses and beholding what their worship was, I durst never be an eyewitness, spectator, or looker on, lest I should have been partaker of Satan's inventions and worships."[48] In Williams's final analysis, Narragansett religion was "false worship," lumped together with all the other "false worships" into which Satan had tricked the Indians of North America.

Undaunted by his lack of success in convincing the Narragansetts that theirs was a false worship, Williams continued his material and spiritual trade with the Narragansetts after the successful publication of the *Key*. Then in early June 1647, Williams learned that Canonicus was dying. The aged sachem was more than eighty years old, so this was hardly a shock, but it may have surprised Williams that Canonicus "sent for me and desired to be buried in my cloth of free gift." So Williams went to his trading house, gathered up some appropriate cloth, and headed to Canonicus's village. There were, according to Williams, "many hundreds" attending the deathbed scene. Just as Williams had written four years earlier in the *Key*, the deathbed scene of an important figure was an event that attracted a great deal of attention. Perhaps Williams uttered some of the expressions he offered in his phrasebook to be used when visiting someone's deathbed: *Paúsawutkitonckquewa, Chachéwunnea.* "He cannot live long, he is near dead." [49] The hundreds of deathbed watchers allowed him to approach the dying man's side. Williams proffered the cloth and after Canonicus died Williams closed the dead man's eyes. As Williams later remembered it, God had "stirred up the barbarous heart of Canonicus to love me as his son to his last gasp." [50] But this was no triumphant model deathbed scene of a Christian Indian, like that of Wequash. Canonicus never embraced any aspect of Christianity, even as he lay dying. Indeed, Canonicus's deathbed scene—without Christian repentance or conversion—served Williams's goals so little that he did not write about it until thirty years after the fact. [51]

Canonicus's funeral was another story. In the rituals that marked the Indian's death, Williams saw parallels with the funeral of another great New England leader, John Winthrop. As he wrote to the General Court of Massachusetts Bay, "In the same most honorable manner and solemnity (in their way) as you laid to sleep your prudent peacemaker Mr. Winthrop, did they honor this their prudent and peaceable prince (mine eyes beheld it)." [52] Williams probably was not referring to the "barrel and a half of the country's store of powder" that was "spent" at Winthrop's funeral, most likely in artillery fire. [53] Instead, Williams seems to have alluded to the fact that, as Nathaniel Morton put it, Winthrop's "body was [buried] with great solemnity and honor." [54] Williams was moved by the similarities between Indian and English funerals for political leaders. The gravity of Canonicus's funeral was further evidence for his belief that in deathways Narragansetts were at their most "humane." But Canonicus's funeral was more "in their [own] way" than Williams let on. True, Canonicus was buried in the cloth "of free gift" that Williams had brought. But overall the burial was in the traditional Narragansett style. Williams's winding sheet simply replaced mats made of reeds and grass. This is not to imply that the use of Williams's cloth in the burial was unimportant; Canonicus clearly felt that the incorporation of freely given English goods into his burial would help demonstrate his status as a man to be reckoned with in two societies.

An encounter with Indian deathways that shows that Williams remained influential in two societies occurred seven years later when, in February 1655, eighty armed Narragansetts met with Williams to demand satisfaction for the desecration of an Indian grave. Grave robbing was a European tradition in New England dating back to the first days of the Plymouth colonists' landfall. Local Indians had not exactly become resigned to the practice, but they knew that occasionally their graves would be opened in a search for buried treasure. This most recent occurrence, however, was so grotesque that it demanded a response from the offended Indians. Not only had a group of Euro-Americans robbed the grave of the sachem Pessicus's sister but the rogues had also stooped to the "mangling of her flesh." This was an unusual and highly offensive form of grave desecration, and Roger Williams knew how this "ghastly and stinking villainy," as he termed it, would anger the Narragansetts.[55] With his knowledge of Narragansett deathways and his desire to keep peace with his Indian allies, Williams was precisely the right person to try to assuage the Indians' ire.

When the eighty Indian warriors marched into Warwick, their first words were of war. They were "so bold as to talk often of men's lives and of fighting with us." Williams was able to talk them out of that threatening posture, but still the Indians "demanded an English child for hostage until satisfaction." This was unacceptable to Williams, so he tried other means to calm the Indians. He asked them who was responsible for the desecration. The Indians named Jan Gereardy, a Dutch trader from New Amsterdam, and "one Samuel a hatter and one Jones a seaman and an Irishman, persons infamous."[56] Williams responded that he would "attach" Gereardy's goods, seizing the Dutchman's trade items until he "made satisfaction." With this promise "it pleased the Lord to satisfy all." The crisis averted, Williams remained true to his word. As president of the colony he had the Providence Court of Trials seize £47 worth of Gereardy's goods to ensure that he would appear at court.[57]

When the date arrived, Gereardy made his way to the court from New Amsterdam, but the Narragansetts did not show up, even though they had been notified by Williams and one of the town deputies. It is hard to understand why, only four months after they were ready to go to war over the grave desecration, the Narragansetts failed to appear before the court. Perhaps they felt they could not meet the court's standard for finding Gereardy guilty: the Indians would "have redress," the court declared, if "evidence should be brought in to prove their charge." What kind of evidence would they be able to muster? Or perhaps the Narragansetts simply did not trust the English court to deliver justice. Whatever the case, the court was forced to declare that Gereardy was "by law cleared from his bonds and engagements of answering to this court." [58]

Williams was frustrated by the inconclusive result. Only two days later he introduced a law against grave robbing that the colony quickly adopted. The new law did not specify Indian graves as the target of desecration, but that was clearly what Williams had in mind; presumably no one would have robbed English graves because they did not contain burial goods. "If any person shall be accused of robbing of any grave," the law stated, "the party or parties offending, shall be fined or suffer corporal punishment, or both, as the General Court of Trials shall judge." [59] There is no record of anyone ever being prosecuted under the statute, but that of course does not mean that Indian graves went unmolested. All that can be said for sure is that Williams expended a fair bit of political capital in the affair, first to assuage the Narragansetts, then to attempt prosecution of Gereardy, and finally to champion the only law that I have found in the mainland British colonies against grave robbing. Twenty-five years after he first arrived in New England, Williams continued to see the importance of deathways to his diplomatic, missionary, and ethnographic projects.

*   *   *

Unlike Roger Williams, John Eliot (1604–90) was not particularly interested in the deathways of non-Christian Indians. Whereas Williams was both a preacher and an ethnographer, Eliot, in his dealings with Indians, was almost single-mindedly concerned with missionary efforts. Despite authoring hundreds of pages devoted to his activities in Massachusetts Bay, Eliot wrote next to nothing about the belief system and religious practices of the region's non-Christian Indians. [60] Eliot's lack of ethnographic writing about non-Christian Indian deathways does not mean, however, that he was uninterested in death as a tool for conversion. In fact, more than perhaps any other missionary in the New World, Eliot placed questions of death and eternal life at the center of his preaching to the Indians. And also unlike Williams, Eliot was not content merely to preach to the Indians. Starting in 1650 he gathered prospective converts into "praying towns" where he could better enforce rules meant to "civilize" them, such as this one aimed at Indian deathways: "They shall not disguise themselves in their mournings, as formerly, nor shall they keep a great noise by howling." [61]

Like other missionaries, Eliot worked among Indians who had been mourning frequently, as they continued to be sickened by European diseases. The Massachusett Indians lost perhaps 75 percent of their population due to disease between 1600 and 1630, and then even more during the 1633–34 smallpox epidemic.[62] These Indians were thus in a state of demographic crisis when Eliot began his missionary work in 1646, their powwaws reeling from their inability to stem the tide of disease and death. Eliot recognized this and exploited the spiritual advantage it gave him. As Eliot wrote in 1657, "It pleaseth God to try them with great sickness and mortality. . . . By the Lord's assistance, they do the more judge themselves for their sins, and cry for mercy, pardon, and grace in Christ." [63] The specter of epidemic disease did not cause all, or even most, Massachusett Indians to embrace Christianity, but enough did so to make Eliot feel that his missionary efforts were shined upon by heaven.

Moreover, even though he did not write much ethnography, Eliot recognized parallels between Indian and English deathways and sought to turn those similarities to his advantage. Eliot believed that Indian ideas about the afterlife readied the natives for conversion to Christianity. "These principles of a twofold estate after this life, for good and bad people, Heaven and Hell, I put amongst the first questions that I instruct them in, and catechize their children in." According to Eliot, the benefits of this strategy were evident. "They do readily embrace it for a truth, themselves by their own traditions having some principles of a life after this life, and that good or evil, according to their demeanor in this life." [64] As discussed in Chapter 1, the evidence about the Indian afterlife is conflicting. But the testimony of English observers suggests that Massachusett Indians had a concept of differing fates for the souls of good and bad individuals. This parallel with Christian belief helped lead several hundred Massachusett people to explore the Christian afterlife as a possible answer to their demographic and spiritual problems.

Eliot arrived in New England in 1631 and very quickly became established as a minister in Roxbury, just outside Boston. It is unclear exactly how Eliot came to be interested in missionary work. As pastor of a settled church he could have focused solely on his Anglo-American parishioners, as almost all of his ministerial colleagues did. But instead in September 1646 he decided to preach to a small gathering of Indians at Neponset, about four miles from Roxbury. Eliot's historic first sermon to the Indians was a complete flop: "They gave no heed unto it . . . and rather despised what I said." [65] Eliot had better luck the following month when he traveled to Nonantum, where the sachem Waban had already expressed curiosity about Christianity. Eliot's words were undoubtedly better received because they had Waban's imprimatur, but his sermon may also have made a better impression because he focused on the issues his audience found most pressing: death and the afterlife. According to minister Thomas Shepard's eyewitness account, Eliot preached for an hour and a quarter and he rarely swerved from his central theme: that Jesus Christ was "the only means of recovery from sin and wrath and eternal death." Eliot painted a glorious picture of the "blessed estate of all those that by faith believe in Christ, and know him feelingly." He waxed eloquent about the "joys of heaven" and in stern tones informed the Indians of "the terrors and horrors of wicked men in hell." Two weeks later Eliot returned to Nonantum and stuck to his script, bringing them the "good news" of Jesus Christ: that "while they live they may be happy, and when they die they may go to God and live in Heaven." [66]

Over the next few months at Nonantum and elsewhere, Eliot continued to preach this simple message, but he also decided that sermonizing alone was not the best approach to conversion. Rather than simply lecturing, he would try another method, so that, in Shepard's vivid phrasing, "we might screw by variety of means something or other of God into them." [67] Eliot's other technique for screwing God into the Indians was to take questions from the floor and to respond directly to the issues that most concerned the Indians. Eliot was flooded with questions about the strange new spirit world he described. The Indians' questions covered a wide range of topics, not all death-related. But many Indians wanted to know precisely what kind of resources Christianity could offer them regarding the next world.

> *When the soul goes to heaven, what doth it say when it comes there? And*
> *   what doth a wicked soul say when it cometh into Hell?*
> *Shall we see God in Heaven?*
> *Now the Indians desire to go to Heaven, what shall we do that we may go*
> *   thither when we die?*[68]

These Indians wondered what the Christian heaven and hell looked like, what happened there, and whether in heaven they would meet this mighty god about whom Eliot spoke at great length. Their questions also pointed to some of the same difficulties with reformed Protestantism that Anglo-American laypeople had.

> *If when men know God, God loves them, why then is it that any one are*
> *afflicted after that they know him?*
> *Whither their little children go when they die, seeing they have not sinned?*
> *If a child die before he sin, whither goeth his soul?*[69]

They asked the classic question of theodicy, wondering why an all-powerful God would allow bad things to happen. Along with their Anglo-American counterparts, they begged for clarification about where the souls of their young children went when they died. In response to this concern, Eliot confidently asserted, "By this question, it did please the Lord, clearly to convince them of original sin, blessed be his name."[70] Eliot offered the orthodox Calvinist interpretation that because of original sin and predestination, infant children were just as likely to go to hell as any other person. This was not a terribly comforting doctrine, and there is substantial evidence that Anglo-American laypeople did not fully accept it, at least when thinking about their own recently deceased infants.[71] Eliot claimed that he was able to "convince" the Massachusett Indians of this point, but this seems unlikely given the resistance of Anglo-American laypeople to this doctrine.

Other questions reveal that even those Indians most interested in Christianity interpreted the new belief system in relation to traditional beliefs.

> *Seeing we see not God with our eyes, if a man dream that he seeth God,*
> *doth his soul then see him?*
> *Whether doth God make bad men dream good dreams?*
> *In wicked dreams doth the soul sin?*[72]

Eliot's interlocutors were keenly interested in the role of dreams in this new spiritual realm. According to the anthropologist Kathleen Bragdon, Indians of southern New England believed they had two souls: a "clear soul," located in the heart, that was an individual's animating force, and a "dream soul" that traveled to the spirit world during dreams. This dream soul was the same one that exited the body and headed to the southwest and the afterlife when a person died.[73] So the Massachusetts posited an intimate connection between dreaming, the spirit world, and the afterlife. Those who were attracted to Christianity wanted to know just how their dreams fit into the new spiritual landscape. Eliot likely answered with the conventional Protestant interpretation of dreams, that they could reveal God's will, but that they could also delude people and should therefore not be relied upon.[74] Whether the questioners were satisfied with this response, we do not know.

Thus, Eliot's brand of reformed Protestantism offered some comfort to Indians concerned about death and the afterlife, with its message of an all-powerful God, a forgiving Christ, and a glorious heaven. But it did not offer only comfort. It raised troubling questions about original sin, infant damnation, and the role of traditional beliefs and practices. As Eliot wrote, "There is another great question that hath been several times propounded, and much sticks with such as begin to pray, namely, If they leave off powwawing, and pray to God, what shall they do when they are sick?"[75]

This might have proven a major stumbling block to Eliot's mission were it not for the unusual healthfulness of the Christian Indians in the first years of the mission. According to Eliot, Christian Indians were much less likely to contract smallpox than their non-Christian neighbors. This certainly strengthened Eliot's efforts to demonstrate that his magic was stronger than that of the powwaws. But despite the healthfulness of Eliot's Christian Indians, they were not, of course, immune to illness. In October 1647 a child in Nonantum died of consumption. The funeral arranged by the Nonantum Christian Indians—without being directed by Eliot—shows Indians using Christianity in ways that both departed from and resonated with traditional practices. This funeral was described by Thomas Shepard, who received the story from a "faithful man" named Edward Jackson, who lived near Nonantum and who understood "a little of their language." After the child died, the Indians sought out Jackson to ask him how the English buried their dead. The Indians took Jackson's advice, "hereupon rejecting," Shepard editorialized, "all their old superstitious observances at such sad times (which are not a few)." But it was not as simple as that. The Nonantum Indians improvised their first Christian funeral ceremony in ways that reveal powerful connections with their previous practices.

First the Indians bought some boards and nails from the English and, after some work, they finished a "pretty handsome coffin." They placed the child into the unadorned box and about forty Indians accompanied it to the gravesite. They dug a grave for the child, placed the coffin within, and covered it with earth. Consistent with the extreme simplicity New Englanders demanded of their burials, there is no mention of a burial marker. Thus far the burial accorded exactly with a standard Puritan funeral of the period.

But then the Indians "withdrew a little from that place, and went all together and assembled under a tree in the woods, and there they desired one Totherswamp a very hopeful [promising] Indian to pray with them." To the modern reader, a prayer gathering after a burial sounds perfectly natural, but this was not the case for the Puritans. Shepard explained, "Although the English do not usually meet in companies to pray together after such sad occasions, yet it seems God stirred up their hearts thus to do." Reformed Protestants wanted to avoid the appearance that they were praying for the deceased's soul to reach heaven; their theology taught them that their prayers could have no influence on the final destination of the soul, contrary to what Catholics believed.

Totherswamp and his fellow Nonantum Indians were not so well versed in the fine points of Calvinist theology, so they saw nothing wrong with a prayer gathering. Surely it is significant that they chose to pray not by the graveside but headed into the woods and prayed "under a tree." For the Indians of southern New England, trees "linked the three realms of the underworld, the surface world, and the sky world," according to Bragdon. Perhaps even more relevant, the forests where trees grew "were likely spots for encounters with the powerful other-than-human beings who dwelt there."[76] Thus, "under a tree" would have been a perfect spot to pray. And while they did so, the Indians mourned in a way not entirely dissimilar to their pre-Christian practices. Totherswamp orated, expressed great "zeal in prayer," and "the woods rang again with their sighs and prayers." The prayers were directed to the Christian god, but the woods rang with their mourning cries in ways reminiscent of pre- or early-contact New England Indian practices.[77]

Totherswamp's zeal may have been fueled in part by memories of his own losses, which helped ready him for an acceptance of the Christian god. As he later recalled in a confession of faith, he was at first resistant to the Englishmen who asked him to pray to their god. "But I thought in my heart, that if my friends should die, and I live, I then would pray to God." Totherswamp had seen enough death among his people to know that such a sad fate was a distinct possibility. Indeed, "soon after, God so wrought, that they did almost all die, few of them left." His reaction was typical of those Indians who embraced Christianity. "Then my heart feared, and I thought, that now I will pray unto God."[78]

These words come from a body of sources that must be examined more closely before being used further. Totherswamp was among a group of Indian men who delivered confessions of faith before Eliot, several other ministers, and a crowd of onlookers in 1652 and again in 1659. A total of eighteen men offered confessions of faith at one or both occasions. These statements pose several problems of interpretation. They were spoken in Massachusett and translated on the fly by Eliot, who admitted that some of the Indians "spoke not so well to my understanding."[79] The statements were gathered together and offered for publication by the man whose reputation depended upon presenting these converts as orthodox Protestants. Thus, Eliot may have fudged a bit as he translated, copied, and recopied these confessions. Nonetheless, the scholarly consensus in recent years has been that these statements, read carefully, can provide valuable information about the ways this small group of especially devoted Christian Indians made sense of their new religion.[80]

The first thing that jumps out of these statements is the constant refrain that death—the deaths of loved ones and fear of one's own death—framed these men's attraction to Christianity.[81] In this Totherswamp's account is entirely typical. Listen to Nookau: "Five years ago, before I prayed I was sick, I thought I should die, at which I was much troubled, and knew not what to do. Then I thought, if there be a God above, and he give life again, then I shall believe there is a God above, and God did give me life, and after that I took up praying to God." And listen to Robin Speene: "I was ashamed because you taught me to pray to God, and I did not take it up. I see God is angry with me for all my sins, and he hath afflicted me by the death of three of my children, and I fear God is still angry, because great are my sins, and I fear lest my children be not gone to Heaven, because I am a great sinner."[82]

Indians, however, were not the only residents of New England whose relationship with Christianity was strengthened by death. Totherswamp's and Nookau's Anglo-American neighbors feared death, mourned the deaths of loved ones, and used their religion to gain some comfort at a time when death struck unpredictably. Anglo–New Englanders also described this relationship between death and piety in their confessions of faith and conversion narratives. In a sample of eighty-eight conversion narratives recorded by Thomas Shepard and John Fiske, thirty individuals (34 percent) stated that their path to Christ was connected to a close encounter with death.[83] This is only half the rate of the Indian narratives—twelve of eighteen Indians (67 percent) drew similar links between death and piety—but it nonetheless shows that many Indians and Anglo-Americans interpreted their spiritual worlds through the lens of death.[84] The Christian Indians of Massachusetts would have understood the explanation that Jane Stevenson of Cambridge offered for her religious convictions. "When the Lord was pleased to convince me of sin," Stevenson told her fellow congregants, "it was by affliction, the plague being in the place . . . and some whom I have been in company with, within 24 hours laid in grave, and yet the Lord spared me, and I knew not but I might be next at grave by reason of my sins." [85]

Also like Anglo-Americans, Indians found that death could not only strengthen their faith but test it as well. Monequassun found that death in his family caused him to question whether the Christian god was paying attention to him. "God laid upon me more trouble," he remembered, "by sickness and death. And then I much prayed to God for life, for we were all sick, and then God would not hear me, to give us life, but first one of my children died, and after that my wife. Then I was in great sorrow, because I thought God would not hear me." [86] Likewise, Antony's faith was tested by death in his family. "My brothers and kindred died," Antony told his audience. "Then my heart said, sure it's a vain thing to pray to God, for I prayed, yet my friends die. Therefore I will run wild, and did cast off praying." [87] For Eliot and his readers on both sides of the Atlantic, the stories of Monequassun and Antony had happy endings: both overcame their doubts and became steadfast Christians. But we should remember that these confessions of faith were delivered by the eighteen most devoted Christian men in Eliot's flock. The crises of faith suffered by Monequassun and Antony shed light on the experiences of the thousands of Indians in New England who remained unmoved by Christianity. "I prayed, yet my friends die." Death led some New England Indians to become Christians, but it caused many others to question the power of the English god.

*   *   *

If only there were more documents left by Indians, in addition to sources redacted by Eliot and Williams and other European observers, we might have a better sense of the totality of the New England Indian encounter with Christian deathways. We might have something to complement the reports about the Indians most devoted to the new religion.

In a sense, those sources do exist, in the form of over three hundred seventeenth- and early eighteenth-century Indian burials unearthed by archaeologists (Table 1). To be sure, these sources are not unmediated: the data have been collected by Euro-American archaeologists with their own biases, most notably an eagerness to find buried evidence of Indian resistance to European culture. Despite this concern, archaeological evidence offers an alternate perspective on the interaction between Indian and English deathways.

TABLE 1. SELECTED NEW ENGLAND INDIAN BURIAL GROUNDS

Site name	Dates in use	Number of individuals
West Ferry, R.I.	1620–60	75
Burr's Hill, R.I.	most burials 1650–75, some early eighteenth century	52+
RI-1000, R.I.	1660–80	47
Long Pond, Conn.	1670–1720	21
Ponkapoag, Mass.	1652–1720	44
Natick, Mass.	1650s–1720s?	25
Pantigo, L.I.	1660–1730s	58

Sources: West Ferry: William Scranton Simmons, *Cautantowwit's House: An Indian Burial Ground on the Island of Conanicut in Narragansett Bay* (Providence, R.I., 1970). Burr's Hill: Gibson, ed., *Burr's Hill*. RI-1000: William A. Turnbaugh, *The Material Culture of RI-1000, A Mid-17th Century Narragansett Indian Burial Site in North Kingstown, Rhode Island* (Kingston, R.I., 1984), and Rubertone, *Grave Undertakings*. Long Pond: Linda Welters et al., "European Textiles from Seventeenth-Century New England Indian Cemeteries," in *Historical Archaeology and the Study of American Culture*, ed. Lu Ann De Cunzo and Bernard L. Herman (Knoxville, Tenn., 1996), 193–232. Ponkapoag: Brenda J. Baker, "Pilgrim's Progress and Praying Indians: The Biocultural Consequences of Contact in Southern New England," in *In the Wake of Contact: Biological Responses to Conquest*, ed. Clark Spencer Larsen and George R. Miller (New York, 1994), 35–45, and John W. Kelley, "Burial Practices of the Praying Indians of Natick, Ponkapoag, and Marlboro" (M.A. thesis, University of Massachusetts Boston, 1999). Natick: Elise Melanie Brenner, "Strategies for Autonomy: An Analysis of Ethnic Mobilization in Seventeenth-Century Southern New England" (Ph.D. diss., University of Massachusetts, 1984). Pantigo: Foster H. Saville, *A Montauk Cemetery at Easthampton, Long Island*, Indian Notes and Monographs, vol. 2, no. 3 (New York, 1920).

The overwhelming majority of southern New England Indian burials from the period 1620 to 1670 were performed according to a logic that owed nothing to Christianity. In a typical burial, the corpse was placed into a roughly meter-deep oval or round grave in a tightly flexed posture resembling the fetal position. No English observer recorded an Indian's explanation for this burial posture, but in New France, Indians explained that the body was buried in a flexed position so "he may be committed to the earth in the same position in which he once lay in his mother's womb."[88] The corpse, in its flexed posture with its hands drawn up near or even in its mouth, was often wrapped in wool blankets or reed matting. It was then ordinarily laid in the grave on its right side with its head pointing toward the southwest, toward Cautantowwit's house, the land of the souls. Many burials included grave goods. Goods were placed either on the body as adornment—as in necklaces, bracelets, and earrings—or in front of the body as it lay on its side, or in a position resembling how the item was used in life, as a pipe placed between the fingers. Most goods were European, including glass beads, bottles of colored glass, pipes, iron hoes, and occasionally weapons like swords or guns. There were some items of aboriginal manufacture: clay vessels, shell beads, and bone tools.

This describes the modal burial from 1620 to 1670, but there are many puzzling exceptions to this pattern that remind us of how little we know about the logic behind these practices. While almost all the individuals were buried with their heads pointing to the southwest, at the RI-1000 site one person was buried along a north-south axis and at Burr's Hill two people's heads pointed to the southeast.[89] Likewise, while most individuals were buried on their right sides, at least one at Burr's Hill and roughly one-quarter (ten of forty-four) at West Ferry lay on their left sides.[90] Was there any significance to these variations in orientation and sidedness? Archaeologists have ventured some fanciful speculations, but the truth is that we just don't know.[91] The same holds for occasional multiple burials. There are no multiple burials at RI-1000, but there is one at West Ferry and several at Burr's Hill.[92] At the latter site one grave contained seven skeletons and another held six. If we focus too much on the typical burials, it downplays the very real variations that occurred, variations with meanings that are now very difficult to reconstruct.

But there is much to be learned from the ordinary burials of 1620 to 1670. Most importantly, despite decades of missionary efforts, the vast majority of southern New England Indians rejected Christian burials. They did not use coffins and, more crucially, they did not place the body into the grave on its back with its legs extended. This, however, does not mean that these burials were untouched by European influence. Indeed, in the clustering of burials in cemeteries and in the inclusion of large amounts of grave goods, these interments departed dramatically from those performed prior to 1500. European goods seem to have played an especially important role in seventeenth-century Indian mortuary rites. There were many times more European than aboriginal items used as grave goods.

The archaeologist Constance Crosby offers the most satisfying explanation of why New England Indians were eager to bury European goods with their dead. She argues that European goods were especially desirable because of their perceived *manit* or spiritual power. Europeans usually translated the Algonquian *manit* (and the closely related *manitou*) as "God" or "god," but according to Crosby a more accurate translation would be "spiritual power manifested in any form." New England Indians perceived material objects as having *manit* when the items were especially useful, such as an iron drill for making wampum, or unusual, like a magnifying glass, or connected with spiritual power, like a crucifix or Bible.[93]

To be sure, most items Indians buried with the dead were rather prosaic in nature: heavily used iron hoes, worn kaolin pipes, and the like. But the excavated graves also reveal Indian interest in the material symbols of Christianity. At least one individual at Burr's Hill and three at RI-1000 were buried with brass "Jesuit" rings, "to which was attached a flat round or oval plaque with a cast or engraved design generally of a religious nature."[94] Jesuits traded these rings, most of which were engraved with a cross and the IHS symbol of the Jesuit order, with Indians they hoped to convert to Christianity. New England Indians probably got their Jesuit rings from Mohawks and other trading partners of the Jesuits, rather than directly from the Jesuits themselves. It is possible, as Patricia Rubertone argues, that when New England Indians acquired and buried Jesuit rings "their earlier symbolism disappeared." But it is also quite possible that the Narragansett man who was buried with six Jesuit rings on his right hand saw these objects—three of which were clearly incised with a cross—as having *manit* as the result of their connection with Christianity. The same holds for a skin shirt buried with a Narragansett man. The shirt was gaudily decorated with brass spirals, glass tubes, and, most intriguingly, thin mica ovals backed with paper printed with an image of Jesus Christ, "quite possibly cut from a larger engraving in an illustrated Bible."[95]

An even more evocative reuse of Christian material culture was discovered in the grave of an eleven-year-old girl at the Long Pond site in Connecticut. The girl lay on her side, arms and legs drawn tightly to her chin, her head pointed to the southwest. Buried alongside her was a six-by-six-inch medicine bundle made of the finest European wool cloth available at the time. Inside the small wool bag a bear paw and a folded page from an English Bible were tucked. On the page was the joyful poetry of Psalm 98 from a 1680 edition of the King James Bible, an edition with type too small to read easily but compact enough to be portable. "O sing unto the Lord a new song, for he hath done marvelous things," the Psalm begins. This extraordinary object raises more questions than it answers. Could the Pequot parents of this child read the Bible? If so, were they drawn to the richly metaphorical language of the Psalms, or of this Psalm in particular, with its nature-based language reminiscent of the metaphors used by Indian orators: "Let the sea roar, and the fullness thereof; the world, and they that dwell therein. Let the clouds clap their hands, let the hills be joyful together." What was the relationship between the bear paw and the page from the Bible? Whatever the answers to these questions, it seems highly unlikely that the page of holy scripture lost its earlier symbolism when it was buried with the child. Much more likely the bear paw and the Psalm were included in the grave because they both possessed *manit*.[96] Indeed, this burial demonstrates an inclusive reaction on the part of at least some Indians toward Christian deathways. They encountered this new religion, were curious about it, and incorporated some aspects of its material culture into their mortuary practices.

The Long Pond burial hints at another dynamic that must be considered: change over time. Because the Long Pond Bible page was printed in 1680 and the cemetery was used until roughly 1720, the medicine bundle dates to 1700 plus or minus twenty years. At this point, in the late seventeenth and early eighteenth centuries, some important changes begin to creep into the archaeological record. In particular, some Indians began to abandon their long-time practice of flexed burials in favor of the Christian model of supine extended burials. There were no extended burials at West Ferry or RI-1000, but there were at least two at Burr's Hill, a cemetery that was used until the early eighteenth century. And at Pantigo on the eastern tip of Long Island, seventeen of thirty-eight burials (45 percent) were extended. It is impossible to date the extended burials at Pantigo with any accuracy, but their location on the periphery of the cemetery suggests the later decades of the cemetery's date range of 1660 to 1730.[97]

Significantly, eight of the seventeen extended burials at Pantigo, and both at Burr's Hill, were buried with grave goods.[98] The percentage of extended burials with grave goods (47 percent) is only slightly lower than the percentage of flexed burials with grave goods (57 percent, or twelve of twenty-one). One typical extended burial at Pantigo included two metal dishes, a stone arrowpoint, an iron knife, a spoon, and some red paint, reminiscent of the red ochre Algonquians had long used to paint their corpses.[99] Thus, around 1700 in Rhode Island and Long Island, some Indians began to adopt the burial orientation of their Euro-American neighbors. At the same time, they continued to place grave goods alongside many of the dead, in opposition to Protestant teachings.[100]

In light of this pattern, James Axtell argues that "extended burials may have constituted only a superficial accommodation to European preferences, designed to placate the invaders in things of little import while preserving the heart of their traditional beliefs intact."[101] But it is unclear why Indians at

Burr's Hill and Pantigo would feel the need to use their burials to "placate" Euro-Americans. There is no evidence that any of these Indian burials were witnessed by Euro-Americans. Moreover, it seems condescending to take Indian burials seriously as evidence of native belief, except when they begin to resemble Christian burials. Rather than viewing extended burials as a ruse, it seems more plausible that this burial orientation represents Indian mortuary practices changing over time, as they had always done. As some Indians began to bury their dead in the Christian supine fashion, they maintained aspects of their previous practices, including the placement of grave goods and the use of red paint. Burials around 1700 therefore reveal Indians gaining spiritual power from a variety of sources.

Perhaps less surprising, supine Indian burials have also been found in the cemeteries of John Eliot's praying towns. In 1988 bulldozers revealed Indian graves in what had been the cemetery of the praying town of Ponkapoag. A quick salvage archaeology was performed on the thirty-two undisturbed burials. Thirty-one of the thirty-two graves were either rectangular or had coffin remains, suggesting a move away from traditional oval and uncoffined burials. Moreover, eight of the ten skeletons observed at the site were supine and extended.[102] Like the Nonantum Indians who in 1647 buried a consumptive child in Christian fashion, most Ponkapoag Indians seem to have adopted some aspects of Christian burials.

But did the Nonantum Indians place grave goods in the consumptive child's coffin? Children's graves were some of the most richly supplied in southern New England, filled with small hawk's bells, thimbles, beads, and spoons.[103] The English observer did not report grave goods at Nonantum, but maybe he did not see that part of the ceremony. What we do know is that the Ponkapoag Indians, despite their intense training by Eliot, did supply their dead with grave goods: pipes, metal pots, and glass beads.[104] Likewise, even at Natick, the first and most steadfast of Eliot's praying towns, Christian Indians placed grave goods alongside their dead. Because the Natick site was excavated long before the advent of professional archaeological techniques, the data are generally poor. However, we can say with certainty that the Natick Christian Indians—like their Catholic counterparts at Sainte-Marie among the Hurons—buried their dead with a wide array of goods. Natick Indians were buried with spoons, glass bottles, glass beads, a skillet, a porringer, a sleigh bell, and much more.[105] Again, supine burials seem not to have been a "superficial accommodation" to Christianity but representative of a complex spirituality that drew on Christian and Indian sources.

*   *   *

The seven burial grounds examined here provide valuable—if sometimes enigmatic—evidence about Indian-English interactions. But although these cemeteries held more than three hundred individuals, the sample is skewed toward areas of intense colonization pressure. Farther west and north of these burial grounds, Indians experienced fewer encounters with English people, English religion, and English deathways. These Indians—Nipmucks, Pocumtucks, Abenakis—likely experienced slower changes in their deathways than the Indians in the seven southeastern burial grounds.

But even in southeastern New England the adoption of certain aspects of Christian burial practices happened slowly and not without contention. Among the Wampanoags and Narragansetts, a split emerged between Christian Indians and traditionalists. Not unlike the rivalries that helped tear apart the Huron confederacy, the tensions in southeastern New England set the stage for the outbreak of King Philip's War in 1675.[106] The complex history of this war—by some measures the bloodiest per capita in American history—is beyond the scope of this discussion. The important point here is that it was in some ways a holy war, waged using the literal and symbolic language of death. Christian Indians, most of whom allied with the English against traditionalist Wampanoags, Narragansetts, Nipmucks, and Pocumtucks, wound up caught in the middle, trusted by neither side.

Like the Powhatans who waged holy war against the Jamestown colonists, New England Indians terrorized their enemies by using their familiarity with English attitudes toward religion, death, and the body. Indians did not stop at killing their English opponents; they violated English beliefs in the sanctity of corpses by mutilating dead bodies and leaving them to rot, naked, in the sun. Virtually every English account of the war focused on corpse desecration: heads crushed or scalped, intestines ripped out, bodies burnt. Perhaps most galling of all, these corpses were denied proper burial, unless the English could recover the bodies, which they often could not. According to the historian Jill Lepore, "All over New England, English bodies were said to have been left to 'lie naked, wallowing in their blood.' "[107] Without coffins or even shrouds to protect them, rotting and mutilated corpses became the dominant English image of Indian savagery, and the leading rationalization for the fury with which they themselves attacked and mutilated Indians.

It is possible that some acts of corpse mutilation were not meant specifically as attacks on English religious scruples regarding the proper treatment of bodies, even if the English interpreted them that way. Many of these deeds were simply how New England Indians waged war and would have happened whether their enemies were English or Mohawks.[108] But there were numerous other instances of Indians deliberately attacking English religion in general, and English ideas about death and the afterlife in particular, in their attempts to defeat the English and thereby retain the autonomy to worship their own gods. For example, in April 1676 1,500 Nipmucks attacked Sudbury, Massachusetts. During the fighting an old English man tried to escape by running into a swamp. A Nipmuck warrior chased him down and took the opportunity to mock the old man's religious beliefs: "Come Lord Jesus, save this poor English man if thou canst, whom I am now about to kill." The Nipmuck man clearly had been exposed to Protestant teachings about the power of prayers to Jesus regarding questions of life and death, and he just as clearly wasn't buying it. No supernatural force intervened, and the Nipmuck killed the English man with a blow to the head. Other Indians taunted the English by using the Christian afterlife against them. Indians reportedly celebrated a victory by mocking those they had killed, saying "they had done them a good turn to send them to heaven so soon." [109]

Some Indians relied on a combination of violence and the symbols of English religion to make a statement about the relative power of the combatants' gods. There were numerous English reports of Indians mutilating Bibles and corpses together. One group of soldiers found a Bible torn apart with the pages "scattered about by the enemy in hatred of our religion." Farther down the road they encountered mutilated corpses, with "heads, scalps, and hands" cut off and "stuck upon poles near the highway." [110] It did not take a great deal of decoding for the English to understand the connection between such violence against religious symbols and violence against corpses. This was also the case when Indians attacked Providence, Rhode Island, in March 1676. There they found an Englishman who was a religious dissenter, of strong beliefs but of no particular denomination. This man "had a strange confidence or rather conceit, that whilst he held his Bible in his hand, he looked upon himself as secure from all kind of violence." The Indians came upon this man in front of his house, refusing to seek the shelter of a garrison and holding his Bible in his hand for protection. It did not work. The Indians killed him, "deriding his groundless apprehension or folly therein, ripped him open, and put his Bible in his belly." [111]

The English responded to such shocking scenes in kind. They too knew how to use righteous violence against their enemies. So it was only fitting that when the English finally killed Metacom—the war's eponymous "King Philip"—they used the symbolism of deathways to show their contempt for the man and his methods. In August 1676 Benjamin Church and his men, including a few Christian Indian allies, surrounded Metacom in a swamp. A Christian Indian named Alderman shot Metacom dead. Church, according to his son's account written forty years later, did not take long to decide what to do with the corpse. He ordered Metacom's corpse "to be pulled out of the mire on to the upland, so some of Capt. Church's Indians took hold of him by his stockings, and some by his small breeches, (being otherwise naked) and drew him through the mud unto the upland, and a doleful, great, naked, dirty beast, he looked like." It was clear what fate this dirty, naked beast deserved. Church declared, "That for as much as he had caused many an English man's body to lie unburied and rot above ground, that not one of his bones should be buried." [112] For the crime of violating English burial norms, Metacom would be denied the flexed, southwest-pointing burial of his people. Church had Metacom beheaded and quartered and he distributed the body parts among his men as trophies.

Because King Philip's War was in some senses a holy war, fought with the symbolism of corpses and Bibles as much as with guns and hatchets, there was precious little room for cross-cultural understanding. Although many Christian Indians allied with the English and served as guides and soldiers, the English remained suspicious of their motivations. As a result, in October 1675 the Massachusetts General Court ordered the Indian residents of Natick interned on Deer Island in Boston Harbor. There they would remain, joined by Christian Indians from the praying towns of Ponkapoag and Nashobah, until May 1676. The roughly five hundred Indians on Deer Island endured horrifying conditions, lacking food and clean water and adequate protection against the cold. [113] The Indians sickened and died at an alarming rate; by the end of winter half the praying Indians on Deer Island were dead. Like their non-Christian counterparts who had suffered a crisis of faith when their powwaws could not stop the dying in 1616 and 1633, the surviving Christian Indians found their faith shaken.

In light of all this, it is hardly surprising that King Philip's War curtailed the missionary project in New England, especially around Boston. The praying Indians were eventually released from their imprisonment, but their numbers were greatly reduced and some undoubtedly turned away from Christianity as a result of the experience. After the war, Eliot, now in his seventies, withdrew from the daily management of the praying towns. His late writings, in the words of the literary scholar Kristina Bross, expressed "his sadness and disappointment with the imminent failure of his work." [114] The number of full church members was steadily declining in the praying towns and Eliot feared that the Christian Indian community would not continue after his death.

Roger Williams, also in his seventies, had even greater reason for self-pity after King Philip's War. In March 1676 a group of Narragansetts attacked Providence. As part of their offensive, they burned many houses, including the one owned by Williams. Williams could hardly believe his eyes as he watched his possessions go up in smoke. His sense of betrayal is palpable in this question to the Narragansetts: how could they burn his house, which "hath lodged kindly some thousands of you these ten years?" The people whose language he had learned, whose culture he had studied, whose leader had been buried in Williams's cloth of free gift, responded in the language of holy war. According to Williams, the Narragansetts asserted that "God was [with] them and had forsaken us [the English], for they had so prospered in killing and burning us far beyond what we did against them." [115] This marked the end of Williams's attempts to Christianize his Indian neighbors. Indeed, after his home burned to the ground Williams was instrumental in having Providence's Indian war captives sold into "involuntary servitude." Williams and several others shared in the profits from selling these Indians into bondage. [116]

*   *   *

If the missionary project around Boston and in the old praying towns was moribund after King Philip's War, one place where the Christian Indian community remained strong was on the island of Martha's Vineyard. There, Experience Mayhew (1673–1758) continued the work that his grandfather, Thomas Mayhew Jr., had begun in 1643. The Mayhews had long practiced a less coercive form of missionary work than Eliot used in his praying towns. Thomas Mayhew Jr. inaugurated a tradition of acceding to Wampanoag desires to retain their cultural traditions, compared with Eliot's attempts to effect wholesale changes in Indian dress, social arrangements, and agricultural practices. Thomas Mayhew Jr. was still a missionary, convinced of the superiority of Christianity, but his conversion tactics placed him closer to Jesuits than to Eliot. Partly as a result of this legacy, English and Indian residents of the island lived in relative harmony. While King Philip's War convulsed the mainland, most Martha's Vineyard denizens sat out the conflict.[117]

Experience Mayhew was two generations removed from the first English missionaries in New England. Whereas Eliot and Williams were in their seventies during King Philip's War, Experience Mayhew was but two years old. Moreover, Experience grew up in a bicultural environment. He seems to have conversed in the Wampanoag language as a native speaker and he moved easily between English and Indian communities. In 1693, only twenty years old, he began preaching to the Indians of Martha's Vineyard, and he would spend the next sixty-five years of his life in this capacity. To call Experience Mayhew a missionary does not quite capture his role; by 1693 most of the island's Indians were Christians. Mayhew preached in the island's various churches not unlike any Puritan minister responsible for several flocks.

After more than thirty years as a preacher, Mayhew published his most enduring work, *Indian Converts* (1727).[118] This nearly three-hundred-page book was published in London and addressed to the Society for the Propagation of the Gospel (SPG), an English charitable organization that supported the work of missionaries worldwide. Mayhew had two reasons for publishing the biographies of ninety-four pious Christian Indians. First, he wanted to demonstrate to readers in England and New England that his family's eighty years of work on the island had not been in vain. Second, he hoped to convince the SPG and other potential donors that his efforts deserved continued funding.

The biographies range from a page to several pages in length. All the Indians who appeared in the book were dead; as the literary scholar Hilary Wyss points out, Mayhew "appropriates their ability to speak for themselves."[119] On the other hand, Mayhew also preserved these Indians' words for posterity. And he did so by relying heavily on native informants. He interviewed survivors to fill in the details about the deceased's lives and dying scenes. As a result, Mayhew was able to describe the deathbed scenes of seventy-seven of the ninety-four Indians he profiled, even though he did not attend nearly that many.

Unsurprisingly, the large majority of the scenes he described were model deaths (sixty-one of seventy-seven, or 79 percent). This was, after all, a compendium meant to show the success of his Christianization efforts. What may be more surprising, in light of the historical literature that has emphasized the differences between Catholic and Protestant missionary efforts, is how similar Mayhew's model deathbed scenes (and those described by other Protestants) were to those written by Jesuits in New France. The parallels can be explained by the deep roots of the model Christian death, roots that extended beneath the subsoil of the split engendered by the Protestant Reformation. The *Ars moriendi* tradition was popular in Catholic England through the first half of the sixteenth century. After the Reformation, the Protestant model death departed in some important ways from the Catholic model (especially in discarding the sacrament of extreme unction), but both religions continued to draw largely on the older traditions.[120] As a result, Catholic and Protestant missionaries fashioned similar models of good Indian deaths. As in Jesuit descriptions of model deaths, Mayhew's Indians were almost uniformly resigned to their deaths. They accepted their impending departure, and any pain they experienced, as God's will. They urged their loved ones to behave well and to continue praying to God. They looked forward with cautious optimism to meeting Jesus in heaven.

But Mayhew also included a surprisingly large number of unorthodox scenes in *Indian Converts*: thirteen (17 percent) were unorthodox and another three (4 percent) were orthodox with an unorthodox moment. As discussed in the previous chapter, unorthodox deathbed scenes are of great interest because in their departures from the script, they offer clearer windows onto what actually happened on Indian deathbeds. These unorthodox scenes have not had their individuality squeezed out of them by an attempt to fit them into the model script.

The unorthodox scenes show that some Wampanoags of Martha's Vineyard had the same doctrinal difficulties with reformed Protestantism that some dying Anglo-Americans had. One similarity between Anglo-American and Indian breaches of the model deathbed scene was when the mortally ill person died in great distress. This was fairly common among Anglo-Americans. Protestant observers became upset when near relations died in anguish. Distress seemed to observers to indicate that the person might not be going to heaven.[121] Mayhew reported that Christian Indians sometimes died without the hopeful optimism that observers would have liked. Take, for example, the 1718 death of a woman whose English name was Katherine but who continued to be called Wuttontaehtunnooh by her fellow Indians. For a full year this woman had been "very frequently miserably distracted [insane]." The duration of her fits of anguish led Katherine "to fear that God had suffered the Devil to take some kind of possession of her." When Katherine finally died, she continued to be "terribly distracted, and under such violent agitations of body as were very uncomfortable to those that tended her." Even as Mayhew tried to argue that one should not judge her final state by her death-bed behavior, he acknowledged the observers' concerns when he wrote, "One would have hoped, that so good a woman as this was, would have had a most comfortable exit." This incident could just have easily occurred as part of an Anglo-American deathbed scene.[122]

Likewise, Indians had similar problems dealing with the doctrine of pre-destination that Anglo-American laypeople did. Among white New England-ers, one of the most common breaches of the model deathbed script was for the dying person to evince far too much confidence about going to heaven.[123] New England ministers wanted their parishioners to be hopeful, but not cer-tain, of reaching heaven. Christian Indians in New England sometimes made the same errors, in the eyes of their ministers. When Mary Manhut died in 1724, Mayhew was unhappy with her statement that she was willing to die, but only if she were going to heaven, not if she were going to hell. As a result, Mayhew reformulated her dying words to express what she really "meant by this." [124]

Whereas some of Mayhew's unorthodox Christian Indian deaths showed that natives could have the same problems adhering to the script as any lay-people, others had meanings shaped by the fact that the dying person was an Indian. In particular, Mayhew recorded several deathbed scenes that included supernatural events with no Anglo-American analogue. Indian observers oc-casionally asserted that they had seen spirits, witnessed inexplicable lights, or heard voices in the vicinity of a loved one's deathbed. Unlike Anglo-American deathbed scenes, during which the *dying person* sometimes had a vision, su-pernatural events were sometimes reported by Indians *observing* a deathbed scene. I have never come across a similar example among Anglo-Americans. These cases suggest that Christian Indians brought a very different sensibility to the deathbeds of their loved ones from that brought by white New En-glanders. There is evidence that early-contact Indians of southern New En-gland considered deathbed observers—in addition to the dying person—to be in a liminal position. When a Narragansett lay dying, the female observers blackened their faces; male observers did so only when the person died.[125] Ac-cording to one anthropologist, the Indians' blackened faces represented their liminality: not only was the dying person believed to be between states (this world and the afterworld) but so were deathbed observers (between an ordi-nary state and a state of mourning).[126] Given the liminality of the mortally ill and those gathered, the spirit world more easily broke in upon this world than usual. Drawing on this cultural inheritance, some Christian Indians on Martha's Vineyard were more receptive than Anglo-Americans to intervention from the spirit world as a person lay dying.

Mayhew recorded a number of these incidents. Of the seventy-seven deathbed scenes he described in *Indian Converts*, thirteen (17 percent) involved supernatural occurrences (dreams, visions, and observers hearing or seeing spirits).[127] Of these thirteen, in seven (9 percent of the total), observers witnessed the supernatural occurrences, compared to zero such cases among the hundreds of contemporary Anglo-American deathbed scenes I have examined.[128] Significantly, supernatural deathbed events were associated with women, both as females lay dying and as observers who saw spirits. Of the seven deathbed scenes in which observers witnessed something supernatural, six (86 percent) of these scenes involved dying females, even though only 48 percent of Mayhew's descriptions were of female Indians. Furthermore, two out of three (67 percent) of the observers of spirits whose sex can be ascertained were women. Though the sample is too small to permit definitive conclusions, these figures suggest that the Christian Indians of Martha's Vineyard may have kept alive what Williams described as an especially female sense of liminality and border crossing associated with deathbeds.[129]

The scenes in which observers witnessed supernatural events fall into two broad categories. First were the cases where people saw spirits. For instance, in 1698 one of the most pious Christian Indians on Martha's Vineyard lay dying. David Wuttinomanomin, a deacon in Japheth Hannit's Indian church, seemed to be on the edge of death due to a grievous sickness. Mayhew did not witness this deathbed scene, but according to oral tradition preserved by the Christian Indians and recorded by Mayhew, spirits descended to the dying man's side: "Some of the persons that tended him in his sickness, and were with him when he died, have with great assurance affirmed, that . . . while one was praying with him, there appeared in the room where he lay far brighter attendants, in human shape, than any which this lower world could have afforded." The phrasing is ambiguous about whether Wuttinomanomin could see the spirits, but it is clear that the observers could. Likewise, an observer saw spirits during Abigail Ammapoo's dying moments in 1710. Ammapoo was attended diligently in her final days by her daughter. Too diligently, thought the mother, who asked her daughter to get some rest. But the young woman would not lie down, opting instead to sit in a chair next to her sleeping mother's bed. As the daughter became drowsy, she was treated to a spectacular supernatural display: she "suddenly saw a light which seemed brighter than that of noon-day; when looking up, she saw two bright shining persons, standing in white raiment at her mother's bedside, who, on her sight of them, with the light attending them, immediately disappeared." [130]

The second type of supernatural events witnessed by Indian observers were those in which voices or inexplicable sounds were heard. Again, these were deathbed scenes at which Mayhew was not present, so he relied on native informants for descriptions. One such case occurred while Margaret Osooit was dying. Osooit was pious and literate; Mayhew noted that she loved to read Lewis Bayley's *Practice of Piety* translated into Massachusett by John Eliot. Likewise, her deathbed scene was pious: "Some Christians that were with her when she was dying, having at her desire commended her to God by prayer, and sung a Psalm of praises to him, she manifested a desire to be gone, and intimated, that the messengers of heaven were already come to receive her: and two persons that were then abroad, near the house where she lay a dying, do affirm, that they then plainly heard a melodious singing in the air, over the house where the woman lay." [131] Inside the house, Osooit felt that spirits were coming to take her to heaven; outside the house, Christian Indians heard the voices of those spirits. Again, it seems that Christian Indians may have been more receptive to intervention from the spirit world than their Anglo-American counterparts.

Mayhew's reactions to these and similar reports are significant. He did not dismiss these accounts; instead, he hedged. Mayhew distanced himself very little from these descriptions, making clear his inclusive assessment of these events. His public stance was that he could not vouch for the veracity of the statements but that he did not greatly doubt them. After offering the account of Wuttinomanomin's death, Mayhew editorialized, "Whether this account be true or false I cannot determine, there being but one witness now living, by whom the affirmative is asserted; yet I doubt not but that the man, to whom the story relateth, 'died in the Lord, and was carried by the angels into Abraham's bosom.'" And after describing a deathbed scene where an observer heard a voice in the air and "supposed it to be a voice from heaven by the ministry of angels," Mayhew essentially turned interpretive responsibility over to his readers: "Query. Whether the person that dreamed the dream now related, ought to take any other notice of it, than she should of any common dream; or what she should think concerning it? A solution of this problem would gratify both the person that had the dream, and him that has related it." [132]

When New England ministers such as Cotton Mather, Ebenezer Parkman, and Isaac Backus were told by laypeople that they had visions of heaven upon their deathbed, these clergymen almost always reacted with skepticism, urging their parishioners to rely on more scriptural sources of hope.[133] Because these ministers seem never to have been presented cases in which deathbed observers witnessed supernatural events, it is impossible to be certain how they would have reacted, yet it is not hard to imagine them scoffing at such claims.

Yet Mayhew, orthodox in most respects, did not dismiss such reports from his Christian Indian flock. It is possible that this resulted from Mayhew absorbing some of these Christian Indians' syncretic sensibilities. The same factors that made Experience Mayhew such an effective and sympathetic minister to the Indians—that he was born on the island, spoke the native language fluently, and knew most of the Indians personally—perhaps led him to adopt a belief characteristic of many Christian Indians: the willingness to accept spiritual intervention during deathbed scenes. This is, admittedly, speculative, but it is hard to account for Mayhew's attitudes otherwise.[134] At the very least, the Indians of Martha's Vineyard influenced Mayhew to the extent that he was willing to include these very unusual scenes in his compendium.

In eighteenth-century New England, however, Martha's Vineyard was the exception, the lone place where Christian Indians had enough of a presence that they might have influenced the beliefs of a minister. Elsewhere, there is basically no evidence of Indians influencing wider Anglo-American deathways. White New Englanders were shaped by the frontier environment in which they lived: like residents of the Chesapeake, they were more likely than those living in England to bury their dead in coffins, due to the abundance of trees.[135] But no Anglo–New Englanders, so far as we know, buried their dead in a flexed position, or smeared corpses with red ochre, or used kaolin pipes and hawk's bells as grave goods. Those practices became increasingly rare as Anglo–New Englanders largely succeeded in their grave mission of Christianizing, killing, or driving out the aboriginal inhabitants of the land.

CHAPTER 6

Across the Waters:
African American Deathways

NEWTON PLANTATION IN Barbados looks much the same today as it did three hundred years ago, the landscape dominated by towering sugar cane. Amid the monoculture one scrubby field stands out, distinctive for its covering of sour grass, used for grazing the Barbadian black-bellied sheep. There is nothing to indicate that beneath this pasture lie the bones of hundreds of slaves, their ends hastened by the brutal work regime enforced by generations of Newton's overseers.

This unremarkable patch of sour grass is perhaps the best spot to begin a consideration of the slow process by which the African deathways that were brought across the waters of the Atlantic became African American deathways. Here, in the 1970s, an archaeological team led by Jerome Handler and Frederick Lange dug into the soil and performed the most thorough analysis to date of a plantation slave cemetery.[1] Since then Manhattan's African Burial Ground has been unearthed and its remains carefully examined, but that cemetery served an urban population of free and enslaved blacks. Handler and Lange's work remains unsurpassed for plantation sites.

Historical archaeology is especially important for understanding African deathways in the Americas, because Euro-Americans were far less interested in the cultural practices of their slaves than of their indigenous neighbors. Even though more Euro-Americans lived in close proximity to people of African descent than to native peoples, colonists left fewer detailed descriptions of African deathways. Largely this was due to a lack of missionary efforts. In Protestant New World colonies, slave masters generally did not want their

slaves exposed to Christ's potentially liberatory message. As a result, missionaries worked sluggishly and haphazardly among the region's slaves, at least
until the second half of the eighteenth century, and therefore did not leave a
body of literature comparable to the *Jesuit Relations* or Roger Williams's *Key
into the Language of America*. Thus, some of the best information we have
about slave deathways comes to us courtesy of those who muddy their hands
in the physical remains of the past. Beneath Newton's sour grass lie clues to
two hundred years of life and death, persistence and adaptation.

*   *   *

The scene is three hundred years ago, give or take a couple of decades. Newton's slaves, more than a hundred of them, have gathered in the evening to
bury one of their own. But this is not the mournful gathering of people who
have lost a beloved friend, or even the joyful festival celebrating the return
of the deceased's soul to Africa. This is something more frightening, more
portentous: the burial of a young woman whose bizarre behaviors have led the
slave community to conclude that she is a witch.

In the decades around 1700, Newton's slave population consisted mostly
of individuals who had been born in Africa. Every year roughly three thousand new slaves were brought in chains from Africa to Barbados to feed the
island's insatiable demand for labor. Sugar was booming and Barbados was
the jewel in England's imperial crown, producing far more revenue than any
other colony. The Royal African Company's concentration of forts and trading posts along the African coast from Accra to Lagos meant that in the first
two decades of the eighteenth century the large majority of Barbadian slaves
came from two regions: the Bight of Benin (39.5 percent) and the Gold Coast
(31.2 percent).[2] As in the rest of the British West Indies, the reliance on Gold
Coast slaves would only increase in subsequent decades. If Newton approxi-
mated the general profile for Barbadian slave imports (and there is no reason
to suspect otherwise), its slave community circa 1700 was made up largely of
people who had been taken from a relatively compact stretch of West Africa
from present-day Ghana to Nigeria.

These people did not all adhere to precisely the same religious beliefs in
their native lands, but there were enough underlying similarities that consensus ordinarily reigned regarding burial practices. Plantation owners in
this period cared very little about their slaves' spiritual lives, so they allowed
slaves a great deal of autonomy in organizing their own burials, as long as

the rites did not interfere with the plantation's work routine. Slaves thus had long experience arranging the burials of their dead. But around 1700 Newton's slave community was faced with an unusual situation: the death of a young woman, about twenty years old, who had been behaving abnormally. Unbeknown to them, she was suffering severe lead poisoning, which may have caused her to experience seizures and episodic paralysis.[3] West Africans often interpreted such physical maladies in supernatural terms, so it is likely that they considered this unfortunate woman either to be a witch or to have been bewitched. The burial they performed suggests they believed her to be a witch.

There may well have been initial disagreements about what rituals to perform in this unusual case; today among the Saramacca of Suriname—descendants of runaway slaves—there is a saying that "there are no burials without argument."[4] But ultimately the community reached consensus and proceeded with the burial. They dug a shallow pit, only a foot and a half deep and not quite long enough for the woman to lay in fully outstretched, in a part of the plantation unsuitable for sugar cultivation that had been set aside as a slave cemetery. They placed her into this pit face-down: the only prone burial of the 104 excavated at Newton, and one of the only prone slave burials found in the New World (none of the more than four hundred bodies found in Manhattan's African Burial Ground were buried face-down). This was a clear sign of the low regard they had for this woman, but what exactly the slaves hoped to accomplish by a face-down burial remains open to speculation. Did they hope that this would prevent her spirit from tormenting them? Might it prevent her soul from returning to Africa? Or was it simply a sign of disrespect?

The slaves decided upon one other way to indicate that this was an unusual burial. Although they placed this woman within the slave cemetery and only twenty feet from other slave burials, they made sure to mark her grave in a singular fashion. Out of soil they built a low circular mound, about twenty-five feet in diameter and three feet high, over the woman's grave. They may have marked the top of the mound with stones or sticks, though if they did no archaeological record exists. With or without markers, the mound remained a visible reminder to generations of Newton's slaves about the fate reserved for a suspected witch. During the next century, a period when hundreds of other slaves were buried in the cemetery, dozens of them only twenty feet away, not a single individual was placed within the area demarcated by the witch's low mound. Despite the horrifying rate of mortality on sugar plantations such as

Newton, and the constant turnover in the slave community as fresh imports replaced dead workers, the memory of this woman's burial remained alive.

In the same decades—before or after the burial of the suspected witch, we do not know—Newton's slaves came together once more to perform an extraordinary burial. This one probably required less negotiation about what rituals to perform because it was less unusual than the witch's burial. Rather, it was more like an intensified version of ordinary burials. For in this case, the person who died was not feared or loathed but respected. He was a man of about fifty years, and based on the goods that accompanied his burial, he was evidently a healer held in high regard by his fellow slaves.

Because the healer's burial resembled ordinary burials except in the number and types of grave goods, it is possible to use European descriptions of other plantation slave funerals in this period to go beyond the archaeological remains and get a sense of what the ritual components of his burial might have been. These descriptions are all taken from the Caribbean through the first half of the eighteenth century, a period when Christianized slaves remained almost nonexistent and when continued importation of Africans meant that slave funerals retained a strongly African character.

We cannot know how Newton's healer experienced his last moments, due to the dearth of deathbed descriptions. Yet the one general account we have from this period conforms with what we know from later periods. In 1740 a Jamaican merchant, Charles Leslie, reported that slaves were generally happy on their deathbeds—and not simply due to their insensibility, as one might expect an English observer to conclude. According to Leslie, "They look on death as a blessing. 'Tis indeed surprising to see with what courage and intrepidity some of them will meet their fate, and be merry in their last moments; they are quite transported to think their slavery is near an end, and that they shall revisit their happy native shores, and see their old friends and acquaintance." Leslie thus attributed deathbed happiness to the slaves' belief in the transmigration of the soul back to Africa. This belief was corroborated by virtually every European commentator on slave attitudes toward death and the afterlife.[5] Transmigration seems to have been a New World modification of the widespread African belief that if a person died away from his homeland and could not be buried in his village, his soul would return to its land of birth.[6] This was a deeply comforting belief for New World slaves. Although we cannot be sure that Newton's healer died happy, we can be almost certain that he died believing that his soul was going to Africa.

Now that the healer was dead, it was imperative for the slave community to prepare his body for burial. According to the 1745 account of a Moravian missionary who long worked among slaves in Suriname, "the more respect a person had amongst them, the more elaborate the ceremonies."[7] But this desire to offer lavish funerals to respected slaves butted up against the material reality of life in slavery. For example, when the healer died, his body was likely washed and prepared for burial in his clothes, not a shroud. Though many West African groups shrouded their dead, especially their esteemed dead,[8] the poverty of enslaved Africans made shrouding impractical in most cases. As a result, burial in clothing seems to have become the general practice.[9] Moreover, archaeological and descriptive evidence indicates that in this period coffins were uncommon, in light of their expense and the lack of widespread African precedents for their use.[10] In this respect, the healer's burial was typical: he was interred without a coffin.[11]

In the tropical heat, rapid interment was necessary. According to Reimert Haagensen, a Danish planter in St. Croix, burial occurred "the same day or evening that [a slave] dies." An early Barbadian informant, Richard Ligon, confirmed in 1673 the prevalence of evening burials among slaves.[12] The preference for evening burials may have been a convergence of African practices and plantation requirements that funerals not interfere with work.[13] So it is likely that on the evening Newton's healer died, he was carried in his clothes, perhaps on a plank or other improvised bier, from his home to the slave cemetery. The procession ordinarily was—as it was in Africa—a noisy affair, at least to European ears. A Barbadian minister wrote, "Most young people sing and dance, and make a loud noise with rattles, as they attend the corpse to its interment."[14]

At Newton the procession headed toward the slave cemetery, and in this the burial was typical of New World slave funerals. Most plantations had grounds set aside for the burial of slaves, usually in marginal land unsuitable to cultivation. But occasionally—we do not know how often—slaves chose to bury their dead within their house-yard compounds instead of in the designated burial grounds. This was a continuation and perhaps modification of the Gold Coast practice of subfloor burial. There are only a handful of documentary references to subfloor burial among slaves. In 1788 the governor of Barbados wrote that among slaves "it is frequent to inter a near relation under the bed-place on which they sleep." Given that Governor Parry's statement is corroborated by only a few other observers, it is possible that this practice was not as "frequent" as he asserted.[15] But there is irrefutable archaeological evidence that such burials were at least occasionally performed. At the Jamaican plantation of Seville, archaeologists have uncovered four burials, not precisely from beneath the bedroom floor, as was the practice along the Gold Coast, but from the house-yard compound within the slave quarters. These burials, dating from the 1720s to the 1750s, were performed outdoors near the slave quarters: two beneath a narrow pathway between houses, and two in the yard.[16]

But at Newton the healer's destination was the slave burial ground, so the procession carried his clothed corpse in that direction. If members of the slave community believed that his death was owing to witchcraft—at the hand of Newton's lead-addled witch, for example—the slaves who carried the healer's corpse would have participated in one of the most distinctively African practices in the entire mortuary program: the "supernatural inquest" discussed in Chapter 1. This procession, a direct carryover from Gold Coast practices, was considered "ludicrous" by Europeans such as Charles Leslie. Nonetheless, Leslie left this account, corroborated by numerous others. "They who bear [the corpse] on their shoulders," wrote Leslie, "make a feint of stopping at every door they pass, and pretend, that if the deceased person had received any injury, the corpse moves toward that house, and that they can't avoid letting it fall to the ground when before the door." [17] The procession would then demand that the "guilty" person either pay a fine, if the injury was monetary, or offer other restitution for injuries caused by magical powers. This was a mechanism for the slave community to police its members, putting pressure on those suspected of deviant behaviors to adhere more closely to community norms.

When the raucous procession finally reached Newton's slave cemetery, the slaves almost certainly "gently put the corpse" into the grave, as an English visitor to Jamaica described in 1687. The corpse bearers laid the healer into a shallow grave that, when filled, left the top of his head only three inches from the surface. The grave had been dug along an east-west axis, and the healer was laid on his back, with his hands resting at his sides, and his head pointed toward the east. Africa lies east of Barbados, so the burial's easterly heading may have been to allow the soul to escape in that direction, but many of the healer's contemporaries were buried with their heads pointed to the west, so the geographical reference of Africa may not have been the issue at all. Perhaps the rising and setting of the sun provided the chief impetus for burial along an east-west axis. The mourners then in all probability placed items in the healer's grave that did not survive to be excavated by twentieth-century archaeologists. Europeans described a range of food, drink, and perishable goods that slaves placed into graves: cassava bread, sugar, rum, tobacco, and cloth.[18]

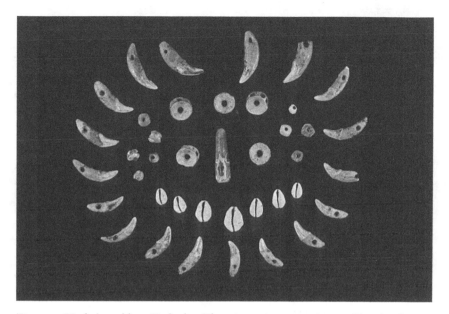

Figure 11. Healer's necklace, Barbados. These items were worn in a necklace by the man presumed to have been a healer among the slaves at Newton Plantation in Barbados. The necklace, unstrung for this photograph, dates to ca. 1700 and was buried with the healer when he died. Around the outside are dog teeth; inside those are cowrie shells from the Indian Ocean, glass beads from Europe, and fish vertebrae. At the very center is a large carnelian bead from India. Courtesy of Jerome S. Handler.

Whether or not they included perishable goods, Newton's slaves buried the healer's body with an unmatched array of durable African and African-inspired items. In this, the healer's burial was atypical. Of Newton's 104 excavated graves, the healer's was by far the most richly appointed. Only nineteen other burials had any artifacts associated with them, some as meager as "one button" or "one metal fastener." [19] Newton's healer, by contrast, was buried wearing three rings on his left-hand middle finger, a copper bracelet on his right forearm, and two brass bracelets on his left arm. He had a six-inch iron knife blade, possibly placed in his hand at burial. Into the grave his friends placed a unique buff-colored short-stemmed earthenware pipe of a kind found along the Gold Coast, nothing like the long-stemmed kaolin (white clay) tobacco pipes found throughout the Anglo Atlantic world. And around his neck the healer wore a necklace inspired by African norms and connected to a globalizing economy (Figure 11). The necklace was strung with seven

Indian Ocean cowrie shells, five vertebrae from a large fish, twenty-one dog teeth, fourteen glass beads made in Europe, and a large (4.2 cm long) reddish-orange carnelian bead made in Khambhat, in southern India. It boggles the mind to consider how this Barbadian slave came to possess such far-flung elements for his necklace. However he acquired them, they were clearly related to his role as a healer. It seems that the necklace was not merely a badge or insignia of the healer's role but a central element in his magical arsenal.[20]

As Newton's slaves arranged the healer's corpse and the grave goods, they continued to make a great deal of noise, as was characteristic of most African funerals. During the interment itself slaves were usually found "clapping and wringing their hands, and making a doleful sound with their voices." Charles Leslie wrote, "While they are covering [the corpse] with earth, the attendants scream out in a terrible manner, which is not the effect of grief but of joy; they beat on their wooden drums, and the women with their rattles make a hideous noise."[21] "Terrible" and "hideous": Leslie's description was typical of most European accounts in its disdain for the clamor of slave funerals.

After Newton's slaves covered the healer with earth, they likely left food and/or drink on top of the grave, an action reported by almost all European informants, and another carryover from African practices. Sometimes these offerings were made right after the burial; other times mourners returned and made offerings in future months and years.[22] Finally, with the healer and his magical goods safely interred in Newton's slave cemetery, the mourners almost certainly returned to their quarters for a loud, expressive, and joyful funeral celebration. According to Haagensen, "the same evening on which a slave is buried" the survivors "dance in his honor." To show their respect for the dead and their happiness at his soul's departure for Africa, members of the slave community "jump around in their crazy ways and sing, in addition to beating their fingers on a skin they have made into a drum."[23] Weary from emotion and from hours of singing and dancing, Newton's slaves made their way back to their quarters for a few hours of sleep before they were roused at dawn to labor once again in the cane fields.

The funerals of Newton's witch and healer, circa 1700, partook of African and African-inspired rituals, beliefs, and material culture. This is not to say that all the mortuary customs from the Newton slaves' various homelands in West Africa were transplanted to the New World. Some material and ritual components of African deathways did not make it across the Atlantic. The mortuary terracottas that formed such an important part of the material culture of death along the Gold Coast after 1600 do not seem to have played much of a role in slave deathways; at least there is no archaeological and very little documentary evidence for the terracottas.[24] In this case one imagines that the local materials and expert craftspeople required for terracotta manufacture were generally not available on slave plantations. It also seems likely that certain African rituals—such as the ceremony described by de Marees in Chapter 1, in which a priest constructed a mortuary fetish and anointed it with the juice of specially prepared leaves—were impossible to reproduce in the New World without the requisite ritual specialists and cosmologically significant plants, animals, and minerals. There is no New World evidence of Gold Coast mortuary fetishes or the leaf-squeezing ritual.

But overall, enough African attitudes toward death crossed the Atlantic in the minds and hearts of slaves to allow for the continuation of many African deathways at Newton Plantation. This is relatively unsurprising, given the recent forced migration of many of Newton's slaves from Africa, and in light of six decades of historical scholarship that has emphasized the African origins of slave culture in the Americas.[25] What is perhaps more surprising is the almost total indifference of Anglo-Americans to the foreign rites in their midst. There are virtually no descriptions of slave funerals before 1800 from the southern British colonies of mainland North America. There are more from the Caribbean, but even these are relatively few and brief, at least compared with the much more voluminous literature on American Indian deathbed scenes, funerals, and mourning practices. This contrast demands explanation.

Several factors seem to account for the difference. First, many accounts of Indian deathways were penned by first- or early-contact travelers, people who reported back to their countrymen about a new land and its marvelous inhabitants. The parallel for this literature is Europeans who traveled to Africa. By the time slavery was established in British colonies, planters were getting down to the business of making money, not writing ethnographies about exotic cultural practices. Slave owners were, for the most part, beyond the stage of initial inclusive and exclusive reactions to unfamiliar deathways. Second, missionaries were much less active among slaves than among Indians. Whereas most British colonies hoped to Christianize their indigenous neighbors, most planters through the eighteenth century did not want their slaves exposed to missionary teachings. Finally, the overall context of the encounter between Anglo-Americans and slaves was more exploitative than that between whites and Indians. Anglo-Americans simply did not need to understand their slaves in order to extract labor from them. They did need to understand Indians if they hoped to use them as allies, or gain land cessions from them, or convert them to Christianity. Once again, deathways are diagnostic of power relations between Europeans and non-Europeans.

This is not to say there was no European interest in the parallels between their own and African American deathways similar to what we have seen in previous chapters. Implicit in the descriptions of slave deathways are comparisons between numerous practices that Europeans and Africans had in common before they arrived in the Americas: belief in an afterlife, careful ritual attention to the corpse, a funeral procession, earth interment along an east-west orientation, variation in funerals according to the status of the deceased, and a gathering after the burial with the (sometimes immoderate) consumption of food and drink. But, in contrast to how they described Indian deathways, Europeans almost never drew explicit notice to the parallels with African American deathways. They were more likely to compare African practices with other peoples—usually non-Christian and less "civilized" ones.[26]

Only very rarely did a European use African American deathways to critique European practices, as was so common in the literature on American Indians. One of the few examples of this was penned by the progressive Jamaican sugar planter William Beckford, who argued in the late eighteenth century for the amelioration of slave conditions as a way to make plantations more profitable. After describing the "cheerfulness" of slave funerals, Beckford argued that the slaves' joyful, intense mourning contrasted favorably with European indifference: "Nor will he be scandalized [by slave funerals] who looks into our cathedrals and houses of mortality, in which so many hundreds are yearly buried without any accompaniment, but a vacant question, 'Who was he? Poor man! I am sorry for him. It is, alas! what we must all come to.'"[27] Thus Beckford used slave funerals to draw attention to the harsh, anonymous conditions in England's growing cities, where so many died without the comparatively humane rites found on a Jamaican sugar plantation.

Far more common than this kind of self-examination was Europeans' use of their knowledge about slave deathways to control and intimidate their laborers. Plantation owners did not bother to learn much about their slaves' deathways, but they learned enough so they could try to use that knowledge to make their workers more docile. Due to the high mortality associated with plantation labor and the numerous resultant slave funerals, masters knew how important proper funerals were to their slaves, even if masters were generally not careful observers of such rituals. They learned about African beliefs in the sacredness of the corpse and the importance of respecting the dead. They thereby discovered a tactic to control their slaves. As Edward Long wrote, "insulting the ashes of the dead" (the remains of the dead) was "esteemed the highest impiety" by slaves, second only to murder.[28] Likewise, in 1751 a Jamaican minister wrote to his superior in England that "to deprive them of their funeral rites by burning their dead bodies, seems to Negroes a greater punishment than death itself. This is done to self-murderers."[29]

This mention of suicide points to a key issue of control over slaves to which masters applied their knowledge of slave deathways. If plantation owners learned anything about their slaves, it was that they believed in the transmigration of their souls to Africa upon their death. This belief led not only to the happy deaths and joyous funerals described by Europeans but also to a more problematic result: suicide. If slaves were brutalized in this life and would return to their homeland after death, why not simply commit suicide? This question troubled countless slave owners. According to Richard Ligon, because slaves believed in transmigration, they "make it an ordinary practice, upon any great fright, or threatening of their masters, to hang themselves." One of Ligon's fellow Barbadian slave owners devised a way to prevent this willful destruction of his property, based on his knowledge of his slaves' deathways:

> Colonel Walrond having lost three or four of his best Negroes this way [by suicide], . . . caused one of their heads to be cut off, and set upon a pole a dozen foot high; and having done that, caused all his Negroes to come forth, and march round this head, and bid them look at it . . . He then told them, that they were in a main error, in thinking they went into their own countries, after they were dead; for, this man's head was here, as they were all witnesses of; and how was it possible, the body could go without a head.

Ligon reported that Walrond's tactic was successful: the slaves "changed their opinions; and after that, no more hanged themselves."[30] There is, of course, no evidence about whether Walrond's slaves actually were convinced by his grisly display.

Walrond was not alone in his tactics. A British ship captain involved in the slave trade wrote in 1754, "Many blacks believe that if they are put to death and not dismembered, they shall return again to their own country."[31] So plantation owners and state authorities pursued this knowledge to its logical and brutal end. They dismembered, burned, and otherwise denied proper burial to the corpses of suicides and other slaves for whom they wanted to show the greatest contempt. Moreover, the state sanctioned and promoted the dismemberment of corpses of runaways and slaves found guilty of crimes such as murder. In 1730, for example, a slave named James was convicted in Richmond County, Virginia, of murdering his master's daughter. That James died in custody was not enough for local officials; they ordered his corpse quartered, the pieces displayed in various locations around the county. They reserved his head to be stuck on a pole at the courthouse.[32]

Some historians have argued that corpse dismemberment was the result of Anglo-American understandings of African deathways, in particular the belief in transmigration.[33] But it was also an extension of European traditions of corpse humiliation as the highest form of disdain. Even though actual dismemberment of corpses was only "rarely performed" in eighteenth-century England, travelers on English highways often found themselves confronted by the "common spectacle" of the decomposing corpses of murderers hanging from gibbets, a practice that did not end in England until 1832.[34]

In addition to learning how corpse desecration might be used to prevent the loss of valuable slaves, plantation owners throughout the British colonies also discovered that slave funerals provided the opportunity for a dangerous level of interplantation communication among slaves. Even the least curious masters realized that slave funerals could provide cover or even inspiration for planning rebellions. As a result towns, counties, and colonies passed laws aimed at restricting slave funerals. The first law of this sort in Anglo-America was passed by the Virginia House of Burgesses in 1680. The act explicitly drew the connection between slave funerals and the potential for violence against whites: "Whereas the frequent meetings of considerable numbers of Negro slaves under pretense of feasts and burials is judged of dangerous consequence, it is enacted that no Negro may carry arms . . . nor go from his owner's plantation without a certificate." The penalty for ignoring this statute was twenty lashes on the bare back, "well laid on." [35]

With this same fear in mind, numerous jurisdictions tried to ban slave funerals from taking place during the evening hours, when slaves could more easily mount a rebellion. Such laws were passed in Westmoreland County, Virginia, in 1687, New York City in 1722, South Carolina in 1745, Antigua in 1757, and Jamaica in 1816.[36] There is some evidence, however, that these laws were difficult to enforce. In 1766, the *Georgia Gazette* ran a public notice written by the colony's Court of General Sessions of the Peace: "We also do present as a grievance, that the Negro Act is not put in force, particularly with respect to their attendance on funerals in large bodies in the night." [37] Ironically, laws requiring daytime funerals may have encountered resistance from slave owners, who probably could not decide which they hated more: the fear of violence threatened by night funerals, or the loss of productivity to daytime funerals.

Government officials in the New World also attempted to legislate a variety of other African American mortuary practices. Colonists in the Danish West Indies seem to have been especially sensitive to the dangers presented by slave deathways. In 1733 they banned African instruments at slave funerals, in 1765 they forbade slave wakes, and in 1778 they limited the number of mourners at a funeral to twelve. In 1731 New York City likewise tried to limit to twelve the number of slaves who could attend a funeral, because at such gatherings slaves "have great opportunities of plotting and confederating together to do mischief." [38] All these laws were aimed at preventing slaves from using funerals to gather and plot violence against their white oppressors.

But, paradoxically, there was another category of funeral regulations that aimed to prevent people of African descent from appropriating the deathways of Euro-Americans. These laws were not as common as those intended to prevent rebellion, but they were widespread enough to indicate white concerns about the symbolic appropriation of their deathways. In Manhattan, for example, it became a crime in 1731 for slaves to show respect for the dead by placing a pall over the deceased's coffin. The law proclaimed that "no pall be allowed or admitted at the funeral of any slave, and if any slave shall hereafter presume to hold up a pall or be a pallbearer at the funeral of any slave, such slave shall be publicly whipped at the public whipping post." South Carolina in 1750 declared that no "negro" could wear a funeral scarf, the distinctive Anglo-American article of mourning apparel that was worn over the shoulder like a sash. Antigua went beyond New York and South Carolina in 1757 by outlawing *both* palls and scarves. [39]

These laws demonstrate that by the middle of the eighteenth century, people of African descent began to adopt some of the material trappings of Euro-American deathways. This development was intertwined with the adoption by some African Americans of the spiritual trappings of Euro-American deathways as well. In this regard, Anglo-American colonies lagged behind their Catholic counterparts. In French, Spanish, and Portuguese colonies, the Catholic Church and the colonial state combined to put much more pressure on slave owners to try to convert their slaves to Christianity. The 1685 Code Noir that regulated slavery in French colonies, for example, demanded that slave owners baptize their slaves and instruct them in the Catholic religion (Article II), and it required that all baptized slaves be buried in consecrated ground (Article XIV).[40] Iberian colonies were even more aggressive about promoting the Christianization of slaves.

This is not to say that slaves in Catholic colonies quickly abandoned African practices; indeed, there is a great deal of evidence for the retention of African deathways. But Catholic practices informed slave deathways earlier than did Protestant ones in English colonies. The distinctive practices of vodou in Haiti, santeria in Cuba, and candomblé in Brazil all combined African and Catholic rituals.[41] And there were many black Catholics in Iberian colonies whose deathways were orthodox Catholic with very little African influence. As early as 1552 Brazil had an *irmandade* (lay sodality or confraternity) organized by Catholics of African descent, and by the end of the colonial period at least 165 black confraternities had been formed in the country.[42] The chief concern of these societies was to provide for the proper Catholic burial of members.[43]

By contrast, there was almost no organized effort to convert slaves to Christianity in the first century of slavery in English plantation colonies. These colonies were dominated by the Church of England, and the Anglican regular clergy did not have the resources or interest to try to Christianize slaves in the face of resistance from plantation owners. This can be seen in the answers given by Anglican officials in each of Barbados' eleven parishes in response to a questionnaire sent to them by the bishop of London in 1723. The bishop asked several questions, including "Are there any infidels, bond or free, within your parish; and what means are used for their conversion?" Edward Brice of St. Lucy's parish answered tersely, "Many. Their conversion must be the work of authority." Brice's meaning is clarified in the response of Oliver Deuchamp of St. Thomas parish. Deuchamp explained to the bishop, "I know not neither do I use any means toward their conversion, nor do I see any practicable method without the authority and concurrence of the civil power." In plantation colonies, the state was controlled by slave owners who had no interest in promoting the Christianization of their slaves.[44]

The exceptions to this rule of indifference are notable for their near-total failure to make an impression on the thousands of slaves in their midst. In 1701 the Anglican Church founded the Society for the Propagation of the Gospel in Foreign Parts (SPG) in hopes of converting indigenous peoples and enslaved Africans in English colonies. One of the most dogged of these

Anglican missionaries was Francis Le Jau, who was sent to South Carolina in 1706 to try to convert Huguenots to Anglicanism, but who soon became interested in trying to teach slaves about Christ. Le Jau quickly realized the difficulties he was up against. The slaves in his parish of St. James worked six days a week for their masters and then on Sundays had no time to learn about Christianity, because they were working in their own gardens and visiting their loved ones on distant plantations.[45]

Moreover, the racism of St. James's white residents and their horror at the idea of Christian slaves made his task doubly difficult. One genteel plantation mistress asked Le Jau, "Is it possible that any of my slaves could go to Heaven, and must I see them there?" A "young gentleman" declared that he would not receive the Lord's Supper if blacks did so.[46] The rare slave owner who attempted to teach her slaves about Christianity was mocked by other planters. Lilia Hague wrote to the SPG in 1715 to complain, "Some of the people here are very averse to the instructing or Christening of their slaves and were pleased to make a jest of me for attempting."[47] It is thus hardly a surprise that Le Jau never counted more than a handful of black communicants—out of the thousands of slaves in St. James—among his small flock.[48] And Le Jau was one of the most active missionaries in the English plantation colonies. Furthermore, slaves sometimes actively resisted Protestant efforts to change their deathways. As John Shipman, a missionary in Jamaica, would later write, "Many refuse to be christened merely because they would not have, in that case, any drumming or dancing at their funerals."[49] There can be no doubt that in the absence of a credible alternative, and in the face of slave efforts to preserve their practices, African deathways persisted in St. James and other Anglican parishes through the first half of the eighteenth century.

The first Protestant missionary group to enjoy any significant success in New World plantation colonies came from an entirely different position from that of the Anglicans, whose ties to the state ultimately rendered them incapable of challenging the slave owners. This new missionary force was the Moravians, who not only stood further outside state power but whose message of Christian love and equality resonated more powerfully with slaves than the Anglican message of hierarchy and order. Moreover, it is possible that the Moravians' distinctive deathways helped make their teachings especially appealing to slaves. Moravians saw death as joyful rather than terrifying; they referred to it as "going to sleep" or "going home to the Lord." In their Christocentric theology, Jesus "plucked flowers from the garden" of the

Moravian community and welcomed them into heaven. Indeed, the Moravians entertained no Calvinist doubt about salvation. All members of the community went to Jesus upon death.[50]

In 1732 the first two German Moravian missionaries sailed to the island of St. Thomas in the Danish West Indies. By the end of the 1730s the Moravians were already gaining some converts from among the island's slaves, not least because of their single-minded focus on deathways as a site for teaching about Christianity. In 1739 a female convert died, which gave the missionary Valentin Löhans the opportunity to conduct a funeral service, the first for a person of African descent led by the Moravians. Understanding the importance of death rituals among the slaves, Löhans, as described by a Moravian historian several decades later, used singing, prayer, and preaching at the funeral to "effect a salutary change in the hearts of many of his listeners, who were thus confronted with the public testimony of the salvation which Christ had purchased for all mankind." [51] Time and again the Moravians used slave funerals to describe the glories of the Christian afterlife to those already converted and those who were simply curious.

In the early years of the Moravian mission on St. Thomas, plantation owners mirrored the skepticism of their Anglo-American counterparts, likewise believing that Christianization could undermine order on the plantation. Some masters even used deathways as a weapon in their arsenal to prevent the Christianization of their slaves. In 1750 a slave recently baptized by the Moravians lay dying. The man's owner was furious that the slave had joined the religious fellowship of this odd band of zealots, and thus he displayed his anger in the most effective way he knew: by denying the slave a good death and burial. As the slave's condition grew worse, the planter refused to get him care. When the dying man begged for some water, the master forbade it. The dying man's wife tried to sneak him some water but the enraged planter struck her on the head with his sword. Finally, mercifully, the slave died, but this did not quench the owner's hatred. "He forbade that the slave's body be given a burial but rather ordered that it be left to rot in the hut." Perhaps this would make his slaves think twice about embracing Christianity, he likely thought. In the end, two missionaries crept into the hut, removed the man's body, placed it into a coffin, and gave it a "proper burial." The owner's rage had passed and he overlooked the defiance of his orders, but the slaves on the plantation did not overlook the courage of the missionaries who risked a great deal to provide a Christian burial for one of their own.[52]

This should not be construed to mean that the Moravians were bold enemies of the slave power. Not only did they own slaves themselves but they repeatedly framed their teachings within the context of obedience to authority.[53] When three Christian slaves ran away in 1755 in order to escape the cruel treatment of their plantation manager, the Moravians did not use this as an opportunity to rail against the barbarity of slavery. Instead, they gathered their charges together and preached a sermon based on 1 Peter 2:18, "Servants, be subject to your masters with all fear; not only to the good and gentle, but also to the froward." As the missionaries put it, the runaways "not only sinned against His holy ordinances, but they also brought shame on their entire religious community." [54]

While this sort of rhetoric may have left some slaves shaking their heads in disbelief, it eventually worked to convince most masters in St. Thomas that Christianization was not a threat to their authority. By the 1760s the Moravians could happily report that slave owners were encouraging their slaves to attend the mission church. Some masters even appropriated the missionary strategy of using deathways to encourage Christianization. One master drew a sharp distinction between his Christian and non-Christian slaves. Those who had been baptized were buried in a coffin when they died, whereas the unbaptized received no such token of respect.[55]

As newly supportive masters used deathways to promote the adoption of Christianity among slaves, Moravian attention turned to the deathbed as an important site for the promotion of Christianity. Similar to the strategy pursued by a variety of missionary groups among American Indians, Moravians used deathbed scenes to highlight the happy ends of those who embraced their faith. By applying this strategy to enslaved Africans, Moravians found themselves nearly alone among New World Protestants. Moravians were the only Protestant denomination that systematically collected reports of slaves' dying moments. Christian Oldendorp included forty-seven of these brief descriptions in his *History of the Mission of the Evangelical Brethren* (1777). Because almost all of these are model deathbed scenes, they are not the best sources for learning about the interplay between African and Christian deathways. But as model scenes they are valuable for understanding what the Moravians considered to be their success stories in the Caribbean.

Oldendorp's 47 deathbed scenes took place between 1741 and 1768. They include descriptions of the deaths of 31 females (66 percent) and 16 males (34 percent), a ratio even more female-dominated than the overall conversions on the island, which in 1768 totaled 1,031 females (57 percent) and 771 males (43 percent). Unlike Jesuit missionaries among the Huron Indians, Moravians were reluctant to baptize children. Only 4 (8.5 percent) of the Moravian scenes identify the deceased as a child or youth. Only two of the Moravian scenes departed from the script for a good death, and in both of those cases only momentarily.

The key to these good deaths, for Oldendorp and the other Moravians, was that the dying person was resigned to God's will, even cheerful about impending death. Naemi died "with joy," Bilha departed "in joy and in consolation of her redemption by Jesus," and Basmath was so happy while she was dying that it could be seen on her corpse: the joy was "still clearly visible in death." [56] Joyful death was the clearest sign that these were sincere Christians, and it was also a selling point to the non-Christian slaves who witnessed these scenes. The missionaries never commented, however, on the parallel between these descriptions and the accounts of non-Christian slaves who died happy in the certainty that their souls were going to Africa.

Likewise, the missionaries on St. Thomas were silent about possible African connections with a component of the model Moravian dying scene that was unique among Christian deathbed descriptions: the importance of music. In the scenes compiled by Oldendorp, singing helped the dying person express love for Christ and demonstrated a willingness to die. Singing also allowed observers to console the dying with reminders of Christ's love. When a woman named Antonette was dying in 1766, her husband Jonathan anxiously kept a vigil by her bedside. As her dying hour approached, he "entertained her with the singing of consoling songs." This pleased her so much that she "asked him to continue singing until her last breath." In Antonette's case we do not know what songs her husband sang, but it is clear from other deathbed scenes that baptized slaves responded to the Moravian focus on Christ's bodily fluids, an emphasis that struck many Europeans and Euro-Americans as peculiar. As Christina drew close to death in 1756 her fellow slave Cornelius sang to her, "The blood of Christ and His righteousness, that is your embellishment and your cloak of honor." Likewise, as Johannes was dying of consumption in 1767, he gathered his last few breaths and "tried to join in singing the verse of the song about 'the sweat of Jesus' face saves you from coming before the tribunal.'" [57] Through song European and African deathways resonated on the deathbed. For people of African descent, whose death practices always incorporated music, the Moravian practice of singing with the dying was powerfully attractive.

Also embraced by dying slaves was the Moravian willingness to allow women important roles as spiritual instructors and exhorters, especially when addressing other women.[58] A common component of these model deathbed scenes involved a woman using the power that derived from the deathbed—where the dying person straddled the boundary between this world and the next—to gain the attention of the people around them. Some of these death-bed speeches resembled those of American Indians who urged their friends and family to hold true to the new faith. Such was the case with Eunica as she grew weaker and weaker in December 1762. According to Oldendorp, "She summoned her friends and acquaintances to her deathbed and exhorted them with the following words: 'I implore you, stay with the Savior and hold firm to Him.'" Likewise, Oldendorp used active language to describe Regina's dying scene. First she "exhorted" her unbaptized children, then she "urged" her baptized daughter to stay true to the faith, and finally she "addressed" the assembled sisters with her parting words.[59] Although she was soon dead, Regina left a memory of active and forceful speech among her family, her fellow slaves, and—through Oldendorp's celebratory writings—a transatlantic audience of readers.

The Moravians did indeed have a great deal to celebrate on St. Thomas. Compared with other Protestant denominations in the New World, they had by midcentury an unrivaled degree of success in Christianizing people of African descent. The Danish West Indies thus became the unlikely incubator for a process by which African deathways became entwined with Protestant practices and thereby transformed into African American deathways. On the North American mainland, missionaries played a less important role than did evangelical revivalist preachers. Where even the most energetic missionaries like Francis Le Jau had but the tiniest effect on the thousands of Africans in their midst, white and black Baptist and Methodist preachers began to capture the attention of people of African descent in the second half of the eighteenth century. In South Carolina and Virginia, whites such as Hugh Bryan and Shubal Stearns, blacks such as George Liele and David George, and countless other anonymous men and women began to preach a version of Christianity with far greater appeal to African Americans than Anglicanism. Focusing on the equality of all believers in the eyes of God and embracing a style of worship that encouraged emotional release, these evangelicals soon counted among their adherents thousands of free and enslaved blacks—such as the Virginia man named James Williams, described in a runaway slave advertisement in 1775 as being "very fond of singing hymns and preaching." [60]

Unfortunately, there is little direct evidence about African American deathways in the southern mainland colonies from these transformative decades. Contemporary observers were nearly silent about these matters; even someone like Reverend Thomas Bacon, who claimed to have "attended several" slave burials, left no details of what he witnessed.[61] Moreover, historical archaeology in the region has focused mostly on slave quarters, with only a small number of African American graves unearthed and analyzed.[62] Virtually all we have to go on are tantalizing written tidbits such as the notation in Charles Pinckney's account book in 1753, indicating that the South Carolinian slave owner paid one pound and ten shillings to have a coffin made and rum and sugar distributed at the burial of a slave child.[63] It is impossible to know from these scant details whether the burial of the child adhered to Christian or non-Christian norms, or some combination of the two. Similarly opaque are the entries in the diary of James Kershaw of Camden, South Carolina:

October 17, 1799: Anthony died.
October 27, 1799: Sunday. Negroes gave Anthony a burial.[64]

Why did Kershaw's slaves wait ten days to bury Anthony? To allow time for slaves to arrive from other plantations, or perhaps to adhere to an African tradition? And why did they finally bury him on a Sunday? Was this to observe the Christian Sabbath, or was it because it was the only day of the week Kershaw allowed them some free time? At a time when mainland African Americans were increasingly likely to be Christians, the death and delayed burial of Anthony stands for the tens of thousands of deaths about which we know next to nothing.

One African-inspired tradition that did leave behind evidence in the South was the practice of placing items such as rocks and shells, along with broken plates and pottery used by the deceased, on top of the grave.[65] Curiously, there are no descriptions of this practice prior to the 1840s. This is probably the result of planter inattention, but the practice may also have become more widespread as slaves and later freedpeople saw their material conditions improve and could afford to leave household items on top of graves. There can be no doubt that grave decorations drew on African traditions. As we saw in Chapter 1, seventeenth-century residents of the Gold Coast and the Kingdom of Kongo decorated their graves with domestic implements, and there was no comparable European tradition to which people of African descent might have been exposed.

If anything, the influence went in the opposite direction: some white southerners seem to have adopted the African practice of grave decoration. Again, the evidence for this comes not from the colonial period but from the nineteenth and twentieth centuries. Scholars have found seashells, jars, and wine bottles on the graves of some Euro-Americans.[66] But this may be the exception that proves the rule that African deathways did not generally influence Euro-American practices. Historians have searched for other examples of African influence on white deathways, but they have found only vague connections such as emotional responses to death or the desire for a happy death, both of which had deep European roots.[67]

Whereas little evidence survives from the southern colonies, archaeological work in Manhattan's African Burial Ground suggests some answers to questions about African American deathways in the eighteenth century, even as it raises other uncertainties. In the middle of the eighteenth century, people of African descent made up between 16 percent and 20 percent of New York City's total population in several different censuses.[68] Despite this large pool of potential converts, missionary activities were desultory, with an Anglican schoolmaster here and an itinerant preacher there seeking to bring the word of Christ to the city's black residents. The converts these preachers inspired were few in number, generally the domestic servants of the city's wealthiest families.[69] Indeed, more vigorous attempts to proselytize the city's black residents ran headlong into the suspicion that Christianity kept slaves from the labor that put money into their masters' pocketbooks. Even an Anglican missionary such as James Wetmore remarked, "Most of them [Negroes] are so vicious that people don't care to trust them in companies together, and some have under pretense of going to catechizing taken opportunity to [be] absent from their masters' service many days."[70] If Christianization occurred only fitfully among black New Yorkers, Anglicization proceeded more rapidly. People of African descent learned the English language, wore English clothes, and, as most of them were bound laborers, took up the artisanal trades of their owners. Their immersion in English material culture was reflected in their deathways.

Like slaves throughout the New World, enslaved New Yorkers were largely free to attend to their dying and dead without a great deal of interference from their masters or from the local clergy. In 1713 the Anglican minister John Sharpe was upset by the lack of ministerial presence at slave deathbeds. He complained that "there is no notice given of their being sick that they may be visited" by the clergy. Once they were dead ministerial inattention continued. People of African descent were, Sharpe grumbled, "buried in the

Common by those of their country and complexion without the office [the Anglican burial liturgy], on the contrary the heathenish rites are performed at the grave by their countrymen."[71] Apparently there were enough Africans of a variety of different ethnic backgrounds that members of each nation could attend to their own dead.

Sharpe's brief reference to burial "in the Common" glossed over the exclusionary Anglican burial policy in the city. In the seventeenth century some whites and blacks—primarily those not members of churches or too poor to afford church burial—had been buried in one of two public cemeteries in Manhattan. The public cemetery that was located just north of the town's wall was incorporated into the burial ground of New York's impressive new Anglican church, Trinity. One of the first orders of business for Trinity's vestrymen was to ban the burials of people of African descent. In 1697, immediately after Trinity was completed, the vestrymen ordered that "after the expiration of four weeks from the dates hereof no Negroes be buried within the bounds and limits of the church yard of Trinity Church . . . and that no person or Negro whatsoever, do presume after the term above limited to break up any ground for the burying of his Negro, as they will answer it at their peril."[72] Unlike evangelical missionaries in the Caribbean, who understood that providing a burial ground was one of the best ways to attract new African converts, New York's Anglicans did not care about appealing to the city's black residents. They certainly did not want to share their burial ground with them. Other denominations were equally committed to segregated burials.[73] As a result, black New Yorkers began to bury their dead "in the Common," a rocky ravine of little use to the city's white residents, a place that would eventually be called the "Negros Burial Ground" on eighteenth-century maps.

This would represent the sum total of our knowledge about African American deathways in colonial New York but for the U.S. government's desire to build a gleaming new federal office building at 290 Broadway in lower Manhattan. With construction just about to start in the summer of 1991, the federal government hired a consulting firm to see if any salvage archaeology needed to be done before the project could get under way. The archaeologists found bones, and then more bones, and soon it became clear that this was the "Negros Burial Ground" that colonial-era maps suggested would be there. Under increasing pressure from black New Yorkers and others, construction was finally halted in 1992 so a full archaeological excavation could be mounted.[74] By the time the work was completed, archaeologists had unearthed 419 individuals from what they now dubbed New York's African Burial Ground.

Because this burial ground was outside the developed part of the city circa 1700, it was fairly large for a colonial-era cemetery: about six acres. It was in use from at least 1712, and perhaps from as early as 1697, until 1795. Archaeologists estimate that the cemetery holds between ten and fifteen thousand bodies.[75] This means that the families and friends of ten to fifteen thousand black New Yorkers considered this marginal patch of land to be sacred space. It also means that many of the million or so black New Yorkers who lived in the city when the burial ground was unearthed were eager to ensure that African Americans took a leading role in handling and analyzing the human remains. Mayor David Dinkins appointed Michael Blakey of Howard University to lead the excavation.[76]

For fifteen years, Blakey and his team published very few of their findings. Those that did appear, especially in *Update: Newsletter of the African Burial Ground*, emphasized the African origins of the material culture unearthed in lower Manhattan: beads, shells, rings, and more. Historians have eagerly followed this lead, seeing in the African Burial Ground artifacts glimpses of a long-hidden African worldview in New York.[77] But when the final archaeological report was published in 2006, it seemed to me that some of the strongest claims about African influence needed to be revised.

The vast majority of the 419 individuals removed from the African Burial Ground were buried in ways identical to those of their white neighbors. Or, to be more precise, the *material remains* of the vast majority of the African Burial Ground interments are identical to those of white New Yorkers. Religious rituals rarely leave a trace in the material record, and thus archaeology is unable to shed light on most of the rites that meant a great deal to those who performed and observed them. Still, it is striking that so few of the burials contain African elements.[78]

Of the individuals whose remains were sufficiently well preserved to allow for analysis, 92 percent (352/384) were buried in coffins, 94 percent (393/419) were single interments, 98 percent (367/375) were buried with the head facing west, and 100 percent (269/269) were supine, that is, lying face-up. This is precisely how white New Yorkers were buried in the eighteenth century: coffined (with perhaps a few exceptions for indigents), west-headed, supine, single interments (except for a few mothers with infant children and children

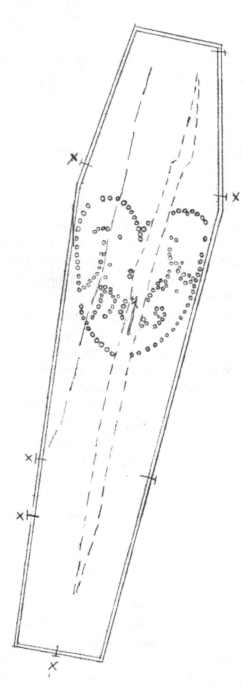

Figure 12. Coffin lid with heart, Burial 101. This coffin was made of larch, a wood similar to pine. The dashed lines represent cracks in the coffin, which make the date (1769?) and deceased's initials difficult to read. Original sketch of in-situ burial, African Burial Ground Collection, Howard University, Montague Cobb Laboratory Record Group. Courtesy of U.S. General Services Administration, New York City.

Figure 13. Heart-shaped design, Burial 101. Made of fifty-one iron tacks, this heart measures about 19 inches high and 18 inches wide. Original sketch of in-situ burial, African Burial Ground Collection, Howard University, Montague Cobb Laboratory Record Group. Courtesy of U.S. General Services Administration, New York City.

who died at the same time). Likewise, 93 percent (351/376) had no personal adornment such as rings, buttons, or cufflinks, and 93 percent (350/376) were not buried with coins, shells, pipes, and other durable objects.[79]

Other aspects of the material record demonstrate fewer connections with Africa than the first reports from the site suggested. In 1995 *Update* published an article by Kwaku Ofori-Ansa, an expert in African art, analyzing the heart-shaped symbol found on the coffin lid of Burial 101, a young man between the ages of twenty-five and thirty-five (Figure 12). The design, about eighteen inches wide and nineteen inches high, was made out of fifty-one iron tacks with heads about 3/8 of an inch in diameter, hammered into the center of the coffin lid (Figure 13). Ofori-Ansa wrote that "it could be safely concluded that the image was meant to be" a Sankofa symbol used by the Akan people of Ghana.[80] The Sankofa symbol is connected with modern-day Akan mortuary practices; the word *Sankofa* translates as "go back to fetch it." This refers to a proverb, "It is not a taboo to return and fetch it when you forget," that describes the connections between the spirit world and this world.[81] For this reason, the Sankofa is one of the hundreds of symbols that are today stamped onto adinkra cloth—meaning "a message one gives to another when departing"— out of which Akan mourning garments are made. Scholars rapidly incorporated this example from the African Burial Ground into their narratives as evidence of African cultural survivals in the New World. Thelma Wills Foote, for example, asserts that archaeologists "discovered a coffin lid displaying the heart-shaped Sankofa symbol," which demonstrates that "a trace of the Akan belief system . . . survived the native Africans' enslavement in colonial New York City." [82]

There are three problems with this interpretation. First, there is no evidence that the Sankofa symbol was a part of eighteenth-century Akan mortuary practices.[83] It is, of course, impossible to disprove the existence of a cultural form in the past. But there is no way to place adinkra cloth definitively in the eighteenth century, and there is evidence that the Sankofa symbol in particular may have emerged as late as the early twentieth century.

African oral tradition dates the arrival of adinkra among the Akan to 1818, at the conclusion of the Asante-Gyaman War. However, the Englishman Thomas Edward Bowdich collected an adinkra cloth in Ghana in 1817, suggesting that adinkra art existed before the traditional starting date of 1818. But ascertaining when adinkra cloth became part of Akan mortuary practices is impossible before 1817. Moreover, surviving nineteenth-century adinkra cloths do not contain the Sankofa. Bowdich's adinkra cloth, which is held by the British Museum, is stamped with fifteen symbols but not the Sankofa (Figure 14).[84] Likewise, another adinkra cloth, commissioned in the mid-1820s by the Dutch governor of the Guinea Coast and now held by the Rijksmuseum voor Volkenkunde in Leiden, is stamped with sixteen symbols but not the Sankofa. And in photographs taken by German missionaries in 1898 of Akan craftsmen making adinkra cloth, there are eighteen symbols visible on two cloths, and again the Sankofa is not among them.[85] The first appearance of the Sankofa is in R. S. Rattray's catalogue of adinkra symbols published in 1927. Rattray, an anthropologist who specialized in the art and religion of what is today Ghana, documented fifty-three symbols that were used on adinkra cloth. He gives two different versions of the Sankofa, one of

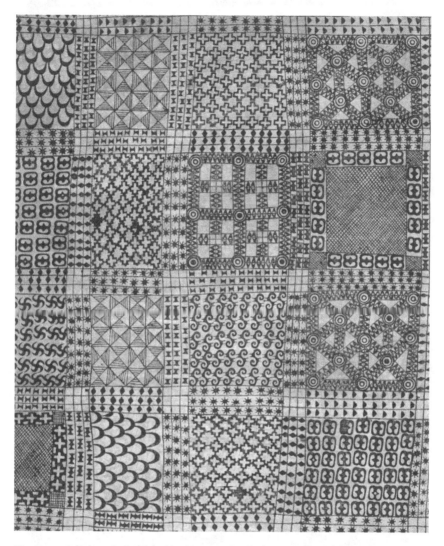

Figure 14. Adinkra cloth. This Akan mourning cloth was collected in Kumasi, a city in south-central Ghana, by Thomas Edward Bowdich in 1817. The patterns were printed on the cotton cloth using carved calabash stamps and a vegetable-based dye. This oldest known example of adinkra art does not include the Sankofa symbol. Instead, it features fifteen stamped symbols, including *nsroma* (stars), *dono ntoasuo* (double Dono drums), and diamonds. Image © Trustees of the British Museum.

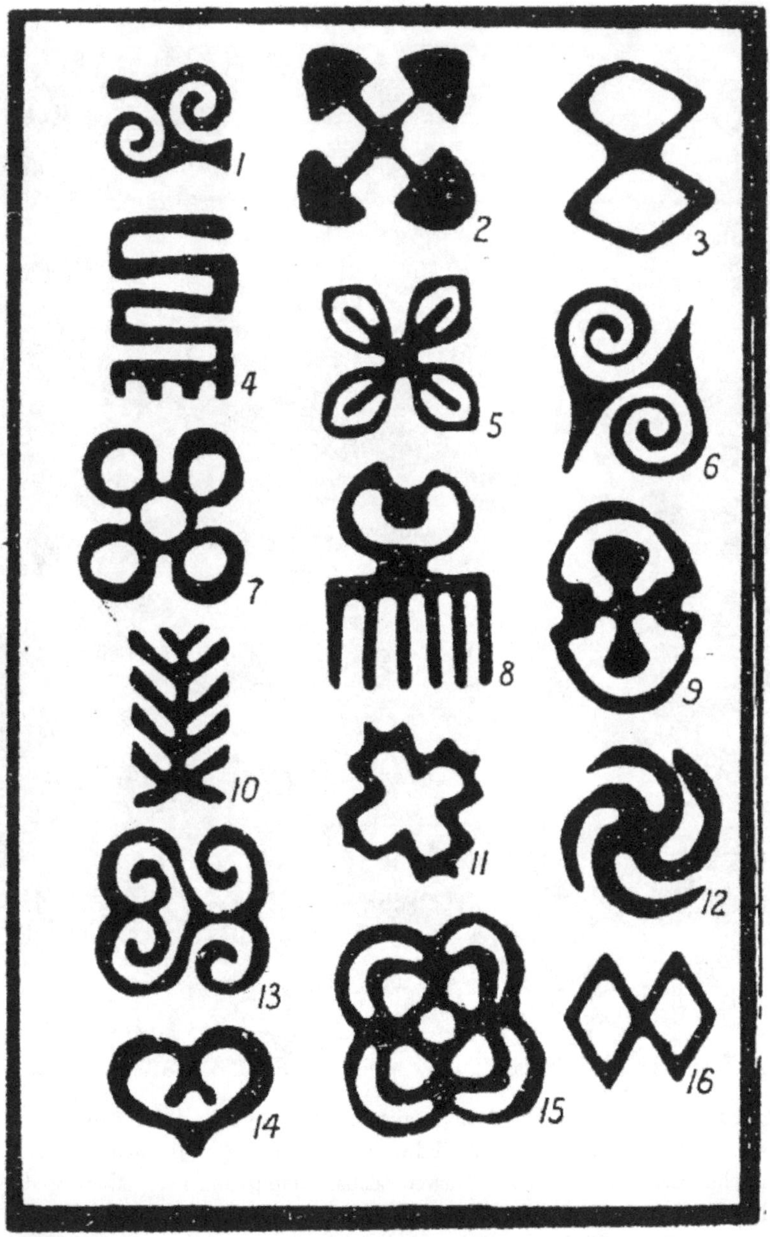

Figure 15. First documented Sankofa symbol. The earliest evidence of the Sankofa is in R. S. Rattray's *Religion and Art in Ashanti* (1927). The two figures in the lower left are both versions of the Sankofa: #14 is a relatively plain heart and #13 is a more elaborate version of the heart motif. In all, Rattray collected fifty-three adinkra stamps. Today there are hundreds of designs.

which is a heart-shaped pattern, the other of which is a more elaborate expression of the heart design (Figure 15).[86]

Thus, even if adinkra art had emerged by the middle of the eighteenth century, there is no evidence that the Sankofa was part of the symbology. Adinkra art has changed and expanded dramatically over the centuries to incorporate many new symbols, including modern commercial logos; one would certainly not want to posit that the eighteenth-century Akan were fanciers of Coca-Cola and Mercedes-Benz based on the presence of these symbols on recent adinkra garments.[87]

Second, even though slaves had a great deal of autonomy in burying their dead, masters were customarily responsible for providing coffins for their slaves. This is apparent in the financial records of plantation owners throughout the Americas, and in the 1753–56 account book of Joshua Delaplaine, a New York cabinetmaker who built coffins for a wide range of customers. His account book records at least eight examples of slave owners purchasing a "coffin for his negro boy" or a "coffin for his negro man" or the like.[88] Sometimes a slave owner spent more than necessary on a coffin, presumably to reward a faithful or well-liked slave. Most adult slave coffins sold by Delaplaine ranged in price from nine to twelve shillings, except for the one purchased by Christopher Fell in 1754: a "black coffin for his negro woman rosined and with screws" cost fourteen shillings.[89] Fell paid a few extra shillings to have his slave's coffin painted black (rather than left unpainted, as most were) and tightly secured with rosin and screws rather than the cheaper nails, probably to show his affection for the deceased. This evidence suggests that if Burial 101 was a slave—and it must be emphasized that he may have been free—it would have been his master's decision to pay extra for the tacks on his lid.

The third problem with seeing the heart as a Sankofa symbol is that hearts made out of tacks were not uncommon on Anglo-American coffin lids. Nathaniel Harrison, for example, who died in 1727 in Surry County, Virginia, was buried in a pine coffin elaborately decorated with brass tacks in the shape of a heart (and a skull and crossbones).[90] When the nineteenth-century local historian Arthur W. Dowe entered the Wainwright family tomb in Ipswich, Massachusetts, he found ten coffins in various states of disintegration. On five coffin lids "were hearts formed with iron nails; and initials and dates with brass nails"; the dates ranged from 1731 to 1798.[91] More recently, when archaeologists removed thirty-four coffins from the Bulkeley family tomb in Colchester, Connecticut, twenty of them (covering the period 1775 to 1826) had lids with heart-shaped designs made out of tacks (Figure 16).[92] Also rel-

Figure 16. Coffin lid of Asa Bulkeley. Archaeologists found thirty-four well-preserved coffins in the Bulkeley family tomb in Colchester, Connecticut, twenty of which had heart-shaped designs made out of brass tacks on the lid. As the design indicates, Asa Bulkeley died at age thirty in 1804. His pine coffin was marked with this heart, as well as tacks around the edges of the coffin, all of which cost extra. Courtesy of John J. Spaulding, Friends of the Office of State Archaeology.

evant is further evidence from Delaplaine. The busy New York coffin maker included in his account book an order for a fancy coffin of expensive "bilsted" or sweet gum wood, almost certainly for a wealthy white individual, for whom Delaplaine had a heart with the deceased's name, age, and date of death "struck" on the lid, presumably with tacks.[93] This description sounds uncannily like the design on the lid of Burial 101's coffin, which included not only a heart but what appear to be the deceased's initials and year of death (1769?).

It is possible that the family and friends of the young man now known only as Burial 101 ascribed meanings to the heart-shaped symbol on his coffin different from, or in addition to, the meanings the same symbol evoked for their Euro-American neighbors. Whereas white New Yorkers used the heart to symbolize the soul and its ascension to the Christian heaven—for the heart was where the soul was believed to reside[94]—black New Yorkers may have replaced or complemented those significations with other meanings. If the Sankofa existed 175 years before its first appearance in the historical record, the symbol on Burial 101's coffin may even have recalled the Akan proverb about crossing from the spirit world to this world. But in the absence of any literary or archaeological evidence supporting the eighteenth-century appearance of the Sankofa, and in the absence of any grave goods in Burial 101's coffin to indicate that this was an African-style burial, and in light of the numerous ways that black New Yorkers incorporated aspects of Anglo-American deathways such as coffins into their own mortuary rituals, that interpretation must remain highly speculative.[95]

By contrast, there are indisputable material links with African practices for a small minority of the African Burial Ground interments. One of the most evocative of these is the adult woman known as Burial 340.[96] Despite her anonymity this woman has left behind a material record that personalizes some of the ways black New Yorkers used their mortuary practices to keep alive their memories of Africa. This woman was between the ages of thirty-nine and sixty-four when she died; her poorly preserved remains prevent any more definitive statement of her age. She is believed to have died before 1735, at a time when a high percentage of black New Yorkers had been born in Africa. This woman almost certainly was one of those forcibly taken from her homeland: her incisors had been filed, one into the shape of an hourglass, another into the shape of a peg, a practice that is usually diagnostic of African birth.[97]

Her grave goods show how objects of European, American, and African origin could be combined to create distinctively African American mortuary practices. Into her grave, near her pelvis, had been placed an unused, white kaolin clay pipe of British or American manufacture. Both white and black New Yorkers enjoyed smoking tobacco, but only people of African descent placed goods into coffins to be used by the deceased in the afterlife. Even more uniquely African were the beads with which the woman was buried. She wore a bracelet around her right wrist made up of forty-one glass beads, and around her hips she wore a string of waist beads consisting of seventy glass beads, one amber bead, and seven cowrie shells. The amber bead, translucent red with fourteen facets, might have been made in Africa; the cowries came from the Indian Ocean coast of Africa; and the glass beads were manufactured in Europe, likely Venice. It is not the origin of the beads that makes them characteristically African but their use as waist beads. The waist beads would have made a delightful visual display while this woman was alive, with greenish-blue beads set off by the gleam of occasional yellow beads and shiny cowries, except for the fact that waist beads were not meant for public viewing. West African women wore waist beads under their garments, as a way to tuck in and hold up their skirts or aprons, and thus they were visible only to a woman's spouse or lover or her female bathing partners.[98] Whoever prepared this woman for burial must have known how important the waist beads were to her and therefore made sure that she was buried with them.

Whereas waist beads were African objects of daily use, conjuring bundles were reserved for spiritual and supernatural purposes. Called *minkisi* (singular *nkisi*) by Kongolese but used elsewhere in Africa and throughout the African diaspora, conjuring bundles were small cloth or fiber bags containing objects with magical or ritual significance.[99] Burial 147 was an old man, fifty-five to sixty-five years old, probably buried in the last decades that the African Burial Ground was in use, sometime after 1776. He was found with four straight pins and fourteen tiny copper-alloy rings—at 11mm in diameter too small to fit on an adult's fingers—between his upper right arm and his chest (Figure 17). It seems likely that the rings had been contained in some kind of small cloth sack pinned to his burial garment. It is impossible to know for what purposes the old man carried his tiny rings in a small sack, or whether he carried them in daily life as in death attached to his arm, although there is evidence of African men in the eighteenth and nineteenth centuries wearing amulets and protective bracelets on their upper arms.[100] But he likely kept his bag of precious, possibly magical rings hidden from the white New Yorkers he interacted with—including, if he was a slave, his master—just as the bag remained hidden from view in his coffin for over two centuries.

Overall the evidence from New York's African Burial Ground paints a

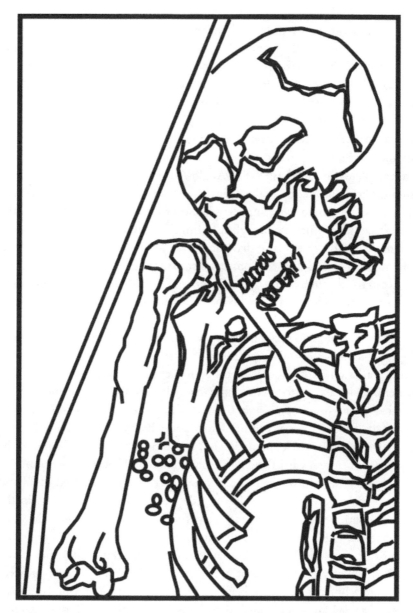

Figure 17. Burial 147, African Burial Ground. Look carefully between the right arm and ribcage to see the tiny rings interred with Burial 147. Archaeologists infer that they were originally contained within a cloth bag that no longer survives. Original sketch of in-situ burial, African Burial Ground Collection, Howard University, Montague Cobb Laboratory Record Group. Courtesy of U.S. General Services Administration, New York City.

more complicated portrait of black life in eighteenth-century New York than is sometimes seen in the historical works that have drawn on evidence from the cemetery. Some of the graves show connections with African material culture or African cosmology, including Burial 147 with his mysterious bundle of rings, Burial 340 with her prized waist beads, and several others not discussed here, such as Burial 328 with a broken pot placed atop the coffin lid, and Burial 397 with oyster shells left on top of the coffin.[101] But the large majority included nothing to distinguish them from contemporary white burials. Indeed, many included aspects of Anglo-American material culture—linen shrouds held together by straight pins, pine coffins secured with iron nails— that were not part of contemporary West African deathways. The material record cannot capture the thoughts, feelings, rituals, or nondurable offerings like food and drink that may have accompanied many of these burials. But the material record also cautions against assuming too great a connection between the deathways of Africa and those of eighteenth-century New York. Such caution is also warranted by the increasing importance of Christianity in the lives of African Americans as the century progressed.

At the same time that Burial 147 was interred with his bundle of rings, in mainland cities from Newport, Rhode Island, to New York, Philadelphia, and Charleston during the last decades of the eighteenth century, fewer and fewer individuals of African descent had any living memory of Africa. Burial 147 had been born around 1720, but for African Americans born in the second half of the eighteenth century Christianity held increasing appeal.[102] Especially as the free black population of New York grew toward the end of the eighteenth century, Christianity and Christian burial became the norm.

Toward the end of the century, free urban blacks in several mainland cities formed benevolent societies in order to further their interests in the face of continued racism. In 1794 New York's free blacks formed the African Society, a group dedicated to "improving . . . morals" and "promoting a spirit of brotherly love" within their community. But before they could reach these lofty goals they first needed to attend to a more pressing need: to secure a burial ground for black New Yorkers. Development within the city had spread far enough north that the African Burial Ground, which had once seemed distant and marginal to whites, now appealed to commercial interests. With this in mind, the African Society petitioned the Common Council in 1795 in order to "procure a place for . . . the interment of people of color."[103] Similar desires animated the free black benevolent societies in Philadelphia and Charleston. Philadelphia's Free African Society, established in 1787, attempted in 1790 to rent the portion of the Strangers' Burial Ground where blacks had long been buried, renewing a quest that had begun with a petition in 1782, even before the society was founded. When their 1790 request was also turned down, they bought a plot of their own.[104] Charleston's Brown Fellowship Society was organized in 1790 by elite free people of color who belonged to the predominantly white St. Philip's Episcopal Church, where they were allowed to be baptized and married but not buried. Not only did the Brown Fellowship Society procure a burial ground for its members and their families but it also oversaw funerals and even deathbed visitations.[105] The men who formed these urban benevolent societies did not forget their African roots; their pride in their heritage was reflected in the way most of the groups were called "African." But these were also committed Christians whose deathways partook of the material and spiritual aspects of Christianity.

This was true for the oldest and most active of the groups, Newport's Free African Union Society, established in 1780. The society concerned itself with a variety of issues of interest to the free black community, including education and recolonization in Sierra Leone, but nothing mattered more to its members than its death-related activities. Members paid small quarterly dues to ensure that when they or their family members died, they would receive a proper Christian burial. A typical funeral followed a pattern laid out in the society's proceedings. When the society learned that one of its members had died, the sexton went through the town and notified all the members when and where the funeral would begin. Each member "being well in body" was expected to attend the funeral. When members arrived, they placed the coffined body onto the society's bier for easier carrying (and to adhere to Anglo-American convention); the society even provided pillows to protect the shoulders of the coffin bearers. With the coffin atop the bier, members then laid the society's pall over the coffin. This was a powerful symbolic moment. In the eighteenth century, at least two jurisdictions—New York City and Antigua—prohibited people of African descent from using palls. Many whites were uncomfortable having their social inferiors appropriate this aspect of European deathways that had its origins in the pomp of heraldic funerals.[106] The pall was a point of great pride for the society's members, who even set up a separate pall company to keep track of the rental fees the pall generated (they rented it to nonmembers) and to keep it in good shape (they paid a shilling to repair a "hole or tear" in 1791).[107]

With the coffin now dignified by its place atop the bier and beneath the pall, the procession began. First came the coffin, carried by the bearers, unless the weather was bad, in which case the society paid for a horse and carriage to carry the coffin. Next came the deceased's family, then the president and officers of the society, and finally the rest of the members. The individuals in the procession dressed in their finest clothes, a requirement that resulted from some bad experiences they had had with Newport's whites. The society required that its members "dress themselves and appear decent" in the procession so "all the spectators may not have it in their power to cast such game contempt, as in times past." The procession made its way through Newport, past many white-owned houses and shops, the society's members undoubtedly proud they could make such an impressive visual statement. Indeed, as the historian John Wood Sweet puts it, the public display of respectability enacted in the funeral processions of Newport's African Americans represented nothing less than a "claim to citizenship." [108]

Finally the procession arrived at the town's African American cemetery, a wedge of land separated from the rest of Newport's Common Burying Ground by a road, where the deceased was given a "decent" Christian burial. After the burial, members gathered to consume the tea, rum, and sugar the society paid five or six shillings to provide, along with other food and drink supplied by the deceased's family. The purchase of rum suggests that this was a festive postburial party, but it likely had little of the unrestrained abandon of slave funerals in the Caribbean at the same time: the society's leaders warned its members that at the funeral "ye be sober, be vigilant because your adversary, the Devil, is a roaring lion walking about seeking whom he may devour." [109]

Shortly after the funeral the deceased's family, if it had the financial means, purchased a stone marker to memorialize the dead and provide a focal point for future cemetery visits. Earlier in the century, when most of Newport's blacks were slaves, masters occasionally purchased gravestones for their most favored slaves. Forty-five of the 245 stones in the burial ground state that the individual buried below was a slave, or "servant" in the preferred euphemism of the period; others were slaves but this is not mentioned on the stone.[110] The oldest surviving stone in the cemetery (1720) remembers "Hector Butcher Negro, late servant to Mrs. Ann Butcher of Barbados" (Figure 18). Several stones indicate the master's fondness for the deceased slave: Edward Collins was "faithful and well beloved" (1739), Hercules Brown was "faithful and beloved" (1762), and Pompey Lyndon, only twenty-eight months and eight days old, was "beloved" (1775). It is impossible to know how deeply

Figure 18. Hector Butcher stone, Newport. This is the oldest surviving stone in the African American section of Newport's Common Burying Ground. The inscription reads, "Here lyeth Hector Butcher Negro, late servant to Mrs Ann Butcher of Barbadoes, aged 37 years and dyed August ye 12th 1720." The lunette and pilasters have been laid out but not carved; perhaps Ann Butcher decided it would be too expensive to complete the stone. Photograph by the author.

masters felt these sentiments so conventionally expressed. Certainly it was not necessary for masters to purchase expensive stones for their deceased slaves, though the markers may have been, as one scholar argues, "objects of conspicuous consumption by elites demonstrating their wealth, rather than their affection for their slaves." [111] Either way, they resonate with the heart-shaped design on the coffin found in New York's African Burial Ground, if indeed that coffin was purchased for a slave by his master. In both New York and Newport, masters went beyond the minimum required by convention and bestowed on favored slaves tokens of esteem drawn from Anglo-American deathways.

The stone of "beloved" little Pompey Lyndon is important because it may

Figures 19 and 20. Pilasters of Cuffe Carr's and Hannah Hayward's gravestones. Stylized foliage in the pilasters of the stones of African American Cuffe Carr (1745), left, and Anglo-American Hannah Hayward (1758), right. Blacks and whites in Newport's Common Burying Ground used similar iconography on their stones. Photographs by the author.

have been carved by Pompey Stevens, an enslaved stonecutter in the shop of John Stevens III. When Pompey Stevens later became free, he changed his first name back to its African original, Zingo. The African American markers cut by Stevens and others mostly partake of Anglo-American iconographic conventions. The lunette (semicircular top) of Pompey Lyndon's stone and many others include winged cherubs, representing the soul of the deceased ascending to heaven, while the lunette of Ann Oliver's 1743 stone and two others contain classic Puritan death's heads. The designs on the pilasters (right and left vertical margins) of most stones include the same stylized tulips and foliage, symbolic of the ephemerality of life, found on contemporary stones from the other side of the road that divided black from white Newport graves (Figures 19 and 20).[112]

But in at least two cases, Newport stonecutters carved images that appear to have been particular to their African American clients. When Pompey Brenton died at age fifty-five in 1772, and when twenty-year-old Dinah Wigneron died in the same year, their families purchased distinctive stones for them. The markers are in the conventional Anglo-American shape, but the cherubs in the lunettes appear to have African features (Figure 21). Along with African names such as Cudjo, Cuffe, Mingo, Quamino, Quarco, and Quash, the seemingly African-featured angels represent the extent to which we can detect African influences in Newport's burial ground. The men and women buried there may have shared the sentiments of Phillis Wheatley, a contemporary urban African American who wrote in 1768,

'Twas mercy brought me from my pagan land
Taught my benighted soul to understand
That there's a God, that there's a Savior too:
Once I redemption neither sought nor knew.[113]

With the proverbial zeal of a convert, Wheatley and others like her in northern cities embraced the teachings—and the deathways—of Protestantism.

Such was not the case to the same extent on Caribbean plantations, where in the decades around 1800 observers continued to report numerous African and African-inspired deathways. Even though Britain legally abolished the slave trade in 1807, M.G. Lewis, the gothic novelist who lived in Jamaica from 1815 to 1817, could still write that "nothing is more firmly impressed upon the mind of the Africans, than that after death they shall go back to Africa."[114] Observers noted that many slaves continued to place grave goods into

Figure 21. Gravestone of Pompey Brenton, Newport. This stone's lunette is carved with a cherub that has seemingly African features: a broad nose and curly hair. Brenton died in 1772, "aged about 55 Years." The stone is signed by John Stevens III, a member of the third generation of Stevens stonecarvers in Newport. Photograph by the author.

the coffin for burial with the deceased.[115] Numerous Europeans wrote about the continued use of the supernatural inquest, probably because it was so different from Anglo-American practices.[116] Many slaves continued to place rum and food on top of graves after the deceased had been buried.[117] And finally, after a burial most slaves returned to their quarters where, as they had done since the start of the plantation era, they held a noisy, festive funeral that featured African drumming, singing, and dancing. The Methodist missionary John Shipman wrote in 1820 that among Jamaican slaves, "eating, drinking, drumming, and dancing are their funeral solemnities; in short every kind of tumult and festivity which was pleasing to the deceased in his lifetime."[118]

But this was also a time of transition in the Caribbean. Even though some people of African descent held funerals that partook strongly of African influences, others slowly began to adopt aspects of Anglo-American deathways. This was partly due to the increasing number of Creoles, born in the Caribbean with no memory of Africa. For some of these individuals, the material and spiritual aspects of Anglo-American funerals became increasingly appealing. The transitional nature of Afro-Caribbean deathways in the second half of the eighteenth century can be clearly observed through the diaries of Thomas Thistlewood, a slave owner in Jamaica who left behind the period's most extensive plantation diary, over 10,000 manuscript pages long. Thistlewood noted the occurrence of numerous "plays," the term white and black Jamaicans used to describe raucous, African-style slave funerals. Thistlewood was not a sensitive ethnographer and he did not leave detailed descriptions of these mortuary activities, except to note, for example, that the 1767 funeral for Frankie's husband Quashe included "singing etc. at the Negro houses," or to mention that when Fanny died shortly after childbirth in 1782 her funeral included "many Negroes and much noise." [119]

The one exception to this lack of interest occurred when Abba, one of Thistlewood's favorite slaves (he forced her to have sex with him 155 times over seven years), suffered the loss of a beloved child. When Abba's son died in January 1771, Thistlewood noticed that Abba was "almost out of her senses." He also paid attention six months later, when he gave her permission "to throw water (as they called it) for her boy Johnie who died some months ago; and although I gave them strict charge to make no noise, yet they transgressed, by beating the coombie [a kind of African drum] loud, singing high, etc. Many Negroes there from all over the country." [120] Historians have not found evidence of African precedents for exactly this sort of six-month "throwing water" ceremony; perhaps it related to the Kongolese belief that water separated the world of the living from the world of the dead. Whatever the exact origins, it is likely that this African ritual of memorialization comforted Abba.

At the same time that African-born slaves like Frankie, Quashe, and Abba continued to practice African deathways, some Jamaican-born slaves began to incorporate the mortuary practices of their English masters. When Mulatto Will was dying in 1758, he called Thistlewood to his side. Will told Thistlewood exactly how he wanted his property divided upon his death. Even though slaves in Jamaica and other English plantation colonies could not legally own property, they had customary rights to acquire goods through their lives and pass them on when they died. [121] Thistlewood obliged and wrote down Will's dying wishes: "Write a memorandum, how Mulatto Will's goods are to be disposed of at his death. His wife's shipmate Silvia to have his cow; her daughter Hester, the heifer," and so on. Will's dying wishes about his burial are significant: "he desires to be buried at Salt River at his mother (Dianah's) right hand, and that no Negroes should sing, etc." [122] Through hard work—and likely through the connections provided him by his white parent—Will had accumulated a significant amount of property, which set him apart from most other slaves. He also distanced himself from African burial practices. Although we do not know if he was baptized a Christian, Will's desire to avoid having his funeral become a "play" suggests that he embraced the religion of the master class.

Will's funeral points to the other reason—in addition to increasing numbers of Creoles—why Afro-Caribbean deathways began to change in the second half of the eighteenth century. The slow adoption of some Euro-American deathways was partly the result of some slaves' interest in Christianity. This was a response to the work of missionaries such as the Moravians discussed earlier, in addition to others who arrived toward the end of the eighteenth century: Baptists and Methodists mostly, but some Anglicans as well. In some cases the shift toward Christian burials was coerced, when missionaries made it their business to prevent any hint of African practices from seeping into the burials of their Christian converts. The Anglican missionary Henry Evans Husbands proudly reported from Barbados in 1789, "I am always at hand to baptize, and never suffer a Christian to be buried any other way than as he ought to be, on which occasions I strictly prohibit any of their rude customs to be afterwards practiced over the corpse." [123]

More often, those slaves who began to embrace the teachings of the missionaries were voluntarily attracted to the religious rituals surrounding Christian burial. When missionaries from dissenting denominations initially came to islands where Anglicanism was the established church, it typically took the dissenters several years to secure their own burial grounds. During this period they were at a competitive disadvantage compared to Anglicans. Isaac Bradnack, a Methodist missionary to Barbados, wrote to his superiors in 1804 letting them know just how dire the situation was without a Methodist burial ground.

> Dear sirs you are not unacquainted with the West Indies, in particular with regard to . . . the very great attention paid to the dead in these islands. It hath been said, not only in Barbados, but also other islands, "If you go to the Methodist Chapel, you shall not be interred in the [Anglican] churchyard." And the fear of this prevents many from hearing the Word. This, no doubt, would be removed, had we a burying place of our own. The want of this prevents us from having any to baptize, or many to hear. [124]

For those people of African descent who were becoming Christians in this period, Christian burial was one of the key attractions of the faith. The threat of being denied Christian burial kept them away from the Methodist fellowship, at least until the dissenters could obtain land for a cemetery of their own.

But even people of African descent who adopted aspects of Anglo-American burial often retained some African customs in this transitional period. One example of this is the syncretic funeral that marked the death in 1806 of Jenny, an elderly African-born washerwoman in Barbados, described by the British naval physician George Pinckard. "The females were neatly clad, for the occasion, and mostly in white," wrote Pinckard. In the Caribbean this color of mourning attire was associated with Christian missionaries. Pinckard further detailed that "the corpse was conveyed in a neat small hearse, drawn by one horse. Six boys, twelve men, and forty-eight women walked behind, in pairs." At the graveside, one aspect of the burial so appealed to Pinckard that he recommended it to his countrymen: "The mould was not shoveled in roughly with the spade, almost disturbing the dead . . . but was first put into a basket, and then carefully emptied into the grave; an observance which might be adopted in England very much to the comfort of the afflicted friends of the deceased." When the earth had been gently placed atop the coffin, Jenny's fellow washerwomen cried out, "God bless you, Jenny! Good-bye! Remember me to all friends t'other side of the sea, Jenny! Tell 'em me come soon!" Was this the Christian god they invoked to bless Jenny in the afterlife? In any case, these early nineteenth-century women of African descent still believed in transmigration.[125]

From Bridgetown, the site of Jenny's funeral procession, we travel five miles east along the rutted path to Newton Plantation, where a century earlier the healer and the witch were buried according to a strictly African logic. By the end of the century, the demographic situation on Newton Plantation, as on other plantations throughout the West Indies, had changed dramatically. In 1796, 242 of Newton's 248 slaves were born on the plantation, three were born elsewhere in Barbados, and only 3 (1.2 percent) were born in Africa. After 1805 there were no Africans on the plantation.[126] Among these Creoles, increasing numbers turned to Christian burials, pointing the way toward the not-so-distant moment in the future when nearly all people of African descent in Barbados would be Christian.

One remarkable family of slaves at Newton Plantation was on the leading edge of this change toward Christian burials. This family was led by Old Doll, a black Barbadian-born slave who served as a midwife, her mulatto half-sister Mary Ann Saer, and her mulatto half-brother, George Saer, the plantation's head cooper. As a hardworking artisan who had mastered a craft essential to the economic success of a sugar plantation—without barrels no sugar or rum could be exported—George Saer was the most important slave at Newton, at least in the estimation of the plantation's manager, Sampson Wood. In July 1798 Wood wrote to Newton's absentee owner in England with bad news: "The Negroes all well, except one, the most valuable of all, poor George Saer, a few days now must put a period to him. I have done every thing, Mrs. Wood too, that the greatest care, affection, and tenderness could." As the forty-seven-year-old man lay dying, Wood knew exactly how he wanted to honor his faithful slave. "I mean to give him," Wood pledged, "a handsome burial, what *they* esteem the best reward of services after death, and his richly deserved any thing, a ready, diligent servant in all points, and an honest man in every degree." [127]

In his role as plantation manager, Wood had long acted on his belief that allowing well-behaved slaves latitude to practice their deathways was a way to keep the slaves happy and, more to the point, to keep the plantation running smoothly and profitably. He had the coopers take time out from their valuable work of making casks to build coffins for slaves when they died. For example, on November 21, 1796, he recorded in Newton's account book the labor of two "coopers making a coffin for Aubah." [128] Perhaps George Saer worked that day to build the coffin for his fellow slave. Even more surprising, Wood gave one or sometimes two days off to slaves who were mourning the loss of a loved one. When Violet died in 1797, Wood noted, "Given the day to 5 of her family." These were all first gang slaves, those doing the hardest and most important field work, and three of them got the next day off as well.[129] Why did Wood have coffins made for the slaves and give them days off for mourning when nothing compelled him to do so? The end of the eighteenth century in Barbados and elsewhere in the British West Indies was marked by the conscious "amelioration" of slave conditions. With the abolition of the slave trade seeming every day more possible, plantation owners strove to make their workforce self-reproducing by treating their slaves more humanely.[130] No island had greater success in improving its birth rate than Barbados, and the attention Wood paid to slave deathways was part of this new philosophy of slave management.

Thus it was with sadness that Wood wrote to his employer three months later, in October 1798, that "George Saer, faithful George Saer, your and my friend is no more." As promised, Wood arranged an impressive Christian

funeral. "I gave him a handsome funeral (as I told you I should) as an encouragement to others, and a small tribute to faithful services. I would make
one request in his name, that, if there be not much expense in it, you would
send over a small plain stone for the head of his grave (he was a Christian)
expressing the approbation of his owners for his faithful services, 'twould, I
think, have a good effect." [131] There is no evidence that the plantation owner
ever sent a "small plain" stone. Nor is there any record of how much Saer's funeral cost, but it likely was expensive. His burial was registered by the Christ
Church Parish, which meant that the plantation had to pay the fees for the
clerk to record the death, for the sexton to dig the grave, and probably for the
minister to perform the burial liturgy.[132] For comparison's sake, when Saer's
nephew Ned Thomas died seven years later, the "funeral fees" came to £1 15s,
equivalent to forty-two days of "negro labor" at the rate that slaves were let
out to other plantations.[133] This sort of expenditure demands explanation.
Wood seems to have been genuinely saddened by the loss of his "friend," but
he also had his eye on the bottom line as he arranged Saer's funeral. One of his
reasons for the elaborate funeral was "as an encouragement to others." And he
believed that marking Saer's grave with a headstone would "have a good effect." Through deathways Wood hoped to improve morale on the plantation
and perhaps to encourage other slaves to become Christians. This support for
deathways is evident with the other enslaved members of Saer's family. Ned
Thomas, Mary Ann Saer, and Old Doll all received pricey Christian burials
paid for by the plantation owners, with Mary Ann's topping out at £3 12s 6d
(eighty-seven days of "negro labor"!), which included not only funeral fees
but "hearse hire." [134] Like Mulatto Will on Thomas Thistlewood's Jamaican
plantation, George Saer and the members of his family almost certainly did
not want their deaths to be marked by African-style "plays." They were on the
leading end of the changes that marked the creation of Afro-Christianity.

*   *   *

In west-central Africa, the site of the Kingdom of Kongo and nearby polities
such as Loango and Mbundu, water played important symbolic and material
roles in people's ideas about death and the afterlife. Broadly speaking, the
universe was believed to be divided between the world of the living and the
world of the dead. When a person died, his or her soul crossed a large body
of water to reach the world of the dead. As a result, water was an integral part
of west-central African religious practices, with various rituals of immersion

and cleansing meant to resonate with the crucial water crossing that souls performed after corporeal death. But the body of water between the living and dead was not conceived of as an impermeable barrier. The spirits of the dead maintained contact with the living, influencing their lives and responding to their supplications and rituals.[135]

Likewise, when Africans crossed the Atlantic Ocean and endured the horrors of the Middle Passage, the ocean did not represent an impermeable barrier between the culture and deathways of Africa and the plantations of the New World. Although slaves could not easily travel back across the body of water, the way spirits of the dead could in west-central African cosmology, Africans were able to bring with them the memories of beliefs and practices that had sustained them when confronted with death in their homeland. Their practices could not be transplanted in their entirety to the New World. Too many ritual specialists, locally made goods, and spiritually significant places had been left behind for that. But enough memories came across the waters to sustain a largely African-inspired mortuary program in the early years of Anglo-American slavery.

The eighteenth century was a crucial period of transition from largely African to newly African American deathways. Even as huge numbers of Africans continued to be ripped from their homelands to serve the needs of New World planters, some people of African descent began to adopt aspects of Anglo-American mortuary practices. First to be appropriated was the material culture of death, including pine coffins, linen shrouds, and slate grave markers. Some of these goods could be used without any fundamental change in worldview, substituting for similar African materials.

Next to be appropriated was the spiritual dimension of death. Although Africans in the New World may not have undergone a "spiritual holocaust," as one scholar has controversially claimed, they did over time—as memories of Africa faded farther into the distance—find a spiritual vacuum in their lives that Christianity eventually filled.[136] The adoption of material and spiritual deathways occurred at varying rates throughout the Americas, depending on the ratio of blacks to whites in the local population, the concentration of African-born individuals in the local black population, the presence or absence of other Africans of the same ethnicity, and simple variations in individual disposition. But by 1800, when even on a sugar plantation such as Newton 99 percent of the slaves were born in the New World, the outlines of an emerging Afro-Christianity could be glimpsed in the deathways of people such as Old Doll, George Saer, and Mulatto Will. This would not be precisely the same version of Christianity their masters practiced. These people would change Christianity as they appropriated it, emphasizing its message of equality and love over and against their masters' favorite passage: "servants be obedient to thy masters." Their Afro-Christianity was inflected with some African sensibilities.[137] But their prayers were now to the Christian god, the cherubs on their headstones were ascending to the Christian heaven, and their deathbed scenes drew on centuries of good death literature going back to the *Ars moriendi*. Through their deathways we can see how Africans became African Americans.

CHAPTER 7

Crossing Boundaries, Keeping Faith: Jewish Deathways

IN CONTRAST TO people of African descent, Jews did not experience a great deal of religious change as they became Jewish Americans. Likewise, contact with Christian deathways in the New World changed Jewish deathways less than such contact shaped the beliefs and practices of Africans or, for that matter, American Indians. There are several reasons for this. Jews were not as frequent targets of missionary activity as were Africans and Indians. This is not to say they entirely escaped the unwanted attention of Christian missionaries, but for the most part they less regularly found their beliefs questioned by outsiders. Moreover, Jews were often in a less exploited or vulnerable position vis-à-vis Christians than were Africans and Indians. Even though the number of Jews in the New World remained small through the seventeenth and eighteenth centuries and their communities included many impoverished families, they did not suffer the kinds of demographic stresses that Indians did, and they were not enslaved as Africans were. In addition, Jews had conservative tendencies regarding deathways. As the historian Jonathan Sarna puts it, specifically in reference to Sephardic (Iberian) Jews but applicable to others as well, Jews believed that "ritual could unite those whom life had dispersed." They wanted any Jew "to feel at home in any Sephardic synagogue anywhere in the world: the same liturgy, the same customs, even the same tunes." [1] Jews consequently frowned on religious innovations, particularly in the realm of deathways. And finally, Jews had a written tradition of biblical and postbiblical laws and commentary regarding deathways to which they could turn for guidance, even in an alien environment.

Jewish deathways, however, were not frozen in time. Their practices were, to a certain extent, shaped by their New World surroundings. For example, in one locale—the plantation colony of Suriname—Jewish deathways were shaped by the novel presence of Jewish mulattos. Even more commonly, because New World Jewish communities were often smaller than their European counterparts, they struggled more with the issue of exogamous marriage, as Jews sometimes chose Christian spouses at least in part due to the dearth of suitable marriage partners. Intermarriage and its continual threat to the community's viability shaped Jewish deathways in one crucial regard: more so than in Europe, deathways served as a means to try to prevent Jews from leaving the community.

But the overall story of Jewish deathways in the New World is one of continuity with European precedents. Because of that relative lack of change over time, this chapter, unlike most others in this book, is organized topically rather than chronologically. As Jews confronted an environment with much that was new to them—plantation agriculture, African slaves, American Indians, imperial laws and officials from unfamiliar lands—they worked to preserve their deathways as a strategy to mark the boundaries between themselves and outsiders, and between observant and nonobservant Jews.

*   *   *

A central fact of Jewish life in the New World was the group's status as a religious minority. In towns from Montreal to Recife (Dutch Brazil), Jews found themselves greatly outnumbered by Christians. In their daily lives, Jewish shopkeepers served Christian customers, Jewish women had tea with Christian neighbors, and Jewish children romped with Christian playmates. Although in religious matters Jews almost always sought out other members of their faith, even in this realm Jews occasionally faced unsubtle pressures from ministers such as Cotton Mather and Ezra Stiles to convert to Christianity.

For New World Jews, this interaction with Christians can be traced back to their European roots, as discussed in Chapter 1. For centuries Jews had been an important part of the economy and culture of the Iberian Peninsula. As the historian Todd Endleman observes, Iberian Jews were not forced to live in physical ghettos and they did not choose to create cultural ghettos; in matters of language and dress they more or less resembled their Christian neighbors.[2] The period when Jews were an important part of Iberian culture and economy ended in 1492 when the Spanish crown issued its infamous decree that Jews must convert to Christianity or face expulsion. Portugal adopted a similar policy in 1497, converting Jews to Christians—at least in name—by fiat.[3] Many Jews left the Iberian Peninsula, but many others remained (especially in Portugal) and became conversos—nominal Christians with varying degrees of covert attachment to Judaism. In 1601, Philip III of the United Provinces (Holland) issued an order stating that in exchange for a large payment of badly needed specie, Jews could migrate. Even though Judaism was not yet officially tolerated in Amsterdam, many Iberian conversos emigrated there in the early seventeenth century. As the seventeenth century progressed, Judaism became tolerated in Amsterdam and, after 1639, Sephardic Jews were able to worship openly for the first time in several generations.

This was the golden age of the Netherlands, and Jews participated in the remarkable expansion of the Dutch overseas empire. When in 1630 the Dutch captured Recife in present-day Brazil from the Portuguese, this seemed to many Amsterdam residents to be an opportunity to cash in on the lucrative sugar economy that already flourished there. Along with numerous Christians, approximately 1,500 Jews migrated from Amsterdam to Recife to try their hand at the mercantile activities in which they specialized in Europe.[4] But when the Portuguese (whom the Sephardim remembered all too well from the Inquisition) retook Recife in 1654, the Jews made haste for their ships. Most left for the Dutch Caribbean island of Curaçao, which would support the largest Jewish community in the New World. But one ship was captured by French pirates and unceremoniously unloaded in New Amsterdam (Manhattan), thus laying the foundation for the first Jewish community on mainland North America.

After 1654, European Jews maintained their interest in the New World, emigrating from Amsterdam and, later, London. Most seventeenth-century Jewish emigrants to the New World were thus Sephardim by way of Amsterdam and London. The eighteenth century, by contrast, saw an increasing number of Ashkenazim, from the German states, Poland, and Lithuania. The more recent arrivals were often poorer and less culturally assimilated than their Iberian coreligionists. By the mid-eighteenth century, Ashkenazim predominated numerically in New York, though Sephardic Jews still dominated throughout the Americas financially and religiously, in terms of determining the liturgy used in synagogues. The tensions between these two groups occasionally played themselves out in deathways.

In the New World, Jews clustered in port towns, where they could continue their mercantile activities. Like Quakers and Huguenots, Jews established far-flung economic ties based on ethnicity and religion. The correspondence of New World Jews is filled with evidence of these Atlantic World connections: family members in New York and Newport wrote to loved ones in Nevis and Barbados; financially strapped congregations in Savannah and Philadelphia pleaded for support from London and Curaçao; merchants in Kingston and Charleston traded with Jews from all of the port towns already mentioned. As Jacob Belmonte of Curaçao stated in 1786 when asked his occupation, "I seek my living on land and sea."[5] For the men and women who made dangerous sea voyages—for trade or to find a marriage partner—this Atlantic identity influenced their ideas about death. This impact was especially acute because of a widespread belief that death at sea was particularly ignominious. This idea emerged from not only the inability to give the corpse a proper earth interment within twenty-four hours but also the folk belief that a small bone in the spine needed to be buried in the earth to ensure resurrection. As a result of this fear of death at sea, many Jewish wills began like that of the New York merchant Abraham de Lucena, who wrote his in 1725 explicitly because he was "proceeding upon a voyage to Jamaica considering the dangers of the sea and the uncertainty of this mortal life."[6]

But wherever they journeyed, Jews were forced by necessity to interact with the Christian residents of port towns. Except for Curaçao, where the island's 1,100 Jews made up a substantial proportion of the population, Jewish communities in the Americas were exceedingly small.[7] New York, with the largest Jewish community in mainland North America, had only three hundred Jews (or 2.5 percent of the town's residents) in 1750. The other towns of British North America had even smaller numbers: Newport had perhaps thirty Jewish households in 1770, Philadelphia had even fewer, and between 1741 and 1762 Savannah's Jewish families could be counted on one hand.

Intensifying the interaction between Jews and Christians was the relatively tolerant atmosphere of the New World. Had Jews been locked into ghettos or otherwise persecuted, their interactions with Christians would have been necessarily limited. But Jews encountered little overt discrimination, though there were some exceptions to this rule: the Puritan colonies of Massachusetts and Connecticut were notoriously hostile to outsiders of all stripes in the seventeenth century, and until 1740 Jamaican Jews were taxed at a higher, discriminatory rate.[8] Moreover, except in New York, Jews could not vote or hold public office until after the American Revolution. Aware of their minority status, Jews continued the tactics they had used in Europe and tried not to antagonize their Christian neighbors. Among the very first bylaws of Curaçao's Mikve Israel, passed sometime before 1671, was the injunction that "no one of this Holy Congregation, whether man or woman, shall in any way dare discuss the subject of another religion or scandalize it by curse words or disparagement of their gods." In similarly self-conscious fashion, the executive committee of this same congregation urged Curaçao's Jews to avoid "scandal" and "private hatreds" when a series of recriminations shook the community in 1721. "We well know," the committee observed, "that those who do not care much for us will take note and with this pretext will withhold the little affection they have for us by saying that we are as hateful as pagans."[9]

But overall, New World Jews encountered greater religious and social toleration than they did in most parts of Europe, which, given the small size of the community, heightened the possibility for intermarriage and other centrifugal tendencies. As one historian asserts, the central dynamic of the early American Jewish community was the tension between the preservation of group distinctiveness and assimilation.[10] Although this was also true in London and Amsterdam, the larger size of those Jewish communities made it easier for them to retain a cohesive group identity.[11]

Rituals and beliefs surrounding death are an especially sensitive barometer for gauging this tension between distinctiveness and assimilation, as deathways were central for defining Jewish identity. When Jews brought their deathways from Europe to the Americas, they strongly desired to retain familiar customs. Although there is not a great deal of extant evidence about Jewish deathbed scenes in the New World, it is clear that this highly charged moment between life and death retained a central place in Jewish death rites. The first New World society for presiding at deathbeds was founded in Curaçao between 1686 and 1692. Likewise, when the much smaller New York congregation of Shearith Israel finally reached sufficient size in 1785, members formed the Hebra Gemiluth Hasadim, or the Society for Dispensing Kindness—specifically for the dying, dead, and bereaved. Men and women paid an initiation fee and a small monthly allowance for the privilege of joining these societies so they could help their fellow Jews in times of distress, and so they could have the pleasure of performing such a valuable *mitzvah* or good deed. But the New York society's organizers did not want the proper performance of deathbed scenes to hinge only upon the goodwill of its members, as this entry in its records indicates: "Fine for not sitting up with the sick when summoned, each time," eight shillings (compared to only one shilling for insulting the treasurer!).[12]

Before the establishment of these groups in Curaçao and New York and in other locales without analogous societies, Jews had to rely on less formal networks to provide the requisite watchers for a deathbed scene. This is why Abigail Franks of New York was so proud of her son Naphtali for his conscientious attendance while his uncle lay dying. "Under that great misfortune," she wrote to Naphtali, "you had the satisfaction of employing your indefatigable endeavors in discharging your last duties to him in such a manner as procured you the commendations of all his friends."[13] Not only his doting mother but also the community at large recognized Naphtali's efforts, which (from this abundant praise) may have included attendance at a longer-than-usual deathbed scene.

That the community paid attention to the dying person's deathbed demeanor is attested by the occasional gravestone, such as these two from Barbados: Esther Pinheiro's 1802 stone reported that she was "resigned in death," and twelve-year-old Sarah Nunes Castello was likewise reported in 1782 to have demonstrated "fortitude in her last illness."[14] Evidence for community interest in deathbed behavior may also be found in obituaries, which often described the dying scene. Like Pinheiro and Castello, Elkaleh Seixas was praised for her strength and resignation to God's will. The obituary for Seixas that appeared in the *New York Packet* in 1785 described her "tedious and afflictive illness" which Seixas "endured with a religious fortitude resigned to the holy will of the Supreme, the God of Israel, in which she confided for salvation."[15]

Even more important than deathbed scenes for a community's collective identity, however, was a Jewish burial ground, for the most scrupulous deathbed attention could be undone if there was no place to bury the corpse with proper attention to ritual laws. This too was a continuation of European practices. Almost all Jews would have agreed with Rachel Luis's desire, expressed in her will of 1737: "I wish and order that after my decease my body be interred in a decent manner after and according to the ceremonies used among the Jewish nation."[16] This required a *beth haim* (literally "home of the living," a pious euphemism for a cemetery), or, as another New Yorker familiarly referred to it in 1792, "our burial ground in the City of New York."[17]

Because of this desire, once Jews took up permanent residence in a New World community, one of their first goals was to establish a cemetery. Indeed,

Figure 22. Touro Synagogue, Newport. This building was not completed until 1763, nearly a century after land was set aside for a cemetery. Designed by the noted Rhode Island architect Peter Harrison, it is the oldest synagogue in the United States. Photograph by the author.

the very first piece of evidence that Jews had settled in Newport is the 1677 record of a land transfer from a gentile to two Jews for the purpose of creating a cemetery (Figure 22).[18] Likewise, New York Jews successfully petitioned Governor Peter Stuyvesant to grant them a plot of land for a *beth haim* just eighteen months after their arrival in North America.

As in Newport and New York, Savannah's Jews had been granted access to a "burial place" at "the first of families settling in this province" in 1733. But in a 1762 petition to the colonial legislature, they made clear the inadequacies of this plot: because the original conveyance of land had been vague, the exact boundaries of the burial ground could not be ascertained. As a result, in direct contradiction of Jewish law, "no enclosure thereof could be made." Without walls this burial place did not adhere to the Talmudic requirement that a *beth haim* be protected against incursions made by rooting animals and disrespectful gentiles. But Savannah's Jews were rebuffed by the legislature in their repeated efforts to obtain an adequate cemetery. Lawmakers seem to have concurred with anti-Semitic sentiments among Savannah's Christian residents. Gentiles argued that their property values would decline due to proximity to a cemetery, but their reasoning went beyond typical "not in my backyard" concerns: "they apprehend no person would choose to buy or rent a house whose windows looked into a burial ground of any kind particularly one belonging to a people who might be presumed, from prejudice of education to have imbibed principles entirely repugnant to those of our most holy religion." [19] In response, the legislature continually tabled the Jewish requests for a new cemetery. In the end Savannah's Jews had to rely on private philanthropy: a Jewish leader, Mordecai Sheftall, donated five acres in 1773 to be used as a *beth haim*.[20] At last, a six-foot-high brick wall could be built around the cemetery. Now properly protected, the *beth haim* served as a magnet for Jews throughout the region. Mrs. Moses Nathans made the journey from Pohetalligo, South Carolina, to die and be buried "where there were Jews." And little Jacob Henry, but a few days old when he died, was carried by his father the 110 miles from Vainsborough, Georgia, so he could be circumcised and properly buried in Savannah.[21]

Even in the relatively open and tolerant atmosphere of the New World, Jewish cemeteries were—as in Savannah—occasionally the focus of Christian resentment. In both 1746 and 1751 Jews placed ads in the New York *Weekly Post-Boy* offering a reward for information about the "malicious and evil-minded persons" who had done "very considerable damage both to the walls and tombs of the Jewish burying-place." In 1751 Philadelphia's *beth haim* was damaged, but in this case Nathan Levy, the author of the notice in the *Pennsylvania Gazette*, blamed "unthinking" individuals who had been "setting up marks, and firing several shots against the fence of the Jews' burying ground," which damaged the fence and a gravestone.[22] Whether the errant marksmen were merely "unthinking" or closer to the "malicious and evil-minded" New Yorkers is unclear. What is certain, however, is that while New World Jews generally received fair treatment from colonial governments, prejudiced individuals occasionally took out their resentments on the physical manifestations of Jewish deathways.[23]

But while isolated acts of hate surely troubled New World Jews, even more threatening to the community's continued viability was, ironically, tolerance, or specifically the possibility for intermarriage with the much larger Christian population. Given the small size of the New World's Jewish communities, it was always at least a theoretical possibility that individuals would assimilate and intermarry to such an extent that a distinctive Jewish identity in the Americas might be lost. For the large majority of Jews who wished to prevent such a situation, burial proved an ideal way of policing religious boundaries. To prevent their members from being swallowed by the surrounding gentile population, many congregations tried to use the desire for proper Jewish burial that still resided in the hearts of many assimilated Jews as a lure to keep people within the fold of the Jewish community. As one historian eloquently puts it, "Time and again, the exigencies of life drew individuals away from their people and their faith, and the mystery of death brought them back." [24]

Congregations therefore used the "mystery of death" as both an inducement for straying members to return and as a punishment for those who strayed too far. For example, in 1752 Congregation Shearith Israel in New York stated that "any person, that in his life time absented himself from the Synagogue, or was no ways a benefactor to the Congregation," would not be buried within the walls of the cemetery unless the elders of the community ruled otherwise. [25] The focus on whether the deceased had been a "benefactor" or regular contributor to the congregation reveals that one motivation behind policing the boundary of who could be buried in the *beth haim* was financial. New World Jews, with the possible exception of those in Curaçao, were continually aware that their congregations were on shaky financial footings. More Jews drifting away from the core community meant more Jews who did not pay to support the synagogue.

Given this reality, most communities passed regulations like the one in New York, restricting burial to those individuals who were in good financial standing with the congregation. When Philadelphia Jews wrote their first synagogal constitution in approximately 1770, they included just such a provision. It was under the authority of this restriction that the *parnass* (president) of the Philadelphia congregation acted in 1793 when a man named Solomon Raphael petitioned for permission to have his child buried in the cemetery. The *parnass* ruled that the corpse could be interred in the *beth haim*, but only if Raphael paid "his 2 years' contribution toward the support of the shoehet [ritual slaughterer], at 30s. per annum, also the sum of two pounds 5s. for his free will offerings, at the time his child was circumcised." [26] For Jews such as Raphael whose poverty or tenuous connections with the Jewish community caused them to avoid paying their dues, this was no choice at all: he made the payments and they buried the child.

But other conflicts reveal that while financial concerns were partly responsible for burial restrictions, the deeper concern was over the definition of the community. Jews who did not follow Jewish laws in life, for example, represented a threat to the traditionalist community. Lion Norden was a Jew born in Amsterdam who lived in Jamaica and eventually moved to Savannah in 1798. When he died he was granted burial within the *beth haim*, but not without controversy. Levi Sheftall, one of Savannah's most prominent Jews, fumed in his diary (and likely with others whose ear he could bend) that Norden "ought not to have been buried amongst the Jews but ought to have lain without the wall" because he "kept no day." Sheftall elaborated on his reasoning as to why Norden should have been buried outside the cemetery's walls: "he kept open his store on all our holy days." [27] This was a case in which the congregation opted for inclusion of a wayward soul, even though at least one leading member of the community favored a more restrictive definition.

In contrast with the inclusive impulse of the Savannah congregation, the sad case of Lunah Arrobus of Barbados demonstrates how burial rituals were used to exclude an individual considered outside the fold. Arrobus was born a Jew and converted to Christianity. But when she died in 1792 her corpse was shunned by both her natal and adoptive communities. Barbadian Christians, apparently unconvinced of the sincerity of her conversion, would not bury her, and so the government ordered the Jews to bury her in the *beth haim*. Aiming to avoid antagonizing the government, Barbadian Jews agreed to do so—but with several important ritual restrictions. Congregants were forbidden to "be concerned in aiding or assisting in digging her grave or washing her." How then would the corpse find its way into the earth? "They will bring negroes to dig her grave." Yet even this potent symbol of outsider status was not enough. The corpse was to be interred in "the Nook," an irregular corner of the cemetery, and furthermore "it was directed that a way should be built to divide the Nook from the Bet Haim and a door to be put at the end in front of the street so that that part shall have not communication with the other." [28] With this elaborate—and costly—solution, Barbadian Jews demonstrated their resolve to stand firm against those congregants who might be considering conversion to Christianity.

But not all burial conflicts among New World Jews pitted observant individuals against their more lax co-religionists. In Curaçao between 1744 and 1750, a dispute within the observant community that originally had nothing to do with burial practices eventually played itself out most dramatically within the walls of the *beth haim*, demonstrating that deathways are among the most potent symbols of group unity and disunity. The late 1740s were turbulent throughout the island. Protestants and Jews had become accustomed to calm prosperity, but this complacency was shaken by a series of disturbing events: several high-profile murders, a terrible drought, war between France and Holland, and finally a slave uprising that led to the execution of thirty-six alleged participants.[29] But for the Curaçaon Jewish community the troubles may be dated to the 1744 arrival from Amsterdam of Samuel Mendes De Sola to serve as *hakham* (sage or rabbi). Almost immediately De Sola alienated a portion of Curaçao's Jews with his abrasive style and his meddling in secular affairs. For several years tensions built between De Sola and the *parnassim* on one side, and several leading families with about seventy supporters making up the opposition.

It became clear that the conflict had reached a new level of animosity when the cemetery became a battleground. De Sola had excommunicated several members of the opposition for a variety of indiscretions. When one of these individuals, Ishac Lopes Dias, died in April 1749, De Sola ordered that his corpse be treated with certain discriminations. The prayers and ceremonies of the burial remained unchanged, but the corpse itself was treated with disrespect. Unfortunately, the records do not specify precisely what was done to the corpse, but the best-informed historians of this community suggest that the coffin may have been dragged rather than carried in the cemetery, or stones may have been cast onto the coffin in a symbolic stoning of the deceased.[30]

Mordechay Alvares Correa had seen enough. This highly respected merchant and moderate oppositionist resigned as leader of the gravediggers' society. But Correa's protest had little effect. In October 1749 two members of the opposition died and at each funeral the corpses were treated with disrespect. To the horror of many, these burial discriminations led to fistfights in the cemetery between the two factions.

The sad scene of Jew pummeling Jew, however, was not nearly as dramatic as the fireworks that followed Correa's death. Perhaps worn down by so much infighting, the sixty-five-year-old Correa contracted what turned out to be his final illness in the early months of 1750. Near death, Correa drew up his will and specified that only his friends were to wash and bury him: he did not want De Sola's faction to have the opportunity to treat his corpse with disrespect. But Correa was not about to take any chances. He included in his will a sizable bequest of 500 florins to the Protestant church hoping that the minister and elders would help prevent any indignities.[31]

When Correa died the evening of May 24, 1750, the Protestant minister declined to intervene, despite the generous bequest. So several of Correa's supporters took matters into their own hands. Under cover of darkness, they broke down the walls of the *beth haim* and removed the gates so De Sola could not lock them out of the cemetery. In response, De Sola begged the Protestant governor of the island, Isaac Faesch, for military support. The governor dispatched twenty-two soldiers to protect the cemetery. But Correa's supporters, according to Faesch's report to the Dutch West Indies Company, "pushed through the guards who had orders not to defend themselves, as this would have started a revolution on the island." De Sola had hoped that the soldiers would keep Correa's supporters away from the cemetery, but the show of force had the opposite effect. According to the governor, from "500 to 600 Christians and Jews, whites as well as coloreds and mulattos" attended the funeral.[32] Correa's dying wish was fulfilled: his corpse received no indignities.

The funeral's impact on the Jewish community was no less important, as the great show of support for Correa put De Sola into an untenable position. So when Prince William of the Netherlands ordered the Curaçaon Jews to cease their infighting, both sides managed to put aside their differences and reach a reconciliation. Perhaps De Sola had learned that it was one thing to harass a dissident faction with fines and sharply worded sermons but quite another to interfere with their deathways.

In the Curaçao burial conflict it is impossible to label one group "insiders" and another "outsiders"; both factions had strong claims to prestige and power within the community. More typically, though, Jewish burial conflicts involved an insider and an outsider group, and such was the case in the conflict that rocked Suriname's Jewish community in the 1790s. But in Suriname, unlike any other place in the New World, the outsiders were Jewish mulattos.

It is a peculiarity of the Jewish experience in the New World that even though some Jews owned slave plantations and some Jewish men undoubtedly had sexual relations with women of African descent, a distinct community of Jewish mulattos formed in Suriname and nowhere else. In Curaçao, Jamaica, and other places where Jews owned slaves, there are almost no recorded examples of Jews trying either to convert their slaves to Judaism or to raise their mulatto offspring as Jews. Nor, outside of Suriname, is there any evidence of individuals of African descent being buried in Jewish cemeteries.[33] Partly this is due to Judaism's nonproselytizing character: this is a religion by birth and not, generally, by conversion. And partly this is because Judaism had for millennia evolved regulations for treating slaves as something less than human, as is clear from this statement in the sixteenth-century Code of Hebrew Law regarding mourning rites for slaves: "For male and female slaves no line [of comforters] is made, nor is consolation offered [to their master], but they say to him, 'May the Lord replace your loss,' even as they say to a man regarding his ox and ass, ['May the Lord replace your loss.']" [34] The question remains, however, why Suriname should be the exception to the rule of not raising mulatto offspring as Jews. Perhaps it is because, compared with the rest of the New World, more Jews in this prosperous Dutch colony in the northeastern corner of South America made their living as plantation owners than as urban merchants. In 1730, Jews owned 115 of Suriname's 401 plantations and held perhaps 20,000 slaves. The average Jewish-owned plantation, therefore, exploited the labor of nearly 175 slaves. By comparison, in the 1760s Curaçao's 159 slave-owning Jews owned only 867 slaves, or roughly 5.5 per owner. [35]

In the cross-cultural interaction between Jews and Africans, it is difficult to say whether African deathways influenced Jews at all. But Jewish influence on Africans is much easier to document. In Suriname one of the most obvious manifestations of this influence was in language: many slaves developed a Creole language called Djoe-tongo, or Jew tongue, which combined African elements with the Portuguese vocabulary of Sephardic slave owners. [36] The other clear outcome of this interaction was the Jewish mulattos themselves, the offspring that resulted from sexual liaisons between Jewish men and African women. In some cases, mulattos were conceived when slave owners sexually abused their female slaves, but these offspring were probably not raised as Jews. More likely to be brought up as Jews were the children who resulted from a "marriage Suriname-style," the contemporary term for a marriage or, more often, cohabitation between a free mulatto woman and a European (Christian or Jewish) man. [37]

By the 1760s there were at least several dozen Jewish mulattos who sought to practice their religion with their white co-religionists. But the leaders of Suriname's Jewish community made it clear that mulattos could participate only as second-class citizens. As early as 1754, the Paramaribo congregation passed a series of rules codifying the lower status of the Jewish mulattos. The mulattos could never be full members, only congregants. They were relegated to the mourners' bench in the synagogue and they could not receive a blessing in the synagogue. Finally, the synagogue had a separate *Porta dos Negros*, "door for blacks," to serve as a physical reminder of the mulattos' inferior status. [38]

Suriname's Jewish mulattos had little choice but to accept these demeaning regulations, though in response they founded in 1759 a religious brotherhood called Darhe Jesarim (Way of the Righteous). This fraternity existed inconspicuously for over thirty years before it became the center of controversy in the 1790s. It began with the April 1790 burial of a Jewish mulatto, Joseph de David Cohen Nassy. The brotherhood, as usual for one of its members, prepared the corpse and organized the procession to the cemetery. But when they arrived at the *beth haim*, they found that the grave opened by the congregation's white gravediggers was "in a swamp" and thus full of water, and dug "only one foot deep." When they protested to the gravediggers they were told, "You cannot give orders here, and if you folks do not shut up we will shut you up." [39]

The mulattos complained to the synagogue's leaders, but they were surprised when the incident caused the leaders to investigate Darhe Jesarim. The inquiry was led by the secretary of the executive committee, David Cohen Nassy. This wealthy Nassy seems to have been the former owner of the poor mulatto Nassy—could he have been the deceased man's father too? If Nassy was the dead man's father, his ruling contained no shred of paternal feeling. Instead Nassy complained that the fraternity was not burying its members according to proper Jewish law. It turned out that the religious brotherhood of mulattos had buried Joseph de David Cohen Nassy—and perhaps others— with ceremonies reserved for a *parnass*. They had used wax candles in the procession, and the mourners themselves, instead of the cantor, had recited the mourning prayers. By these small gestures the members of Darhe Jesarim had tried to add a hint of pomp to an otherwise humble burial. David Cohen Nassy and the congregation's other white leaders would not allow such usurpations of the postmortem symbols of esteem, and in 1793 they proscribed and disbanded the Way of the Righteous. [40]

If Jewish mulattos raised troubling questions of identity in Suriname, the issue that most threatened Jewish identity in the rest of the New World was intermarriage with Christians. Exogamous marriage had always been considered problematic by observant Jews; indeed, in folk custom, one's child who married outside the Jewish fold was mourned as if dead. [41] It is important to remember, though, that from the perspective of the Jew who took a Christian spouse this did not necessarily or even usually mean a renunciation of Judaism. Consider the case of Michael Judah. This modest merchant left New York City in the 1740s to take up business in the less competitive atmosphere of Fairfield, Connecticut. Although Judah married a Christian woman, he tried to keep a kosher house. And when he died, he left his Christian son only £5 and divided the remainder of his estate equally between "the Synagogue in New York" and "the poor widows and orphans of my own nation, living in New York."[42]

But in the New World context, with the ever-present possibility of being swallowed up by the much larger Christian population, most Jews were unsatisfied with such gestures. For the large majority that worked very hard to find themselves and their children suitable Jewish spouses, this issue was not to be taken lightly, which is reflected in the group's deathways. In 1778, for example, Montreal's congregation confronted this sensitive situation: Ezekiel Solomons, a Jew who had married a gentile, sought burial within the walls of the *beth haim* for his recently deceased uncircumcised son. The elders were presented with "several circumstances favorable to the said Ezekiel Solomons," but they feared setting a dangerous precedent, so they engineered a Solomonic compromise. The child could be buried, "but," they announced, "no man or boy, whomsoever shall be, after sixty days from this date, [shall] be buried in the burying place of this congregation unless circumcised."[43] This declaration, the congregation hoped, would blunt the tendency of Jews who married outside the faith to raise their children as Christians.

Philadelphia's Jews grappled with a similar case in 1785, but in this instance Solomon met his Jereboam, with explosive results for the community. On March 15 the congregation learned that Benjamin Moses Clava, a local merchant, had died. A man of "great Jewish learning," Clava had married a gentile some years before in a civil ceremony. In their wedded state this interfaith couple had produced two daughters. Despite all of this, while alive, Clava expressed his desire to be buried in the Jewish cemetery.[44]

This was no time for leisurely perusal of Jewish laws and debate with rabbis far and wide; "the corpse was waiting to be buried." But the situation also presented the congregation with the opportunity to make a statement about their disapproval of intermarriage. Indeed, their decision was made explicitly within the context of preserving Jewish identity despite a growing tide of assimilation: "Since many, to our sorrow, are in the same predicament, some mode of burial ought to be adopted different from the usual way of burying good Jews." Perhaps denial of burial rites would prevent others from migrating out of the camp of "good Jews."

But a complete denial of Jewish burial struck those assembled as too harsh, so they forged a compromise: "The dead man shall be buried in a corner of the cemetery, without ritual washing, without shrouds, and without a ceremony, but four boys shall carry him to the grave and bury him, and the shrouds that have been prepared shall be put into the casket, but he shall not wear them." Despite these tough measures, the corpse would still be interred within the walls of the cemetery. And—key for policing the boundaries of the community—this decision would permanently apply "to all transgressors who shall marry out of the faith."

All seemed well. A reasonable decision had been reached, and all that remained was for the *parnass*, Benjamin Nones, to go to the house of mourning to deliver the congregation's verdict. But Nones was shocked by what he found: several men had already begun to ritually prepare the corpse. The ringleader of this dissident group was Mordecai Moses Mordecai, a native of Lithuania already entangled in a dispute with the congregation. Nones warned the men to stop, but Mordecai disregarded the *parnass* and quoted Jewish laws to support his position. Nones grabbed the shrouds and cut them to shreds but his efforts were futile: Mordecai and his allies washed the body and clothed it as well as they could in the mangled linen. It is unclear what happened next, but somehow the coffined Clava was interred in the *beth haim*.

For those who formulated the original compromise, this incident was sadly representative of the "great lack of discipline that prevails in our generation." Mordecai's actions, they felt, were nothing less than a direct attack on the congregation's power to determine who were "good Jews" who deserved full burial rites. But Mordecai may have simply been offering another response to the problem of assimilation in the New World. A man "well learned in Jewish law," Mordecai had, after all, been touched closely by the issue of intermarriage. His niece had eloped with a gentile and been married in a Christian ceremony in May 1782. To effect a reconciliation between the young woman and her incensed father (Mordecai's brother), Mordecai remarried the couple in a Jewish ceremony. Though the congregation strenuously objected, citing his lack of authority to perform such a ceremony, Mordecai's actions paralleled what he would do three years later in the Clava affair: offer a creative and nonpunitive solution to the dilemmas encountered by Jews in a Christian land.[45]

Although Benjamin Moses Clava's Christian wife presumably did not sit shivah for him, most New World Jews followed European traditions and could expect their loved ones to mourn their death according to Jewish laws. Unfortunately, records describing these practices are hard to find for the seventeenth and eighteenth centuries. But in addition to distinctively Jewish customs, Jews borrowed some mourning traditions from Christians, especially regarding material culture. In Jewish law there was no requirement for a distinctive mourning costume for men or women: ordinary garments were rent in grief, and the rent itself served as a badge of deep mourning. Nonetheless, when well-off Jews wrote their wills they often provided funds for mourning attire. Isaac Pinheiro of Nevis left £10 in his 1710 will to two of his "loving friends" so they could each purchase a "mourning suit." Samuel Myers Cohen, a wealthy New York merchant, left £25 to each of his executors in 1743 for a "mourning suit," whereas a less prosperous New Yorker asked that his brothers and sisters make do with only £5 each. Some Jews also provided mourning rings for their loved ones: one man named six recipients of mourning rings and Samuel Myers Cohen lavished rings valued at forty shillings each on nine different people.[46] Historians have not identified any Jewish mourning rings from the eighteenth century, but because this aspect of material culture was borrowed from Christians, the rings likely employed standard Christian iconography such as winged death's heads. Mourning suits and rings were not required by Jewish laws, but neither did they transgress the letter or spirit of the laws.

One way Jewish mourning differed from Christian mourning in the eighteenth century was in the broader range of sources of wisdom and comfort Jews drew upon. With forebears from European locales as divergent as the Iberian Peninsula and Poland, and with continued contact with friends and relatives around the Atlantic, New World Jews called upon an impressive array of ideas to cope with death. The case of New Yorker Abigail Franks is instructive. Franks was by no means a typical Jewish woman in the eighteenth-century Atlantic: she was literate in English (we know about her mostly from her extensive correspondence with her son), she read widely in European sources such as the London-based *Gentleman's Magazine*, and, though she kept kosher and observed the Sabbath, she was uncomfortable with some Jewish customs she felt were mere "Superstitions."[47]

As a result, when she was confronted with the death of a loved one, Franks relied on a variety of traditions to make sense of the situation. In response to the "melancholy" news that her relative Bilah Franks had died in 1748, Abigail worried that Bilah's husband Aaron would be distraught. But she remembered that "in Scripture we find these Words[,] And Judah lost his wife and was comforted." Abigail herself found comfort in these words from Genesis 38, as it made her think Aaron would not be overly upset. But she also relied on a Spanish folk saying: "dolor de' Codo Y: dolor de Esposo Devello mucho mas duro poco," to the effect that "a pain in the elbow and the pain for a [lost] spouse hurts a great deal, but lasts a short time."[48] At another time, Franks responded to the death of a close relation both by holding out the promise of the afterlife (from "this world to a state of bliss where all is at rest and cares preside no more") and by quoting from *The Dispensary*, a poem written in 1726 by the Englishman Sir Samuel Garth. Though atypical in being able to quote Georgian poets from memory, Franks shared with other Jews a wide-ranging repository of ideas to employ in mourning.

Atlantic-world Jews also drew on a wide range of sources when they memorialized the dead. Some of these sources were distinctively Jewish and followed European patterns. Sephardic naming practices were meant to honor one's forebears and to remember them after they died. Traditionally, the first-born son was named after his paternal grandfather and the second-born son received the name of his mother's father. Likewise, the first-born daughter was named after her paternal grandmother, while the second-born daughter bore the name of her mother's mother. In eighteenth-century Suriname, for example, 90 percent of recorded Jewish births followed this pattern. Furthermore, if one of these children named after a grandparent died, the next child born of the same sex would receive the same name, sometimes with the addition of *Haim* (life), a plea to God to grant the newborn child life. In Curaçao, Benjamin Da Costa de Andrade lost three sons named after his father: Yosseph died in 1716; "Do segundo Yosseph," the second Yosseph, died in 1719; and little "Yosseph Haim de Benjamin," who was not granted a long life, died in 1720.[49]

The importance of these naming practices is revealed in wills. Aged relatives often left especially generous bequests to their namesakes—born or unborn—because these youngsters allowed the memory of their elders to live on. Esther Senior of Curaçao, for example, left her identically named niece Esther Senior "for bearing my name . . . a slave Suzanna with her son Matthias . . . a gold ring, a pair of earrings with white stones and all my clothing." Joseph Hisquiau Rodrigues da Costa, also of Curaçao, went so far as to make his bequest conditional. His 1756 will specified that the unborn son of his brother Isaac Haim would receive 500 pesos, so long as he was named Joseph.[50] One generally does not find Christians of the same era making similar demands.

Whereas these naming practices were distinctly Jewish, another facet of memorialization owed some of its inspiration to Christian influence. Jews believed that memorial prayers (usually Kaddish) offered by survivors helped the soul of the deceased attain peace in the hereafter. This belief, according to the historian Jacob Rader Marcus, "certainly harked back to the medieval

Catholic theology to which all European Jews had been exposed for over a millennium." [51] Indeed, the *hashkabah*, or prayer of repose (called an "escaba" by many Sephardim), was motivated by a belief in the purgatory-like Gehenna: memorial prayers helped the soul safely reach heaven after a year-long sojourn in Gehenna.

As in Europe, New World Jews counted on their family members—and in particular their children—to ensure that Kaddish was said for them during the year after their death. But if one did not have any children, or just wanted a little extra insurance, one might include a bequest in one's will in exchange for someone offering prayers. In some cases this could be a form of charity, as in 1737 when the Jamaican merchant Mordecai da Silva willed £5 to a young orphan boy "for to say a funeral prayer used in our Synagogue during the time of eleven month after my decease." [52] Though da Silva, like most testators, did not explicitly state his reasons for paying for memorial prayers, Abraham Mendes de Castro of Curaçao did. According to his 1752 will, de Castro left 100 pesos for memorial prayers simply so that "God may receive me." Because this goal was so important, some Jews worried that those they entrusted to say Kaddish for them would neglect their duties. As a result, some testators made their bequests provisional. Before Jacob Hisquiau de Leon of Curaçao died in 1760, he included this legacy in his will: "I leave Jeudah Alva the sum of one hundred pesos to say 'Cadis' for me only on condition that he say it for the eleven months [of mourning] when he shall be paid, and in default thereof this bequest shall remain null and void." [53] No leaving such an important matter to chance for de Leon.

Starting among the Jews of seventeenth-century Amsterdam, a new memorialization practice emerged. Some individuals began to leave bequests so that memorial prayers would be said on their behalf in perpetuity. This practice lagged a bit in the New World: it was not common in Curaçao until 1700 or so and it did not become common in New York until the middle of the eighteenth century. But after those dates comfortably well-off Jews often left a sum of money to the synagogue in return for one or more yearly escabas said in their memory. Colonial New York's Jews would be happy to know that Congregation Shearith Israel continues to honor their wishes. Early New Yorkers who continue to be memorialized include Isaac Gomez, whose 1770 will left £15 to the synagogue in exchange for several yearly escabas, and the merchant Sampson Simson, who asked for a yearly escaba in return for his bequest of £20. [54] Cash-strapped congregations soon grasped the fundraising potential of these perpetual mourning prayers. When Philadelphia's Jews were trying to raise money in 1782 to erect a synagogue (after several decades of worshipping in people's homes), they auctioned off the privilege of underwriting the four cornerstones. In anticipation of the auction, the congregation noted that the four highest bidders "shall be entitled to have an *escoba* on each anniversary day of the dedication and on every Kippur night forever." [55]

But some congregations began to find that people's strong desire for perpetual memorialization led to some problems. In Kingston, Jamaica, the congregation was faced with at least two individuals who wanted their memorial prayers to be set off from those of the common hordes. David Bravo left the hefty sum of £100 to his synagogue in 1749 in exchange for an annual "prayer called Scava," but he attached the following proviso: "I do hereby further direct that no other person or persons name or names shall be named or read in the reading [of] the said Scava but my own." It seems that the congregation accepted this rather self-aggrandizing restriction, though they may have regretted the decision, for less than five years later Abraham Gonsales demanded similar treatment in return for his own bequest of £100. The synagogue could collect the cash "upon this condition, that there be had for me an Escava on our fast day called Kippur in the same manner as was done for the late David Bravo deceased." [56] The congregation may have decided to nip this trend in the bud and refuse Gonsales's money, as there are no further examples of Jamaican testators invoking the Bravo precedent.

As with naming practices and memorial prayers, Jewish cemeteries were likewise central to remembering the dead—and they similarly display a wide range of influences. In New World Jewish cemeteries, one finds gravestones with inscriptions in Hebrew, English, Spanish, Portuguese, Judeo-Portuguese, even Latin. Moreover the iconography combines Jewish and Christian images, oftentimes on the same stone. Common images unique to Jewish cemeteries include hands raised in blessing as a symbol of the *Cohanim*, or the priestly caste, a synagogue scene portraying three Levites performing their ritual service, and carvings incorporating the biblical figure whose name the deceased bore. This latter group includes numerous stones of individuals named Abigail, David, Esther, Mordecai, Moses, and others. But New World Jews were also comfortable using Christian symbols of the transience of life such as winged hourglasses and death's heads (Figure 23). In the second half of the eighteenth century, Jews followed the Anglo-American shift away from glowering death's heads and toward chubby cherubim.

In this multiplicity of influences, New World Jewish cemeteries differed little from those in London and Amsterdam. [57] Indeed, due to a dearth of

Figure 23. Ishac Haim Senior gravestone, Curaçao. Senior died in 1726 and his stone (on the left) contains several human figures. At the top Senior is represented by Isaac Aboab da Fonseca, an Amsterdam rabbi, as copied from a 1686 engraving by a Christian artist, Aernout Naghtegael. At the bottom is a deathbed scene, presumably Senior's, with several weeping observers. The Portuguese epitaph indicates that he "suffered infinite martyrdoms of illness" while he lay dying. The stone on the right contains several images of the transience of life usually associated with Christian gravestones, including a winged hourglass and two skulls. Courtesy of Jacob Rader Marcus Center of the American Jewish Archives.

local carvers with the facility to render Hebrew letters accurately, New World Jews often ordered their stones from Europe. In his 1722 will, Isaac Henriques Alvin of Jamaica declared that his executors should "as soon as conveniently can be after my decease purchase in Great Britain three new large marble tombstones of dark blue color and of a good thickness to be sent to Jamaica to cover three graves": his own, his brother's, and his sister's.[58] Most other Jamaican Jews joined Alvin in this practice; the apparently homemade stone of Jacob Torres from 1696, carved from local sandstone with a crudely cut inscription, is unique.[59] Like their co-religionists in Jamaica, the Jews of Barbados, New York, and Newport seem to have imported their stones from London, while Curaçao's Jews sent out to Amsterdam.[60]

Despite these similarities in origins, the gravestones in each of these New World cemeteries reflected, to an extent, local circumstances. The stones in Newport and New York were relatively restrained in terms of stone carving; they appear downright dowdy when compared with the exuberant carving present on Jamaican and Curaçaon stones.[61] This may reflect the relative wealth and size of the different communities, as New York's and Newport's Jews were decidedly less prosperous on the whole than their Caribbean counterparts. But there may have been other factors at work. In particular, Jews in New York seem to have adhered more closely than other communities to the Jewish principle of equality in death. Without elaborate carvings, the stones of the wealthiest differed little from the stones of their humbler neighbors. Moreover, the New Yorkers may have been less comfortable with human images on their gravestones, which perhaps seemed to transgress the Second Commandment's stricture against "graven images."

Such concerns apparently did not trouble Caribbean Jews. As relatively recent returnees to rabbinic Judaism (after more than a century in the Iberian Peninsula when the open practice of Judaism was prohibited), they embraced the iconographic traditions of the lands in which they lived. In Jamaica many gravestones can be found with skulls and crossbones, numerous stones depict a hand descending from the clouds to fell a tree (Figure 24), and at least two represent the faces of angels.[62] A Barbadian gravestone goes so far as to seemingly represent God—with face and body visible—cutting down the Tree of Life.[63] Curaçaon stones, like their counterparts in Amsterdam's *beth haim* at Ouderkerk, are even more likely to depict human figures. Abraham Henriques's monument, made in Amsterdam from expensive Carrara marble in 1726, shows him confidently piloting his ship through a light chop. Other stones represent the deathbed scene of the deceased. In some of these cases,

Figure 24. David Senior gravestone, Curaçao. Unlike many Curaçaon stones, Senior's is carved only in Portuguese. His year of death is reckoned by both the Jewish calendar (5492) and the Christian one (1731). The image of God chopping down the tree of life usually represents a life cut short. This is a horizontal slab, lying flat over the tomb it covers, as were all the markers in Curaçao's Jewish Cemetery. Courtesy of Jacob Rader Marcus Center of the American Jewish Archives.

the deathbed scene is allegorized, represented as a biblical story to distance it from the actual deathbed. Sara Hana's stone of 1761, for example, shows a woman dying while giving birth in a tent under a tree. Hana surely did not die in a tent; the reference is to the biblical Rachel, who in Genesis 35:18 died giving birth to Benjamin while traveling through the desert.[64] The 1726 monument to Ishac Haim Senior, by contrast, depicts the deathbed scene more realistically, with observers sitting in period chairs and weeping into handkerchiefs as Senior points toward heaven (Figure 23).

Ishac Senior included another depiction of a recognizable human character: he is represented by Isaac Aboab da Fonseca, an Amsterdam rabbi, as copied from a 1686 mezzotint by the artist Aernout Naghtegael (Figure 23). If a Christian's engraving of a rabbi seems an unlikely source for a Jewish Curaçaon stone, consider the source for the human figures on Esther Senior's 1714 marker. The representation of the biblical Esther pleading her case before King Ahasuerus (Figures 25 and 26) is "almost a line-for-line copy" of a woodcut from a Christian Latin Bible published in Lyon in 1581![65] Jews today are often surprised by the profusion of images that would now be considered by many to be transgressions of the Second Commandment. But eighteenth-century Caribbean Jews, remembering the dark decades when Sephardim were forced to convert or keep their beliefs secret, seem to have rejoiced in their ability to proclaim to the world their faith and their varied cultural inheritances.

Like iconography, epitaphs also demonstrate the wide range of influences on New World Jews. In this period the languages on the stones change over time: in the seventeenth century markers are usually inscribed in Portuguese (or Spanish) and Hebrew; then English is added to the mix on many early eighteenth-century stones; finally, by the end of the eighteenth century, Portuguese and Spanish appear less and less, and most stones are cut in Hebrew and English or English only. But in all these permutations, one constant remains: epitaphs are almost never translated from one language to the other. Instead, New World Jews adhere to the conventions of each language, demonstrating their flexibility in adopting the local vernacular to their own needs and desires. Two admittedly extreme examples of this flexibility may be found in the Caribbean. On the Dutch island of St. Eustatius, home to a small but prosperous Jewish community, the gravestone of Hannah Mears declares that she "departed this life Jan[ua]ry the 18th A D 1768." To use the abbreviation for *anno Domini*, "the year of the Lord," was a concession to Christian conventions that very few Jews were willing to make. A similar example of

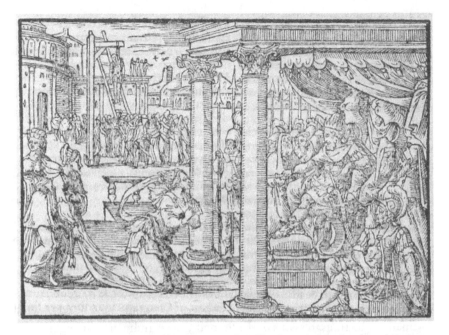

Figures 25 and 26. "Esther before Ahasuerus," *Biblia Sacra* (1581), above, and Esther Senior's gravestone, Curaçao, right. The woodcut, by Pierre Eskrich, is from a Latin Bible published in Lyon, France. This image served as the model for the carving on Esther Senior's 1712 gravestone. Like virtually all stones in the cemetery, this one was carved in Amsterdam and shipped to Curaçao. Courtesy of New York Public Library, Astor, Lenox, and Tilden Foundations (Figure 25), and Jacob Rader Marcus Center of the American Jewish Archives (Figure 26).

cultural flexibility may be found in the Barbados *beth haim*, on a 1699 stone carved in Hebrew, Portuguese, and English. In Portuguese the deceased is referred to as "Joseph Jessurun Mendez," while in English he is called "Mr Lewis Dias." Mendez/Dias, perhaps in order to be "respected by *all* men in his time" as his tombstone asserts he was, apparently went by two different appellations in the two vernacular languages he used in his business life.[66]

While this level of flexibility in terms of self-presentation was unusual, the different languages on Jewish gravestones typically adhere to different epitaph formulas. In English, for example, Jewish stones follow the historical shifts in epitaph conventions of the broader Anglo-American world. From the late seventeenth century through the middle of the eighteenth century,

most English-language Christian stones begin with some version of "here lies the body of" or "here lies interred." [67] After that, many Christian stones open with "in memory of" or "sacred to the memory of" the deceased. English-language Jewish stones follow this pattern. No doubt this is partly because the stone carvers who incised these monuments did so according to prevailing conventions. But presumably Jews could have requested alternate wording if the conventions troubled them; they apparently did not make such requests.

Take the stones in Jamaica. In 1692 Moses de Lucena was buried beneath a stone with an inscription in Hebrew, Portuguese, and English. The monument's English border states, "Here lieth interred the body of Mr Moseh de Lusena merchant who departed this life the 21 of August 1692." Aside from the Sephardic name, nothing in this English epitaph suggests the deceased's religion: insert the name "John Smith" and you have a perfectly conventional Christian stone of the period. A century later the conventions had changed. A 1781 stone begins in typical late eighteenth-century fashion, "Sacred to the Memory of Moses Gutteres." [68] By the late eighteenth century other English conventions appear on Jamaica's Jewish gravestones, including a general turn toward more Romantic language. Thus one sees phrases like "this gloomy Grave" in 1791 and "a disconsolate Mother" in 1794. [69] There were, of course, exceptions to this pattern—one occasionally finds "Hebrewisms" in English, such as when Rebeca Cohen Belefante of Barbados was referred to on her 1774 stone as "Rebeca of happy Memory"—but much more common was a strict adherence to the standard epitaph formulas of the language in question. [70]

Conventional language was thus not limited to English epitaphs. The Portuguese portion of an epitaph was not a translation of the English but its own entity, adhering to Portuguese conventions. Returning to the stone of Moses de Lucena, the Portuguese section declares,

Sa
Do Bem Aventurado de Moseh
de Lusena faleceo em 11 de
elul 5452
que correpsonde a 21 de
Agosto 1692
SUA ALMA GOZE DA
GLORIA

"SA" is an abbreviation for "sepultura," tomb. So strong were Portuguese epitaph conventions that many words and phrases were simply abbreviated. Almost all start with "SA," and most end with "S A G D G" or "S B A G D G" for "Sua [bemdita] alma goze da gloria," may his [blessed] soul enjoy glory. Lucena's stone was unconventional in actually spelling this out. Thus his Portuguese epitaph reads, "Tomb of the blessed Moses de Lucena, who died 11 Elul 5452, which corresponds to 21 August 1692. May his soul enjoy glory." When compared with Lucena's English epitaph, the conventional aspects of both languages become clear. Nowhere in Portuguese is Lucena's occupation as a merchant mentioned, nor is any reference made to his body. The English epitaph does not use the Jewish date of Lucena's death and it does not refer to him as blessed, "bem aventurado." This last designation was so common in Portuguese that it was sometimes abbreviated, as in "Sᴀ Da B.A. Abigail."[71]

It was in Hebrew, though, that New World Jews were best able to express their esteem for the deceased. There were, to be sure, conventional phrases that continually reappeared in Hebrew epitaphs, as discussed in the first chapter. One finds repeatedly phrases such as "the pious and honored woman," the "venerable and honorable," the "modest and pious." There were conventional expressions regarding the memory of the deceased: "May his memory be a blessing" and "May the memory of this righteous person be a blessing" were but two of the most common formulas.[72] But in Hebrew Jews could also be much more creative and literary. The 1719 stone of the New Yorker Samuel Levy, the *parnass* of his congregation, contains a complicated double acrostic on his name. The lengthy acrostic honoring Isaac Adolphus in 1774 includes such distinctive lines as "A lover of the poor, whom he clothed, and fed with / Meat for the hungry and drink for the thirsty."[73]

Even though most epitaphs were highly stylized, it is possible to glean from them some of the concerns central to New World Jews. Indeed, stylized language is of great utility for understanding the ideas and concepts most valued by the community. The theological issue that most often finds its way onto Jewish gravestones is an unwavering belief in the afterlife. This could be expressed differently in different locales. Newport's Jews, when writing in Hebrew, most often described the deceased as "liberated for Paradise" on the day of death. New Yorkers, on the other hand, preferred the Hebrew phrasing that the deceased "went to her eternal home." And in Curaçao, that island's wealthy elite had a taste for poetic images in Hebrew, such as this beautiful epitaph on Jahacob Alvares Correa's 1714 stone: "Although turned into dust in the grave / This Jacob the young man, the chosen of the land / Will shine like the bright sun in Paradise / And his reward and share will be exalted."[74]

If belief in the afterlife was the most common theological position staked out on gravestones, what did Jews believe about why they merited salvation? Again, gravestones provide clues. For Hana Sarah Lopes Laguna of Curaçao, the ticket to paradise was her Job-like faith in spite of adversity. According to her 1742 stone, Laguna, "having suffered several martyrdoms in this life, God wanted to receive her for the better world." Indeed, Laguna suffered these martyrdoms with such patience precisely "in order that she merit and enjoy the place reserved for the virtuous." For another Curaçao woman, charity rather than patience was her key claim for salvation. Lea Hana Carilho's stone announced that she "has always acted charitably; thus her blessed soul was transported from this hemisphere for eternal glory." [75]

These last two gravestones begin to give a sense of the virtues that were especially prized in the Jewish women of the New World. Reflecting the modest circumstances of Jews in their first few decades of residence in the New World, early stones were inscribed with relatively brief epitaphs. Family members were content to describe female virtues with a few phrases, as on a typical 1733 Jamaican stone remembering a "loveing wife & a tender mother," or the 1745 monument to Rachel Valverde, described in English simply as "charitable." [76] These were the conventional virtues praised on early stones: charity, piety, and love for husband and children.

Starting in the second half of the eighteenth century, Jewish gravestones followed the Euro-American trend toward lengthier and more elaborate epitaphs—at least for those who could afford them. This change was spurred by the Romantic cult of memory, which sought to paint more individualized portraits of the deceased. In general, the female virtues praised on these stones remained similar to earlier epitaphs; the wording simply became more flowery. Thus was Abigail Lopez of Newport remembered for piety and charity on her 1792 stone: "her unaffected piety and benevolence of heart, ever replete with afecting sensibility for the indigent and destitute has erected a lasting monument to her virtuous character." [77]

But on both early and late stones, whether brief or prolix, Jewish women—like their Christian neighbors—were almost always described in relation to men. Conventionally, Rachel Lopez of Newport (daughter of the Abigail mentioned above), who died in 1789, was situated within the community as "the beloved consort of David Lopez" and the "third daughter of the Late worthy Mr. Aaron Lopez." Rachel Lopez was further singled out for being "exemplary for conjugal affection." [78] If a woman never got a chance to express "conjugal affection," this was cause for comment as well. Sarah Pereira Henriques of Barbados died in 1774, thirty-six years old and never married. Her parents' sense that her life was incomplete without husband and children echoes through this sad couplet:

Cutt off in the prime of youth & life
Er'e her Virtues could Shine as wife [79]

The emphasis on the connections between the deceased woman and the men in her life was taken to its logical end on the 1740 New York stone of Grace Hays. In Hebrew the epitaph declared that Hays was the daughter of Samson Mear; in English Hays is described not only as the wife of David Hays but also as "formerly wife of" Moses Levy.[80]

Men were more likely to stand on their own two feet in epitaphs, though they too were often situated within family contexts. Boys and young men were especially likely to be described in terms of their lineage. Though an extreme example, the epitaph of nine-day-old Isaac Martins of Jamaica gives a sense of the importance of lineage to Jewish families in the New World. Young Isaac was described on his stone as the son of Moses and Esther Martins, the grandson of Isaac Martins (his namesake), and "Great Grandson to the late Moses and Leah Martins."[81]

As with this concern for lineage, Jews resembled Christians in the conventional male qualities cited on gravestones. Men were singled out for having good judgment, for being benevolent, and (especially in the second half of the eighteenth century) for being virtuous. They were cited for their love of family and their good deeds. But in at least one way did Jewish epitaphs differ from their Christian counterparts. With so many Jews being merchants and shopkeepers, their epitaphs were much more likely to cite honesty and skill in business as noteworthy traits. With the characteristic brevity of early stones, Jacob Alvares of Jamaica was described in 1723 simply as "a fait[h]ful dealer." Later stones made the same point more elaborately. "As a Trader" David Nunes Castello was remembered in 1775 to be "punctual & honest," while visitors to Newport's *beth haim* learned that Jacob Rivera, who died in 1789, observed "the strictest integrity in extensive commerce."[82]

Thus, Jewish cemeteries in the New World stand as silent reminders of the wide range of cultural influences Jews used to construct their identity. Some conventions—winged hourglasses, opening lines of epitaphs—were borrowed comfortably from Christian models, just as Jews did in Amsterdam and London. Other conventions of iconography and epitaph were uniquely Jewish. Where else in the Americas besides a *beth haim* would one find shapely Hebrew letters carved alongside an image of the pitcher and basin of the Levite? On gravestones as in other aspects of Jewish deathways, Jews in the Americas were able to preserve many of the traditions they brought with them from Europe.

*   *   *

New World Jews, like Africans and Indians, faced pressures to change their deathways in light of new demographic and cultural contexts. But for the most part Jews were more successful in preserving their mortuary customs. Uniquely Jewish practices—including rending garments at death-bed scenes, sitting shivah, saying Kaddish, and erecting gravestones with Hebrew inscriptions—persisted virtually unchanged in the Americas.

Perhaps most distinctively Jewish of all, though, was the multiplicity of cultural traditions Jewish deathways drew upon. Though a legacy of a sadly restless history, with Sephardim and Ashkenazim forced to flee on the whim of a monarch or with the stench of a pogrom in their nostrils, this inheritance became a source of strength in the New World. When Jews in the Americas faced death, they were sustained by traditions reaching back to Moses and forward to the Romantic poets. They therefore had the cultural flexibility to incorporate into their own practices elements of Christian deathways—such as mourning rings and gravestones with winged hourglasses and death's heads—and to deal with novel New World phenomena such as Jewish mulat-tos. In this encounter between centuries of Jewish laws and the experience of life in the predominantly Christian and partially African port towns of the Atlantic world, death was not a destructive force but rather a generative one. The rituals and beliefs that surrounded death were at the very heart of the Jewish community's ability to sustain itself.

CHAPTER 8

Burial and Condolence in the Seven Years' War

ON JULY 9, 1755, Major General Edward Braddock and his troops suffered an infamous defeat at the hands of French and Indian forces on the Monongahela River in western Pennsylvania. Anglo-American soldiers ran screaming from the real and imagined cruelties committed by their enemies; hundreds could not escape being slaughtered by muskets and hatchets. This was not a good moment for cross-cultural understanding on the early American frontier.

But three days earlier on the Braddock campaign an event took place that puts a different face on cross-cultural encounters in the Seven Years' War. On July 6, after being killed by friendly fire in a small skirmish, a young Oneida ally of the British forces was buried with greater pomp than any common soldier—regular or provincial—could ever hope for. An attempt to reach across cultural boundaries, this funeral used elements of European battlefield funerals for high-ranking officers to communicate a message of solidarity and sympathy with Indian allies. Nor was this an isolated event. When enemy gunfire killed an Indian sachem during the building of Fort Stanwix in 1758, the English likewise designed his funeral to make a statement about cross-cultural solidarity. The burial pageantry was a complex blending of European officer funerals and Iroquois deathways.

An even more common occurrence than an extraordinary burial was Euro-American participation in Iroquois condolence rituals. Over a period of eight days in June 1756, for example, Sir William Johnson, the British superintendent for Indian affairs, took part in remarkably intricate Iroquois mourning rituals for the leading Onondaga sachem. This condolence was more firmly rooted in Iroquois traditions than the extraordinary burials, but it too was a cross-cultural affair, with Anglo-American as well as Iroquois participants and material culture.

This chapter unravels the multiple meanings of these extraordinary burials and condolence ceremonies. As it does so it addresses a curious paradox regarding the Seven Years' War. This "First World War" was a time of shocking violence that generated intense hatred across cultural boundaries. Yet there were also moments of curiosity, learning, and understanding regarding other peoples—especially on the subject of deathways. By this point in our narrative, individuals were long past the point of initial inclusive and exclusive reactions to unfamiliar deathways. Rather, the English, French, and Indian participants in the Seven Years' War built on nearly two centuries of interactions in North America, during which time they had come to understand a great deal about each others' deathways.[1] Through two centuries of shared experiences and observation these groups had discovered how other peoples buried their wartime dead, how they honored fallen warriors, and how they thought about death and the afterlife. Sometimes, as in the extraordinary burials and condolences, they used this knowledge to build bridges across cultural chasms. Other times, as with corpse mutilation, they used this knowledge to horrify their enemies.

This perspective complicates our understanding of cross-cultural encounters in the Seven Years' War. For 250 years writers have mostly emphasized misunderstandings and brutality in their accounts of the war. Even recent works that see the war as a "theater of intercultural interaction" focus on the inability of different peoples to communicate effectively.[2] This is, for the most part, a valid interpretation. But even though the possibilities for death-inspired cross-cultural communication had attenuated from the first years of European-Indian encounters, the potential for understanding remained very much alive in the second half of the eighteenth century. This was true even—perhaps especially—during wartime, when all groups involved sought allies across cultural lines, and when the heightened presence of death forced all participants into a conversation about their most profound beliefs. "Death diplomacy" was therefore crucial to the outcome of the war.

*   *   *

By the middle of the eighteenth century, most of the Indian groups discussed earlier in this book had been considerably weakened compared to their position in the early seventeenth century. The Huron Confederacy had been destroyed in 1649, its people scattered in a far-flung diaspora. Powhatans and Wampanoags had experienced no similar dramatic destruction but instead witnessed the slow decrease of population—and with it power—due to disease, dispersal, and intermarriage. In sharp contrast, the Six Nations of Iroquois thrived in their position in central New York, between the French and English empires in North America. Especially after the Grand Settlement of 1701 put an end to the destructive conflict between Anglophile and Francophile Iroquois, and after the 1713 Treaty of Utrecht brought several decades of peace between France and England, the Iroquois had been able to consolidate power, playing the two European empires off one another in order to advance their own interests. The Iroquois will therefore play a lead role in this chapter, with other Indian groups cast in supporting parts.

During two centuries of interactions, French Catholics, English Protestants, and Christian and non-Christian Indians found many things about which they could disagree, yet they were frequently struck by the real and perceived similarities in their approaches to death. In wartime, with these groups variously composed as allies and enemies, these congruences were expressed in several concrete forms.[3] First of all, Indians, Frenchmen, and Englishmen adhered to (at least in the ideal) what might be called a "warrior ethic." This ethic maintained, simply enough, that men should be willing to fight and possibly die for their cause. Although desertion and flight from battles demonstrated that the warrior ethic was not universal, many fighters sincerely maintained this belief.

Europeans often admired the bravery of their Indian allies, though it is true that Indians, especially the Iroquois, may have been less willing to embrace dying in battle than most Europeans. Because the Iroquois believed that the souls of those killed in battle could not enter the villages of the dead and were therefore doomed to wander for eternity, they placed a premium on escaping battles with as few casualties as possible.[4] Nonetheless, even the Iroquois believed that death on the battlefield should be faced bravely. Therefore, during the Seven Years' War, Indians—including Iroquois—often gave voice to the warrior ethic in terms very similar to those used by Europeans. One conventional example of this rhetoric was offered in 1756 by Waadory (also known as Thomas), an Oneida who had previously allied himself with the French. To demonstrate his sincerity to William Johnson, Waadory offered a "very large" belt of prized purple wampum and his pledge that he was "ready on every occasion to sacrifice my life in the cause of my brethren the English."[5]

Even if Johnson was somewhat skeptical about these words, he understood their cultural import, for he too often gave voice to the warrior ethic. As reported in 1758 by Louis Antoine de Bougainville, a high-ranking French officer, Johnson once "swore by his halberd and tomahawk he would conquer or die." And Bougainville, as a French officer, almost certainly clung to this warrior ethic just as fervently as Johnson. Bougainville would have heartily agreed with his countryman General Louis-Joseph Montcalm's avowal in a letter of 1758: "I shall willingly shed the last drop of my blood, and give up the last breath of my life for his [the king's] service."[6]

It is more difficult to ascertain whether rank-and-file soldiers held these ideals as strongly as their officers. Yet by their frequently brave and self-sacrificing actions on the battlefield, common soldiers suggested that they too were willing to die on the battlefield. And, for New England's provincial forces at least, their religious culture prepared them to die for a righteous cause. According to the historian Ann Little, these men had long listened to artillery sermons—preached at each town's annual militia muster—that taught that "manhood in battle was proved by a display of courage in the face of possible or even certain death."[7] Although the existence of a warrior ethic among those engaged in battle may be unsurprising, it is important to note because beliefs about life, death, and honor were shared by Indians, Englishmen, and Frenchmen. This widespread ethic was the foundation of understanding and even respect among these groups.

That a key component of the warrior ethic was a willingness to die for one's cause proved valuable, since many men lost their lives in the war. When their fellow fighters died in battle, surviving combatants usually went to great pains to bury their fallen comrades. This was true for Indians, the English, and the French (though there are some hints that the English were less scrupulous about burying their dead than were Indians and the French). Again, although the desire to bury one's fallen comrades might not be unexpected, the reasons behind these actions should be analyzed rather than assumed, for these too reveal deep parallels in beliefs among the three groups.

By all accounts, Indians were assiduous about taking care of corpses on the battlefield, either by removing them or by burying them. In the colonial Northeast, Indians' preferred method of dealing with their dead was to carry them off the battlefield. In 1758 Caleb Rea, the surgeon of a provincial regiment, reported this after a battle: "Afterward when Major Gage with a party went out to bury their [own] dead they found where the Indians had made a number of biers to carry off their dead and wounded." Seth Metcalf, an enlisted man from Massachusetts, adds some detail to Rea's account with a description from 1757. After a lightning raid by Indians against some soldiers outside a fort, an English force was dispatched to hunt down the offending Indians. The scouting party, though unsuccessful, noticed "where the Indians cut beans and peeled bark to carry their dead and wounded." [8] The Indians, probably French-allied Iroquois, evidently used bean poles with peeled bark stretched between them to serve as litters for the dead and wounded. There is archeological corroboration for this practice, in the form of a headless body, presumed to be a warrior, apparently brought back to his village for burial.[9] Significantly neither Rea nor Metcalf witnessed these scenes firsthand but heard about them from others who found these details noteworthy. Rea, Metcalf, and their comrades were likely interested in both the tactical significance of Indians carrying off their dead—which prevented enemies from gaining scalps for trophies and from gathering information on the number slain— and in the evidence of another culture's deathways.

Like Indians, the French had the reputation of being very careful to accord battlefield casualties special treatment. In English reports, the French were linked with their Indian allies in their desire to carry their dead off the battlefield. In 1758, 900 Frenchmen and 200 Indians attacked the English forces encamped at Pennsylvania's Fort Ligonier, just east of the French Fort Duquesne. After several hours of bombardment that did little damage to the English fort, the French "retreated a little, and carried away their dead and wounded . . . and then marched five miles off." [10] Not only did the French expend the effort of carrying off their dead; they sometimes risked further casualties by burying their dead, occasionally even with the English in pursuit. Such was the case at Oswego after a French attack on the fort in 1759. A similar case from the previous year earned a stinging rebuke from the British commander. Brigadier General John Forbes complained that even though he "had above 1500 effective men within . . . our breastwork exclusive of sick," his men "shamefully allowed [the French] to bury the few they had killed," that is, the few French who had been killed.[11] The French, eager to bury their dead, risked pursuit by the British. In this instance their gamble paid off and they managed to avoid further casualties.

The English, like the French and Indians, believed that corpses generated in battles should, ideally, be buried. English agreement with French beliefs can be seen in the truces that were negotiated specifically to bury the dead. The sieges typical of eighteenth-century warfare could last weeks and result in the deaths of hundreds of soldiers. During the ferocious bombardment of Quebec in July 1759 that led up to the famous battle on the Plains of Abraham, the combatants were able to agree upon a truce to discuss what would be done with the dead on both sides. Likewise, during the 1758 siege of Fortress Louisbourg, the bitter foes took several pauses to bury the dead. On July 8, after the English killed some French defenders of the fort, the French sent out the red flag of truce (to distinguish it from the white Bourbon flag) so they could bury their dead. The very next day, after a long night of shelling, an English officer reported that "this morning the enemy sent out a flag of truce to bury their dead which we sent half way to them where there were biers brought for to carry them off." [12] Not only did the combatants agree to suspend fighting in order to pay proper respects to the dead but the English were also thoughtful enough to carry the dead halfway to the fort so the French could retrieve them. When the siege was finally over, the English continued in this generous spirit. Louisbourg surrendered on July 26 but the British forces did not enter the walled city until July 29, "the French having liberty to bury their dead and to clear away the rubbish." [13]

Thus the English understood perfectly the French desire to bury their wartime dead, and, in the context of the conventions that governed eighteenth-century European warfare, they accepted truces and granted surrender terms to allow this to happen. Indeed, in at least one instance, English and French concern for the dead seems to have affected the outcome of a battle. In the summer of 1758 a column of Anglo-American scouts nearly a mile long trudged "Indian file" through the heat toward Fort Edward on the headwaters of the Hudson River. Ambushed by a large contingent of French and Indians, the vanguard of the column was in danger until the soldiers in the rear, led by the near-mythical scout Robert Rogers, came to their aid. According to a later secondhand account, "as soon as the enemy perceived Rogers' party flanking upon 'em they retreated carrying off their dead and wounded what they could, our men pursued them not[,] but took care of their dead and wounded and came off[,] so that it seems rather a drawn battle than either party victorious." [14]

But this case was something of an exception, for unlike the French and Indians, the English generally chose to return to the scene of a skirmish or small battle to retrieve corpses rather than taking the dead with them as they retreated. In these instances, the English and their provincial allies would send out a small scouting party to find the corpses. They would then bring the bodies back to camp or to the fort for burial. [15] One of the motivations for this was to prevent the corpses from being scalped, which would provide the enemy with trophies. But this was not the only motivation, as attested by the numerous times scalped corpses were brought back for burial. To cite just one example, in October 1759 a Massachusetts soldier at Louisbourg recorded the following gruesome incident: "Four men went out for to get wood a mile from the block house and they was waylaid by Indians who killed three outright and the other came in alive and the picket [a detachment of soldiers] went out and brought in the dead, one having lost his head, the others were stripped and scalped—a sad accident." [16]

If preventing scalping was the only motivation for burial, then these scalped and headless corpses might as well have been left to rot. But for the English, as for the other combatants, mutilated corpses served an important purpose: they were valuable symbols, too valuable to be left as carrion. Mutilated corpses—brought back for all to see, inspect, talk about, and write about—warned the men and women in camp to be careful and to be hateful. Officers used these corpses as examples to urge their charges to be more vigilant; many of these incidents occurred when soldiers did not exercise due caution while gathering wood, looking for berries, or relieving themselves. But there was a broader lesson to be learned as well. The English, like their French counterparts, used examples of corpse desecration to highlight the barbarous nature of their enemies. The Seven Years' War was, after all, a quasi-religious war. Though its primary ends were geopolitical in nature, the fact that this conflict pitted Catholic against Protestant—with both using ostensibly "heathen" Indians as allies—lent the whole affair the air of a crusade.[17] It was important to maintain religious rituals in a crusade, and the easiest and most useful ritual was burial of the dead. Mutilated corpses were doubly effective in instilling a sense of outrage among the troops.

Bringing corpses back to camp was most practical when the individuals had been killed in an ambush or small skirmish. After a pitched battle, however, gathering hundreds of corpses and carting them to a fort was simply not feasible. In such cases, the English would usually return to the battlefield for the "most melancholy piece of business" of interring the dead. This eloquent description of the aftermath of the Battle of Lake George in 1755, penned by a provincial officer, Seth Pomeroy, was no doubt sincere. But as a lieutenant colonel, Pomeroy likely did not soil his hands on the 136 corpses bloating for two days in the unseasonably hot September sun. This was left to the 400 men in Pomeroy's "command," ordinary soldiers who would have gained small comfort knowing that they might rifle the dead men's pockets for a little booty.[18]

Usually the English followed this pattern after a large battle, sending out a large contingent of ordinary soldiers to bury the dead. But there is some evidence that the English were not as vigilant about interring battlefield corpses as were their French and Indian enemies. After what is usually considered to be the very first engagement of the Seven Years' War, when George Washington was forced to surrender the ill-constructed Fort Necessity in 1754, a French engineer reported that "the savages took twenty scalps from the dead whom the English had not buried." [19] A more respectful final disposition awaited those English and provincial troops left dead on the field after the Battle of Ticonderoga in July 1758. On the day after this epic battle a French officer noted in his diary, "The day was devoted to . . . burying our dead and those the enemy had left on the field of battle." [20]

Thus, the French, English, and Indians all felt that the dead on the battlefield deserved burial, but the English may have been the most likely to abandon that general rule when confronted with the exigencies of battle. If so, this could be explained by the tenets of Protestantism. According to Catholicism and most Indian religions of the Eastern woodlands, a good burial was crucial in assisting the soul or spirit of the deceased to the afterlife. Protestantism, on the other hand, argued that the actions of the living did not affect whether the deceased's soul went to heaven or hell. Although Protestants went to great lengths to honor their dead, they nonetheless believed that the final state of the soul was not dependent upon a good burial.

Not only did Indians, Catholics, and Protestants all desire to bury their wartime dead; they also buried them according to a similar logic: individuals of higher rank received more elaborate funerals. This was more strongly expressed among Europeans and colonists than among Indians, who had fewer gradations of rank. Indians buried their leaders more elaborately than common people, but they did not make distinctions among generals, captains, sergeants, and ordinary soldiers. Outside of wartime, European and American burials varied by rank; elaborate funerals cost a great deal of money and were available only to the well-off. There were exceptions to this rule, as individuals occasionally opted for burials less grand than they might have afforded, to make a statement about the desirability of simplicity. Such ostentatiously simple burials would become especially common a decade later during the imperial crisis between Britain and its North American colonies.[21] But on the battlefield, rank was even clearer than in civilian life, and this was reflected in death.

When a general died, especially one beloved by his men, Euro-Americans pulled out all the stops. The death of the universally revered General George Augustus Howe at the Battle of Ticonderoga inspired not only unprecedented lamentations but also remarkable attention to his corpse. The officers who served under Howe brought his body to Mutton Island in Lake George, the site of a camp hospital, where it was embalmed and then sent to Albany for temporary burial. The corpse was later disinterred and removed to England for reburial.[22] Likewise, Brigadier General John Forbes generated enormous good will after he led the building of his eponymous road through the Pennsylvania backcountry to Fort Duquesne, all the while suffering intensely from what was likely some kind of abdominal cancer. Upon his death in 1759, Philadelphians organized a remarkably elaborate funeral procession, which included several regiments of troops, heavy artillery, the governor and members of the assembly, and "a led horse, covered with black, conducted by a groom." [23]

Lower-ranking French and English officers who died during the war were not treated with as much pomp as were their generals, but officer funerals generally proceeded with a level of display commensurate with the deceased's rank. This almost always meant burial in a coffin, even in times when wood was scarce. Officer funerals could also include a pall, the firing of minute guns (artillery fired with a mournful minute between shots), a volley of small arms fire, and a procession of men in arms. All this was meant to honor the manly virtues the officer embodied in life, particularly his warrior ethic expressed in his willingness to die for his cause. For example, after the French officer Daniel-Hyacinthe-Marie Liénard de Beaujeu was killed on the Monongahela during Braddock's defeat, he was "buried with all the marks of honor due to his bravery" in a coffin specially made for the purpose. Attention was also paid to the demeanor of those attending the funeral: a burial with "decency" was paramount for officers. Seth Pomeroy took great pains to make the funeral of his fellow provincial officer, Captain Elisha Hawley, worthy of his rank. Pomeroy ordered a coffin to be made, appointed bearers, and had a minister read a prayer. Pomeroy was gratified to note that "the funeral was attended with decency and order." [24]

Indeed, officers' impulse to give one another decent and honorable funerals got out of control, at least according to the high command of the British forces. In 1758 Lord Loudon decreed that "when an officer dies, (of any rank whatsoever) he may be buried with as little expense as possible, and no scarves to be allowed to any person, except to the clergyman." Fashionable eighteenth-century Britons and Americans demonstrated their largesse and status by giving large scarves, worn over the shoulder, to mourners at funerals. Loudon aimed to stifle this expensive habit that officers brought with them from their civilian lives.[25]

Ordinary soldiers, by contrast, could not hope for scarves to be distributed at their funerals. Nor could they wish for a pall, the firing of minute guns, or a procession of men in arms. Indeed, they were lucky to get a coffin. The attention to rank and status during burials is vividly illustrated by an incident narrated by the Reverend Gideon Hawley, a minister who served in the 1756 campaign with the provincial army. An officer and several soldiers had been killed in an ambush, and Hawley was called upon to officiate. The slain captain, "being a worthy man and a good officer, loved while he lived and lamented now he is dead, a coffin was provided for his corpse and orders to bury him under arms etc." Three additional men lost their lives with their captain, but their mutilated corpses did not fare so well. "For we could not afford coffins for them," Hawley noted, "they were obliged to be exposed. No, so far from it that we could not allow them blankets to be wrapped in, their legs and arms all naked and besmeared with blood appeared very ghastfully."

Reverend Hawley tried to reconcile his orthodox Protestantism with this assault on his sensibilities: "Though tis true that [it] little matters to persons after they are dead what becomes of their bodies, yet I could not but be something affected."[26] Hawley believed there was no theological reason for worrying about the lack of a coffin, but he could not get over his deeply ingrained cultural response. And this was not an isolated incident. Ordinary soldiers were usually buried without coffins, often naked as the day they came into the world. Though soldiers on burial duty may have become inured to this indignity, it could still shock the uninitiated. Thomas Barton, an Anglican chaplain serving in the Pennsylvania backcountry, betrayed his sensitivity in his description of an incident similar to Hawley's: "Buried a Virginian soldier this day. He was launched into a little hole out of a blanket, and there left naked. And when I remonstrated against the inhumanity as well as indecency of it, a sergeant informed me that he had orders not to return without the blanket. Upon which I got some small bushes cut, and thrown over him, till I performed the service."[27] The exigencies of the battlefield sometimes meant that good burials were impossible, but a lifetime of absorbing the rules for a good burial could not easily be overcome.

Indians likewise buried their slain leaders with greater pomp than ordinary warriors received. As with Europeans, this was a reflection of peacetime practices: Indians of the Eastern woodlands in the seventeenth and eighteenth centuries generally buried high-ranking individuals in an elaborate fashion. For the Iroquois, for example, this was a new development in the period after European contact. Before contact, Iroquois burials were relatively simple; corpses were accompanied with little in the way of grave goods. Archaeological evidence starting in the 1560s shows a dramatic change in Iroquois mortuary practices, similar to that which occurred among the Hurons. Grave goods—especially beads, pipes, and copper objects—increased exponentially in number.[28]

This development allowed for greater differentiation between high- and low-ranking individuals. According to Adriaen van der Donck's 1653 *Description of New Netherland*, "if he was a person of some standing" a deceased Iroquois was buried "with variations according to his position."[29] Thus, by the time of the Seven Years' War, Iroquois sachems were commonly buried with greater attention than ordinary men and women, and, as the French traveler François Marbois wrote in 1784, "If he is a famous warrior, they paint his face with startling colors so that when he arrives in the other country, its guardians will receive him without hesitation and assign him an honorable place."[30] Moreover, as attested by another eighteenth-century French observer, leading Iroquois warriors were eulogized with a funeral oration narrating the man's deeds and remembered with a special grave marker: "a small white pole representing the dead man, on which they carve the number of men he killed, the prisoners he took, and the war parties he commanded."[31]

Indian warriors shared one more trait with English and French soldiers: the knowledge that committing violent acts on corpses was a grimly effective way of cross-cultural communication. Because all three groups placed a premium on good burials, all understood that violation of these norms could shock or appall their enemies, as we have already seen in the Powhatan uprising of 1622 and King Philip's War—and in the European responses to both. Violence upon corpses was the easiest way to prevent a good burial. Indian acts of corpse mutilation during the Seven Years' War are so well known as to warrant only a brief discussion. Indeed, the popular understanding of the war is tightly bound up with scalping, torture, and the "massacre" at Fort William Henry that provided the inspiration for James Fenimore Cooper's *Last of the Mohicans*.[32] Nonetheless, there is an important analytical point to be made about scalping: Indians used corpse mutilation as a form of communication. As the historian Hal Langfur argues in another geographical context, violence between Indians and Europeans "did not represent the cessation of cultural interaction on th[e] colonial frontier; rather, it was an essential means by which that interaction occurred." [33] This accounts for the irony that cross-cultural interactions and understanding promoted the practice of corpse mutilation. When Indians practiced their campaign of civilian terror in the Pennsylvania backcountry in 1755 and 1756, they understood full well that Euro-American colonists would be especially shocked and frightened— and, more to the point, likely to abandon their homes—if residents were not merely killed but tortured, mutilated, and left for others to find.

Europeans, too, were adept at employing the semiotics of corpse mutilation. Several times in late 1755, after Indians killed settlers in the Pennsylvania backcountry, outraged Euro-Americans carted the mutilated corpses to Philadelphia to "show the inhabitants the barbarities that are committed on our fellow subjects." When dragging scalped corpses to urban centers proved impractical, Euro-Americans instead published accounts describing the various forms of postmortem humiliation Indians used to communicate their anger. These published descriptions became so common, and so stereotyped in their use of stock images and phrases, that the historian Peter Silver argues they became a recognizable genre, which he has dubbed the "anti-Indian sublime." [34]

For Europeans, this focus on corpse mutilation did not remain relegated to print culture during the Seven Years' War. English and French soldiers eagerly adopted the Indian practice of scalping. James Wolfe notoriously ordered in 1759, "The general strictly forbids the inhuman practice of scalping, except where the enemy are Indians." Not only did European troops participate in "uncivilized" acts such as scalping and plundering corpses but they also used brutal treatment of the dead to send messages to their own troops. Floggings were sickeningly violent and sometimes resulted in the death of the accused. One can only imagine the horror of ordinary soldiers as they watched a man, then a corpse, receive its five hundred or one thousand lashes. Executions weren't pretty either. Lemuel Wood, a teenaged provincial soldier, described a fairly typical execution in July 1759. The only thing unusual about this case is the vividness of the surviving description: "The prisoner was brought and set before one of the platoons and kneeled down upon his knees, he clenched his hand, the platoon of 6 men each of them fired him through the body, the other platoon then came up instantly and fired him through the head and blowed his head all to pieces, they then dug a grave by his side and tumbled him in and covered him up." [35]

Whereas executions represented intracultural knowledge about how to make an impression on one's own men, other incidents demonstrate intercultural understanding of the symbolic meaning of corpses. As William Johnson was the European perhaps most adept at Indian diplomacy, it is not surprising that he was a master of this trope. One revealing example of this comes from a speech Johnson made at Onondoga in 1756. "I . . . sharpen your knife to cut our enemy's throat or take their scalps off," proclaimed the diplomat in a ringing endorsement of corpse mutilation. But Johnson went even further: "And as I know it is an old custom amongst you to feast on your enemies' flesh I present you those kettles for that purpose." In order to avoid offending Englishmen who might find their gorge rising due to Johnson's apparent promotion of cannibalism, the secretary who recorded this speech hurriedly noted, "(This is meant figuratively, and some meat is boiled in the kettles, which they eat and call it French Men's Flesh, so when drink is given it is called blood of their enemies)." [36] This wartime parody of Catholic communion, linked with Iroquois traditions of anthropophagy, received universal assent from the assembled Iroquois. Johnson's actions demonstrate the utility of using the language of death to promote cross-cultural communication.

Likewise, extraordinary burials of Indians by Europeans performed similar functions of "death diplomacy." Extraordinary burials were not invented during the Seven Years' War and were not confined to just one European power. When "the chief of the Indians of L'Isle Royale [Cape Breton Island]" died in 1737, he was buried in Fortress Louisbourg and "given several honors" by the French, including a "detachment with a sergeant" who presumably fired over the burial.[37] But such burials reached their peak of importance during the Seven Years' War, with nothing less than the imperial fate of North America hanging in the balance. In particular, because the English were so dependent upon their Iroquois allies for manpower and intelligence, they went out of their way to use deathways to communicate their indebtedness to and respect for the Iroquois. I now return to the two burials mentioned at the outset of this chapter to tease out their significance in light of broader deathways.

The first took place during General Edward Braddock's ill-fated march from backcountry Virginia to the French Fort Duquesne, where Pittsburgh now stands. Braddock had been advised to bring along Indian warriors to serve as scouts and soldiers, but he wound up with only eight or ten warriors. Fifty warriors from the Ohio country had proved to be more than Braddock, convinced of the superiority of English military tactics, could bear. He sent away all but the most trusted handful of Indians, a group of "fighting men and lads" that included the Oneida diplomat Scarouady and his thirteen-year-old son.[38]

On the morning of July 6, Scarouady's son proved why he had, despite his youth, garnered the trust and admiration of American officers. Along with several other Indian advance scouts, he came upon a French man in a canoe. Though the lone man did not pose a threat on his own, if he alerted the French forces at Duquesne to the English position, all hope for surprise would be lost. To avoid having the canoeist's valuable scalp sink with him to the bottom of the river, the sachem's son waited until the man came ashore and then shot and scalped him. The young warrior brought his trophy directly to Braddock, who likely had kind words for this act of bravery.[39]

Several hours later, though, this boy's bravery would be his undoing. As the Anglo-American troops marched through the woods, they "startled a parcel of the French Indians" who began to fire on the column's right flank.[40] Hearing the commotion, the Indians siding with the English boldly sprang to action. This confused the soldiers: even though they had only eight or ten Indian allies to keep track of, they did not recognize these warriors. Tragically thinking they were more enemy Indians, the soldiers unleashed a volley from their muskets. Cut down by the friendly fire were three Indians, two wounded and one killed. Receiving a fatal wound was Scarouady's son.

The English officers immediately recognized that this was a potential diplomatic disaster. No Indian had been a more committed ally to the English than Scarouady. In 1754, two people had been awarded medals by the Virginia lieutenant governor, Robert Dinwiddie, after the Fort Necessity campaign: Scarouady and George Washington. Indeed, the connections between Scarouady and Washington ran deep. Washington referred to Scarouady as "our good friend" and one among "brothers." Another member of the Virginia gentry called Scarouady a man of "power and skill" and went so far as to suggest that Scarouady take the name "Washington."[41] Clearly Scarouady had done much to earn the trust and respect of the English, and here his young son had been killed by English troops.

The remedy was obvious: an extraordinary burial. The boy's corpse was placed into a wagon and carried back to Thicket Run, the most recent camp and an area away from the skirmish with enough open space to permit some ceremony. As one eyewitness put it, that evening "we had him buried with all the decency in our power," which, according to another chronicler, meant that "the soldiers fired over him, the same as though he was a Christian."[42] The English understood that their Indian allies used elaborate funerals to mark the demise of noted warriors, so the English reached out with a gesture of cross-cultural solidarity. Unable or unwilling to reach all the way across the cultural divide and appropriate Iroquois burial practices, the English settled instead for a tribute usually reserved for European officers: a volley fired over the burial by soldiers in arms.

It is unclear whether this gesture mollified Scarouady. On the one hand, according to a British officer, the extraordinary burial was a success: "the Indians seem much pleased with" it. On the other hand, this same officer reported Scarouady's lingering anguish. Remarking that Scarouady "undoubtedly is a very good man," the officer admitted that the Oneida sachem "was hardly able to support his loss; he said had [his son] been killed by the French it would have been trifling, but what he regretted most was his being killed by our own people."[43] This sentiment, imbued with the warrior ethic, likely resonated with the British officer and induced him to call Scarouady a "very good man." Like Scarouady, the officer had been socialized in a culture in which death at the hands of one's enemy in battle was a noble death, but death by friendly fire was a waste.

At this moment the British officer felt a strong bond with Scarouady. Both were good men fighting a just war against a hated enemy. Maybe the officer was a father; in any case he could sympathize with Scarouady's loss and also admire his willingness to sacrifice his son in battle. But his attempts to bridge a cultural divide in words and deeds, an attempt symbolized in death rituals, was undercut by his ignorance regarding the Oneidas. The officer's comment that the young warrior's burial was carried out "the same as though he was a Christian" is doubly ironic. First, there is nothing uniquely or necessarily Christian about firing guns at a funeral. There is no scriptural basis for this practice; moreover, numerous non-Christian cultures fire weapons at funerals.[44] Second, there is evidence that Scarouady's son was, at least nominally, Christian.

In September 1753, Scarouady's eleven-year-old son was "christened" and given the name "Dinwiddie" in honor of Virginia's lieutenant governor.[45] To qualify for Anglican christening, the boy most likely would have been required to demonstrate at least a basic grasp of Christianity and its concepts of death and the afterlife. Such knowledge would not have been at all unusual for a mid-eighteenth-century Oneida boy, as his people had been hearing the words of Christian missionaries for nearly a century. The rationale underlying this christening ritual was the same that George Washington voiced in 1754 for a proposal to have Indian women and children live among the colonists:

so "their children may imbibe the principles of love and friendship in a stronger degree which if taken when young is generally more firm and lasting." [46] Like a latter-day Pocahontas, Scarouady's son found himself an important player in the geopolitical drama that whirled around him since his birth. Christened "Dinwiddie" at age eleven, fighting with George Washington at age twelve, fighting and dying with Edward Braddock at age thirteen—this boy's commitment to his father's cause could not have been more "firm and lasting."

In the weeks following his son's death and burial, Scarouady seems to have become increasingly embittered with his English allies. Three days after the boy was committed to the earth, Braddock suffered his infamous rout at the hands of the French. Wounded, leaking blood, and festering with maggots and infection, Braddock finally died on July 13, four days after the battle. Rather unlike the European pomp of Scarouady's son's funeral, Braddock's body met an ignominious end, buried in the road so enemy Indians could not find the grave and scalp the corpse—Braddock's men motivated by the same fear that led de Soto's lieutenants to consign his body to the Mississippi.[47] But having the general's corpse run over by wagons and shit upon by horses was not, in Scarouady's opinion, infamy enough. A month later he stood before the Pennsylvania provincial council and offered this anti-eulogy to Braddock: "He is now dead; but he was a bad man when he was alive; he looked upon us as dogs, and would never hear any thing what was said to him." [48]

In response the council tried to make amends for Scarouady's loss by offering him a condolence present of a saddle and a new beaver hat. Like the extraordinary burial on the Monongahela, this attempt at cross-cultural communication was not entirely successful: Scarouady had to endure the humiliation of being grilled under oath about his son's death before he could collect the goods.[49] This indignity put the lie to the familial language with which the council had earlier honored Scarouady and six other Indians who fought with "spirit and valor" on the Monongahela: "We see you consider yourselves as our flesh and blood, and fight for us as if we were of your own kindred." Scarouady knew what it meant to lose his flesh and blood in battle, and he would know it again, losing his son Nica-anawa in the Battle of Lake George just three weeks after he heard these words. Scarouady knew that among the Iroquois—among flesh and blood—mourning gifts were not contingent upon a sworn oath, as if one might lie about a death to receive the symbolic goods of condolence.[50]

If the extraordinary burial of and condolence for Scarouady's son only partially bridged cultural divisions, the burial of the Oneida sachem Kindaruntie was somewhat more successful. Kindaruntie had been active in diplomacy with the French, English, and with other Six Nations Indians—including those loyal to the French—since at least 1751.[51] Unlike his fellow Oneida Scarouady, however, Kindaruntie was initially tepid in his support for the English. Kindaruntie sat on the fence for much of the Seven Years' War, formally allying himself with the English but waiting to see which imperial power proved more successful and thus more deserving of his people's support.

In March 1758 William Johnson's frustration with Kindaruntie reached the boiling point. At a conference with Iroquois leaders at Fort Johnson, the superintendent of Indian affairs publicly and privately gave the sachems—Kindaruntie among them—"several severe rebukes for their past conduct," demanding firmer allegiance. But in his patented style of playing both the good cop and the bad cop, Johnson the very next day "reinstated Kindarundie . . . before all the Oneida sachems with the usual ceremony and marks of distinction giving him a strict charge at the same time to behave deserving that notice taken of him, and the rank he now bore."[52] The "marks of distinction" likely included a medal stamped with the likeness of George II and a certificate attesting to the bearer's "repeated proofs of . . . attachment to his Britannic Majesty's interests."[53]

Though Kindaruntie was, first and foremost, attached to his own people's interests (as he perceived them) over and above the king's interests, Johnson's ceremony seems to have had the desired impact. Five months later the English began building the fort that would eventually be named Stanwix in the heart of Oneida country, and the Oneidas helped defend the fort from its beginning. On August 23 the "first stick of timber" of the fort was laid, and on September 1 "a great number of Indians came from the Oneida castle." Even though an attack by the French and their Indian allies was rumored to be imminent throughout the month of September, the mood at the fort was optimistic. Four times that late summer "joyful" news was brought of English military success—at Cape Breton, St. Malo (France), Fort Frontenac, and Crefeld (Westphalia)—and all four times twenty-one guns were fired and the Anglo-American troops shouted three huzzahs.[54] The Oneidas likely did not join the huzzahs, but the festivities probably helped convince them that they were, in fact, casting their lot with the winning side.

This fragile cross-cultural camaraderie was shattered by a blow from the French-allied Indians. On October 6 shouts announced that Kindaruntie, out with several other Indians "fetching some bark to make a hut," had been killed by a scalping party of some thirty French Indians. The news "caused an alarm in the camps," and it is easy to see why: if not handled properly, the death of a leading sachem could cause the rest of his people's support to evaporate. As with the death of Scarouady's son in 1755, the situation demanded an extraordinary burial.[55]

Within thirty minutes of his death, Kindaruntie's scalped corpse was brought back to the fort. Twenty-four hours then passed before his burial. Like William Johnson's ceremony "reinstating" Kindaruntie as chief, the funeral was a combination of Iroquois and Anglo-American cultural forms. At four o'clock in the afternoon, the Oneida sachem's coffined corpse, "with his gun and hatchet by his side," was buried inside the fort. The firing of three doleful minute guns gave the proceedings a somber air.

The officers at Fort Stanwix used the funeral to make several statements about cross-cultural solidarity. Burial within the walls of the fort was highly unusual, as the cemetery outside the fort was the typical burying ground. Gunfire offered the pageantry and mournfulness usually reserved for European officers, and minute guns were even more highly esteemed than the volley of small arms fire that graced the interment of Scarouady's son. The coffin provided for Kindaruntie's remains likewise was an attempt to raise the level of the funeral to that of a European officer. But the coffin was an even more complex symbol than that. The Iroquois had not used coffins prior to European contact and for a century and a half had shown almost no interest in adopting this European artifact. But archaeological and documentary evidence demonstrates that by the second half of the eighteenth century, some Iroquois individuals desired coffined burials. For example, in 1753 two Moravian missionaries traveling to Onondaga were asked by an Iroquois leader to make a coffin for his deceased wife.[56] The coffin was thus a European item that was just beginning to be adopted by some Iroquois to symbolize their high status or their links with Christianity and Euro-American society.

But Kindaruntie—or more precisely, those Oneidas who prepared his corpse for burial—did not opt for all the trappings of a European officer funeral and leave it at that. The Oneidas chose to place the sachem's gun and hatchet by his side in the coffin. These two weapons are apt symbols of the syncretism not only of this burial but of warfare on the North American frontier. Even though hatchets symbolized Indian warfare and guns epitomized European weaponry, the reality during the Seven Years' War was more complex. Indians used guns, of course, and Euro-American soldiers were routinely outfitted with hatchets. Moreover, the very presence of the weapons within the coffin signaled the cross-cultural nature of this funeral. Missionaries who first encountered the Indians of the Eastern woodlands mocked the native practice of depositing grave goods with corpses.[57] What use, asked the Black Robes, did the soul have for kettles and furs? But even after almost a century of exposure to the barbs of Christian missionaries, Kindaruntie's people asserted that a fallen warrior deserved grave goods.

Kindaruntie's extraordinary burial seems to have been successful, at least from the perspective of the fort's officers. There was no great defection of Oneida warriors from Fort Stanwix in the weeks that followed Kindaruntie's murder. Ironically, though, the funeral seemed to William Johnson to have been all too effective at assuaging the Oneidas' grief. Johnson wanted to use Kindaruntie's death to help incite the Oneidas against the French and their Indian allies. This seemed to Johnson to be the perfect opportunity to get the wavering Oneidas fully on board as English allies. But the Oneidas were not reacting to Kindaruntie's murder with as much bloodlust as Johnson hoped. Johnson went so far as to criticize the Oneidas for not adhering to the "former and once established engagements and customs" of condolence when they delayed telling the English-affiliated Mohawks of Kindaruntie's death.[58] At first Johnson played the bad cop, giving the Oneidas a puny three strings of wampum as a gift condoling Kindaruntie's death. Finally, though, Johnson realized he had to believe the Oneidas when they said they were going to avenge the death of their sachem, and, reverting back to his good cop role, gave the Oneidas a much more appropriate condolence gift: a belt made from three thousand highly valued purple wampum beads and a French scalp. Combined with the extraordinary burial, this impressive condolence tribute satisfied the Oneida leaders and helped cement the alliance, at least for the time being.

Johnson had learned the language of death diplomacy during his long years among the Six Nations, and his deft touch at Kindaruntie's condolence had been likewise demonstrated two years earlier. In June 1756 Johnson had participated in an unusually well-documented condolence ceremony after the death of the Onondaga sachem the English called Red Head but whose Iroquois name was Kakhswenthioni, that is, "Hanging Wampum Belt." Kakhswenthioni first appears in the historical record in 1748, at a conference of Iroquois with the governor of Canada in Montreal.[59] In the late 1740s and early 1750s, the Onondaga sachem—baptized a Catholic—staunchly supported the French. Indeed, in 1751 Kakhswenthioni thanked the Canadian governor for participating in a condolence ritual, using the familial language that marked the French-Iroquois alliance: "Father, You have had the goodness to send persons to meet us at Lachine to wipe away our tears and clear our throats; we thank you for your kindness; permit us to do the same in your presence." But by 1753 many Onondagas were beginning to feel uncomfortable in their position between the French and English empires. Kakhswenthioni complained, "We are so hemmed in by both [French and English], that we have hardly a hunting place left. In a little while, if we find a bear in a tree, there will immediately appear an owner for the land to challenge the property, and hinder us from killing it which is our livelihood." As a result of these concerns, by 1755 Kakhswenthioni had made a dramatic reversal: he now supported the English, believing they were more likely to prevail in their conflict with the French, and that they were more likely to respect Six Nations claims in the Ohio River Valley.[60]

It was thus with great anguish that Johnson learned about Kakhswenthioni's death in June 1756. The cause of death is not mentioned in the records, which points to natural causes, because if the sachem had died in battle or been murdered this almost certainly would have been noted. Whatever killed Kakhswenthioni, this was a delicate moment: an ally was dead, but not just any ally, a Catholic (at least nominally) who had changed sides and lent his considerable prestige to the English. Plus, the war was not going well for the English. There had been Braddock's disaster the year before and the campaigns of 1756 were not going much better. Too much more bad news and the English risked losing their Iroquois allies. Johnson therefore knew that he would have to participate in the "ancient custom" of condolence, and do so with a flourish.[61]

By the 1750s both Indians and Europeans conceived of condolence as "ancient," but in fact historians do not know when the ritual began to be used. It seems likely that what might be called "personal condolence" emerged prior to "diplomatic condolence." A personal condolence occurred within a given village. If an individual died, his or her lineage mourned. In response, another lineage group within the village—called the "clearminded" because they were not bereaved—was responsible for assuaging the mourners' grief. It was necessary to attend to the bereaved because the Iroquois believed that death could cause the grief-stricken to lose their reason and become dangerously angry. In this state, the bereaved might do damage to themselves, to the community, or, in the case of someone who died due to warfare or murder, to the person responsible for the death. To help curb this potentially destructive grief, the Iroquois had developed a protocol whereby the clearminded offered gifts and ritualized words of comfort to the bereaved.[62]

At some point after the establishment of the Iroquois Great League of Peace and Power in the fifteenth or sixteenth century, diplomatic condolences emerged. When any one of the fifty sachems of the Great League died, the clearminded half of the confederacy condoled the mourning half and raised up a new sachem to replace the deceased one. Thus, as the historian Jon Parmenter has recently argued, the condolence ceremony was not about stasis but about change: it provided a framework for dealing with change in the wake of a sachem's death.[63] This function was essential to maintaining the peace among the Iroquois nations, which had long warred with one another before the founding of the league. Diplomatic condolences further evolved when Europeans began participating in them: first the French, starting in 1645, and later the English in the eighteenth century. Moreover, just as seventeenth-century Algonquian-speaking groups such as the Ojibwa adopted the Huron Feast of the Dead, some of the Iroquois' Algonquian neighbors—including the Delawares, Shawnees, and Ottawas—began to practice the diplomatic condolence.[64]

This perspective—that the condolence ceremony changed over time, in terms of its protocols and participants—differs from the dominant interpretation of the ritual. The scholars most interested in condolence have been anthropologists and ethnologists. As they are disciplinarily inclined to do, they have been especially concerned with continuities, and indeed there are striking similarities between the condolence ceremonies performed today and those in which William Johnson participated.[65] But between 1645, when the first European-attended condolence ceremony appears in the historical record, and the outbreak of the Seven Years' War, the condolence ritual—at least as it was performed with Europeans—changed in important ways.

First, the ritual evolved differently depending on whether the French or the English participated with the Iroquois. For example, it seems that the French sometimes literally covered the graves of dead sachems with wampum, as opposed to the English, who did so only metaphorically.[66] Second, there is evidence that all the death caused by the Seven Years' War, combined with Johnson's commitment to the condolence ritual, led to a sort of "golden age" of condolence in the middle of the eighteenth century, with the ritual performed more frequently and over a more widespread area of North America than ever before. As Kakhswenthioni himself told Johnson after a condolence in 1755, "We are much obliged to you for renewing our ancient forms."[67] And third, the material culture of condolence changed over time. The firing of guns, which was never reported in early condolences, became common by the middle of the eighteenth century. Wampum, which had always been a part of the ritual, was used in ever greater quantities as Europeans and Indians had easier access to "wampum factories" on Long Island Sound and elsewhere. And Europeans seem to have initiated the practice of offering goods such as shirts, handkerchiefs, and strouds (coarse woolen blankets) to the bereaved. Europeans gave these goods to "cover" the deaths of allied Indians, and, unlike wampum, these goods were not meant to be returned.

Nonetheless, even though condolence was incorporating new elements of European material culture, it was still very much an Indian ceremony, propelled by Indian logic, in which the French and English participated. Because condolence was an Iroquois ritual, Europeans often complained that its hours and even days of speeches, songs, and gift giving were "tedious," "trifling," and "fatiguing."[68] Except William Johnson, that is. Johnson was an Irishman who had arrived in the Mohawk River Valley in 1738 as a merchant. Through a combination of guile and self-interest he became a successful trader, learning that the key to earning the trust of the Iroquois was to learn their language and adhere to as many native protocols as possible. Few Europeans were as willing as Johnson to do so. He quickly gained a reputation—among Indians and Euro-Americans—as a person who could get things done in Indian country. The Mohawks dubbed him Warraghiyageh, which meant "in the midst of affairs."[69] In 1746 the governor of New York recognized Johnson's unique position in the midst of Indian business by naming him the colony's sole commissioner for Indian affairs.

Even though Johnson was comfortable participating in Iroquois rituals on their own terms—at least when it furthered his own interests—his understanding of condolence was no doubt aided by some deep similarities between it and English mourning practices. The terminology of "clearminded" and "mourners" may have been unfamiliar, but the idea that the community should support the bereaved was not. Speechmaking after someone died, whether in the form of a eulogy or funeral sermon, was standard practice in eighteenth-century England and America. Songs and hymns were likewise often a part of the European and Euro-American funerals with which Johnson was familiar. And it was common to give gifts at Anglo-American funerals, although the items were usually given by the mourners rather than the clearminded. So in the early 1750s, when Johnson began to participate in condolence rituals as the representative of first New York and later the British crown, he not only understood Iroquois practices but in his reports was able to translate them into terms his superiors could understand.

As soon as Johnson heard of Kakhswenthioni's death, he knew that there was little time to waste and therefore immediately headed for Onondaga. But first he stopped at Oneida on June 13, where he met representatives of the clearminded half of the Iroquois confederation (clearminded, that is, because the dead man was not from their nations): the Oneidas, Tuscaroras, Cayugas, and their non-Iroquois allies the Nanticokes. This side, referred to as the "Four Brothers," would condole the mourning half of the confederation: the Onondagas, Senecas, and Mohawks, or "Three Brothers." [70] Tesanonda, the speaker for the Four Brothers, greeted Johnson with the "At the Woods' Edge Ceremony" to condole Johnson for the losses the British had recently suffered: "I by this string of wampum wipe off your tears, clear your throat, and open your heart that you may speak without constraint." Johnson was polite enough not to mention it in his official report, but Tesanonda breached protocol by giving Johnson only one string of wampum—instead of the customary three—to accompany the Woods' Edge Ceremony. Perhaps there was a wampum shortage at Oneida. Johnson, however, was not offended, and later that evening when he returned Tesanonda's greeting he gave the traditional three strings of wampum. "I also sweep away the blood out of your council room which hath been spilt by our common enemy the French." [71]

Then it was off to Onondaga. Johnson and the representatives of the Four Brothers reached the outskirts of the settlement on June 18. But before they could enter, messengers from the village met the group "and a halt was made for two hours, to settle the formalities of the condolence." The ritual had a general outline to which all condolences roughly adhered, but there was a great deal of room for negotiating the particulars of a given ceremony. It was just this sort of time-consuming haggling that so many European officials found "tedious." The issues settled, Johnson marched "at the head" of the Four Brothers sachems, who were "singing the condoling song which contains the names, laws, and customs of their renowned ancestors." [72] The words and musical notation to this song were transcribed only two years earlier by François Piquet, a Sulpician priest at Oswegatchie on the St. Lawrence River. The score is marked "Air Funébre, très Lent" (Funereal Air, very Slow). It begins:

Hear us, alas alas!
You who founded it, alas!
You who established the Great Law, alas!
Which should be observed always, alas![73]

After the clearminded sachems were finished singing this mournful song, they began "praying to god that their deceased brother might be blessed with happiness in his other state." Here Johnson elided a crucial issue. To what "god" did the sachems "pray"? Kakhswenthioni had been baptized a Christian, as had several of the participating sachems (including Abraham, who led the ceremony). Protestant and Catholic missionaries mostly disapproved of the condolence ceremony. On the one hand, nothing in it explicitly countered Christianity: it was simply a ritual to comfort the bereaved. For this reason a literate Christian Delaware Indian such as Joseph Peepy felt no conflict when he "went through the ceremony of condolence" in April 1767. On the other hand, the ceremony seemed to suggest that Christian practices such as hymns and prayers were not sufficient to address pressing questions of death and the afterlife, and it was in this realm that missionaries were especially eager to have Christian norms replace older ones. When the Jesuit Jean Pierron attended a Mohawk condolence in 1669, he was disgusted. "If these customs were holy and virtuous," he regaled the assembled group, "they would be respected, and I would do everything imaginable to oblige you to retain them. But to see you pass all your lives in such execrable crimes, that is what I cannot make up my mind to do."[74] This brings us back to the question: Did the sachems at Kakhswenthioni's condolence pray to the Christian god, an Iroquois god or gods, or some combination? Johnson either did not know or would not tell.

After the song and prayers, the clearminded continued on the road, now within sight of Onondaga. But they were stopped in their tracks by a vanguard of Onondaga's "head sachems and warriors," sitting in complete silence, having arranged themselves into the shape of a half moon across the road. Another song commenced, this one about an hour long. Only now did the Onondaga sachems and warriors greet Johnson and the clearminded representatives, shaking their hands and welcoming them through the palisade.

Johnson and the Four Brothers entered the town, the Indians continuing to sing the condoling song. The Onondaga fired their guns to salute the clearminded in a relatively recent addition to the condolence protocol. The clearminded fired a salvo in answer. The mourning Three Brothers led the new arrivals to a "green bower adjoining to the deceased sachem's house prepared on purpose," where all parties were probably relieved to be able to sit down. Typically the mourners and the clearminded sat on the opposite sides of a fire. The Woods' Edge Ceremony was performed to open the lines of communication. "This ended his introduction," the records pithily state.[75] Hours of negotiations, singing, and marching, and this was just the introduction!

The next day everyone reconvened for the condolence ceremony proper. It was led by "Old Abraham the head sachem of the Mohawks." Here was another deviation from the traditional script. As one of the mourning Three Brothers, Abraham technically should not have performed the ceremony. It should have been led by a clearminded Four Brothers sachem.[76] The reason for this breach of protocol was not given—perhaps it was simply that Abraham was the most respected person present, or perhaps he was the Indian most trusted by Johnson—but it again shows the adaptability of the ritual.

Abraham made a speech and "with a large belt covered the grave of the deceased." This was a wampum belt, which contained many times more beads than a wampum string. The "covering" of the grave was metaphorical; it is possible that Kakhswenthioni's body had been buried miles away, if he had died while hunting or on the warpath. Even if Kakhswenthioni lay in the village cemetery, this would have been outside the palisade, not under the bower next to his longhouse. Next, Abraham gave a belt of wampum to comfort Kakhswenthioni's "relations." By this the Iroquois, with a more expansive notion of family ties than Europeans, meant more than simply parents and children. They most likely meant all members of the dead man's lineage and even clan.[77] The next belt was probably the most important in Johnson's eyes: Abraham gave the third belt to the mourners and urged them to continue their friendship with the English. Having only recently convinced Kakhswenthioni and other Onondagas to join the English side in the war, Johnson did not want their grief to weaken the alliance. Abraham gave the fourth and fifth belts to the mourners to dispel the clouds during the day and the night respectively, so that meetings and deliberations could be held "with their usual tranquility."[78]

Evidently there were speeches that went unrecorded, because the final tally of presents was eleven belts, three strings, and a "scalp of the enemy to replace the deceased." It is unclear whether this was the scalp of a French person or a French-allied Indian. In either case it took the place of a captive to be adopted into the village, which had been the practice during the "mourning wars" of the seventeenth and early eighteenth centuries. Perhaps a scalp could not "replace" the deceased as effectively as a captive, but the desire for adopting captives had led to a vicious cycle of wars, deaths, and captives for the Iroquois and their enemies, and the practice was now less common than in the past. Finally, with all the belts given and speeches made, a glass of rum was passed around "to wash down all sorrow and grief." This was clearly another relatively recent addition to the ritual and it ended the ceremony for that day. All that remained was for everyone to meet again the following morning—June 20, the eighth day of Johnson's participation in this elaborate event—so the Onondagas could offer their thanks for the condolence by presenting "as many belts of wampum as were given them yesterday." [79] Thus there was no net gain or loss of wampum for the participants, but in the hours of speeches and attention to ritual forms something more precious was exchanged between the mourning Iroquois and the English: cross-cultural understanding.

Compared with the extraordinary burials of Scarouady's son and Kindaruntie, the condolence for Kakhswenthioni seems to have been even more successful at sustaining the alliance. There was no grilling of a participant, as there had been with Scarouady, and the Onondagas continued in their support for the British. The ritual owed its success to several factors. Because condolence was an Indian ritual—albeit with some newly added touches of European material culture—it was more likely than an extraordinary burial to convince Indians of Europeans' goodwill. For this same reason it was a much tougher ritual for Europeans to master, and sometimes there could be problems, as in September 1755 when the Mohawks chided Johnson for covering their dead and then immediately asking them to go into battle, without the requisite period of mourning. But when Europeans adhered to protocol it meant a great deal to the Iroquois. As the Oneidas declared during a condolence several weeks after the ceremony for Kakhswenthioni, "it was a convincing proof of his [Johnson's] regard for them, to find he did not neglect those necessary ceremonials at a time too when they knew he was much hurried and full of business." [80] Thus was communication between Indians and Europeans facilitated by the knowledge of deathways held by both groups.

* * *

The death diplomacy of extraordinary burials and condolences during the Seven Years' War was remarkably significant in world historical terms. It is not too far-fetched to argue that without proper attention to Indian ideas about death, mourning, and the afterlife, the British might have lost the support of their Indian allies. This could have led to a very different outcome for the war, which when it was settled with the 1763 Treaty of Paris rewrote the map of North America, altered the political landscape in Europe, and set the stage for the colonization of South Asia. To get from Kakhswenthioni's condolence to the late eighteenth-century Bengali rice trade requires only a slight interpretive leap.

Yet viewed with the benefit of hindsight, it is also clear that the extraordinary burials and condolences of the Seven Years' War had little long-term ameliorating impact on Anglo-American treatment of Indians. When the war ended, Anglo-American farmers, eager to sink their plows into the dark soil of the Mohawk River Valley and the Ohio River Valley, migrated by the thousands into former Indian lands. Thus began further decades of war with Indians, displacement, and removal. But from the vantage point of the 1750s, the burials and condolences represent only the most dramatic of numerous attempts by all participants in the conflict to speak in terms their allies and enemies could understand. Hard-won knowledge about deathways, the result of centuries of conflict and comity in the New World, was at the very center of the story.

Ways of Living, Ways of Dying

BY 1800, THE New World was not so new anymore. As a result, ethnographic encounters and curiosity about unfamiliar deathways gave way to relatively peaceful coexistence among a variety of mortuary traditions and eschatological beliefs. In religious matters, Christianity dominated the portion of the hemisphere that has been the subject of this book: the eastern third of North America and the Caribbean. People's attachment to Christianity was not always as strong as clergymen wished, even among individuals of European descent, and there continued to exist groups like the Iroquois whose deathways retained important non-Christian components. Yet for most residents of this region, some version of Christianity now provided the primary interpretive framework for answering questions about life and death, for shaping ways of living and ways of dying.

One can begin to understand the interaction of peoples in the New World by tracing the history of cross-cultural encounters with death. When Indians, Africans, and Europeans met in the New World, interest in unfamiliar deathways combined with real and perceived parallels in mortuary practices to allow for communication and even understanding across cultural boundaries. These sorts of exchanges with strangers had occurred for millennia before Columbus, and they produced a range of reactions along a spectrum from inclusive to exclusive, from tolerant and curious to judgmental and dismissive. These reactions were not, however, scattered randomly along the spectrum. Rather, they tended toward the inclusive end. Observers noticed differences in details and sometimes were repulsed by them, but they paid more attention to deep structural similarities between their own and outsiders' mortuary practices. Observers usually focused on the common humanity of strangers, which included the inescapable facts that all must die and all societies must do something with dead bodies.

This tendency toward inclusivity continued after 1492. Indians, Africans, and Europeans were all curious about the deathways of those they encountered in the New World. Some individuals asked questions about unfamiliar practices and even occasionally participated in them. As they gained an understanding of others' deathways, it soon became apparent to some that this knowledge could be put to use against their adversaries. For New World encounters resulted from a system of European colonization that was fundamentally based upon exploiting land and people. Most Europeans who went to the New World hoped to gain wealth; a much smaller group hoped to win non-European souls for Christ. In this context knowledge about deathways provided a means to an end. For some Europeans this meant building alliances with non-Europeans, for others it meant trying to convert them to Christianity, while for others this knowledge offered an advantage in gaining physical or military dominance. Indians and Africans responded in kind, marshaling their knowledge of European deathways to their own ends. But these latter groups were at distinct disadvantages: Indians faced the challenges of colonization even as they endured devastating epidemics, while Africans arrived in the Americas in chains.

Over the course of the next several centuries, death was among the most important channels of communication between peoples of different cultures. It was not the only one, of course: food, music, sex, and language were all exchanged by participants in colonial encounters. But none of these other cultural categories were invested with as much significance by the people of the early modern Atlantic world, and therefore none of them have left the volume of records—material and literary—that allow us to glimpse the process of change over time. By the end of the eighteenth century, Indians, Africans, and Europeans had long been using the language of death to communicate with one another, and they were all, to varying degrees, changed as a result.

Those Indians who had early and intense interactions with Europeans found themselves greatly weakened by 1800 due to a combination of disease, warfare, and land dispossession. In southeastern New England, Narragansetts and Wampanoags managed to hold on to some of their aboriginal territory, defying the predictions of their white neighbors that they would soon disappear. Nonetheless, their economic and demographic positions remained precarious. In this difficult situation, many turned to evangelical Christianity, with its emotional preaching and message of equality in God's eyes. Indian ministers who continued to preach the word in native languages, such as the Wampanoag Zachariah Howwoswee Jr., saw their congregations shrink as fewer and fewer could understand the language of their ancestors. In contrast, evangelical Indian preachers such as the Baptist Thomas Jeffers used English-language sermons to appeal to a wide range of Indians, young and old, male and female. There is, unfortunately, little evidence about the deathways of these evangelical Indians. Presumably their burials adhered to Christian practices, though without archaeological evidence it is nearly impossible to know how many pre- or early-contact traditions persisted. At least one related practice with deep roots survived: the use of memorial cairns, piles of rocks used to mark sacred places. Not precisely an aspect of deathways, as the cairns did not mark graves but rather sites that had important historical meanings, these memorials caused the Christian Indians of New England to be "ridiculed" by whites for being "idolatrous." Instead of giving up on the cairns, however, Indians simply hid them from their mocking neighbors.[1]

Micmacs in Nova Scotia likewise combined Christianity with a few aboriginal practices in the first decades of the nineteenth century. Due to the efforts of Pierre Biard and subsequent Jesuit and Franciscan missionaries, the Micmacs embraced Roman Catholicism instead of Protestantism. Micmac spirituality revolved around the mother of the Virgin Mary, St. Anne, whom the Micmacs referred to as *Se'ta'n* in their language and portrayed as an Indian woman who was born when the French first came to the region. The annual festival of St. Anne in July became the most important religious day of the year.[2]

Other groups saw their numbers reduced even more than the Micmacs, Narragansetts, and Wampanoags. The various peoples who had made up the Powhatan chiefdom in the seventeenth century lived on small reservations in early nineteenth-century Virginia. The Nansemonds had long been Christianized by that point, while the Pamunkeys were more recent converts. Both groups, like their counterparts in New England, found that evangelical denominations best fulfilled their desire for a message of spiritual equality.[3] Again, though, almost no evidence survives to document the deathways of these individuals. The same holds true for the descendants of the Hurons. After the destruction of the Huron confederacy in 1649, the Huron diaspora scattered in three directions. Several hundred made their way to Jesuit reserves near the town of Quebec. A smaller number headed west, where they would rename themselves the Wyandot and ultimately relocate to Oklahoma.

And perhaps several thousand eventually joined the Iroquois, either through capture or voluntary migration to central New York, where within a generation they became assimilated into Iroquois society.[4]

Because the Iroquois retained so much power and autonomy in the eighteenth century—in part due to their willingness to incorporate outsiders and thereby increase their numbers—they did not face the same pressures to adopt Christian deathways. As we saw in Chapter 8, French and British officials hoping to cultivate the Iroquois as allies had to participate in the condolence ceremony, even as this ritual absorbed European influences over time. In their burials, the Iroquois retained syncretic forms far longer than their counterparts in New England and the Chesapeake. These hybrid burials were not unlike those found in New England Indian cemeteries around 1700, and they could be found well into the nineteenth century. One excavation from the Canawaugus reservation, some twenty miles south of Rochester, demonstrates the longer persistence of syncretic practices. Archaeologists unearthed six burials dating to roughly 1800, all of which exhibit European and Euro-American influences. Three were extended supine burials, two were interred in coffins, and all have goods of European or Euro-American manufacture such as brass kettles and iron knives. But the fact that all these individuals were buried with grave goods, including some of native manufacture such as wooden ladles and vermillion paint, shows that in 1800 the Iroquois retained aspects of their early-contact mortuary practices.[5]

People of African descent faced a demographic situation in 1800 that differed greatly from that of American Indians. African Americans could be counted by the millions, and their numbers continued to grow, both through natural increase in the United States and through continued importation until 1807 (in British colonies) and 1808 (in the United States). Compared with Indians, much more is known about African American deathways in the early part of the nineteenth century. In northern cities, blacks embraced Christian deathways, with very little apparent African influence. In the plantation South and the British West Indies, a wider range of practices obtained. Funerals increasingly showed the impact of Afro-Christianity, with predominantly Christian practices combined with aspects of earlier traditions. Some graves were decorated with broken plates and other items that had belonged to the deceased. And some individuals continued to believe in the transmigration of souls to Africa. But the future of African American deathways lay with Christian beliefs and practices, even in areas with high concentrations of blacks. In the words of one archaeologist, "African American burials by the mid-nineteenth century, and in some cases well before that date, had become indistinguishable from the burials of any other ethnic group in America."[6]

Jews, by contrast, constituted a tiny portion of the hemisphere's population in the early nineteenth century. In the United States, there were only about 2,700 Jews in 1820, barely 0.03 percent of the total population. In a few towns, Jewish communities that thrived in the eighteenth century disappeared in the nineteenth. Newport's Jewish community shrank dramatically after the American Revolution, with services at the synagogue ceasing in 1792 and the last Jew moving to New York in 1822. In the Caribbean the relative proportion of Jews in the population was higher, though the absolute numbers were small. Curaçao retained the largest community, with roughly 900 Jews in the 1820s.[7] Throughout the hemisphere Jews continued to struggle with the issue of exogamous marriage and the threat it represented to the survival of American Jewry, using deathways to police the boundaries of their community. In 1820, for example, Charleston Jews issued a rule that those who married outside the faith would be denied burial in the *beth haim*.[8] Yet Jews were able to use their centuries of written rules regarding deathways to maintain their practices despite such a shaky demographic foundation. They formed and continued burial societies to pass down the knowledge that allowed these traditions to survive.

This does not mean that Jewish deathways were changeless in this period. Indeed, the broader Euro-American world, including Western Europe and the former and remaining European colonies in the Americas, witnessed important changes in attitudes toward death and the afterlife in the early nineteenth century. Jews, Christians of European descent, and Christians of African and American Indian descent all participated in the changes ushered in by what the historian Philippe Ariès has called the "Age of the Beautiful Death." A more Romantic style of describing death and dying first began to emerge among the elites of Western Europe toward the end of the eighteenth century and rapidly spread across the social spectrum in the nineteenth. Observers now judged deathbed scenes less on how well the dying adhered to the old scripts derived from the *Ars moriendi*, with their attention to Christian resignation, and more on the magnificence of the dying person's struggle with death and the beauty of the corpse. Thus a French woman wrote in her journal in 1825, "The death of Madame de Villeneuve was *sublime*," choosing a word that was not used in this context before the nineteenth century.[9] The Christian afterlife also evolved, with heaven being domesticated, portrayed as an extension of one's home where the dead could continue their friendships and familial relationships. At the same time, hell was shorn of some of its terrors, especially with the more optimistic theology that came to dominate American Protestantism during the Second Great Awakening. Burial grounds also began to change, as they were moved out of the center of towns and cities due to fear of contagion and, starting in the 1830s in the United States, into rural cemeteries. The term "cemetery" itself is instructive: derived from the Greek for "sleeping chamber," it gradually overtook the older terms "burial ground" and "churchyard." The use of "cemetery" in the nineteenth century represented death as sleep; one could almost imagine the bloom remaining on the cheeks of the dead.[10]

Despite these important changes, there remained numerous continuities with earlier Euro-American deathways. Deathbed scenes continued to be observed with great attention, even if they were now described in more Romantic terms. The corpse remained the focus of the postmortem proceedings. People still sat up and watched the corpse for signs of life; perhaps they did so with even greater vigilance than in previous centuries, due to the increasing fears of burial alive that writers such as Edgar Allan Poe both drew upon and stoked. The body continued to be prepared for earth inhumation by female relatives and servants, though in the second half of the nineteenth century these functions would increasingly be taken over, especially in the urban North, by professional undertakers.[11]

Another continuity was that people remained fascinated by unfamiliar deathways, although now they experienced this sense of curiosity and wonder mostly in the comfort of their parlors, as they read the accounts of travelers and ethnographers. Readers who picked up Charles Darwin's *Voyage of the Beagle* (1839) would not have been surprised that on the young naturalist's first landfall, on the Cape Verde Islands, the very first thing he visited were the graves of the Catholic "governors and captain-generals of the islands" whose tombstones dated back to the sixteenth century.[12] Likewise, those who enjoyed the works of Lewis H. Morgan, a widely read nineteenth-century anthropologist, learned a great deal about others' deathways. In his classic *League of the Ho-Dé-No-Sau-Nee or Iroquois* (1851), Morgan informed his readers about the Iroquois condolence councils, burial customs, and Dance of the Dead. Few nineteenth-century readers would have disagreed with Morgan that "the burial customs of every people interest the mind."[13]

Indeed, the professional discipline of anthropology that emerged in the early twentieth century drew on its roots in nineteenth-century practitioners like Morgan and their interest in deathways. Two of the most important early twentieth-century works of anthropology, Arnold van Gennep's *The Rites of Passage* (1909) and Robert Hertz's *A Contribution to the Study of the Collective Representation of Death* (1907), placed death at the center of their analyses. Van Gennep's hugely influential work argued that several rituals of transition from one state to another—including funerals—involved a tripartite structure of separation from one status (alive), then a liminal period between statuses (dying), and finally reincorporation into a new status (dead). This insight allowed anthropologists to compare death practices from around the world. Hertz too anticipated the structuralism that dominated much of twentieth-century anthropology. Hertz focused on societies that practiced secondary burial, finding that in these societies individuals saw a sharp contrast between corruptible flesh and perdurable bones. Hertz's broader insight, as described by two recent anthropologists, shaped his field for decades: that "close attention to the combined symbolic and sociological contexts of the corpse yields profound insights regarding the meaning of death and life." [14]

Yet even as professional anthropologists circled the globe looking for ever more obscure deathways to catalogue, the general public began to lose interest in reading about unfamiliar mortuary practices. This resulted from a sea change in attitudes, a shift from the nineteenth century's "Age of the Beautiful Death" to the mid-twentieth century's "Denial of Death." [15] Reacting against the senseless slaughter of two world wars, Western Europeans and North Americans adopted an extreme reticence about death. Professionals now handled every aspect of dying and death, from doctors and nurses in hospitals to funeral directors who embalmed the corpse, prettified it with makeup, and took care of its burial or cremation. In this period the word "cancer" was not spoken in polite company and doctors rarely talked with their patients about end-of-life issues. Mourning costume, which had reached elaborate heights during the Victorian period, was now worn very briefly, if at all. As the etiquette writer Amy Vanderbilt explained in 1952, "We are developing a more positive social attitude toward others, who might find it difficult to function well in the constant company of an outwardly mourning person." [16] In other words, manifestations of grief were an imposition on those who were not bereaved. In this cultural context, reading about deathways seemed grotesque.

More recently, since roughly the 1990s, Americans have begun to talk more about death and dying. American Indians and African Americans are an important part of this trend. Both groups have shown increasing interest in connecting deathways from previous centuries to their lives today. New

York's African Burial Ground, now run by the National Park Service, annually attracts tens of thousands of visitors, a large percentage of whom are black.[17] A few African American graves, especially in the U.S. South, continue to be decorated with broken ceramics, glassware, and bowls—or, in the case of a North Carolina mechanic, a car wheel with two wrenches welded to it.[18] Other African Americans consciously honor their African heritage in their deathways. The Batesville Casket Company's Kente Line, featuring African-inspired fabrics lining the coffin and even serving as burial garments for the deceased, is popular among black baby boomers.[19]

For American Indians, the issue is not so much honoring a distant homeland as it is trying to bring scattered bones back to ancient homelands. Indians have held a special reverence for the remains of ancestors for millennia; Europeans first encountered this when Columbus observed the Taino zemis incorporating human skulls. For the better part of the twentieth century, Indians tried to reclaim bones that had been taken by professional archaeologists and amateur pot hunters. This movement gained steam in the 1980s and culminated in the 1990 passage of the Native American Graves Protection and Repatriation Act (NAGPRA). This law has been a mixed blessing for Indians. Even though NAGPRA is "one of the most powerful human rights mechanisms in United States history," in the words of one scholar, it "has been nothing less than a nightmare" for many who have tried to have human remains repatriated under the act.[20]

More broadly, Americans of all ethnicities have become increasingly interested in talking about death. With the aging of the baby-boom generation, more families are discussing living wills and "do not resuscitate" orders. Hospice care, which treats the symptoms of the terminally ill without trying to extend their lives, has boomed in the United States. An astonishing 39 percent of all deaths in the United States now take place under hospice care, which often is provided in the dying person's home with the help of the dying person's family and friends. In 2007, more than 1.4 million Americans received hospice care, which means that over a million families each year are now involved in the medical, physical, and spiritual aspects of caring for the dying. More and more, ways of living are intertwined with ways of dying.[21]

In this changing cultural climate, more Americans are again reading about deathways, and not just in Mitch Albom's *Tuesdays with Morrie* (1997), which spent 206 weeks on the *New York Times* hardcover nonfiction bestseller list. There seems to be an uptick in interest in unfamiliar deathways. In one recent twelve-month stretch, articles appeared in the *New York Times*

Figure 27. Martyrs' Shrine, Midland, Ontario. Built in 1926, this church commemorates the North American Martyrs, the eight Jesuits who were killed while working as missionaries in present-day Ontario and New York. Photograph by the author.

on Indonesian, Japanese, and Korean deathways. Like nineteenth-century consumers of travel narratives, twenty-first-century readers of the *Times* were transported far away to learn about the use of wooden figurines in Korean burials, about the declining influence of Buddhism on the Japanese funeral industry, and about the elaborate pageantry of a Balinese royal funeral.[22] Even more telling has been a recent boomlet in historical books about death. If one thinks of the "past as a foreign country," one can see these books as responding to the reading public's rejuvenated interest in unfamiliar deathways. For example, Drew Gilpin Faust's *This Republic of Suffering* (2008) and Mark Schantz's *Awaiting the Heavenly Country* (2008), both on death in the U.S. Civil War, were jointly reviewed in the *New Yorker* and the *New York Review of Books*.[23]

The recent interest in unfamiliar deathways, past and present, has its hold on me as well, so I planned a trip to Midland, Ontario, in the heart of what used to be Huronia, to visit the Martyrs' Shrine (Figure 27). This Catholic church was built in 1926 to honor the seventeenth-century Jesuits killed while preaching the word of Christ to the Indians of New France. As a thoroughly secular person, I wanted to try to better understand the Catholic belief in the power of holy bones. When I learned that the shrine holds some of Jean de Brébeuf's relics, I headed north.

I entered the church on a crisp September morning. With the sun filtering through the stained glass, the brown interior of the church looked like leather. When I located the reliquaries I was surprised by the abundance of bones. I've seen reliquaries that hold no more than a splinter, but these were more plentifully supplied, containing holy bones belonging not only to Brébeuf but also Charles Garnier and Gabriel Lalemant. The larger reliquary stopped me in my tracks. Inside was Brébeuf's skull, peering out at me (Figure 28). Even though I have decidedly mixed feelings about Brébeuf's role in the history of the Huron people, the skull captivated me. Holy or not, its power as bone, as previously living human tissue, connected me with the dead from three and a half centuries ago as the *Jesuit Relations* never could.

Someone informed me that the 10:30 a.m. Mass was about to begin, and that worshippers would be blessed by the bones of the saints. Did I want to stay? "Yes, of course," I answered, even though I feared that my notebook gave me away as an interloper. I was put off by the priest's opening prayer, imploring his god to change the minds of Catholics in the Canadian Parliament who were voting for "sinful" legislation (allowing gay marriage, I assumed), but when the sacrament of the Eucharist began the solemnity of the ancient

Figure 28. Jean de Brébeuf's skull. This reliquary at the Martyrs' Shrine displays bone fragments from Gabriel Lalemant and Charles Garnier, but Brébeuf's skull holds pride of place. When Pope John Paul II visited the shrine in 2004, he prayed over Brébeuf's skull. Photograph by the author.

ritual touched me. The priest then invited us to come up to be blessed by the holy bones. After a moment's hesitation, fearing once again that I would be unmasked as a nonbeliever, I took my place in line with about two dozen others. The priest held in his hand what looked like a brass doorknob. One side was flat and glass. Underneath the glass, on a background of what appeared to be red velvet, were tiny bone fragments from Brébeuf, Garnier, and Lalemant. When I reached the front of the line I was surprised to find myself shaking and sweating. The priest pressed the bones to my forehead and quickly asked for my protection "through the prayers of God's holy martyrs."

Leaving the dim church and stepping into the blindingly bright morning sun, I began to glimpse the power of holy bones. My interest in unfamiliar deathways whetted, I headed toward the nearby graves, wondering, "How do they bury their dead?"

NOTES

INTRODUCTION

Punctuation and spelling have been modernized in all quotations. Biblical passages are from the King James Version. All dates are New Style.

1. Anthony Grafton, *New Worlds, Ancient Texts: The Power of Tradition and the Shock of Discovery* (Cambridge, Mass., 1992), 40; Herodotus, *The Histories*, trans. Robin Wakefield (New York, 1998), 87 (Babylonians), 149 (Laocdonians). Other examples: 94, 126–28, 211, 246, 258–59, 266, 299, 305, 306, 371–72.

2. A.W. Pollard, ed., *The Travels of Sir John Mandeville* (New York, 1964), 133. See also 112, 114–15, 117–18, 129, 166, 203–4. On Mandeville's "capacious, theoretical, alienated tolerance," see Stephen Greenblatt, *Marvelous Possessions: The Wonder of the New World* (Chicago, 1991), chap. 2, esp. 49.

3. Pollard, ed., *The Travels of Sir John Mandeville*, 227.

4. Harold Hickerson, "The Feast of the Dead among the Seventeenth Century Alongkians of the Upper Great Lakes," *American Anthropologist* 62 (1960): 81–107. See also the diffusion of the Calumet Ceremony, which had its "origins . . . in mourning ritual." Robert L. Hall, "Calumet Ceremonialism, Mourning Ritual, and Mechanisms of Inter-Tribal Trade," in *Mirror and Metaphor: Material and Social Constructions of Reality*, ed. Daniel W. Ingersoll Jr. and Gordon Bronitsky (Lanham, Md., 1987), 29–43, quotation at 31.

5. On perceptions of cultural congruences, see Richard White, *The Middle Ground: Indians, Empires, and Republics in the Great Lakes Region, 1650–1815* (New York, 1991), 52–53. For a comparable approach in the Pacific, see John Gascoigne, *Captain Cook: Voyager between Worlds* (London, 2007), esp. chap. 8.

6. Anthony Pagden, *The Fall of Natural Man: The American Indian and the Origins of Comparative Ethnology* (New York, 1982), chap. 1; Pagden, *European Encounters with the New World: From Renaissance to Romanticism* (New Haven, Conn., 1993), esp. 10–11; and Margaret T. Hodgen, *Early Anthropology in the Sixteenth and Seventeenth Centuries* (Philadelphia, 1964), chap. 8.

7. Roger Williams, *A Key into the Language of America; or, An Help to the Language of the Natives in That Part of America, Called New-England* (London, 1643), 193.

8. Neal Salisbury, *Manitou and Providence: Indians, Europeans, and the Making of New England, 1500–1643* (New York, 1982), 50. See also Francis Jennings, *The Invasion of America: Indians, Colonialism, and the Cant of Conquest* (New York, 1976), esp. 39–40; and Charles Hudson, *The Southeastern Indians* (Knoxville, Tenn., 1976), esp. 97–102.

9. Winthrop D. Jordan, *White over Black: American Attitudes toward the Negro, 1550–1812* (Chapel Hill, N.C., 1968).

10. John K. Thornton, *Africa and Africans in the Making of the Atlantic World, 1400–1680* (New York, 1992), 236. See also Mechal Sobel, *The World They Made Together: Black and White Values in Eighteenth-Century Virginia* (Princeton, N.J., 1987); and Sylvia R. Frey and Betty Wood, *Come Shouting to Zion: African American Protestantism in the American South and British Caribbean to 1830* (Chapel Hill, N.C., 1998), esp. 82–85.

11. Allan Greer, *Mohawk Saint: Catherine Tekakwitha and the Jesuits* (New York, 2005), x–xi. See also Joyce E. Chaplin, *Subject Matter: Technology, the Body, and Science on the Anglo-American Frontier, 1500–1676* (Cambridge, Mass., 2001); Karen Ordahl Kupperman, *Indians and English: Facing Off in Early America* (Ithaca, N.Y., 2000); Ann M. Little, *Abraham in Arms: War and Gender in Colonial New England* (Philadelphia, 2007); and John Wood Sweet, *Bodies Politic: Negotiating Race in the American North, 1730–1830* (Baltimore, 2003).

12. Nancy Shoemaker, *A Strange Likeness: Becoming Red and White in Eighteenth-Century North America* (New York, 2004), 3.

13. James Axtell, *The Invasion Within: The Contest of Cultures in Colonial North America* (New York, 1985); Denys Delage, *Bitter Feast: Amerindians and Europeans in Northeastern North America, 1600–64*, trans. Jane Brierley (Vancouver, 1993); Matthew Dennis, *Cultivating a Landscape of Peace: Iroquois-European Encounters in Seventeenth-Century America* (Ithaca, N.Y., 1993); and the many works that support the Tannenbaum thesis, such as Jane Landers, *Black Society in Spanish Florida* (Urbana, Ill., 1999).

14. J. H. Elliott, *Empires of the Atlantic World: Britain and Spain in America, 1492–1830* (New Haven, Conn., 2006); and Jorge Cañizares-Esguerra, *Puritan Conquistadors: Iberianizing the Atlantic, 1550–1700* (Stanford, Calif., 2006).

CHAPTER I

1. The one exception is an eleventh-century ossuary found on Cape Cod. Francis P. McManamon, James W. Bradley, and Ann L. Magennis, *The Indian Neck Ossuary* (Boston, 1986).

2. Kathleen J. Bragdon, *Native People of Southern New England, 1500–1650* (Norman, Okla., 1996), 232; Elise M. Brenner, "Sociopolitical Implications of Mortuary Ritual Remains in 17th-Century Native Southern New England," in *The Recovery of Meaning: Historical Archaeology in the Eastern United States*, ed. Mark P. Leone and Parker B. Potter, Jr. (Washington, D.C., 1988), 154–55.

3. Bragdon, *Native People of Southern New England*, 232–33; Brenner, "Sociopolitical Implications," 156.

4. George Parker Winship, ed., *Sailors Narratives of Voyages along the New England Coast, 1524–1624* (Boston, 1905), 19; Alexander Young, ed., *Chronicles of the Pilgrim Fathers of the Colony of Plymouth, from 1602 to 1625* (Boston, 1841), 313, 362. Winslow's account was originally published in 1624. See also Roger Williams, *A Key into the Language of America* (London, 1643), 188.

5. Williams, *A Key into the Language*, 192–93.

6. James Hammond Trumbull, *Natick Dictionary* (Washington, D.C., 1903), 37, 98.

7. Williams, *A Key into the Language*, 193; Bragdon, *Native People of Southern New England*, 229.

8. See, for example, Williams, *A Key into the Language*, 119, 190; John Josselyn, *An Account of Two Voyages to New-England* (London, 1674), 134–35; and Edward Winslow, *The Glorious Progress of the Gospel, Amongst the Indians in New England* (1649), in *Collections of the Massachusetts Historical Society*, 3d ser. (1834): 4, 77.

9. Williams, *A Key into the Language*, 116-17.

10. Young, *Chronicles of the Pilgrim Fathers*, 363; Williams, *A Key into the Language*, 195.

11. William Wood, *New Englands Prospect* (London, 1634), 105; Williams, *A Key into the Language*, 122; Edward Winslow, *Good Newes from New England* (London, 1624), 53. See also Bragdon, *Native People of Southern New England*, 188–91.

12. Wood, *New Englands Prospect*, 104.

13. Charles Francis Adams, Jr., *New English Canaan of Thomas Morton* (New York, 1883), 170; Williams, *A Key into the Language*, 195.

14. Young, *Chronicles of the Pilgrim Fathers*, 363; Patricia E. Rubertone, *Grave Undertakings: An Archaeology of Roger Williams and the Narragansett Indians* (Washington, D.C., 2001), 143–47.

15. Young, *Chronicles of the Pilgrim Fathers*, 153–54.

16. Wood, *New Englands Prospect*, 104. See also Young, *Chronicles of the Pilgrim Fathers*, 362.

17. Josselyn, *An Account of Two Voyages*, 132 (quotation); Wood, *New Englands Prospect*, 104. On keening, see Clodagh Tait, *Death, Burial and Commemoration in Ireland, 1550–1650* (New York, 2002), 35–38.

18. Blackening: Williams, *A Key into the Language*, 193; Wood, *New Englands Prospect*, 104; Adams, *New English Canaan*, 170; and David B. Quinn and Alison M. Quinn, *The English New England Voyages, 1602–1608* (London, 1983), 350. Hair cutting: Young, *Chronicles of the Pilgrim Fathers*, 363.

19. Wood, *New Englands Prospect*, 104; Adams, *New English Canaan*, 170; and Quinn and Quinn, *English New England Voyages*, 350–51.

20. Williams, *A Key into the Language*, 193–94. See also Adams, *New English Canaan*, 170.

21. For example, Mechal Sobel, *The World They Made Together: Black and White Values in Eighteenth-Century Virginia* (Princeton, N.J., 1987), 171–72; Jerome S. Handler and Frederick W. Lange, *Plantation Slavery in Barbados: An Archaeological and Historical Investigation* (Cambridge, Mass., 1978), 200, 206, 209–15.

22. Handler and Lange, *Plantation Slavery in Barbados*, 184–85, 197–98, 199, 205.

23. David Eltis, "The Volume and Structure of the Transatlantic Slave Trade: A Reassessment," *William and Mary Quarterly* 58, no. 1 (January 2001): 44.

24. These European descriptions are not without their problems. In addition to the usual ethnocentrism, these men had an especially powerful incentive to view Africans as savages, because the Europeans were almost all involved in the slave trade. Moreover, when different authors provide similar accounts it is sometimes difficult to disentangle whether the later reports corroborate the earlier ones or simply repeat their claims. But these problems are not insurmountable. Many seventeenth-century authors strove to provide objective accounts, sometimes explicitly to counter the wild claims of earlier observers. And the problem of plagiarized sources has been addressed by these texts' editors and translators, who have meticulously cross-checked the sources to learn what is fresh and what is merely a restatement of earlier authors. See, for example, Adam Jones's translation of Michael Hemmersam's description of his years on the Gold Coast. Jones omits the portion of Hemmersam's account plagiarized from de Marees. Jones, ed., *German Sources for West African History, 1599–1669* (Wiesbaden, 1983), 97–98.

25. William Bosman, *A New and Accurate Description of the Coast of Guinea: Divided into the Gold, the Slave, and the Ivory Coasts*, ed. John Ralph Willis, J. D. Fage, and R. E. Bradbury (London, 1967), 455.

26. P. E. H. Hair, Adam Jones, and Robin Law, eds., *Barbot on Guinea: The Writings of Jean Barbot on West Africa, 1678–1712*, 2 vols. (London, 1992), 1:274; Nicolas Villault, Sieur de Bellefond, *A Relation of the Coasts of Affrick Called Guinee*, 2d ed. (London, 1670), 184; Jones, ed., *German Sources for West African History*, 118, 158; Adam Jones, ed., *Olfert Dapper's Description of Benin (1668)* (Madison, Wis., 1998), 26; and Pieter de Marees, *Description and Historical Account of the Gold Kingdom of Guinea (1602)*, ed. Albert van Dantzig and Adam Jones (Oxford, 1987), 67–68.

27. De Marees, *Description and Historical Account*, 69–70.

28. On supernatural inquests, see Vincent Brown, *The Reaper's Garden: Death and Power in the World of Atlantic Slavery* (Cambridge, Mass., 2008), 66–69.

29. Hair et al., eds., *Barbot on Guinea*, 590; de Marees, *Description and Historical Account*, 180.

30. Jones, ed., *German Sources for West African History*, 257; Villault, *Relation of the Coasts of Affrick*, 190; de Marees, *Description and Historical Account*, 180; Bosman, *New and Accurate Description*, 228.

31. Bosman, *New and Accurate Description*, 448; Jones, ed., *German Sources for West African History*, 123, 257; de Marees, *Description and Historical Account*, 180.

32. Jones, ed., *German Sources for West African History*, 257.

33. Negative comments: Bosman, *New and Accurate Description*, 231; Hair et al., eds., *Barbot on Guinea*, 640. Nineteenth century: Christopher R. DeCorse, *An Archaeology of Elmina: Africans and Europeans on the Gold Coast, 1400–1900* (Washington, D.C., 2001), 100; Sandra E. Greene, *Sacred Sites and the Colonial Encounter: A History of Meaning and Memory in Ghana* (Bloomington, Ind., 2002), 71.

34. Jones, ed., *German Sources for West African History*, 42.

35. DeCorse, *Archaeology of Elmina*, 188.

36. Among the nineteenth-century Anlo, just to the east of the Akan in Ghana, subfloor burial was denied to those who died a "bad death," including hunchbacks and adults who died before having children, and those who died "in blood," which included those who died as a result of war, snakebites, and diseases such as smallpox and tuberculosis. Greene, *Sacred Sites*, 67.

37. Villault, *Relation of the Coasts of Africk*, 193 (household stuff); de Marees, *Description and Historical Account*, 182 (straw hut). See also Bosman, *New and Accurate Description*, 156, 232; and Jones, ed., *German Sources for West African History*, 31, 258.

38. Adam Jones, ed., *Brandenburg Sources for West African History, 1680–1700* (Stuttgart, 1985), 186. See also de Marees, *Description and Historical Account*, 182; Villault, *Relation of the Coasts of Africk*, 195; Bosman, *New and Accurate Description*, 230.

39. Jones, ed., *Brandenburg Sources for West African History*, 88; Jones, ed., *German Sources for West African History*, 42; Hair et al., eds., *Barbot on Guinea*, 591.

40. De Marees, *Description and Historical Account*, 180–83.

41. Jones, ed., *German Sources for West African History*, 257; Bosman, *New and Accurate Description*, 229, 230; Jones, ed., *Brandenburg Sources for West African History*, 127.

42. Birgit Meyer, *Translating the Devil: Religion and Modernity among the Ewe in Ghana* (Edinburgh, 1999), 10.

43. DeCorse, *Archaeology of Elmina*, 189; James O. Bellis, *The "Place of the Pots" in Akan Funerary Custom* (Bloomington, Ind., 1982).

44. John Vogt, *Portuguese Rule on the Gold Coast, 1469–1682* (Athens, Ga., 1979), 213.

45. On supernatural inquests in other regions of West Africa, see André Álvares de Almada, *Brief Treatise on the Rivers of Guinea*, ed. P. E. H. Hair (1594; Liverpool, 1984), 69–70, 105; Manuel Álvares, *Ethiopia Minor and a Geographical Account of the Province of Sierra Leone*, ed. P. E. H. Hair, 2 vols. (Liverpool, 1990), I:3:4, I:7:13–14, II:3:5; John Ogilby, *Africa: Being an Accurate Description* (London, 1670), 500; and John Matthews, *A Voyage to the River Sierra-Leone* (1788; London, 1966), 122.

46. Sylvie Anne Goldberg, *Crossing the Jabbok: Illness and Death in Ashkenazi Judaism in Sixteenth- through Nineteenth-Century Prague*, trans. Carol Cosman (Berkeley, Calif., 1996), 8–9, 20; Robert Goldenberg, "Bound Up in the Bond of Life: Death and Afterlife in the Jewish Tradition," in *Death and Afterlife: Perspectives of World Religions*, ed. Hiroshi Obayashi (Westport, Conn., 1992), 99–100.

47. Some scholars believe the *Semahot* appeared as late as the eighth century, but Dov Zlotnick argues convincingly for the earlier date. Zlotnick, ed., *The Tractate "Mourning" (Semahot): Regulations Relating to Death, Burial, and Mourning* (New Haven, Conn., 1966), 4–9.

48. Miriam Bodian, *Hebrews of the Portuguese Nation: Conversos and Community in Early Modern Amsterdam* (Bloomington, Ind., 1997), 30. The edition of this code that I use is Chaim N. Denburg, ed., *Code of Hebrew Law: Shulhan 'Aruk* (Montreal, 1954), cited by chapter and paragraph. Another valuable prescriptive work is the *Ma'avar Yabbok*, a book of death and burial ritual written in 1626 by Aaron Berachia of Modena. I

rely on the discussion of this text in Goldberg, *Crossing the Jabbok*, 102–28. These two texts are supplemented with Leo Modena, *The History of the Rites, Customs, and Manner of Life, of the Present Jews, throughout the World* (London, 1650), which has the great advantage of having been written by a rabbi; Johann Buxtorf, *The Jewish Synagogue; or, An Historicall Narration of the State of the Jewes* (London, 1657), which is marred by its Swiss author's explicit desire to convert Jews to Christianity but is still valuable due to Buxtorf's close study of Jewish law and customs; and, for a slightly later period, Bernard Picart, *The Ceremonies and Religious Customs of the Various Nations of the Known World*, 7 vols. (London, 1733–37), which relies heavily on Modena and Buxtorf but also includes some of the author's own observations.

49. Goldberg, *Crossing the Jabbok*, 108.

50. *Shulhan 'Aruk*, 338 § 2 (quotation); Elliott Horowitz, "The Jews of Europe and the Moment of Death in Medieval and Modern Times," *Judaism* 44, no. 3 (Summer 1995): 271 (proper burial); Goldberg, *Crossing the Jabbok*, 106.

51. Modena, *History of the Rites*, 234; Goldberg, *Crossing the Jabbok*, 111–12.

52. Modena, *History of the Rites*, 235 (meritorious work); Robert Bonfil, *Jewish Life in Renaissance Italy*, trans. Anthony Oldcorn (Berkeley, Calif., 1994), 281.

53. *Shulhan 'Aruk*, 344 § 1.

54. Picart, *Ceremonies and Religious Customs*, 1:243. See also Modena, *History of the Rites*, 237; and Goldberg, *Crossing the Jabbok*, 116. This custom seems not to have existed in the thirteenth century, but by the sixteenth century it was integral to Jewish burial practices. Goldberg, *Crossing the Jabbok*, 133–35.

55. Goldberg, *Crossing the Jabbok*, 38–39.

56. Zlotnick, *Tractate "Mourning,"* 33 (suicide); *Shulhan 'Aruk*, 345 § 1, 345 § 4 (excommunicant).

57. Picart, *Ceremonies and Religious Customs*, 1:244.

58. Babylonian Talmud, *Mo'ed Katan*, 15a-b. See also Zlotnick, *Tractate "Mourning,"* 48, 78–80.

59. *Shulhan 'Aruk*, 387 § 2.

60. Isaac S. Emmanuel, *Precious Stones of the Jews of Curaçao: Curaçaon Jewry, 1656–1957* (New York, 1957), 89.

61. Bonfil, *Jewish Life in Renaissance Italy*, 281.

62. Goldberg, *Crossing the Jabbok*, 23–27.

63. D. Henriques de Castro, *Keur van grafstenen op de Portugees-Israëlische begraafplaats te Ouderkerk aan de Amstel* (Ouderkerk aan de Amstel, 1999), 33.

64. Goldberg, *Crossing the Jabbok*, 124–25.

65. Quoted in A. N. Galpern, *The Religions of the People in Sixteenth-Century Champagne* (Cambridge, Mass., 1976), 19.

66. Natalie Zemon Davis, "Ghosts, Kin, and Progeny: Some Features of Family Life in Early Modern France," *Daedalus* 106 (Spring 1977): 92. This section of the chapter focuses on French deathways. Spanish Catholics held essentially the same beliefs about the afterlife, with some differences in funeral customs and the veneration of saints. See Carlos

E. M. Eire, *From Madrid to Purgatory: The Art and Craft of Dying in Sixteenth-Century Spain* (New York, 1995); Laura Vivanco, *Death in Fifteenth-Century Castile: Ideologies of the Elites* (Woodbridge, Eng., 2004); and, more generally, William A. Christian, Jr., *Local Religion in Sixteenth-Century Spain* (Princeton, N.J., 1981).

67. Jacques Le Goff, *The Birth of Purgatory*, trans. Arthur Goldhammer (Chicago, 1984).

68. Norman P. Tanner, ed., *Decrees of the Ecumenical Councils*, 2 vols. (London, 1990), 2:710.

69. Louis Chatellier, *The Europe of the Devout: The Catholic Reformation and the Formation of a New Society*, trans. Jean Birrell (New York, 1989), 204–5.

70. Peter Brown, *The Cult of the Saints: Its Rise and Function in Latin Christianity* (Chicago, 1981), esp. chap. 4.

71. Tanner, ed., *Decrees of the Ecumenical Councils*, 2:776.

72. R. Po-Chia Hsia, *The World of Catholic Renewal, 1540–1770*, 2d ed. (New York, 2005), 219.

73. Mary Catharine O'Connor, *The Art of Dying Well: The Development of the Ars moriendi* (New York, 1942), 114. See also Brad S. Gregory, *Salvation at Stake: Christian Martyrdom in Early Modern Europe* (Cambridge, Mass., 1999), 52–55.

74. This point is made about English Catholics in Eamon Duffy, *The Stripping of the Altars: Traditional Religion in England, c. 1400–c. 1580* (New Haven, Conn., 1992), 316–18.

75. Tanner, ed., *Decrees of the Ecumenical Councils*, 2:710.

76. John Bossy, *Christianity in the West, 1400–1700* (New York, 1985), 27, 32, 28–29.

77. Vanessa Harding, *The Dead and the Living in Paris and London, 1500–1670* (Cambridge, 2002), 200.

78. "Funeral Provision of Jeanne Passavent, 1582," in Harding, *Dead and Living in Paris and London*, 295–96.

79. Galpern, *Religions of the People*, 23.

80. Geoffrey Rowell, *The Liturgy of Christian Burial: An Introductory Survey of the Historical Developments of Christian Burial Rites* (London, 1977), 66, 71–72. The elements in this description not found in Passavent's will are taken from the Roman Ritual of 1614, which though compiled after Passavent's funeral merely formalized many of the changes to the medieval burial liturgy that had already taken place. Thus it may reasonably be used as a source for a 1582 funeral. For a vivid description of the requiem Mass, see Michael Camille, *Master of Death: The Lifeless Art of Pierre Remiet, Illuminator* (New Haven, Conn., 1996), 179–88.

81. The following description is based on Ralph E. Giesey, *The Royal Funeral Ceremony in Renaissance France* (Geneva, 1960), 1–17.

82. "Funeral Provision of Jeanne Passavent," in Harding, *Dead and Living in Paris and London*, 295. On burial *ad sanctos*, see Philippe Ariès, *The Hour of Our Death*, trans. Helen Weaver (New York, 1981), 32–40; and Caroline Walker Bynum, *The Resurrection of the Body in Western Christianity, 200–1336* (New York, 1995), chap. 5.

83. Harding, *Dead and Living in Paris and London*, 69, 72–74, 102. Charnel houses were a relatively recent development; the first reference is from the 1160s. Bynum, *Resurrection of the Body*, 203–4.

84. Davis, "Ghosts, Kin, and Progeny," 92–96; and Bossy, *Christianity in the West*, 29–30. For a slightly earlier period, see Jean-Claude Schmitt, *Ghosts in the Middle Ages: The Living and the Dead in Medieval Society* (Chicago, 1998), esp. 187–94.

85. R.C. Finucane, *Appearances of the Dead: A Cultural History of Ghosts* (Buffalo, 1984), 98. This example is taken from Pierre le Loyer's *Livres des spectres* (1568).

86. On Catholic attitudes toward corpse dismemberment, see Elizabeth A.R. Brown, "Authority, the Family, and the Dead in Late Medieval France," *French Historical Studies* 16, no. 4 (Autumn 1990): 803–32; and Bynum, *Resurrection of the Body*, esp. 320–29. For Protestants, see Peter Marshall, *Beliefs and the Dead in Reformation England* (Oxford, 2002), 224–31.

87. Natalie Zemon Davis, "The Rites of Violence," in *Society and Culture in Early Modern France* (Stanford, Calif., 1975), 179; and Barbara B. Diefendorf, *Beneath the Cross: Catholics and Huguenots in Sixteenth-Century Paris* (New York, 1991), 93–106. Davis asserts that while many tales of corpse desecration were exaggerated or even fabricated for propaganda purposes, there can be no doubt that the practice was very real.

88. Richard A. Etlin, *The Architecture of Death: The Transformation of the Cemetery in Eighteenth-Century Paris* (Cambridge, Mass., 1984), 3–5 (quotation); Bossy, *Christianity in the West*, 31; Camille, *Master of Death*, 158–60.

89. The traditional view, that the Protestant Reformation occurred quickly and with the enthusiastic participation of the people, is found in A. G. Dickens, *The English Reformation* (New York, 1964). Revisionist accounts, which stress the health of the late medieval Catholic Church in England and emphasize the slow and uneven process by which the people adopted Protestant beliefs, include J. J. Scarisbrick, *The Reformation and the English People* (Oxford, 1984), and Christopher Haigh, *English Reformations: Religion, Politics, and Society under the Tudors* (Oxford, 1993). Analyses of deathways that are part of the revisionist turn include Duffy, *Stripping of the Altars*, and Marshall, *Beliefs and the Dead*.

90. Craig M. Koslofsky, *The Reformation of the Dead: Death and Ritual in Early Modern Germany, 1450–1700* (New York, 2000), 34–39.

91. Ibid., 19–39; Marshall, *Beliefs and the Dead*, 47–92.

92. William D. Maxwell, ed., *The Liturgical Portions of the Genevan Service Book* (Westminster, Eng., 1965), 161.

93. Haigh, *English Reformations*, 167.

94. Duffy, *Stripping of the Altars*, 567.

95. In the 1980s debate over predestination in the Tudor-Stuart period, I am persuaded by Peter Lake's insistence on the "Calvinist predominance" in the Elizabethan and Jacobean churches, and by Nicholas Tyacke's assertion that "by the 1590s Calvinism was dominant in the highest reaches of the established church." This is not to deny that there were some Elizabethan theologians who would have disagreed with my portrayal of

predestination's impact on deathbed scenes, especially regarding assurance. Peter Lake, "Calvinism and the English Church, 1570–1635," *Past and Present* 114 (February 1987): 32–76, quotation at 34; Nicholas Tyacke, "The Rise of Arminianism Reconsidered," *Past and Present* 115 (May 1987): 201–16, quotation at 202.

96. William Perkins, *A Salve for a Sicke Man; or, A Treatise Containing the Nature, Differences, and Kindes of Death* (1595; London, 1638), 29. On England's good death literature, see Nancy Lee Beaty, *The Craft of Dying: A Study in the Literary Tradition of the* Ars moriendi *in England* (New Haven, 1970).

97. Perkins, *Salve for a Sicke Man*, 29.

98. Edgar C. S. Gloucester, ed., *The First and Second Prayer-Books of King Edward the Sixth* (London, 1910), 264–65, 421; John E. Booty, ed., *The Book of Common Prayer, 1559: The Elizabethan Prayer Book* (Charlottesville, Va., 1976), 306.

99. F. E. Brightman, ed., *The English Rite: Being a Synopsis of the Sources and Revisions of the Book of Common Prayer*, 2 vols. (London, 1915), 2:818–19; Booty, ed., *Book of Common Prayer*, 300.

100. For a slightly later period in one London parish, the seven longest delays between death and burial (each over two weeks, with one of forty-four days) pertained to wealthy individuals whose families were presumably organizing elaborate funerals. Stephen Porter, "Death and Burial in a London Parish: St. Mary Woolnoth, 1653–99," *London Journal* 8, no. 1 (1982): 76–80, esp. 79.

101. Julian Litten, *The English Way of Death: The Common Funeral since 1450* (London, 1991), 12; Clare Gittings, *Death, Burial, and the Individual in Early Modern England* (London, 1984), 114–15, 240; Cressy, *Birth, Marriage, and Death*, 433–35; Harding, *Dead and Living in Paris and London*, 140–45; and Houlbrooke, *Death, Religion, and the Family*, 339–41.

102. Gittings, *Death, Burial, and the Individual*, 106 (quotation). See also Cressy, *Birth, Marriage, and Death*, 427–28; and Houlbrooke, *Death, Religion, and the Family*, 277.

103. This point is made in Duffy, *Stripping of the Altars*, 475, although he goes too far in claiming the "disappearance of the corpse" from the Protestant liturgy.

104. Koslofsky, *Reformation of the Dead*, 46 (Luther), 40–77 (extramural burial).

105. Houlbrooke, *Death, Religion, and the Family*, 334.

106. Marshall, *Beliefs and the Dead*, 296–98; Harding, *Dead and Living in Paris and London*, 55.

107. Andrew Spicer, "'Defyle not Christ's kirk with your carrion': Burial and the Development of Burial Aisles in Post-Reformation Scotland," in *The Place of the Dead: Death and Remembrance in Late Medieval and Early Modern Europe*, ed. Bruce Gordon and Peter Marshall (Cambridge, 2000), 149–69.

108. Historians differ about the chronology of gravestone usage. Cressy states that "permanent outdoor headstones were rare before the eighteenth century, even for the gentry." Cressy, *Birth, Marriage, and Death*, 470. Gittings concurs, noting that wooden markers were sometimes used before gravestones came into fashion. Gittings, *Death,*

Burial, and the Individual, 143–44. Houlbrooke places the transition earlier, saying that the "erection of substantial memorials in the churchyard" became "widespread only from about 1650 onwards." Houlbrooke, *Death, Religion, and the Family*, 362.

109. Cressy, *Birth, Marriage, and Death*, 445.

110. Thomas Becon, *The Sycke Mans Salve* (London, 1561), 176.

111. Marshall, *Beliefs and the Dead*, 128–32.

112. Cressy, *Birth, Marriage, and Death*, 438.

113. Claire S. Schen, *Charity and Lay Piety in Reformation London, 1500–1620* (Aldershot, Eng., 2002), 156–59; and Houlbrooke, *Death, Religion, and the Family*, 248–49.

114. Bruce Gordon and Peter Marshall, "Introduction: Placing the Dead in Late Medieval and Early Modern Europe," in *The Place of the Dead*, ed. Gordon and Marshall, 13, n. 33; Diarmiad MacCulloch, *Reformation: Europe's House Divided, 1490–1700* (London, 2003), 578–79; Cressy, *Birth, Marriage, and Death*, 408; Houlbrooke, *Death, Religion, and the Family*, 297–98.

115. Keith Thomas, *Religion and the Decline of Magic* (New York, 1971), 589.

116. Marshall, *Beliefs and the Dead*, 232–64.

117. James Fitch, *The First Principles of the Doctrine of Christ* (Boston, 1679).

CHAPTER 2

1. J. H. Elliott, *Empires of the Atlantic World: Britain and Spain in America, 1492–1830* (New Haven, Conn., 2006), 66.

2. John Cummins, *The Voyage of Christopher Columbus: Columbus' Own Journal of Discovery Newly Restored and Translated* (New York, 1992), 94.

3. J. M. Cohen, ed., *The Four Voyages of Christopher Columbus* (London, 1969), 56, 64.

4. Cummins, *Voyage of Christopher Columbus*, 100 (quotation), 94.

5. Onorio Montás, Pedro José Borrell, and Frank Moya Pons, *Arte Taíno* (Santo Domingo, Domincan Republic, 1983), 38–39.

6. Ramón Pané, *An Account of the Antiquities of the Indians*, ed. José Juan Arrom, trans. Susan C. Griswold (Durham, N.C., 1999), 21.

7. Cohen, ed., *Four Voyages*, 192. Information on the second voyage was compiled by Columbus's son Hernando Colon for his *Life of the Admiral*, from originals written by Columbus but now lost. The population figure is from Irving Rouse, *The Tainos: Rise and Decline of the People Who Greeted Columbus* (New Haven, Conn., 1992), 7.

8. Rouse, *Tainos*, 13–14, 116–21. On cohoba, see Pané, *Account of the Antiquities*, 15, n.70.

9. Cohen, ed., *Four Voyages*, 193. For more on Taino burials, see Rouse, *Tainos*, 13–14, and Pané, *Account of the Antiquities*, 23–25.

10. Cohen, ed., *Four Voyages*, 194.

11. Geoffrey Symcox and Blair Sullivan, eds., *Christopher Columbus and the Enterprise of the Indies: A Brief History with Documents* (Boston, 2005), 163.

12. James Lockhart, ed., *We People Here: Nahuatl Accounts of the Conquest of Mexico* (Berkeley, Calif., 1993), 96, 98. This is a translation of book 12 of the Florentine Codex, the common name given to Bernadino de Sahagún's *General History of the Things of New Spain*. Sahagún compiled his monumental work between 1547 and 1569 using Nahua informants. On the challenges presented by this source, see "A Question of Sources," Inga Clendinnen, *Aztecs: An Interpretation* (New York, 1991), 277–93.

13. A note on terminology: *Nahuatl* is the language that was spoken in central Mexico, *Nahua* refers to those who spoke the language, and *Mexica* are the subset of Nahautl speakers who lived in the imperial cities of Tenochtitlan and Tlatelolco.

14. J. Bayard Morris, ed., *Five Letters of Cortés to the Emperor* (New York, 1969), 50.

15. Ibid., 87, 88.

16. Bernardino de Sahagun, *Florentine Codex: General History of the Things of New Spain*, trans. Arthur J. O. Anderson and Charles E. Dibble, 13 parts (Santa Fe, N.M., 1950–82), 3:165–80. The figure of 71 is my count of Mexica temples, not including skull frames (religious sites where severed heads were allowed to decompose) and the small fasting houses called *calpulli*.

17. Morris, ed., *Five Letters*, 89, 90.

18. Ibid., 90.

19. Carlos E. M. Eire, *From Madrid to Purgatory: The Art and Craft of Dying in Sixteenth-Century Spain* (New York, 1995), 343.

20. Morris, ed., *Five Letters*, 90–91.

21. Sahagun, *Florentine Codex*, 3:184.

22. Clendinnen, *Aztecs*, 262–63.

23. Jorge Cañizares-Esguerra, "Engtangled Histories: Borderland Historiographies in New Clothes?" *American Historical Review* 112, no. 3 (June 2007): 787–99, esp. 796; and Fernando Cervantes, *The Devil in the New World: The Impact of Diabolism in New Spain* (New Haven, Conn., 1994), 30.

24. Lockhart, *We People Here*, 257.

25. Bernal Díaz del Castillo, *The Discovery and Conquest of Mexico, 1517–1521*, ed. Hugh Thomas (New York, 1996), 252; Morris, ed., *Five Letters*, 92.

26. Morris, ed., *Five Letters*, 199; Díaz, *Discovery and Conquest*, 352.

27. Lockhart, *We People Here*, 180, 182.

28. Hugh Thomas, *Conquest: Montezuma, Cortés, and the Fall of Old Mexico* (New York, 1993), 445.

29. On traditional Mexica deathways, see Claudio Lomnitz, *Death and the Idea of Mexico* (New York, 2005), 157–77, 161 (earth gods); and David Iguaz, "Mortuary Practices among the Aztec in the Light of Ethnohistorical and Archaeological Sources," *Papers from the Institute of Archaeology* 4 (1993): 63–76.

30. On the importance of Indian allies in the conquest, see Matthew Restall, *Seven Myths of the Spanish Conquest* (New York, 2005), 44–51.

31. Bernal Díaz refers to Maxixcatzin as "Mase Escasi." Díaz, *Discovery and Conquest*, 129, 336.

32. Eire, *From Madrid to Purgatory*, 151–56, quotations at 153, 155. See also Laura

Vivanco, *Death in Fifteenth-Century Castile: Ideologies of the Elites* (Woodbridge, Eng., 2004), 169.

33. James Lockhart, *The Nahuas after the Conquest: A Social and Cultural History of the Indians of Central Mexico, Sixteenth through Eighteenth Centuries* (Stanford, Calif., 1992), 203–60. On deathways, see 213–14; and Lomnitz, *Death and the Idea of Mexico.*

34. Charles Hudson, *Knights of Spain, Warriors of the Sun: Hernando de Soto and the South's Ancient Chiefdoms* (Athens, Ga., 1997), 40–41.

35. For one example of de Soto's brutality in Peru, see John Hemming, *The Conquest of the Incas* (New York, 1970), 70.

36. Ian K. Steele, *Warpaths: Invasions of North America* (New York, 1994), 13.

37. Rodrigo Rangel, "Account of the Northern Conquest and Discovery of Hernando de Soto," in *The De Soto Chronicles: The Expedition of Hernando de Soto to North America in 1539–1543*, ed. Lawrence A. Clayton, Vernon James Knight, Jr., and Edward C. Moore, 2 vols. (Tuscaloosa, Ala., 1993), 1:278.

38. John Grier Varner and Jeannette Johnson Varner, eds., *The Florida of the Inca* (Austin, Tex., 1951), 311. On the challenges of using the de Soto chronicles, see Patricia Galloway, "The Incestuous Soto Narratives," in *The Hernando de Soto Expedition: History, Historiography, and "Discovery" in the Southeast*, ed. Galloway (Lincoln, Neb., 1997), 11–44; and Hudson, *Knights of Spain*, 441–55. Galloway is much more skeptical of the sources, especially Garcilaso, than Hudson.

39. Luys Hernández de Biedma, "Relation of the Island of Florida," in Clayton et al., eds., *De Soto Chronicles*, 1:230–31.

40. Rangel, "Account," 1:279.

41. Ibid. (openings); Hernández, "Relation," 1:231 (adipose tissue).

42. Varner and Varner, eds., *The Florida of the Inca*, 438.

43. Vivanco, *Death in Fifteenth-Century Castile*, 141–42.

44. On Spanish veneration of relics, see William A. Christian, Jr., *Local Religion in Sixteenth-Century Spain* (Princeton, N.J., 1981), esp. 126–41.

45. This encounter is analyzed most thoughtfully in Kathleen DuVal, *The Native Ground: Indians and Colonists in the Heart of the Continent* (Philadelphia, 2006), 29–41.

46. Varner and Varner, eds., *The Florida of the Inca*, 438–39, 445. See also Rangel, "Account," 1:301.

47. Gentleman of Elvas, *True Relation of the Hardships Suffered by Governor Fernando de Soto and Certain Portuguese Gentlemen during the Discovery of the Province of Florida*, trans. James Alexander Robertson (DeLand, Fla., 1933), 231.

48. Varner and Varner, eds., *The Florida of the Inca*, 502.

49. Elvas, *True Relation*, 228–29; Varner and Varner, eds., *The Florida of the Inca*, 503–4. DuVal writes that de Soto was buried in either the Mississippi River or the Arkansas River, while Hudson asserts that it was the Mississippi. DuVal, *Indian Ground*, 44; Hudson, *Knights of Spain*, 350.

50. Vivanco, *Death in Fifteenth-Century Castile*, 127.

51. The Englishman William Strachey was still writing about the Strait of Anian in

his 1612 history of Virginia. William Strachey, *The Historie of Travell into Virginia Britania (1612)*, ed. Louis B. Wright and Virginia Freund (London, 1953), 32.

52. Charlotte M. Gradie, "The Powhatans in the Context of the Spanish Empire," in *Powhatan Foreign Relations, 1500–1722*, ed. Helen C. Rountree (Charlottesville, Va., 1993), 155–56.

53. Karen Ordahl Kupperman, *The Jamestown Project* (Cambridge, Mass., 2007), 103–5; James Horn, *A Land as God Made It: Jamestown and the Birth of America* (New York, 2005), 1–9; Paul E. Hoffman, *A New Andalucia and a Way to the Orient: The American Southeast during the Sixteenth Century* (Baton Rouge, 1990), 182–87, 261–66; Gradie, "The Powhatans in the Context"; Charlotte M. Gradie, "Spanish Jesuits in Virginia: The Mission That Failed," *Virginia Magazine of History and Biography* 96, no. 2 (April 1988): 131–56; and Helen C. Rountree, *Pocahontas's People: The Powhatan Indians of Virginia through Four Centuries* (Norman, Okla., 1990), 15–20. An exception is Clifford M. Lewis and Albert J. Loomie, eds., *The Spanish Jesuit Mission in Virginia, 1570–1572* (Chapel Hill, N.C., 1953). Lewis and Loomie were Jesuits.

54. Hoffman, *New Andalucia*, 184 (servant), 186 (many times).

55. Gradie, "The Powhatans in Context," 168–69.

56. Lewis and Loomie, *Spanish Jesuit Mission*, 89.

57. On the religion of Virginia's Indians at the time of European contact, see Helen C. Rountree, *The Powhatan Indians of Virginia: Their Traditional Culture* (Norman, Okla., 1989), 126–39; Rountree, *Pocahontas's People*, 3–28; and Stephen R. Potter, *Commoners, Tribute, and Chiefs: The Development of Algonquian Culture in the Potomac Valley* (Charlottesville, Va., 1993), 210–20.

58. On drought's impact on native and European populations in this period, see Kupperman, *Jamestown Project*, 169–71.

59. Lewis and Loomie, *Spanish Jesuit Mission*, 89.

60. Ibid., 89–90.

61. Ibid., 92.

62. Ibid., 109–10.

63. Ibid., 110.

64. Allan Greer, "Colonial Saints: Gender, Race, and Hagiography in New France," *William and Mary Quarterly* 57 (April 2000): 330.

65. Lewis and Loomie, *Spanish Jesuit Mission*, 110, 136, 159–60. See also 182 for further elaborations. On the trope of skulls used as cups or chalices in a demonic inversion of the Eucharist, see Jorge Cañizares-Esguerra, *Puritan Conquistadors: Iberianizing the Atlantic, 1550–1700* (Stanford, Calif., 2006), 92, 111.

66. Lewis and Loomie, *Spanish Jesuit Mission*, 159.

67. Ibid., 110. Like the killing of the Jesuits, their burial also received increasingly detailed descriptions. See 136 and 160.

68. Rountree, *Powhatan Indians of Virginia*, 121–25.

69. This recalls the experience of the French Recollet missionary Louis Hennepin. In 1680 Algonquian Indians of Wisconsin took his chasuble (Mass vestment) to wrap

the bones of a deceased leader. Louis Hennepin, *A New Discovery of a Vast Country in America*, ed. Reuben Gold Thwaites, 2 vols. (Chicago, 1903), 1:255–56.

70. This scholarly tradition dates back at least to the work of the anthropologist Marcel Mauss in the 1920s. For a more recent treatment of Indian attitudes toward exchange, see Neal Salisbury, "The Indians' Old World: Native Americans and the Coming of Europeans," *William and Mary Quarterly* 53 (July 1996): 435–58, esp. 449–57.

71. Lewis and Loomie, *Spanish Jesuit Mission*, 111.

72. Ibid., 112.

73. George E. Ganss, ed., *Ignatius of Loyola: The* Spiritual Exercises *and Selected Works* (New York, 1991), 138.

74. Cañizares-Esguerra, *Puritan Conquistadors*, 110–15.

75. Lewis and Loomie, *Spanish Jesuit Mission*, 160.

76. Ibid., 108–9, 120–21.

77. The best narratives of Roanoke are Michael Leroy Oberg, *The Head in Edward Nugent's Hand: Roanoke's Forgotten Indians* (Philadelphia, 2008); Karen Ordahl Kupperman, *Roanoke: The Abandoned Colony*, 2d ed. (Lanham, Md., 2007); and David Beers Quinn, *Set Fair for Roanoke: Voyages and Colonies, 1584–1606* (Chapel Hill, N.C., 1985). All the extant sources, along with valuable annotations, may be found in David Beers Quinn, ed., *The Roanoke Voyages, 1584–1590*, 2 vols. (London, 1955).

78. Quinn, *Roanoke Voyages*, 82.

79. Ibid., 108.

80. Oberg, *Head in Edward Nugent's Hand*, 50–51.

81. Ibid., 67.

82. Quinn, *Roanoke Voyages*, 375.

83. Ibid., 384, 379–80.

84. Ibid., 373.

85. Ibid., 373, n. 4.

86. Ibid., 374.

87. Ibid. Joyce Chaplin places Harriot's discussion of Indian resurrection within the context of English debates about natural philosophy. Joyce E. Chaplin, *Subject Matter: Technology, the Body, and Science on the Anglo-American Frontier, 1500–1676* (Cambridge, Mass., 2001), 31–32.

88. Quinn, *Roanoke Voyages*, 374.

89. This differed from what English Puritans argued: that there was not a direct link between one's behavior and the final resting place of one's soul.

90. Karen Ordahl Kupperman, *Indians and English: Facing Off in Early America* (Ithaca, N.Y., 2000), 39.

91. Peter Marshall, *Beliefs and the Dead in Reformation England* (Oxford, 2002), 232–64.

92. *The Most Lamentable and Deplorable Accident Which on Friday Last June 22 Befell Laurence Cawthorn* (London, 1661); *A Full and True Relation of a Maid Living in Newgate-Street, in London* (London, 1680); and *News from Basing-Stoak, of One Mrs. Blunden a Maltsters Wife, Who Was Buried Alive* (London, 1680). A well-researched popular account

of this literature is Jan Bondeson, *Buried Alive: The Terrifying History of Our Most Primal Fear* (New York, 2001).

93. Richard Watkins, *Newes from the Dead; or, A True and Exact Narration of the Miraculous Deliverance of Anne Greene* (Oxford, 1651).

94. Quinn, *Roanoke Voyages*, 367.

95. H. Trawick Ward and R. P. Steven Davis, Jr., eds., *Time before History: The Archaeology of North Carolina* (Chapel Hill, N.C., 1999), 216; Thomas C. Loftfield, "Ossuary Interments and Algonquian Expansion on the North Carolina Coast," *Southeastern Archaeology* 9, no. 2 (Winter 1990): 116–23; David Sutton Phelps, *Archaeology of the Chowan River Basin: A Preliminary Study* (Greenville, N.C., 1982), 25–39; Phelps, *Archaeology of the Tillett Site: The First Fishing Community at Wanchese, Roanoke Island* (Greenville, N.C., 1984), 30–39; and Phelps, "Archaeology of the North Carolina Coast and Coastal Plain: Problems and Hypotheses," in *The Prehistory of North Carolina: An Archaeological Symposium*, ed. Mark A. Mathis and Jeffrey J. Crow (Raleigh, N.C., 1983), 40–43. An older ossuary, farther south in present-day Carteret County, North Carolina, and dating between the tenth and twelfth centuries, contained a few more grave goods: a turtle shell, a small greenstone cup, and several hundred marginella shell beads. Elizabeth I. Monahan, "Bioarchaeological Analysis of the Mortuary Practices at the Broad Reach Site (31CR218), Coastal North Carolina," *Southern Indian Studies* 44 (1995): 37–69, esp. 45.

96. Quinn, *Roanoke Voyages*, 421.

97. Ibid., 425–27.

98. Ibid., 103.

99. The best account of English royal funerals is Jennifer Woodward, *The Theatre of Death: The Ritual Management of Royal Funerals in Renaissance England, 1570–1625* (Woodbridge, Eng., 1997). See also Anthony Harvey and Richard Mortimer, eds., *The Funeral Effigies of Westminster Abbey* (Woodbridge, Eng., 1994); Clare Gittings, *Death, Burial, and the Individual in Early Modern England* (London, 1984), 216–34; Vanessa Harding, *The Dead and the Living in Paris and London, 1500–1670* (Cambridge, 2002), 254–63; and Paul S. Fritz, "From 'Public' to 'Private': The Royal Funerals in England, 1500–1830," in *Mirrors of Mortality: Studies in the Social History of Death*, ed. Joachim Whaley (London, 1981), 61–79. On similar practices in France, see Ralph E. Giesey, *The Royal Funeral Ceremony in Renaissance France* (Geneva, 1960). All these works are ultimately indebted to Ernst H. Kantorowicz, *The King's Two Bodies: A Study in Mediaeval Political Theology* (Princeton, N.J., 1957), esp. 314–450.

100. Elizabeth had requested not to be embalmed, but the long wait before her funeral probably made embalming necessary. Woodward, *Theatre of Death*, 173. Elizabeth's desire to avoid this invasive procedure was not unusual for her time; in the late sixteenth century there was "a minor revolt against embalming, particularly by various aristocratic women." Peter C. Jupp and Clare Gittings, eds., *Death in England: An Illustrated History* (New Brunswick, N.J., 2000), 156.

101. Woodward, *Theatre of Death*, 116.

102. Ibid., 109, 87, 90, 88.

103. Quinn, *Roanoke Voyages*, 372.

104. Ibid., 376–77.

105. Ibid., 277.

106. Ibid., 275, 278.

107. Michael Leroy Oberg, *Dominion and Civility: English Imperialism and Native America, 1585–1685* (Ithaca, N.Y., 1999), 43–44. After Granganimeo died, Wingina changed his name to Pemisipan. The significance of this change is unclear. I will continue to use the name "Wingina" for the sake of continuity.

108. Quinn, *Roanoke Voyages*, 281.

109. Harding, *The Dead and the Living*, 169. Quinn incorrectly states that "month's mind" meant that Catholics practiced a "monthly" commemoration of the dead. Kupperman follows this mistake to assert that the Carolina Algonquians had a "monthly" ceremony to mark their leaders' deaths. Quinn, *Roanoke Voyages*, 281, n. 4; Kupperman, *Roanoke*, 54.

110. David Cressy, *Birth, Marriage, and Death: Ritual, Religion, and the Life-Cycle in Tudor and Stuart England* (New York, 1997), 398 (wills); Gittings, *Death, Burial, and the Individual*, 162–63 (phrase).

111. Quinn, *Roanoke Voyages*, 281, 282.

112. Ibid., 285, 287–88.

113. Ibid., 530.

114. Karen I. Blu, *The Lumbee Problem: The Making of an American Indian People* (Cambridge, 1980), 36–44, 134–37. On the various theories regarding the Lost Colonists, see Horn, *A Land as God Made It*, 145–46; and Kupperman, *Roanoke*, 173–78.

CHAPTER 3

1. Smith included these accounts in his *Generall History of Virginia* (1624). Philip L. Barbour, ed., *The Complete Works of Captain John Smith (1580–1631)*, 3 vols. (Chapel Hill, N.C., 1986), 2:73, 74, 79, 80, 81.

2. George Percy, "'A Trewe Relacyon': Virginia from 1609–1612," *Tyler's Quarterly Magazine* 3 (1921–22): 264.

3. For a similar argument regarding trading practices, see Martin H. Quitt, "Trade and Acculturation at Jamestown, 1607–1609: The Limits of Understanding," *William and Mary Quarterly* 52 (April 1995): 227–58, esp. 258.

4. Philip L. Barbour, ed., *The Jamestown Voyages under the First Charter, 1606–1609*, 2 vols. (Cambridge, 1969), 135.

5. Ibid.

6. Ibid., 218.

7. William Strachey, *The Historie of Travell into Virginia Britania (1612)*, ed. Louis B. Wright and Virginia Freund (London, 1953), 57. Strachey gave Powhatan's age as eighty, but Rountree and Turner put it closer to seventy. Helen C. Rountree and E. Randolph Turner III, *Before and after Jamestown: Virginia's Powhatans and Their Predecessors* (Gainesville, Fla., 2002), 37.

8. Barbour, ed., *Jamestown Voyages*, 143 (flux and swelling); Barbour, ed., *Works of*

John Smith, 1:33 (malice). See also Carville V. Earle, "Environment, Disease, and Mortality in Early Virginia," in *The Chesapeake in the Seventeenth Century: Essays on Anglo-American Society and Politics*, ed. Thad W. Tate and David L. Ammerman (Chapel Hill, N.C., 1979), 96–125.

9. Barbour, ed., *Works of John Smith*, 1:33.

10. For example, Daniel Defoe, *A Journal of the Plague Year* (1722; Baltimore, 1966), 96–97; and William Bradford, *Of Plymouth Plantation, 1620–1647* (New York, 1981), 97, 105, 302.

11. Barbour, ed., *Jamestown Voyages*, 144.

12. William M. Kelso, *Jamestown: The Buried Truth* (Charlottesville, Va., 2006), 141–60, 141 (quotation).

13. Barbour, ed., *Works of John Smith*, 1:247.

14. Ibid., 1:224–25.

15. E. Randolph Turner III, "The Virginia Coastal Plain during the Late Woodland Period," in *Middle and Late Woodland Research in Virginia: A Synthesis*, ed. Theodore R. Reinhart and Mary Ellen N. Hodges (Richmond, Va., 1992), 118. See also Donna C. Boyd and C. Clifford Boyd, Jr., "Late Woodland Mortuary Variability in Virginia," in ibid., 249–75; T. D. Stewart, "The Finding of an Indian Ossuary on the York River in Virginia," *Journal of the Washington Academy of Sciences* 30, no. 8 (1940): 356–64; and Rountree and Turner, *Before and after Jamestown*, 58–62, 67–68. Ossuaries seem to have been more prevalent among the Indians of what would become Maryland, where archaeologists have found thirty-two ossuaries, at least twelve of which held more than one hundred individuals. Dennis C. Curry, *Feast of the Dead: Aboriginal Ossuaries in Maryland* (Myersville, Md., 1999), 10–13.

16. Boyd and Boyd, "Late Woodland Mortuary Variability," 261.

17. Barbour, ed., *Works of John Smith*, 1:169.

18. Henry Spelman's account of commoners receiving scaffold burial, which is sometimes used to describe Powhatan Indian practices, is better used for more northerly groups along the Potomac River, as that is where Spelman lived for a year. Edward Arber, ed., *Travels and Works of John Smith: President of Virginia, and Admiral of New England, 1580–1631* (Edinburgh, 1910), cx.

19. Stanley Pargellis, ed., "An Account of the Indians in Virginia," *William and Mary Quarterly* 16, no. 2 (April 1959): 228–43; Barbour, ed., *Works of John Smith*, 1:169; and Strachey, *Historie of Travell into Virginia*, 94–95.

20. Pargellis, ed., "Account of the Indians," 231.

21. Barbour, ed., *Works of John Smith*, 1:169.

22. This is also attested to by an early eighteenth-century writer, who rooted around in a temple for an hour while the local Indians were away. Robert Beverley, *The History and Present State of Virginia*, ed. Louis B. Wright (Chapel Hill, N.C., 1947), 195–97. Confusingly, though, Beverley went on to describe the burial of leaders in Virginia in terms clearly borrowed from Harriot's description of Carolina. Ibid., 214–16.

23. Strachey, *Historie of Travell into Virginia*, 94. Since ancient Egypt, cedar oil has been used to embalm corpses.

24. Jeffrey P. Blick, "The Huskanaw and Ossuary Rituals of the Quiyoughcohannock Indians of Southeastern Virginia," *Quarterly Bulletin of the Archaeological Society of Virginia* 42, no. 4 (December 1987): 200–201.

25. Vanessa Harding, *The Dead and the Living in Paris and London, 1500–1670* (Cambridge, 2002), 64–65; Peter Marshall, *Beliefs and the Dead in Reformation England* (Oxford, 2002), 40–41.

26. Michel Foucault, *Discipline and Punish: The Birth of the Prison*, trans. Alan Sheridan (New York, 1979).

27. G. A. Williamson, ed., *Foxe's Book of Martyrs* (Boston, 1965), 258–59.

28. Robert Latham and William Matthews, eds., *The Diary of Samuel Pepys*, 11 vols. (Berkeley, Calif., 1970–86), 2:26–27.

29. Beverley, *History and Present State of Virginia*, 84.

30. Barbour, ed., *Works of John Smith*, 2:148. The outcome of this incident is unclear.

31. Ibid., 1:262.

32. Ibid., 266.

33. Ibid., 270 (monuments); Percy, "A Trewe Relacyon," 263 (decore).

34. J. Frederick Fausz, "An 'Abundance of Blood Shed on Both Sides': England's First Indian War, 1609–1614," *Virginia Magazine of History and Biography* 98, no. 1 (January 1990): 3–56, esp. 4 ("holy war" and casualty figures) and 22 (ransacking of temples). Rountree disagrees with Fausz's characterization of events, seeing no evidence of a link between the temple desecration and the Anglo-Powhatan War. Rountree, *Pocahontas's People*, 296, n. 188. I find Fausz's argument convincing.

35. Percy, "A Trewe Relacyon," 265; Jill Lepore, *The Name of War: King Philip's War and the Origins of American Identity* (New York, 1998), 95–96.

36. This is Rountree's estimate of mortality (*Pocahontas's People*, 53), which is significantly less dramatic—but probably more accurate—than Percy's commonly cited figure of only sixty survivors from five hundred alive at the start of winter. Percy, "A Trewe Relacyon," 269.

37. Barbour, ed., *Jamestown Voyages*, 282; Percy, "A Trewe Relacyon," 267.

38. Percy, "A Trewe Relacyon," 267. On European discourses of cannibalism, see Peter Hulme, *Colonial Encounters: Europe and the Native Caribbean, 1492–1797* (London, 1986); and Jean de Léry, *History of a Voyage to the Land of Brazil*, trans. Janet Whatley (Berkeley, Calif., 1990).

39. Barbour, ed., *Works of John Smith*, 2:232–33.

40. Percy, "A Trewe Relacyon," 269.

41. Fausz, " 'Abundance of Blood Shed,' " 33.

42. Edmund S. Morgan, *American Slavery, American Freedom: The Ordeal of Colonial Virginia* (New York, 1975), 94; Rountree, *Pocahontas's People*, 66.

43. Historians used to argue that Opechancanough was Paquiquineo/Don Luís. Opinion has turned against this contention. Karen Ordahl Kupperman, *The Jamestown Project* (Cambridge, Mass., 2007), 340, n.50.

44. Barbour, ed., *Works of John Smith*, 2:293; Percy, "A Trewe Relacyon," 280.

45. Rountree, *Pocahontas's People*, 61.

46. Samuel Purchas, *Hakluytus Posthumus; or, Purchas His Pilgrimes*, 20 vols. (Glasgow, 1905), 19:157.

47. Morgan, *American Slavery, American Freedom*, 97–98; Michael Leroy Oberg, *Dominion and Civility: English Imperialism and Native America, 1585–1685* (Ithaca, N.Y., 1999), 71.

48. George Thorp to Edwin Sandys, May 15, 1621, in *The Records of the Virginia Company of London*, 4 vols., ed. Susan Myra Kingsbury (Washington, D.C., 1906–35), 3:446.

49. Edward Waterhouse, *A Declaration of the State of the Colony and Affaires in Virginia* (London, 1622), 15–16.

50. William Capps to John Ferrar, March 31, 1623, in Kingsbury, ed., *Records of the Virginia Company*, 4:76.

51. The Council in Virginia to the Virginia Company, January 20, 1623, in ibid., 4:10.

52. Ibid.

53. Rountree (*Pocahontas's People*, 71 and 302, n. 45) dates this event five months earlier, but I follow John Smith (2:293) and J. Frederick Fausz, "The Powhatan Uprising of 1622: A Historical Study of Ethnocentrism and Cultural Conflict" (Ph.D. diss., College of William and Mary, 1977), 358, in placing it in early March. This squares better with Opechancanough's mid-March protestation that peace still reigned.

54. Barbour, ed., *Works of John Smith*, 2:293.

55. J. Frederick Fausz and Jon Kukla, eds., "A Letter of Advice to the Governor of Virginia, 1624," *William and Mary Quarterly* 34 (January 1977): 117.

56. Waterhouse, *Declaration*, 13.

57. I follow Fausz's calculation of 325 to 330 deaths, which is more accurate than Waterhouse's list of 347 dead. Fausz, "The Powhatan Uprising," 399.

58. See, for example, Horn, *A Land as God Made It*, 255.

59. Ivor Noël Hume, *Martin's Hundred* (New York, 1982), 243–45.

60. Ivor Noël Hume and Audrey Noël Hume, *The Archaeology of Martin's Hundred*, 2 vols. (Williamsburg, Va., 2001), 1:67.

61. Barbour, ed., *Works of John Smith*, 2:295.

62. Waterhouse, *Declaration*, 14.

63. Ibid., 17.

64. Francis Wyatt's commission to George Yeardley, June 20, 1622, in Kingsbury, ed., *Records of the Virginia Company*, 3:656; William Capps to John Ferrar, March 31, 1623, in ibid., 4:76; William Capps to Thomas Wynston, March or April 1622, in ibid., 38.

65. Hume, *Martin's Hundred*, 211.

66. Quoted in Fausz, "The Powhatan Uprising," 465.

67. William Walter Hening, ed., *The Statutes at Large: Being a Collection of All the Laws of Virginia, from the First Session of the Legislature in the Year 1619*, 13 vols. (New York, 1820–23), 1:123.

68. Quoted in Fausz, "The Powhatan Uprising," 408.

69. Sir Francis Wyatt's proclamation, September 10, 1622, in Kingsbury, ed., *Records of the Virginia Company*, 3:678.

70. Council for Virginia to the Governor in Virginia, August 1, 1622, in ibid., 671–72.

71. Purchas, *Hakluytus Posthumus*, 19:229.

72. Morgan, *American Slavery, American Freedom*, 100.

73. Rountree, *Pocahontas's People*, 89.

74. Kelso, *Jamestown*, 163–66.

75. Hening, ed., *Statutes at Large*, 1:122–23, 161, 185, 227.

76. Hugh Jones, *The Present State of Virginia* (London, 1724), 66 (intelligent persons).

77. Susie M. Ames, ed., *County Court Records of Accomack-Northampton, Virginia, 1632–1640* (Washington, D.C., 1954), 54.

78. June Purcell Guild, ed., *Black Laws of Virginia: A Summary of the Legislative Acts of Virginia Concerning Negroes from Earliest Times to the Present* (New York, 1969), 40.

79. Hening, ed., *Statutes at Large*, 1:160, 243.

80. Ibid., 243. See also Ames, ed., *Court Records of Accomack*, 54, 101.

81. Dell Upton, *Holy Things and Profane: Anglican Parish Churches in Colonial Virginia* (Cambridge, Mass., 1986), 73.

82. Harding, *Dead and the Living in Paris and London*, 119–75; and Clare Gittings, *Death, Burial, and the Individual in Early Modern England* (London, 1984), 140–42.

83. Strachey, *Historie of Travell into Virginia*, 94.

84. Gittings, *Death, Burial, and the Individual*, 151–65.

85. Susie M. Ames, ed., *County Court Records of Accomack-Northampton, Virginia, 1640–1645* (Charlottesville, Va., 1973), 382, 399.

86. For gun ownership, see Kathleen M. Brown, *Good Wives, Nasty Wenches, and Anxious Patriarchs: Gender, Race, and Power in Colonial Virginia* (Chapel Hill, N.C., 1996), 177.

87. Hening, ed., *Statutes at Large*, 1:401–2.

88. Wooden coffins were not unknown in England before the sixteenth century but were quite rare. Ralph Houlbrooke, *Death, Religion, and the Family in England, 1480–1750* (Oxford, 1998), 339–40; Harding, *Dead and the Living in Paris and London*, 140–45; and Gittings, *Death, Burial, and the Individual*, 114–15, 240.

89. Brent Warren Tharp, "'Preserving Their Form and Features': The Role of Coffins in the American Understanding of Death, 1607–1870" (Ph.D. diss., College of William and Mary, 1996), 53.

90. Ames, ed., *Court Records of Accomack*, 170.

91. Kingsbury, ed., *Records of the Virginia Company*, 4:231.

92. Hening, ed., *Statutes at Large*, 1:157–58. Physicians likewise had to be enjoined to help the dying in a 1646 law. Joyce E. Chaplin, *Subject Matter: Technology, the Body, and Science on the Anglo-American Frontier, 1500–1676* (Cambridge, Mass., 2001), 182.

93. Jones, *Present State of Virginia*, 101. There is also evidence from neighboring North Carolina that family and friends could not be counted on for deathbed succor. Several times individuals—presumably not relations—sued a deceased's estate to recover the costs associated with, for example, "attendance and accommodating the said Butler

in his [final] sickness." Mattie Erma Edwards Parker, ed., *North Carolina Higher-Court Records, 1697–1701* (Raleigh, N.C., 1971), 393. See also 84, 95.

94. Jones, *Present State of Virginia*, 67–68. See also John K. Nelson, *A Blessed Company: Parishes, Parsons, and Parishioners in Anglican Virginia, 1690–1776* (Chapel Hill, N.C., 2001), 225–28.

95. Quoted in Rountree, *Pocahontas's People*, 108.

96. Beverley, *History and Present State of Virginia*, 9. Emphasis in original.

97. All quotations and descriptions from ibid., 195–97.

98. *Oxford English Dictionary*, 2d ed.

99. John Lawson, *A New Voyage to Carolina*, ed. Hugh Talmage Lefler (Chapel Hill, N.C., 1967), 185. On the importance of coats in English-Algonquian interactions, see Laurel Thatcher Ulrich, *The Age of Homespun: Objects and Stories in the Creation of an American Myth* (New York, 2001), 57–58.

100. Beverley, *History and Present State of Virginia*, 201–2. John Clayton's 1689 description supports part of Beverley's account. According to Clayton, in the Indian heaven, among other delights, "their women never grow old." But Clayton had nothing to say about wicked Indians being tormented by old women in the afterlife. Pargellis, ed., "Account of the Indians," 236.

101. Peter Kolchin, *American Slavery, 1619–1877* (New York, 1993) n ju.

102. Guild, *Black Laws of Virginia*, 45–16

103. Sylvia R Fr., and Betty Wood, *Come Shouting to Zion: African American Protestantism in the American South and British Caribbean to 1830* (Chapel Hill, N.C., 1998), 55.

CHAPTER 4

1. For a complementary discussion, see Allan Greer, *Mohawk Saint: Catherine Tekakwitha and the Jesuits* (New York, 2005), chap. 1. On "beautiful death," see Philippe Ariès, *The Hour of Our Death*, trans. Helen Weaver (New York, 1981), 307–12.

2. Ramsay Cook, ed., *The Voyages of Jacques Cartier* (Toronto, 1993), 20; Harald E. L. Prins, *The Mi'kmaq: Resistance, Accommodation, and Cultural Survival* (Fort Worth, Tex., 1996), 46.

3. Reuben Gold Thwaites, ed., *The Jesuit Relations and Allied Documents*, 73 vols. (Cleveland, 1896–1901), 1:75. Hereafter JR. When quoting from the *Jesuit Relations*, I have followed Allan Greer's lead and rendered the French *sauvage* as "Indian" rather than "Savage," as it is translated in the Thwaites edition. I have also replaced "thee" and "thy" with "you" and "your." See Allan Greer, ed., *The Jesuit Relations: Natives and Missionaries in Seventeenth-Century North America* (Boston, 2000), vi.

4. JR 2:23. Membertou's beard has led to speculation about whether he had a French father. Maureen Korp, "Problems of Prejudice in the Thwaites' Edition of the *Jesuit Relations*," *Historical Reflections/Reflexions Historiques* 21, no. 2 (Spring 1995): 272, n. 46.

5. H. P. Biggar, ed., *The Works of Samuel de Champlain*, 6 vols. (Toronto, 1922–36), 1:384.

6. JR 3:133.

7. Ibid., 1:167, 169.

8. Ibid., 169.

9. Ibid., 1:169, 3:123.

10. Ibid., 3:129.

11. Ibid., 129–31.

12. Ibid., 177.

13. Vanessa Harding, *The Dead and the Living in Paris and London, 1500–1670* (Cambridge, 2002), 25. For the impact of epidemics on European deathways, see Michel Vovelle, *La mort et l'occident de 1300 à nos jours* (Paris, 1983), 184.

14. Laurence Brockliss and Colin Jones, *The Medical World of Early Modern France* (Oxford, 1997), 69–70.

15. Prins, *The Mi'kmaq*, 219.

16. JR 2:95.

17. R. Po-Chia Hsia, *The World of Catholic Renewal, 1540–1770* (New York, 1998), 186–87.

18. JR 2:17–19; see also 2:95.

19. Susan C. Karant-Nunn, *The Reformation of Ritual: An Interpretation of Early Modern Germany* (London, 1997), 193. Karant-Nunn uses the term to refer to all rituals, not just burial rituals.

20. Harding, *Dead and the Living*, 216; and Bernard Picart, *The Ceremonies and Religious Customs of the Various Nations of the Known World*, 7 vols. (London, 1733–37), 2:106. For a slightly later period, see John McManners, *Death and the Enlightenment: Changing Attitudes to Death in Eighteenth-Century France* (New York, 1981), 276–77.

21. JR 2:17.

22. Norman P. Tanner, ed., *Decrees of the Ecumenical Councils*, 2 vols. (London, 1990), 2:774.

23. JR 2:17.

24. On the importance of relics for the Jesuit missionaries in New France, see Dominique Deslandres, *Croire et faire croire: Les missions françaises au XVIIe siècle (1600–1650)* (Paris, 2003), 414–27. Jesuits in Paraguay likewise placed bones at the center of their missionary efforts. Dot Tuer, "Old Bones and Beautiful Words: The Spiritual Contestation between Shaman and Jesuit in the Guaraní Missions," in *Colonial Saints: Discovering the Holy in the Americas, 1500–1800*, ed. Allan Greer and Jodi Bilinkoff (New York, 2003), 77–97, esp. 90–91.

25. JR 2:19.

26. Ibid.

27. Patrick J. Geary, *Living with the Dead in the Middle Ages* (Ithaca, N.Y., 1994), 41.

28. JR 3:121. The classic account of the origins of this tradition is Peter Brown, *The Cult of the Saints: Its Rise and Function in Latin Christianity* (Chicago, 1981).

29. Tanner, ed., *Decrees*, 2:774.

30. The sources on Membertou's deathbed scene must be discussed. Biard penned three separate accounts of the scene, two in January 1612 and one in May 1614. All three

accounts agree on the basic narrative but differ in certain details. The other description was written by the younger Biencourt in a letter to his father. Although Lucien Campeau, the Jesuit historian who compiled this and other sources, criticizes Biencourt for his "distortion of the facts," I find Biencourt's account no more self-serving than Biard's. Indeed, that the descriptions of the two bitter rivals agree on so many points is good evidence for their essential verity. Thus I have used both to create a composite description. The criticism of Biencourt is in Lucien Campeau, *Jesuit Mission to the Souriquois in Acadia, 1611–1613*, trans. William Lonc and George Topp (Midland, Ont., 2002), 325. Because this was an unorthodox deathbed scene, due to Membertou's initial refusal of Christian burial, I analyze the evidence ethnohistorically, as discussed below.

31. Ignatius of Loyola, *The Constitutions of the Society of Jesus*, trans. George E. Ganss (St. Louis, 1970), 275. See also John W. O'Malley, *The First Jesuits* (Cambridge, Mass., 1993), 174–78.

32. JR 2:21. See also, for example, Roger Williams, *A Key into the Language of America; or, An Help to the Language of the Natives in That Part of America, Called New-England* (London, 1643), 193.

33. JR 2:21, 7.

34. Campeau, *Jesuit Mission*, 327; JR 3:205. Consecrated ground: Jacqueline Thibaut-Payen, *Les morts, l'église et l'état: Recherches d'histoire administrative sur la sépulture et les cimetières dans le ressort du parlement de Paris aux XVIIe et XVIIIe siècles* (Paris, 1977), 78.

35. Campeau, *Jesuit Mission*, 327.

36. Philip T. Weller, ed., *The Roman Ritual in Latin and English with Rubrics and Planechant Notation*, 3 vols. (Milwaukee, 1950), 1:339–41. See also the description in Picart, *Ceremonies and Religious Customs*, 2:93–94.

37. JR 2:23. Biencourt's chronology differs slightly. In his account, Membertou received extreme unction, then declared that he wanted to be buried with his ancestors, then changed his mind the following morning.

38. Campeau, *Jesuit Mission*, 327.

39. JR 2:99.

40. Ibid., 3:131.

41. Ibid., 2:23, 99.

42. A. Lynn Martin, *The Jesuit Mind: The Mentality of an Elite in Early Modern France* (Ithaca, N.Y., 1988), 180. This incident took place in 1570.

43. Vovelle, *La mort et l'occident*, 339.

44. JR 2:25.

45. McManners, *Death and the Enlightenment*, 285.

46. Picart, *Ceremonies and Religious Customs*, 102–5.

47. See, for example, Jacques Baudoin, *La sculpture flamboyante en Bourgogne et Franche-Comté* (Nonette, France, 1996), 100. For a similar example from the Low Countries, see Jeroen Stumpel, "The Case of the Missing Cross: Thoughts on the Context and Meaning of the Nassau Monuments in Breda," in *Care for the Here and the Hereafter: Memoria, Art, and Ritual in the Middle Ages*, ed. Truus van Bueren (Turnhout, Belgium, 2005), 107–24, esp. 108. Thanks to Jonathan Dewald for these citations.

48. Campeau, *Jesuit Mission*, 328–29.

49. Biggar, ed., *Works of Samuel de Champlain*, 1:443–46; Marc Lescarbot, *The History of New France*, trans. W. L. Grant, 3 vols. (Toronto, 1911), 3:273–83. Champlain called him "Panonias," Lescarbot called him "Panoniac."

50. Lescarbot, *History of New France*, 3:275.

51. Biggar, ed., *Works of Samuel de Champlain*, 1:444. On the complex aftermath of this funeral, see Alvin H. Morrison, "Membertou's Raid on the Chouacoet 'Almouchiquois': The Micmac Sack of Saco in 1607," in William Cowan, ed., *Papers of the Sixth Algonquian Conference, 1974* (Ottawa, 1975), 141–58.

52. Prins, *The Mi'kmaq*, 219. For later descriptions of Micmac deathways, see Nicolas Denys, *The Description and Natural History of the Coasts of North America (Acadia)*, trans. William F. Ganong (1672; Toronto, 1908), 410, 437–41; Chrestien Le Clercq, *New Relation of Gaspesia*, trans. William F. Ganong (1691; Toronto, 1910), 207–14, 219–20, 299–303; and N. de Diereville, *Relation of the Voyage to Port Royal in Acadia or New France*, ed. John Clarence Webster (1708; Toronto, 1933), 77–78, 161.

53. Population from Gary Warrick, *A Population History of the Huron-Petun, A.D. 500–1650* (New York, 2008), 223.

54. On Brébeuf's height, see Denis A. Hegarty, "The Excavation of the Indian Church at Ste. Marie," *CCHA Report* 22 (1955): 73.

55. John Steckley, ed., *De Religione: Telling the Seventeenth-Century Jesuit Story in Huron to the Iroquois* (Norman, Okla., 2004), 32.

56. JR 8:137. See also 11:131.

57. Weller, ed., *Roman Ritual*, 2:5.

58. On Huron ceremonial dress, see Bruce G. Trigger, *The Children of Aataentsic: A History of the Huron People to 1660* (Montreal, 1976), 39, 70.

59. JR 8:137.

60. On the arrival of European goods in Huronia, see W. C. Noble, "The Sopher Celt: An Indicator of Early Protohistoric Trade in Huronia," *Ontario Archaeology* 16 (1971): 42–47. On burial practices changing over time, see Peter G. Ramsden, "Rich Man, Poor Man, Dead Man, Thief: The Dispersal of Wealth in Seventeenth Century Huron Society," *Ontario Archaeology* 35 (1981): 35–40; and Richter, *Facing East from Indian Country*, 46. On this dynamic elsewhere in North America, see James Axtell, "Last Rights: The Acculturation of Native Funerals in Colonial North America," in *The European and the Indian: Essays in the Ethnohistory of Colonial North America* (New York, 1981), 110–28, esp. 115–16.

61. Ronald F. Williamson and Susan Pfeiffer, eds., *Bones of the Ancestors: The Archaeology and Osteobiology of the Moatfield Ossuary* (Gatineau, Quebec, 2003), 101–3, 140; Trigger, *Children of Aataentsic*, 137–39, 147.

62. A fifth nation seems to have joined in 1640. Warrick, *Population History*, 9–11.

63. James Axtell, *The Invasion Within: The Contest of Cultures in Colonial North America* (New York, 1985), 46–47; Conrad Heidenreich, *Huronia: A History and Geography of the Huron Indians, 1600–1650* (Toronto, 1971), 232–37.

64. JR 8:121. See also 10:265.

65. Ibid., 10:143. See also Gabriel Sagard, *The Long Journey to the Country of the Hurons*, ed. George M. Wrong (1632; Toronto, 1939), 172.

66. JR 10:147.

67. Sagard, *Long Journey*, 213–14. Champlain made a similar observation in 1615, the first European description of the Feast. Biggar, ed., *The Works of Samuel de Champlain*, 3:162.

68. Harold Hickerson, "The Feast of the Dead among the Seventeenth Century Alongkians of the Upper Great Lakes," *American Anthropologist* 62 (1960): 81–107.

69. Harding, *Dead and the Living*, 72–73, 111–12.

70. Sagard, *Long Journey*, 213. See also 75.

71. Ibid., 207.

72. JR 10:283. Sagard gives an account of the Feast that agrees in all important details with Brébeuf's description. Sagard, *Long Journey*, 211–14.

73. JR 10:283.

74. Ibid., 285.

75. Martin, *Jesuit Mind*, 211–13.

76. JR 10:143.

77. Kenneth E. Kidd, "The Excavation and Historical Identification of a Huron Ossuary," *American Antiquity* 18 (April 1953): 359–79.

78. JR 10:293.

79. The total of eighteen is my count of saints with "direct" relics in the table in Delandres, *Croire et faire croire*, 417.

80. Joyce Marshall, ed., *Word from New France: The Selected Letters of Marie de l'Incarnation* (Toronto, 1967), 299–300. According to Julia Boss, it was a "hagiographic commonplace" in this period that a holy woman's corpse should give off a sweet fragrance. The degree to which Marie de l'Incarnation's narrative was shaped by hagiographic conventions is not central to my concerns, as I am using this description to ascertain the attitudes of French men and women religious toward holy bones. Julia Boss, "Writing a Relic: The Uses of Hagiography in New France," in *Colonial Saints: Discovering the Holy in the Americas, 1500–1800*, ed. Allan Greer and Jodi Bilinkoff (New York, 2003), 211–33, esp. 218.

81. M. Anne Katzenberg and Randy White, "A Paleodemographic Analysis of the *Os Coxae* from Ossossané Ossuary," *Canadian Review of Physical Anthropology* 1 (1979): 12.

82. Kidd, "Excavation and Historical Identification," 367–68.

83. Sagard, *Long Journey*, 212.

84. JR 10:301.

85. Greer, *Mohawk Saint*, 5–7, 16–17.

86. McManners, *Death and the Enlightenment*, 191.

87. Ignatius, *Constitutions*, 265. See also Picart, *Ceremonies and Religious Customs*, 2:95. On Jesuit demonology, see Peter A. Goddard, "The Devil in New France: Jesuit Demonology, 1611–50," *Canadian Historical Review* 78 (March 1997): 40–62.

88. Pierre Chaunu, *La mort à Paris: 16e, 17e, 18e siècles* (Paris, 1978), 275–80, 491–96, esp. 492.

89. The only sustained analyses of Indians' dying speeches are by literary scholars: David Murray, *Forked Tongues: Speech, Writing and Representation in North American Indian Texts* (London, 1991), 34–35; Laura M. Stevens, *The Poor Indians: British Missionaries, Native Americans, and Colonial Sensibility* (Philadelphia, 2004), 178–92; and Kristina Bross, *Dry Bones and Indian Sermons: Praying Indians in Colonial America* (Ithaca, N.Y., 2004), 186–205.

90. Allan Greer notes that the seventeenth century was "one of the last great periods of European (especially French) hagiography." This genre saw "death as the central event in the subject's life." Greer, "Colonial Saints: Gender, Race, and Hagiography in New France," *William and Mary Quarterly* 57 (April 2000): 323–48, quotations at 323 and 330.

91. These findings are presented in greater detail in Erik R. Seeman, "Reading Indians' Deathbed Scenes: Ethnohistorical and Representational Approaches," *Journal of American History* 88 (June 2001): 17–47.

92. Three influential ethnohistories are Francis Jennings, *The Invasion of America: Indians, Colonialism, and the Cant of Conquest* (New York, 1976); James Lockhart, *The Nahuas after the Conquest: A Social and Cultural History of the Indians of Central Mexico, Sixteenth through Eighteenth Centuries* (Stanford, Calif., 1992); and Richard White, *The Middle Ground: Indians, Empires, and Republics in the Great Lakes Region, 1650–1815* (New York, 1991). Literary scholars skeptical of European sources include Stephen Greenblatt, *Marvelous Possessions: The Wonder of the New World* (Chicago, 1991); and Eric Cheyfitz, *The Poetics of Imperialism: Translation and Colonization from* The Tempest *to* Tarzan (New York, 1991).

93. JR 15:135, 10:267. See also Joseph François Lafitau, *Customs of the American Indians Compared with the Customs of Primitive Times,* trans. William N. Fenton and Elizabeth L. Moore, 2 vols. (1724; Toronto, 1974), 2:227.

94. Trigger, *Children of Aataentsic,* 69–75.

95. JR 10:265–67, 11:103–5, 13:55–57, 20:65, 29:171, 34:113, 51:263. See also Lafitau, *Customs of the American Indians,* 2:227.

96. JR 10:147, 153, 12:11.

97. Ibid., 37:155, 32:243, 47:163, 23:129.

98. On the European art of dying tradition, see Chaunu, *La mort à Paris,* 275–85, 491–96; Ariès, *The Hour of Our Death,* 95–139, 297–313; and Mary Catharine O'Connor, *The Art of Dying Well: The Development of the* Ars moriendi (New York, 1942).

99. JR 19:91, 15:33. See also 12:237–39.

100. Ibid., 13:207–9. See also 13:199, 221, 14:33, 41.

101. On this dynamic in the Euro-American context of New England, see Erik R. Seeman, *Pious Persuasions: Laity and Clergy in Eighteenth-Century New England* (Baltimore, 1999), 44–45, 71–72.

102. JR 13:149–51. See also 10:147, 153–55, 12:11.

103. Ibid., 13:151–53.

104. Ibid., 227–31.

105. Ibid., 13:259, 10:163–65.

106. Ibid., 10:267, 15:67.

107. Trigger, *Children of Aataentsic*, 565.

108. JR 23:129.

109. Lalemant did not witness this scene firsthand but heard it from the head of the mission. JR 30:105–7. See also, for example, 11:107, 31:159, 62:39–41. On the importance of baptism, see Kenneth M. Morrison, "Baptism and Alliance: The Symbolic Mediations of Religious Syncretism," *Ethnohistory* 37 (Fall 1990): 416–37; and John Webster Grant, *Moon of Wintertime: Missionaries and the Indians of Canada in Encounter since 1534* (Toronto, 1984), 35.

110. Wilfrid Jury and Elsie McLeod Jury, *Sainte-Marie among the Hurons* (Toronto, 1954), 16; Kenneth E. Kidd, *The Excavation of Ste Marie I* (Toronto, 1949), 12; JR 33:75, 34:197.

111. Warrick, *Population History*, 227, 236.

112. JR 26:289–91; see also 26:211 for other examples.

113. Ibid., 207.

114. Ibid., 23:31.

115. Ariès, *Hour of Our Death*, 305–6.

116. Jury and Jury, *Sainte-Marie*, 93. Problems with the Jury excavation are outlined in Jeanie Tummon and W. Barry Gray, eds., *Before and beyond Sainte-Marie: 1987–1990 Excavations at the Sainte-Marie among the Hurons Site Complex (circa 1200–1990)* (Dundas, Ont., 1995). Jury's poorly substantiated assertions involve not the burials but the non-Christian longhouse and the five-sided bastion.

117. Jury and Jury, *Sainte-Marie*, 93.

118. JR 29:275.

119. Trigger, *Children of Aataentsic*, 722–23.

120. JR 30:27–31.

121. Trigger, *Children of Aataentsic*, 739.

122. Ibid., 661.

123. JR 34:141 (former captives). The deaths of Brébeuf and Lalemant were described by several Christian Hurons "worthy of belief" (JR 34:29), who had also been captured by the Iroquois, were eyewitnesses to the torture, and escaped to tell the tale. They reported the events to donné Christophe Regnaut, who then composed his "Veritable Account" based on these statements and his subsequent examination of the remains (JR 34:23–35). There is no doubt that Regnaut's narrative was influenced by Catholic hagiographic conventions, but the essentials of the story seem entirely plausible. The tortures mostly fit with well-documented Iroquois practices of torture and anthropophagy. The elements of the story that seem most likely to have been exaggerated for effect are the precise words of the torturers and their victims. For a different interpretation of this narrative, emphasizing the "artfully arranged correspondences with the Passion of Christ," see Greer, "Colonial Saints," 334–35, quotation at 335.

124. JR 34:35.

CHAPTER 5

1. The most influential statement of this argument is James Axtell, *The Invasion Within: The Contest of Cultures in Colonial North America* (New York, 1985). See also Peter A. Dorsey, "Going to School with Savages: Authorship and Authority among the Jesuits of New France," *William and Mary Quarterly* 55 (July 1998): 399–420, esp. 408–9; Cornelius J. Jaenen, *Friend and Foe: Aspects of French-Amerindian Cultural Contact in the Sixteenth and Seventeenth Centuries* (Toronto, 1976), esp. 191–92; and Francis Jennings, *The Invasion of America: Indians, Colonialism, and the Cant of Conquest* (New York, 1976), 56–57. For a work that explores the commonalities between Catholic and Protestant missionaries, see Neal Salisbury, "Religious Encounters in a Colonial Context: New England and New France in the Seventeenth Century," *American Indian Quarterly* 16 (Fall 1992): 501–9.

2. There is no contemporary source that connects the start of the 1616 epidemic with the cicada infestation. But in 1633, seventeen years after 1616, Indians told William Bradford that the return of the cicadas presaged an epidemic. The Indian interpretation was almost surely the result of the coincidental arrival of cicadas and disease in 1616. William Bradford, *Of Plymouth Plantation, 1620–1647*, ed. Francis Murphy (New York, 1981), 290.

3. Neal Salisbury, *Manitou and Providence: Indians, Europeans, and the Making of New England, 1500–1643* (New York, 1982), 101–6.

4. Charles Francis Adams, Jr., *New English Canaan of Thomas Morton* (New York, 1883), 132.

5. Phineas Pratt, "A Declaration of the Affairs of the English People That First Inhabited New England (1662)," *Collections of the Massachusetts Historical Society*, 4th ser., 4 (1858): 478.

6. William Bradford, *A Relation or Journal of the Beginning and Proceedings of the English Plantation Settled at Plimoth in New England* (London, 1622), 6.

7. Beth Bower, "Aboriginal Textiles," in *Burr's Hill: A Seventeenth-Century Wampanoag Burial Ground in Warren, Rhode Island*, ed. Susan G. Gibson (Providence, R.I., 1980), 89–91.

8. Bradford, *Relation*, 11. See also Patricia E. Rubertone, *Grave Undertakings: An Archaeology of Roger Williams and the Narragansett Indians* (Washington, D.C., 2001), 173–74.

9. Neal Salisbury asserts that this sailor was "apparently" a member of Captain Thomas Dermer's crew that reconnoitered Cape Cod in 1619. Salisbury does not explain his reasoning and I see no reason why this might not have been a crewman from an earlier voyage. Salisbury, *Manitou and Providence*, 113.

10. Pratt, "Declaration," 479.

11. Bradford, *Relation*, 17.

12. Edward Winslow, *Good Newes from New England* (London, 1624), 25–26.

13. William Perkins, *A Salve for a Sicke Man; or, A Treatise Containing the Nature, Differences, and Kindes of Death* (1595; London, 1638), 108–9, 140–52, quotation at 108.

14. Winslow, *Good Newes*, 27.

15. Ibid., 28–29.

16. Ibid., 29–32.

17. Adams, *New English Canaan of Thomas Morton*, 170, 247; Ivor Noël Hume, *Martin's Hundred* (New York, 1982), 81.

18. Roger Williams, *A Key into the Language of America; or, An Help to the Language of the Natives in That Part of America, Called New-England* (London, 1643), 195.

19. Adams, *New English Canaan of Thomas Morton*, 170; Winslow, *Good Newes*, 33.

20. *A Directory for the Publique Worship of God, Throughout the Three Kingdoms of England, Scotland, and Ireland* (London, 1645), 73–74.

21. Adams, *New English Canaan of Thomas Morton*, 171, 170.

22. Ibid., 248.

23. Pratt, "Declaration," 485.

24. For example, Neal Salisbury contrasts Williams's relatively generous views regarding Indian land and religion with the more self-interested views of the Plymouth and Massachusetts Bay colonists. Salisbury, *Manitou and Providence*, 136–37, 193–202.

25. The 5:1 ratio must be considered a very rough estimate, based on a figure of 52,000 Europeans and Daniel Gookin's 1674 guess of 8,600 Indians. Jennings, *Invasion of America*, 30–31.

26. John Winthrop to John Endecott, January 3, 1634. Allyn Bailey Forbes, ed., *Winthrop Papers*, 5 vols. (Boston, 1929–47), 3:147.

27. The phrase is how John Winthrop twice described Canonicus in his journal. Richard S. Dunn, James Savage, and Laetitia Yeandle, eds., *The Journal of John Winthrop, 1630–1649* (Cambridge, Mass., 1996), 54, 77.

28. Rubertone, *Grave Undertakings*, 14.

29. Glenn W. LaFantasie, ed., *The Correspondence of Roger Williams*, 2 vols. (Hanover, N.H., 1988), 75, n.5. Williams wrote this sentiment in Latin: "morosus aeque ac barbarus senex." LaFantasie, *Correspondence*, 72.

30. Ibid., 72.

31. Salisbury, *Manitou and Providence*, 209–10.

32. Williams wrote that he "possessed" Canonicus of the truth of this assertion. At the time "possessed" was a synonym for "convinced." *Oxford English Dictionary* online, "possess," definition 9b.

33. LaFantasie, *Correspondence*, 72, 76, n.6.

34. On Narragansett desires for cloaks and looking glasses, see Williams, *Key into the Language*, 152, 157. On Williams's trading post as a missionary site, see Rubertone, *Grave Undertakings*, 14.

35. Rubertone, *Grave Undertakings*, 92.

36. Roger Williams, *Christenings Make Not Christians* (1645), in *The Complete Writings of Roger Williams*, ed. Perry Miller, 7 vols. (New York, 1963), 7:29–41, esp. 37–40.

37. Williams, *Key into the Language*, 195–96.

38. Letter of May 7, 1668, to the General Court of Massachusetts Bay, in LaFantasie, *Correspondence*, 577.

39. Williams, *Key into the Language*, 196, 53. *Oxford English Dictionary* online, "personal," definition 5a. Thanks to Kristina Bross for calling this to my attention.

40. Williams, *Key into the Language*, 193, 195, 196 (emphasis added).

41. Ibid., 123.

42. Ibid., 127–28.

43. *New Englands First Fruits* (1643), in *The Eliot Tracts*, ed. Michael P. Clark (Westport, Conn., 2003), 61 (hereafter ET). John Winthrop's body count was somewhat lower: he reported that 150 Pequot "fighting men" and 150 "old men, women, and children" were killed. Dunn, Savage, and Yeandle, eds., *Journal of John Winthrop*, 220.

44. Williams, *Key into the Language*, xi. On the attempts to use Wequash's deathbed scene to make political points, see Kristina Bross, *Dry Bones and Indian Sermons: Praying Indians in Colonial America* (Ithaca, N.Y., 2004), 190–92.

45. *New Englands First Fruits*, in ET, 62 (poisoned); Williams, *Key into the Language*, xi (naughty heart); Dunn, Savage, and Yeandle, eds., *Journal of John Winthrop*, 401 (comfortably).

46. *New Englands First Fruits*, in ET, 62; Williams, *Key into the Language*, x.

47. Rubertone, *Grave Undertakings*, xiv–xv, 132.

48. Williams, *Key into the Language*, 121, 119–20.

49. Ibid., 192–93. The date of Canonicus's death is uncertain. John Winthrop learned of it on June 4, 1647. John Winthrop, *The History of New England from 1630 to 1649*, ed. James Savage, 2 vols. (Boston, 1825–26), 2:308.

50. Testimony of June 18, 1682. John Russell Bartlett, ed., *Letters of Roger Williams, 1632–1682*, 6 vols. (Providence, R.I., 1874), 6:407.

51. The details about hundreds of spectators and the freely given cloth are from a letter of November 1677, and the detail about closing his eyes is from a letter of June 1678. LaFantasie, *Correspondence*, 752, 761.

52. Williams to the General Court of Massachusetts Bay, October 5, 1654, in LaFantasie, *Correspondence*, 412.

53. Nathaniel B. Shurtleff, ed., *Records of the Governor and Company of the Massachusetts Bay in New England* (Boston, 1854), 3:162.

54. Nathaniel Morton, *New-Englands Memoriall* (Cambridge, Mass., 1669), 131. Thanks to Francis Bremer for this citation.

55. Roger Williams to John Winthrop, Jr., February 15, 1655, in LaFantasie, *Correspondence*, 425.

56. Ibid.

57. The £47 figure is found in *Rhode Island Court Records: Records of the Court of Trials of the Colony of Providence Plantations, 1647–1662*, 2 vols. (Providence, R.I., 1920), 1:10.

58. Ibid., 1:9–10.

59. *Records of the Colony of Rhode Island and Providence Plantations in New England*, 10 vols. (Providence, R.I., 1856–65), 1:319–20.

60. Richard W. Cogley, *John Eliot's Mission to the Indians before King Philip's War* (Cambridge, Mass., 1999), 243–44.

61. *The Clear Sun-shine of the Gospel* (1648), in ET, 116.

62. This figure is necessarily speculative. For a discussion of the competing estimates, see Dane Morrison, *A Praying People: Massachusett Acculturation and the Failure of the Puritan Mission, 1600–1690* (New York, 1995), 203, n.9.

63. Wilberforce Eames, ed., *John Eliot and the Indians, 1652–1657: Being Letters Addressed to Rev. Jonathan Hanmer of Barnstaple, England* (New York, 1915), 26. Quakers had a different response to Indian death. See Richard W. Pointer, *Encounters of the Spirit: Native Americans and European Colonial Religion* (Bloomington, Ind., 2007), chap. 6.

64. *The Glorious Progress of the Gospel* (1649), in ET, 153.

65. *Clear Sun-shine*, in ET, 124.

66. *The Day-Breaking . . . of the Gospel* (1647), in ET, 84, 88. See also 91.

67. Ibid., 84.

68. *Glorious Progress*, in ET, 155–56. For similar questions asked by the Indians of Martha's Vineyard, see Len Travers, ed., "The Missionary Journal of John Cotton, Jr., 1666–1678," *Proceedings of the Massachusetts Historical Society* 109 (1997): 52–101.

69. *Clear Sun-shine*, in ET, 136, 129; *The Light Appearing More and More* (1651), in ET, 194.

70. *Light Appearing*, in ET, 194.

71. Erik R. Seeman, *Pious Persuasions: Laity and Clergy in Eighteenth-Century New England* (Baltimore, 1999), 52–53.

72. *Glorious Progress*, in ET, 155, 156, 161.

73. Bragdon, *Native People of Southern New England*, 190–91.

74. Seeman, *Pious Persuasions*, 53–54.

75. *Clear Sun-shine*, in ET, 129.

76. Bragdon, *Native People of Southern New England*, 220. Thanks to David Silverman for making this point.

77. *Clear Sun-shine*, in ET, 137–38. Early-contact practices: Josselyn, *An Account of Two Voyages*, 132; Wood, *New Englands Prospect*, 104.

78. *Tears of Repentance* (1653), in ET, 269.

79. *A Further Account of the Progress of the Gospel* (1660), in ET, 374.

80. Charles L. Cohen, "Conversion among Puritans and Amerindians: A Theological and Cultural Perspective," in *Puritanism: Transatlantic Perspectives on a Seventeenth-Century Anglo-American Faith*, ed. Francis J. Bremer (Boston, 1993), 235–36; and Daniel K. Richter, *Facing East from Indian Country: A Native History of Early America* (Cambridge, Mass., 2001), 117. For a contrary view, see Joshua David Bellin, "'A Little I Shall Say': Translation and Interculturalism in the John Eliot Tracts," in *Reinterpreting New England Indians and the Colonial Experience*, ed. Colin G. Calloway and Neal Salisbury (Boston, 2003), 52–83. Bellin argues that the Eliot tracts are not the transparent sources historians would like them to be.

81. Other scholars have pointed to this connection. Jean M. O'Brien, *Dispossession by Degrees: Indian Land and Identity in Natick, Massachusetts, 1650–1790* (New York, 1997), 54–57; Neal Salisbury, "'I Loved the Place of My Dwelling': Puritan Missionaries and Native Americans in Seventeenth-Century Southern New England," in *Inequality in*

Early America, ed. Carla Gardina Pestana and Sharon V. Salinger (Hanover, N.H., 1999), 117–18; Cogley, *John Eliot's Mission to the Indians*, 242–44; Cohen, "Conversion among Puritans and Amerindians," 253–54; and Richter, *Facing East*, 129.

82. *Tears of Repentance*, in ET, 291, 285. There are numerous other similar cases. See, for example, ET, 271, 292–93, 369–70.

83. George Selement and Bruce C. Woolley, eds., *Thomas Shepard's* Confessions (Boston, 1981), includes 51 narratives recorded between 1636 and 1644; Mary Rhinelander McCarl, ed., "Thomas Shepard's Record of Relations of Religious Experience," *William and Mary Quarterly* 48 (July 1991): 432–66, consists of 16 narratives from 1648–49; and Robert G. Pope, ed., *The Notebook of the Reverend John Fiske, 1644–1675* (Salem, Mass., 1974), has 21 narratives from 1644–66. Of 159 eighteenth-century narratives examined, 39 (25 percent) showed a similar link. Seeman, *Pious Persuasions*, 46.

84. In seven conversion narratives offered in 1666 by Indians at the Mashpee native church, three (43 percent) drew links between death and attraction to Christianity. J. Patrick Cesarini, ed., "John Eliot's 'A breif History of the Mashepog Indians,' 1666," *William and Mary Quarterly* 65, no. 1 (January 2008): 101–34, esp. 127, 129, 133.

85. McCarl, "Thomas Shepard's Record of Relations," 442.

86. *Tears of Repentance*, in ET, 278.

87. *A Further Account*, in ET, 365.

88. Reuben Gold Thwaites, ed., *The Jesuit Relations and Allied Documents*, 73 vols. (Cleveland, 1896–1901), 1:263.

89. Rubertone, *Grave Undertakings*, 133; Gibson, ed., *Burr's Hill*, 17.

90. Gibson, ed., *Burr's Hill*, 13; Simmons, *Cautantowwit's House*, 67–68.

91. Simmons guesses that "if the left side of the wigwam was allocated to men and the right side to women, and if both slept facing the fire, a difference might be expected in the direction in which the person lay at the time of death." Simmons, *Cautantowwit's House*, 67–68.

92. Gibson, ed., *Burr's Hill*, 13, 17–18; Simmons, *Cautantowwit's House*, 82.

93. Constance Crosby, "From Myth to History, or Why King Philip's Ghost Walks Abroad," in *The Recovery of Meaning: Historical Archaeology in the Eastern United States*, ed. Mark P. Leone and Parker B. Potter, Jr. (Washington, D.C., 1988), 183–85, quotation at 184. See also David J. Silverman, *Faith and Boundaries: Colonists, Christianity, and Community among the Wampanoag Indians of Martha's Vineyard, 1600–1871* (New York, 2005), 27–29.

94. Quotation from Nora Groce, "Ornaments of Metal: Rings, Medallions, Combs, Beads, and Pendants," in *Burr's Hill*, ed. Gibson, 111. RI-1000 rings reported in Turnbaugh, *Material Culture of RI-1000*, 49–50.

95. Rubertone, *Grave Undertakings*, 160, 139.

96. Kevin A. McBride, "Bundles, Bears, and Bibles: Interpreting Seventeenth-Century Native 'Texts,'" in *Early Native Literacies in New England: A Documentary and Critical Anthology*, ed. Kristina Bross and Hilary E. Wyss (Amherst, Mass., 2008), 132–41. See also Welters et al., "European Textiles," 225–28; and Joyce E. Chaplin, *Subject Matter:*

Technology, the Body, and Science on the Anglo-American Frontier, 1500–1676 (Cambridge, Mass., 2001), 280–81, 295–96.

97. Gibson, ed., *Burr's Hill*, 13; Saville, *Montauk Cemetery*, 75, map facing p. 74. Pantigo is included in this sample (and in the work of archaeologists studying New England) because the eastern end of Long Island resembled New England in many ways: its Algonquian Montauk Indians shared cultural traits with their neighbors across the Sound, and the English settlers were of the same reformed Protestant stock as those who populated New England.

98. Gibson, ed., *Burr's Hill*, 13; Saville, *Montauk Cemetery*, 80–84.

99. Saville, *Montauk Cemetery*, 83–84.

100. For other syncretic early eighteenth-century Indian burials, see John Wood Sweet, *Bodies Politic: Negotiating Race in the American North, 1730–1830* (Baltimore, 2003), 26, 29–30.

101. James Axtell, "Last Rights: The Acculturation of Native Funerals in Colonial North America," in *The European and the Indian: Essays in the Ethnohistory of Colonial North America* (New York, 1981), 123–24. Other scholars also read resistance into supine burials. See Christina J. Hodge, "Faith and Practice at an Early-Eighteenth-Century Wampanoag Burial Ground: The Waldo Farm Site in Dartmouth, Massachusetts," *Historical Archaeology* 39, no. 4 (2005): 73–94, esp. 85. On evidence of resistance more generally in Indian burials, see Rubertone, *Grave Undertakings*, 139; and Brenner, "Strategies for Autonomy," esp. 229–33.

102. Baker, "Pilgrim's Progress and Praying Indians," 39. For at least one more seemingly Christian Indian burial with grave goods from Ponkapoag, see the site reports in Accession File 969–37, Peabody Museum of Archaeology and Ethnology, Cambridge, Massachusetts.

103. Rubertone, *Grave Undertakings*, 143–45.

104. Baker, "Pilgrim's Progress and Praying Indians," 39; Kelley, "Burial Practices," 94.

105. Brenner, "Strategies for Autonomy," 206; Kelley, "Burial Practices," 118.

106. On King Philip's War as—at least in part—a "civil war" between praying Indians and traditionalists, see Harold W. Van Lonkhuyzen, "A Reappraisal of the Praying Indians: Acculturation, Conversion, and Identity at Natick, Massachusetts, 1646–1730," *New England Quarterly* 63 (September 1990): 396–428, esp. 419–20.

107. My analysis is heavily indebted to Jill Lepore, *The Name of War: King Philip's War and the Origins of American Identity* (New York, 1998), esp. chap. 4, quotation at 79.

108. Williams, *Key into the Language*, 181. See also James Axtell, "Scalping: The Ethnohistory of a Moral Question," in *The European and the Indian*, 207–41, esp. 213.

109. Come Lord Jesus: Anon., *A True Account of the Most Considerable Occurrences That Have Happened in the War Between the English and the Indians in New-England* (London, 1676), 2–3. Send them to heaven: quoted in Lepore, *The Name of War*, 104.

110. Lepore, *The Name of War*, 105.

111. N[athaniel] S[altonstall], *A New and Further Narrative of the State of New-*

England (London, 1676), 6–7. See also Lepore, *The Name of War*, 105; and Edward G. Gray, *New World Babel: Languages and Nations in Early America* (Princeton, 1999), 79–80.

112. T[homas] C[hurch], *Entertaining Passages Relating to Philip's War* (1716), in *So Dreadfull a Judgment: Puritan Responses to King Philip's War, 1676–1677*, ed. Richard Slotkin and James K. Folsom (Middletown, Conn., 1978), 451.

113. Daniel Gookin, "An Historical Account of the Doings and Sufferings of the Christian Indians in New England," *Transactions and Collections of the American Antiquarian Society* 2 (1836): 472–73, 485–86.

114. Bross, *Dry Bones and Indian Sermons*, 195.

115. Roger Williams to [Robert Williams?], April 1, 1676. LaFantasie, *Correspondence of Roger Williams*, 722. There are some concerns about this letter's authenticity. See 717–20.

116. Rubertone, *Grave Undertakings*, 16; LaFantasie, *Correspondence of Roger Williams*, xliii.

117. David Silverman cautions historians not to exaggerate the degree to which the Mayhews were noncoercive. Silverman, *Faith and Boundaries*, chap. 3, esp. 73–74.

118. For an accessible version, see Laura Arnold Leibman, ed., *Experience Mayhew's Indian Converts: A Cultural Edition* (Amherst, Mass., 2008).

119. Hilary E. Wyss, *Writing Indians: Literacy, Christianity, and Native Community in Early America* (Amherst, Mass., 2000), 63.

120. Nancy Lee Beaty, *The Craft of Dying: A Study in the Literary Tradition of the* Ars moriendi *in England* (New Haven, Conn., 1970), 2–16; Philippe Ariès, *The Hour of Our Death*, trans. Helen Weaver (New York, 1981), 95–139, 297–313; and Mary Catharine O'Connor, *The Art of Dying Well: The Development of the* Ars moriendi (New York, 1942).

121. New England ministers urged parishioners not to place too much weight on how people died for determining whether they went to heaven, but many laypeople persisted in drawing links between deathbed behavior and elect status. Seeman, *Pious Persuasions*, 64–65. For people dying in great distress in England, see Houlbrooke, *Death, Religion, and the Family*, 198–99.

122. Experience Mayhew, *Indian Converts; or, Some Account of the Lives and Dying Speeches of a Considerable Number of the Christianized Indians of Martha's Vineyard, in New-England* (London, 1727), 172. It is possible that the Indian observers of this scene were doubly dismayed by the woman's agitated state, if they still maintained the earlier Indian belief in the importance of deathbed stoicism.

123. Seeman, *Pious Persuasions*, 69–71.

124. Mayhew, *Indian Converts*, 210.

125. Williams, *A Key into the Language*, 193.

126. Bragdon, *Native People of Southern New England*, 229.

127. Mayhew, *Indian Converts*, 33, 44, 58, 147, 150, 160, 201, 211, 214, 221, 233, 241, 262. Although I have not carefully quantified a control group, I would estimate that no more than 2–3 percent of contemporary Anglo-American deathbed scenes included the dying person having dreams or visions.

128. Ibid., 33, 147, 150, 201, 214, 221, 241.

129. See also Wyss, *Writing Indians*, 73–75.

130. Mayhew, *Indian Converts*, 33, 150.

131. Ibid., 199–200, 201.

132. Ibid., 33, 148. See also 201.

133. Seeman, *Pious Persuasions*, 44–45, 71–72.

134. Mayhew's openness to Christian Indian syncretism is further suggested by his membership—as a congregant, not a missionary—in a Christian Indian church. Charles Edward Banks, ed., "Diary of Rev. William Homes of Chilmark, Martha's Vineyard, 1689–1746," *New England Historic Genealogical Register* 48 (1894): 414. I am grateful to Douglas Winiarski for sharing this source with me. My reading thus differs from that of Ann Marie Plane, who argues that "Mayhew himself did not dare to represent the full syncretism of this encounter." Plane, "Falling 'Into a Dreame': Native Americans, Colonization, and Consciousness in Early New England," in *Reinterpreting New England Indians*, ed. Calloway and Salisbury, 84–105, quotation at 95.

135. Gordon E. Geddes, *Welcome Joy: Death in Puritan New England* (Ann Arbor, Mich., 1981), 118.

CHAPTER 6

1. Jerome S. Handler and Frederick W. Lange, *Plantation Slavery in Barbados: An Archaeological and Historical Investigation* (Cambridge, Mass., 1978).

2. Ibid., 22, 24.

3. Jerome S. Handler, "A Prone Burial from a Plantation Slave Cemetery in Barbados, West Indies: Possible Evidence for an African-type Witch or Other Negatively Viewed Person," *Historical Archaeology* 30, no. 3 (1996): 79.

4. Richard Price, *Alabi's World* (Baltimore, 1990), 212.

5. Charles Leslie, *A New and Exact Account of Jamaica*, 3rd ed. (Edinburgh, 1740), 323–24. See also Richard Ligon, *A True and Exact History of the Island of Barbadoes* (London, 1673), 51; Hans Sloane, *A Voyage to the Islands Madera, Barbados, Nieves, S. Christophers, and Jamaica*, 2 vols. (London, 1707), xlviii; Alexander Gunkel and Jerome S. Handler, eds., "A German Indentured Servant in Barbados in 1652: The Account of Heinrich von Uchterlitz," *Journal of the Barbados Museum and Historical Society* 33, no. 3 (May 1970): 94; and numerous commentators from later periods and other regions.

6. See, for example, John Atkins, *A Voyage to Guinea, Brasil, and the West-Indies* (London, 1735), 105.

7. Price, *Alabi's World*, 401.

8. Pieter de Marees, *Description and Historical Account of the Gold Kingdom of Guinea (1602)*, ed. Albert van Dantzig and Adam Jones (Oxford, 1987), 180; Adam Jones, ed., *German Sources for West African History, 1599–1669* (Wiesbaden, 1983), 257; Jason R. Young, *Rituals of Resistance: African Atlantic Religion in Kongo and the Lowcountry South in the Era of Slavery* (Baton Rouge, 2007), 149.

9. Handler and Lange, *Plantation Slavery in Barbados*, 185.

10. Reimert Haagensen, *Description of the Island of St. Croix in America in the West Indies*, ed. Arnold R. Highfield (St. Croix, 1995), 60.

11. Jerome S. Handler, "An African-Type Healer/Diviner and His Grave Goods: A Burial from a Plantation Slave Cemetery in Barbados, West Indies," *International Journal of Historical Archaeology* 1, no. 2 (June 1997): 98.

12. Haagensen, *Description of the Island of St. Croix*, 60; Ligon, *True and Exact History*, 50.

13. Evidence of African preference for evening burials mostly comes from Sierra Leone. P. E. H. Hair, "Sources on Early Sierra Leone: (13) Barreira's Report of 1607–1608—The Visit to Bena," *Africana Research Bulletin* 8, no. 2 (June 1978): 95; Manuel Álvares, *Ethiopia Minor and a Geographical Account of the Province of Sierra Leone*, ed. P. E. H. Hair, 2 vols. (Liverpool, 1990), 2:8:6; and John Matthews, *A Voyage to the River Sierra-Leone* (1788; London, 1966), 121.

14. Griffith Hughes, *The Natural History of Barbados* (London, 1750), 15.

15. Quoted in Handler and Lange, *Plantation Slavery in Barbados*, 174. See also J. B. Moreton, *West India Customs and Manners* (London, 1793), 162; J. Stewart, *A View of the Present State of the Island of Jamaica* (London, 1823), 267; and Arnold R. Highfield and Vladimir Barac, eds., *C. G. A. Oldendorp's History of the Mission of the Evangelical Brethren on the Caribbean Islands of St. Thomas, St. Croix, and St. John* (Ann Arbor, Mich., 1987), 264.

16. Douglas V. Armstrong and Mark L. Fleischman, "House-Yard Burials of Enslaved Laborers in Eighteenth-Century Jamaica," *International Journal of Historical Archaeology* 7, no. 1 (March 2003): 33–65.

17. Leslie, *New and Exact Account*, 325; see also Hughes, *Natural History of Barbados*, 15; and Vincent Brown, *The Reaper's Garden: Death and Power in the World of Atlantic Slavery* (Cambridge, Mass., 2008), 66–69.

18. J. Taylor, quoted in Handler, "African-Type Healer/Diviner," 112, 113; Sloane, *Voyage to the Islands*, xlviii; Price, *Alabi's World*, 401.

19. Handler and Lange, *Plantation Slavery in Barbados*, 166.

20. Handler, "African-Type Healer/Diviner," 104–9, 119.

21. Ligon, *True and Exact History*, 50; Leslie, *New and Exact Account*, 325–26. See also Sloane, *Voyage to the Islands*, xlviii.

22. Immediate offerings: Price, *Alabi's World*, 401; Leslie, *New and Exact Account*, 326; and Sloane, *Voyage to the Islands*, xlviii. Delayed offerings: Arthur Holt, letter of March 7, 1729, Fulham Papers, 15:266 (originals at Lambeth Palace Library; read on microfilm, Barbados Department of Archives); Hughes, *Natural History of Barbados*, 15.

23. Haagensen, *Description of the Island of St. Croix*, 60. See also Leslie, *New and Exact Account*, 326; and Price, *Alabi's World*, 401.

24. For two nineteenth-century quotations mentioning figurines in black burial grounds, see Brown, *Reaper's Garden*, 247.

25. Dating back at least to Melville J. Herskovits, *The Myth of the Negro Past* (1941; Boston, 1958). On deathways, see 197–206. Some of this literature has overreached in its

attempts to find evidence of African survivals in African American deathways. Herskovits, for example, argues that "to evaluate frankly at a funeral the characteristics of the dead" is an aspect of African American deathways derived from "West African rituals" (204). Similarly poorly substantiated claims may be found in David R. Roediger, "And Die in Dixie: Funerals, Death, and Heaven in the Slave Community, 1700–1865," *Massachusetts Review* 22 (Spring 1981): 163–83, esp. 170–71; Joseph E. Holloway, "The Sacred World of the Gullahs," in *Africanisms in American Culture*, ed. Holloway, 2d ed. (Bloomington, Ind., 2005), 194–95; and Margaret Washington Creel, *"A Peculiar People": Slave Religion and Community-Culture among the Gullahs* (New York, 1988), 320. To be fair, this problem results at least partly from the dearth of good archaeological work on Africa, which makes it easy to overgeneralize about West African deathways. See Merrick Posnansky, "West Africanist Reflections on African-American Archaeology," in *"I, Too, Am America": Archaeological Studies of African-American Life*, ed. Theresa A. Singleton (Charlottesville, Va., 1999), 21–37, esp. 33–34.

26. Such as Romans, highland Scots, and ancient Irish. Hughes, *Natural History of Barbados*, 15; Edward Long, *The History of Jamaica*, 3 vols. (London, 1774), 2:422; and Moreton, *West India Customs and Manners*, 155.

27. William Beckford, *A Descriptive Account of the Island of Jamaica*, 2 vols. (London, 1790), 390.

28. Long, *History of Jamaica*, 2:416. Definition 2.4.a of "ash" in the online *Oxford English Dictionary* is "mortal remains, buried corpse." This sense goes back to the year 1275.

29. John Venn to Bishop Sherlock, June 15, 1751, quoted in Brown, *Reaper's Garden*, 134.

30. Ligon, *True and Exact History*, 51.

31. Quoted in Sylvia R. Frey and Betty Wood, *Come Shouting to Zion: African American Protestantism in the American South and British Caribbean to 1830* (Chapel Hill, N.C., 1998), 39.

32. Peter Charles Hoffer and William B. Scott, eds., *Criminal Proceedings in Colonial Virginia* (Athens, Ga., 1984), 133–34.

33. Douglas R. Egerton, "A Peculiar Mark of Infamy: Dismemberment, Burial, and Rebelliousness in Slave Societies," in *Mortal Remains: Death in Early America*, ed. Nancy Isenberg and Andrew Burstein (Philadelphia, 2003), 149–60, esp. 153–54; and Brown, *Reaper's Garden*, 133–34.

34. Diana Paton, "Punishment, Crime, and the Bodies of Slaves in Eighteenth-Century Jamaica," *Journal of Social History* 34, no. 4 (2001): 939 (rarely performed); V. A. C. Gatrell, *The Hanging Tree: Execution and the English People, 1770–1868* (New York, 1994), 267, 268 (common spectacle).

35. June Purcell Guild, ed., *Black Laws of Virginia: A Summary of the Legislative Acts of Virginia concerning Negroes from Earliest Times to the Present* (New York, 1969), 45–46.

36. Frey and Wood, *Come Shouting to Zion*, 55; Herbert L. Osgood, ed., *Minutes of the Common Council of the City of New York, 1675–1776*, 8 vols. (New York, 1905), 3:296; Philip D. Morgan, *Slave Counterpoint: Black Culture in the Eighteenth-Century Chesa-*

peake and Low Country (Chapel Hill, N.C., 1998), 641; David Barry Gaspar, *Bondmen and Rebels: A Study of Master-Slave Relations in Antigua* (Baltimore, 1985), 145; and Alexander Barclay, *A Practical View of the Present State of Slavery in the West Indies* (London, 1828), 158.

37. *Georgia Gazette*, December 24, 1766.

38. Neville A. T. Hall, *Slave Society in the Danish West Indies: St. Thomas, St. John, and St. Croix* (Kingston, Jamaica, 1992), 57, 63, 64; Osgood, ed., *Minutes of the Common Council*, 4:88–89. In 1721, Boston allowed only one bell to be tolled for African American funerals in order to reduce attendance. William D. Piersen, *Black Yankees: The Development of an Afro-American Subculture in Eighteenth-Century New England* (Amherst, Mass., 1988), 78.

39. Osgood, ed., *Minutes of the Common Council*, 4:89 (New York); Supplement to *South Carolina Gazette*, July 2, 1750, quoted in Nicholas M. Beasley, *Christian Ritual and the Creation of British Slave Societies, 1650–1780* (Athens, Ga., 2009), 129; Gaspar, *Bondmen and Rebels*, 145 (Antigua). On funeral scarves, see Lou Taylor, *Mourning Dress: A Costume and Social History* (London, 1983), 101.

40. 1685 Code Noir, trans. John Garrigus, www.vancouver.wsu.edu/fac/peabody/codenoir.htm, viewed June 24, 2007.

41. On vodou deathways, see Hein Vanhee, "Central African Popular Christianity and the Making of Haitian Vodou Religion," in *Central Africans and Cultural Transformations in the American Diaspora*, ed. Linda M. Heywood (New York, 2002), 243–64, esp. 262; on candomblé deathways, see João José Reis, *Death Is a Festival: Funeral Rites and Rebellion in Nineteenth-Century Brazil*, trans. H. Sabrina Gledhill (Chapel Hill, N.C., 2003), 145.

42. James H. Sweet, *Recreating Africa: Culture, Kinship, and Religion in the African-Portuguese World, 1441–1770* (Chapel Hill, N.C., 2003), 206. Sweet cautions that the African adoption of Catholicism was not as quick or widespread as sometimes believed.

43. See, for example, Kenneth Mills, William B. Taylor, and Sandra Lauderdale Graham, eds., *Colonial Latin America: A Documentary History* (Wilmington, Del., 2002), 280–96, esp. 285–86.

44. Fulham Papers, 15:204, 205. See also Frey and Wood, *Come Shouting to Zion*, chap. 3.

45. Frank J. Klingberg, ed., *The Carolina Chronicle of Dr. Francis Le Jau, 1706–1717* (Berkeley, Calif., 1956), 54.

46. Ibid., 102.

47. Lilia Hague to SPG, July 15, 1715, quoted in Annette Laing, "'Heathens and Infidels'? African Christianization and Anglicanism in the South Carolina Low Country, 1700–1750," *Religion and American Culture* 12, no. 2 (2002): 214.

48. In 1712, for example, he counted "5 Negroes" among his "actual communicants." Klingberg, ed., *Carolina Chronicle*, 120.

49. John Shipman, "Thoughts on the Present State of Religion among the Negroes in Jamaica" (1820), 5, MS in Wesleyan Methodist Missionary Society, London; viewed on microfiche.

50. Craig D. Atwood, "The Joyfulness of Death in Eighteenth-Century Moravian Communities," *Communal Societies* 17 (1997): 39–58, quotations at 48. On Moravians in the West Indies, see Jon F. Sensbach, *Rebecca's Revival: Creating Black Christianity in the Atlantic World* (Cambridge, Mass., 2005), esp. chap. 3.

51. Highfield and Barac, eds., *Oldendorp's History of the Mission*, 373–74.

52. Ibid., 472–73.

53. On Moravian ownership of slaves in St. Thomas, see Sensbach, *Rebecca's Revival*, 106–9.

54. Highfield and Barac, eds., *Oldendorp's History of the Mission*, 494.

55. Ibid., 555, 556.

56. Ibid., 418, 547, 418.

57. Ibid., 575, 496, 575. On the importance of singing at Moravian deathbeds, see Atwood, "Joyfulness of Death," 51. On slave interest in Moravian blood imagery, see Sensbach, *Rebecca's Revival*, 86.

58. Aaron Spencer Fogelman, "Jesus Is Female: The Moravian Challenge in the German Communities of British North America," *William and Mary Quarterly*, 60, no. 2 (April 2003): 295–332, esp. 317–21; and Sensbach, *Rebecca's Revival*, 47–49.

59. Highfield and Barac, eds., *Oldendorp's History of the Mission*, 548, 576–77.

60. *Virginia Gazette*, September 8, 1775, 3. See also Frey and Wood, *Come Shouting to Zion*, chap. 4.

61. Frey and Wood, *Come Shouting to Zion*, 51.

62. The project at Utopia Quarter, James City County, Va., found all but one of twenty-five slaves buried in European-style wooden coffins. Four were buried with grave goods: one with a necklace made out of amethyst-colored glass beads and three with clay pipes. Lorena S. Walsh, *From Calabar to Carter's Grove: The History of a Virginia Slave Community* (Charlottesville, Va., 1997), 105–6.

63. Morgan, *Slave Counterpoint*, 641.

64. James Kershaw Diaries, South Caroliniana Library, Columbia, South Carolina. For similar examples, see Albert J. Raboteau, *Slave Religion: The "Invisible Institution" in the Antebellum South* (New York, 1978), 230–31.

65. Robert Farris Thompson, *Flash of the Spirit: African and Afro-American Art and Philosophy* (New York, 1983), 132–42; Mechal Sobel, *The World They Made Together: Black and White Values in Eighteenth-Century Virginia* (Princeton, N.J., 1987), 219–21; John Michael Vlach, *The Afro-American Tradition in Decorative Arts* (Cleveland, 1978), 139–47; Young, *Rituals of Resistance*, 162–66.

66. D. Gregory Jeane, "The Upland South Cemetery: An American Type," *Journal of Popular Culture* 11, no. 4 (Spring 1978): 895–903; Sobel, *World They Made Together*, 219.

67. Sobel, *World They Made Together*, 223–25.

68. Edna Greene Medford, ed., *The New York African Burial Ground: History Final Report* (Washington, D.C., 2004), 82, hereafter *ABG History*.

69. Berlin, *Many Thousands Gone*, 189.

70. James Wetmore to the SPG, December 3, 1726, quoted in Thelma Wills Foote,

Black and White Manhattan: The History of Racial Formation in Colonial New York City (New York, 2004), 140.

71. Rev. John Sharpe, "'Proposals for Erecting a School, Library and Chapel at New York,' 1712–13," *New-York Historical Society Collections* 13 (1880): 355.

72. Trinity Church Vestry Minutes, October 25, 1697, quoted in Warren R. Perry, Jean Howson, and Barbara A. Bianco, eds., *New York African Burial Ground: Archaeology Final Report*, 2 vols. (Washington, D.C., 2006), 1:42, hereafter *ABG Archaeology*.

73. Historians have found records of only nine churchyard burials of blacks in eighteenth-century New York: five at the Dutch Reformed Church, two at Trinity Lutheran, and two at the Moravian Church. *ABG Archaeology*, 1:43.

74. Anne-Marie Cantwell and Diana diZerega Wall, *Unearthing Gotham: The Archaeology of New York City* (New Haven, Conn., 2001), 277–88.

75. *ABG Archaeology*, 1:87.

76. Cantwell and Wall, *Unearthing Gotham*, 285.

77. See, for example, Jill Lepore, *New York Burning: Liberty, Slavery, and Conspiracy in Eighteenth-Century Manhattan* (New York, 2005), 231–32; Craig Steven Wilder, *In the Company of Black Men: The African Influence on African American Culture in New York City* (New York, 2001), 33; Cantwell and Wall, *Unearthing Gotham*, 290–91; and Thelma Wills Foote, *Black and White Manhattan*, 141–43.

78. This is also recognized by the authors of the final historical report on the African Burial Ground: "the deceased were laid to rest in a manner not unlike that of white New Yorkers." *ABG History*, 184.

79. *ABG Archaeology*, 1:134–44, 382, 419.

80. Kwaku Ofori-Ansa, "Identification and Validation of the Sankofa Symbol," *Update: Newsletter of the African Burial Ground and Five Points Archaeological Projects* 1, no. 8 (Summer 1995): 3. For additional context, see Erik R. Seeman, "Reassessing the 'Sankofa Symbol' in New York's African Burial Ground," *William and Mary Quarterly* 67, no. 1 (January 2010): 101–22.

81. W. Bruce Willis, *The Adinkra Dictionary: A Visual Primer on the Language of Adinkra* (Washington, D.C., 1998), 188. The most thoroughly researched work on *adinkra* is Daniel Mato, "Clothed in Symbol: The Art of Adinkra among the Akan of Ghana" (Ph.D. diss., Indiana University, 1986).

82. Foote, *Black and White Manhattan*, 143. For similar interpretations, see Andrea E. Frohne, "Reclaiming Space: The African Burial Ground in New York City," in *"We Shall Independent Be": African American Place Making and the Struggle to Claim Space in the United States*, ed. Angel David Nieves and Leslie M. Alexander (Boulder, Colo., 2008), 489–510, esp. 495, 500; Richard E. Bond, "Shaping a Conspiracy: Black Testimony in the 1741 New York Plot," *Early American Studies* 5, no. 1 (Spring 2007): 63–94, esp. 92; Sheila S. Walker, "Introduction: Are You Hip to the Jive? (Re)Writing/Righting the Pan-American Discourse," in *African Roots/American Cultures: Africa in the Creation of the Americas*, ed. Sheila S. Walker (Lanham, Md., 2001), 1–42, esp. 26–27; and Theresa A. Singleton, "Before the Revolution: Archaeology and the African Diaspora on the

Atlantic Seaboard," in *North American Archaeology*, ed. Timothy R. Pauketat and Diana DiPaolo Loren (Oxford, 2004), 319–36, esp. 331.

83. See Walter C. Rucker, *The River Flows On: Black Resistance, Culture, and Identity Formation in Early America* (Baton Rouge, La., 2006), 50, for a similar point.

84. Bowdich wrote that "the white cloths . . . they paint for mourning with a mixture of blood and a red dye wood. The patterns are various, and not inelegant." T. Edward Bowdich, *Mission from Cape Coast Castle to Ashantee* (London, 1819), 310.

85. Mato, "Clothed in Symbol," 79 (fifteen symbols), 100 (sixteen symbols), 174 (eighteen symbols).

86. R. S. Rattray, *Religion and Art in Ashanti* (London, 1927), 265.

87. Willis, *Adinkra Dictionary*, 28. For other modern designs, see Mato, "Clothed in Symbol," unpaginated appendix: figure 196 (steering wheels), figure 205 (U.S. flag), figure 206 (Volkswagen logo).

88. *ABG Archaeology*, 1:254. There are several other ambiguous entries, such as when John Stephens purchased a "black coffin for a negro child." Stephens could have been a master purchasing a coffin for his slave, or a free black man buying it for his offspring.

89. Ibid.

90. Brent W. Tharp, " 'Preserving Their Form and Features': The Commodification of Coffins in the American Understanding of Death," in *Commodifying Everything: Relationships of the Market*, ed. Susan Strasser (New York, 2003), 124.

91. Arthur W. Dowe, "Col. John Wainwright's Tomb," *Ipswich Antiquarian Papers* 2 (March 1881): 2. Many thanks to Jason LaFountain for this citation.

92. Kristen Bastis, "Health, Wealth, and Available Material: The Bioarchaeology of the Bulkeley Tomb in Colchester, Connecticut" (M.A. thesis, University of Connecticut, 2006), 46, 48–51.

93. *ABG Archaeology*, 1:253. See also an 1818 coffin from Cornwall, Connecticut: "Going Home: Henry Opukaha'ia Returns to Hawaii," *Digging In: Office of State Archaeology and Connecticut Historical Commission*, no. 2 (Fall 1993). On the importance of heart imagery in early American Protestantism, see Sally M. Promey, "Mirror Images: Framing the Self in Early New England Material Piety," in *Figures in the Carpet: Finding the Human Person in the American Past*, ed. Wilfred M. McClay (Grand Rapids, Mich., 2007), 71–128, esp. 109–16.

94. Promey, "Mirror Images," 113.

95. Elsewhere, following the interpretations of Rachel Frankel and Aviva Ben-Ur, I suggested that hearts and upside-down hearts on Jewish gravestones in Suriname might be Sankofa symbols. I now believe there is not enough evidence to make such an assertion. Erik R. Seeman, "Jews in the Early Modern Atlantic: Crossing Boundaries, Keeping Faith," in *The Atlantic in Global History, 1500–2000*, ed. Jorge Cañizares-Esguerra and Erik R. Seeman (Upper Saddle River, N.J., 2007), 39–59, esp. 53–55; Rachel Frankel, "Antecedents and Remnants of Jodensavanne: The Synagogues and Cemeteries of the First Permanent Plantation Settlement of New World Jews," in *The Jews and the Expansion of Europe to the West, 1450–1800*, ed. Paolo Bernardini and Norman Fiering (New York, 2001), 394–436, esp. 425–26; Aviva Ben-Ur, "Still Life: Sephardi, Ashkenazi, and

West African Art and Form in Suriname's Jewish Cemeteries," *American Jewish History* 92, no. 1 (March 2004): 31–79.

96. This burial is described to extraordinary effect in Lepore, *New York Burning*, 231–32.

97. *ABG Archaeology*, 1:154. According to Handler and Lange, *Plantation Slavery in Barbados*, 117, a filed incisor "strongly indicates African birth."

98. *ABG Archaeology*, 1:387, 403, 410, 393. See also Cheryl J. LaRoche, "Beads from the African Burial Ground, New York City: A Preliminary Assessment," *Beads* 6 (1994): 3–20, esp. 14–15; and Linda France Stine, Melanie A. Cabak, Mark D. Groover, "Blue Beads as African-American Cultural Symbols," *Historical Archaeology* 30, no. 3 (1996): 49–75, esp. 53, 54.

99. Patricia Samford, "The Archaeology of African-American Slavery and Material Culture," *William and Mary Quarterly* 52, no. 1 (January 1996): 87–114, esp. 107–9; Sweet, *Recreating Africa*, chap. 6; Young, *Rituals of Resistance*, chap. 3.

100. *ABG Archaeology*, 1:432–33.

101. Ibid., 420.

102. Leslie M. Harris, *In the Shadow of Slavery: African Americans in New York City, 1626–1863* (Chicago, 2003), 51–52, 81–84; Graham Russell Hodges, *Root and Branch: African Americans in New York and East Jersey, 1613–1863* (Chapel Hill, N.C., 1999), 180–86; Joyce D. Goodfriend, *Before the Melting Pot: Society and Culture in Colonial New York City, 1664–1730* (Princeton, N.J., 1992), 132; and Foote, *Black and White Manhattan*, 145–47. On Philadelphia, see Gary B. Nash, *Forging Freedom: The Formation of Philadelphia's Black Community, 1720–1840* (Cambridge, Mass., 1988), chap. 4.

103. Quoted in *ABG History*, 214. See also Harris, *In the Shadow of Slavery*, 83–84; and Hodges, *Root and Branch*, 183.

104. William Douglass, *Annals of the First African Church, in the United States of America* (Philadelphia, 1862), 33–34; Berlin, *Many Thousands Gone*, 251–52; Nash, *Forging Freedom*, 94; Richard S. Newman, *Freedom's Prophet: Bishop Richard Allen, the AME Church, and the Black Founding Fathers* (New York, 2008), 61–62.

105. Robert L. Harris, Jr., "Charleston's Free Afro-American Elite: The Brown Fellowship Society and the Humane Brotherhood," *South Carolina Historical Magazine* 82, no. 4 (October 1981): 289–310, esp. 292–97. Richmond's African Burial Ground Society was founded slightly later, in 1815. Marie Tyler-McGraw and Gregg D. Kimball, *In Bondage and Freedom: Antebellum Black Life in Richmond, Virginia* (Richmond, Va., 1988), 40.

106. Ralph Houlbrooke, *Death, Religion, and the Family in England, 1480–1750* (Oxford, 1998), 260; Ivor Noël Hume, *Martin's Hundred* (New York, 1982), 80–82.

107. William H. Robinson, *The Proceedings of the Free African Union Society and the African Benevolent Society: Newport, Rhode Island, 1780–1824* (Providence, R.I., 1976), 78, 79, 83, 93–94.

108. John Wood Sweet, *Bodies Politic: Negotiating Race in the American North, 1730–1830* (Baltimore, 2003), 335.

109. The preceding three paragraphs are based on the society's prescriptions for fu-

neral processions, Robinson, *Free African Union Society*, 61–62, 123–24. Pillows for the shoulders, 86; rum, 43, 119; the Devil, 62, which paraphrases 1 Peter 5:8.

110. Ann Tashjian and Dickran Tashjian, "The Afro-American Section of Newport, Rhode Island's Common Burying Ground," in *Cemeteries and Gravemarkers: Voices of American Culture*, ed. Richard E. Meyer (Logan, Utah, 1992), 164–96, esp. 166, 169.

111. James C. Garman, "Viewing the Color Line through the Material Culture of Death," *Historical Archaeology* 28, no. 3 (1994): 83.

112. Tashjian and Tashjian, "Afro-American Section," 172.

113. Julian D. Mason, Jr., *The Poems of Phillis Wheatley*, rev. ed. (Chapel Hill, N.C., 1989), 53. See also "On Virtue" (1766), 51–53, esp. 52.

114. M. G. Lewis, *Journal of a West India Proprietor, 1815–17*, ed. Mona Wilson (Boston, 1929), 287. See also George Pinckard, *Notes on the West Indies*, 3 vols. (London, 1806), 1:273.

115. Letter of Rev. John Wray from Berbice, October 30, 1813, in Alvin O. Thompson, ed., *A Documentary History of Slavery in Berbice, 1796–1834* (Georgetown, Guyana, 2002), 159; Robert J. Allison, ed., *The Interesting Narrative of the Life of Olaudah Equiano, Written by Himself* (New York, 1995), 145; Beckford, *Descriptive Account*, 2:388–89; and Thomas Atwood, *The History of the Island of Dominica* (London, 1791), 268.

116. Atwood, *History of the Island of Dominica*, 268–69; John Luffman, *A Brief Account of the Island of Antigua* (London, 1789), 112–13; Rev. Mr. Smith, *A Natural History of Nevis, and the Rest of the English Leeward Charibee Islands in America* (Cambridge, 1795), 231; Allison, ed., *Interesting Narrative of the Life of Olaudah Equiano*, 43; Long, *History of Jamaica*, 2:421; Moreton, *West India Customs and Manners*, 162; and Lewis, *Journal*, 88.

117. Letter from Wray in Thompson, *Documentary History*, 159; Beckford, *Descriptive Account*, 2:389; and Susan E. Klepp and Roderick A. McDonald, eds., "Eliza Chadwick Roberts: A Voyage to Jamaica, 1805," *William and Mary Quarterly* 58, no. 3 (July 2001): 669.

118. Shipman, "Thoughts on the Present State of Religion," 4.

119. Douglas Hall, *In Miserable Slavery: Thomas Thistlewood in Jamaica, 1750–86* (London, 1989), xvii, 145, 292. For examples of plays noted by Thistlewood, see Trevor Burnard, *Mastery, Tyranny, and Desire: Thomas Thistlewood and His Slaves in the Anglo-Jamaican World* (Chapel Hill, N.C., 2004), 128–29, 206.

120. Hall, *In Miserable Slavery*, 184, 185–86. Thistlewood recorded a similar example two years earlier: in 1769 Daniel threw water "for his boy, Fortune, killed by Paradise mill last crop." Hall, *In Miserable Slavery*, 216. For more on Abba, see Burnard, *Mastery, Tyranny, and Desire*, 221–27.

121. Roderick A. McDonald, *The Economy and Material Culture of Slaves: Goods and Chattels on the Sugar Plantations of Jamaica and Louisiana* (Baton Rouge, La., 1993), 110; Burnard, *Mastery, Tyranny, and Desire*, 200, 236–37.

122. Hall, *In Miserable Slavery*, 83. Mulatto Will was not Thistlewood's son.

123. Quoted in J. Harry Bennett, Jr., *Bondsmen and Bishops: Slavery and Apprenticeship on the Codrington Plantation of Barbados, 1710–1838* (Berkeley, Calif., 1958), 97.

124. Letter of Isaac Bradnack, April 30, 1804. Original held by the Methodist Mis-

sionary Society, London. Photocopies viewed at the Barbados Department of Archives, "Missionaries' Letters and Papers from Barbados," X/10/6.

125. Pinckard, *Notes on the West Indies*, 1:271–74. White mourning attire: Luffman, *Brief Account of the Island of Antigua*, 110–13.

126. Handler and Lange, *Plantation Slavery in Barbados*, 68. Newton had a somewhat lower percentage of Africans in its workforce than the rest of the island, where in 1817 7 percent of the slave population was African-born. Hilary McD. Beckles, *A History of Barbados: From Amerindian Settlement to Nation-State* (New York, 1990), 55.

127. Sampson Wood to Thomas Lane, July 18, 1798, Newton Papers, University of London Library, 523/352/1. Viewed on microfilm, West Indies Collection, University of the West Indies, Cave Hill, Barbados. Emphasis in original. For a helpful family tree, see Karl Watson, *A Kind of Right to Be Idle: Old Doll, Matriarch of Newton Plantation* (Cave Hill, Barbados, 2000), 31.

128. November 21, 1796, "Newton's 1796/7" (account book), Newton Papers 523/110. See also March 9, 1797. See also November 17, 1796, and November 21, 1796, in "Seawell's 1796/7" (account book), Newton Papers 523/111. Seawell was a nearby plantation also owned by Thomas Lane and managed by Sampson Wood.

129. January 11 and 12, 1797, "Seawell's 1796/7." See also November 17 and 18, 1796.

130. J. R. Ward, *British West Indian Slavery, 1750–1834: The Process of Amelioration* (Oxford, 1988), esp. 61–64 on Barbados; and Beckles, *History of Barbados*, 85–88.

131. Sampson Wood to Thomas Lane, October 19, 1798, Newton Papers 523/381/1.

132. Register of Burials in the Parish of Christ Church, 1643–1825, 175, Barbados Department of Archives.

133. Ned Thomas's funeral fees are found in Newton Plantation Journal, 1805–1841, 10, Barbados Museum and Historical Society. The daily rate of labor is calcuated from a December 1805 entry, p. 11, that lists "12 days Negro labor" costing ten shillings.

134. Newton Plantation Journal, 10 (Ned Thomas), 37 (Mary Ann Saer), 70 (Old Doll).

135. Sweet, *Recreating Africa*, 104; Young, *Rituals of Resistance*, 82–85, 156. For the persistence of these beliefs in the diaspora, see Monica Schuler, "Liberated Central Africans in Nineteenth-Century Guyana," in *Central Africans*, ed. Heywood, 319–52, esp. 346–48.

136. Jon Butler, *Awash in a Sea of Faith: Christianizing the American People* (Cambridge, Mass., 1990), chap. 5.

137. See, for example, Raboteau, *Slave Religion*.

CHAPTER 7

1. Jonathan D. Sarna, "The Jews in British America," in *The Jews and the Expansion of Europe to the West, 1450–1800*, ed. Paolo Bernardini and Norman Fiering (New York, 2001), 522.

2. Todd M. Endelman, *The Jews of Britain, 1656 to 2000* (Berkeley, 2002), 35.

3. Miriam Bodian, *Hebrews of the Portuguese Nation: Conversos and Community in Early Modern Amsterdam* (Bloomington, Ind., 1997), 9–10.

4. Wim Klooster, *The Dutch in the Americas, 1600–1800* (Providence, R.I., 1997), 6–67.

5. Isaac S. Emmanuel, *Precious Stones of the Jews of Curaçao: Curaçaon Jewry, 1656–1957* (New York, 1957), 108.

6. Leo Hershkowitz, ed., *Wills of Early New York Jews (1704–1799)* (New York, 1967), 33. Christians, of course, also wrote wills in advance of sea voyages. On the bone in the spine, see Robert Goldenberg, "Bound Up in the Bond of Life: Death and Afterlife in the Jewish Tradition," in *Death and Afterlife: Perspectives of World Religions*, ed. Hiroshi Obayashi (Westport, Conn., 1992), 101.

7. The figure of 1,100 Jews is from the mid-eighteenth century. R. G. Fuks-Mansfeld, "Enlightenment and Emancipation from c.1750 to 1814," in J. C. H. Blom, R. G. Fuks-Mansfeld, and I. Schöffer, eds., *The History of the Jews in the Netherlands*, trans. Arnold J. Pomerans and Erica Pomerans (Oxford, 2002), 173.

8. Eli Faber, *A Time for Planting: The First Migration, 1654–1820* (Baltimore, 1992), 17. Eighteenth-century Jamaican Jews were prevented from practicing law. Jacob R. Marcus, *The Colonial American Jew, 1492–1776*, 3 vols. (Detroit, 1970), 106.

9. Isaac S. Emmanuel and Suzanne A. Emmanuel, *History of the Jews of the Netherlands Antilles*, 2 vols. (Cincinnati, 1970), 545, 561. See also 56–58.

10. Faber, *A Time for Planting*, 2.

11. By 1750 Amsterdam was home to some 16,800 Jews, about 8.5 percent of the city's population. Jonathan I. Israel, "The Republic of the United Netherlands until about 1750: Demographic and Economic Activity," in *History of the Jews in the Netherlands*, 100. At the same time, London had between 7,000 and 8,000 Jews. Endelman, *The Jews of Britain*, 41.

12. Emmanuel, *Precious Stones*, 60; David de Sola Pool, *Portraits Etched in Stone: Early Jewish Settlers, 1682–1831* (New York, 1952), 99.

13. Leo Hershkowitz and Isidore S. Meyer, eds., *Letters of the Franks Family (1733–1748)* (Waltham, Mass., 1968), 57.

14. E. M. Shilstone, *Jewish Monumental Inscriptions in the Burial Ground of the Jewish Synagogue at Bridgetown, Barbados* (New York, 1956), 163, 164. See also Emmanuel, *Precious Stones*, 381.

15. Pool, *Portraits Etched in Stone*, 250.

16. Hershkowitz, ed., *Wills of Early New York Jews*, 51. See also, for example, Jacob A. P. M. Andrade, *A Record of the Jews in Jamaica from the English Conquest to the Present Time* (Kingston, Jamaica, 1941), 179, 180, 181, 182.

17. Hershkowitz, *Wills of Early New York Jews*, 202.

18. Holly Snyder, "A Sense of Place: Jews, Identity, and Social Status in Colonial British America, 1654–1831" (Ph.D. diss., Brandeis University, 2000), 61.

19. Allen D. Candler, ed., *The Colonial Records of the State of Georgia* (Atlanta, 1907), 13:758 (December 1762); 17:573 (April 1770).

20. David T. Morgan, "Judaism in Eighteenth-Century Georgia," *Georgia Historical Quarterly* 58, no. 1 (Spring 1974): 46.

21. Malcolm H. Stern, ed., "The Sheftall Diaries: Vital Records of Savannah Jewry (1733–1808)," *American Jewish Historical Quarterly* 54, no. 3 (March 1965): 251, 255.

22. Pool, *Portraits Etched in Stone*, 58, 50. The gates of Savannah's Jewish cemetery were damaged in 1800 and 1812. William Pencak, *Jews and Gentiles in Early America, 1654–1800* (Ann Arbor, 2005), 170.

23. Pencak overstates the number of incidents of cemetery desecration. He writes, "In early America, the most visible, and violent, evidence of anti-semitism was the desecration of Jewish graveyards in each of the five major communities" (New York, Newport, Charleston, Savannah, and Philadelphia). Pencak, *Jews and Gentiles*, 2. Pencak's chapter on Charleston contains no description of cemetery desecration, and no evidence of such an attack exists. Pencak, personal communication, January 7, 2009. Furthermore, Pencak's evidence of the desecration of the Newport cemetery (106, 282, n. 47) is highly circumstantial. A typescript paraphrase of the account book of Aaron Lopez, the Newport congregation's treasurer, states, "The Sedakah [treasurer] secures a padlock for the burying place. Evidently the gate was kept locked to keep the kids out, and vandals out." Entry of March 27, 1775, Aaron Lopez account book, typescript at American Jewish Archives. The sentence that begins with "evidently" is the editorial addition of the transcriber. A similar claim about the Newport cemetery is made in Frederic Cople Jaher, *A Scapegoat in the Wilderness: The Origins and Rise of Anti-Semitism in America* (Cambridge, Mass., 1994), 112.

24. Jonathan D. Sarna, *American Judaism: A History* (New Haven, 2004), 10.

25. "Minute Book of the Congregation Shearith Israel," *Publications of the American Jewish Historical Society* 21 (1913): 67. For a similar rule in Curaçao, see Emmanuel and Emmanuel, *Jews of the Netherlands Antilles*, 233.

26. Jacob Rader Marcus, ed., *American Jewry: Documents, Eighteenth Century* (Cincinnati, 1959), 96, 186–87.

27. Stern, "Sheftall Diaries," 268–69.

28. Shilstone, *Jewish Monumental Inscriptions in Barbados*, vii–viii. Contrast with this the case of Sara Israel, a Protestant who converted to Judaism in Jamaica and was buried in 1753—without discriminations—in the Curaçao *beth haim*. Emmanuel, *Precious Stones*, 319–20.

29. Emmanuel and Emmanuel, *Jews of the Netherlands Antilles*, 203.

30. Ibid., 196. The second suggested discrimination seems especially likely in light of the widely heeded recommendations of the *Shulhan 'Aruk*.

31. Emmanuel, *Precious Stones*, 309.

32. Emmanuel and Emmanuel, *Jews of the Netherlands Antilles*, 200, 201.

33. Jonathan Schorsch, *Jews and Blacks in the Early Modern World* (New York, 2004), 237.

34. *Shulhan 'Aruk*, 377 § 1.

35. Suriname: Marcus, *Colonial American Jew*, 159. Curaçao statistics calculated from Emmanuel and Emmanuel, *Jews of the Netherlands Antilles*, 1036–45. A 1680 census of

Bridgetown, Barbados, demonstrated a similarly small number (3.0) of slaves per Jewish household. Richard S. Dunn, *Sugar and Slaves: The Rise of the Planter Class in the English West Indies, 1624–1713* (Chapel Hill, N.C., 1972), 107.

36. Marcus, *Colonial American Jew*, 160. This language has now absorbed more English elements and is called Saramaccan by linguists. John Holm, *Pidgins and Creoles*, 2 vols. (New York, 1989), 2:438–39.

37. Robert Cohen, *Jews in Another Environment: Surinam in the Second Half of the Eighteenth Century* (Leiden, Neth., 1991), 158.

38. Ibid., 161; Schorsch, *Jews and Blacks*, 252.

39. Cohen, *Jews in Another Environment*, 163. These quotations are from the mulattos' 1793 letter to the governor.

40. Ibid., 165–67. For more on Jewish deathways in Suriname, see Aviva Ben-Ur and Rachel Frankel, *Remnant Stones: The Jewish Cemeteries of Suriname* (Cincinnati, 2009).

41. Edith Gelles, "Dear Hertsey: The Letters of Abigail Levy Franks (1733–1748)," paper presented at the Omohundro Institute of Early American History and Culture Conference, New Orleans, June 2003, 20, n. 47.

42. Marcus, ed., *American Jewry*, 138.

43. Ibid., 107.

44. All quotations are from ibid., 140–41. Two documents contain the details of this story. The first is found in the minute book of the Philadelphia congregation and translated from broken English by Marcus. The second is a letter written in Yiddish to an Amsterdam rabbi asking for advice, translated by Marcus.

45. On Mordecai, see Edwin Wolf 2nd and Maxwell Whiteman, *The History of the Jews of Philadelphia from Colonial Times to the Age of Jackson* (Philadelphia, 1956), 128–31, 128 (well-learned). An incident similar to the Clava affair divided Curaçaon Jews so bitterly in 1750 that the dissident group created its own *beth haim* adjacent to the original one. See *They That Are Born Are Destined to Die and the Dead Brought to Life Again: The Jewish Cemetery Beth Haim Curaçao* (Curaçao, 2001), 16.

46. Hershkowitz, ed., *Wills of Early New York Jews*, 24, 67, 70, 140, 67.

47. Hershkowitz and Meyer, eds., *Letters of the Franks Family*, 66.

48. Ibid., 139. The translation appears on 139, n. 3.

49. Cohen, *Jews in Another Environment*, 60–61; Emmanuel, *Precious Stones*, 98.

50. Emmanuel, *Precious Stones*, 98–99.

51. Marcus, *Colonial American Jew*, 949.

52. Snyder, "A Sense of Place," 234–35.

53. Emmanuel and Emmanuel, *Jews of the Netherlands Antilles*, 1097; Emmanuel, *Precious Stones*, 92.

54. Hershkowitz, ed., *Wills of Early New York Jews*, 130, 140.

55. Marcus, ed., *American Jewry*, 120.

56. Will of David Bravo, June 1, 1749, and Will of Abraham Gonsales, November 1, 1753, "Jamaica Wills, 1692–1798," American Jewish Archives, Cincinnati.

57. L. Alvares Vega, *Het Beth Haim van Ouderkerk: Beelden van een Portugees-Joodse begraafplaats* (Amsterdam, 1975); D. Henriques de Castro, *Keur van grafstenen op de Por-*

tugees-Israëlische begraafplaats te Ouderkerk aan de Amstel (Ouderkerk aan de Amstel, Neth., 1999).

58. Richard D. Barnett and Philip Wright, *The Jews of Jamaica: Tombstone Inscriptions, 1663–1880* (Jerusalem, 1997), 3. See also the 1721 will of Daniel Lopez Laguna of Kingston, in Andrade, *Record of the Jews in Jamaica*, 180.

59. Barnett and Wright, *Jews of Jamaica*, 3.

60. Pool, *Portraits Etched in Stone*, 166; Shilstone, *Jewish Monumental Inscriptions in Barbados*, xxviii; Emmanuel, *Precious Stones*, 129.

61. See the markers reproduced in Pool, *Portraits Etched in Stone*.

62. The first two motifs are too numerous to cite. For angels, see Barnett and Wright, *Jews of Jamaica*, 49, 89.

63. Karl Watson, "The Iconography of Tombstones in the Jewish Graveyard, Bridgetown, Barbados," *Journal of the Barbados Museum and Historical Society* 50 (December 2004): 195–212, esp. 203–4.

64. *They That Are Born*, 3, 1.

65. Rochelle Weinstein, "Stones of Memory: Revelations from a Cemetery in Curaçao," in *Sephardim in the Americas: Studies in Culture and History*, ed. Martin A. Cohen and Abraham J. Peck (Tuscaloosa, Ala., 1993), 118, and illustrations pp. 88 and 107 (Naghtegael); 124 and illustrations pp. 86 and 125 (Ahasuerus).

66. Emmanuel and Emmanuel, *Jews of the Netherlands Antilles*, 1055; Shilstone, *Jewish Monumental Inscriptions in Barbados*, 17–18 (emphasis added).

67. Dickran Tashjian and Ann Tashjian, *Memorials for Children of Change: The Art of Early New England Stonecarving* (Middletown, Conn., 1974).

68. Barnett and Wright, *Jews of Jamaica*, 6, 105. A similar trajectory may be traced in New York. See Pool, *Portraits Etched in Stone*, 214, 215, 216, 218, for early "here lies the body of" stones, and 241, 246, 260, 262 for later "in memory of" stones.

69. Barnett and Wright, *Jews of Jamaica*, 86, 87.

70. Shilstone, *Jewish Monumental Inscriptions in Barbados*, 109. See also 110 for David Nunes Castello "of happy Memory."

71. Barnett and Wright, *Jews of Jamaica*, 33.

72. Castro, *Keur van grafstenen*, 33.

73. Pool, *Portraits Etched in Stone*, 192–93, 243.

74. Newport: *Publications of the American Jewish Historical Society* 21 (1913): 192; New York: Pool, *Portraits Etched in Stone*, 209; Curaçao: *They That Are Born*, 14.

75. Emmanuel, *Precious Stones*, 109.

76. Barnett and Wright, *Jews of Jamaica*, 57; Shilstone, *Monumental Inscriptions*, 11.

77. *Publications of the American Jewish Historical Society* 21 (1913): 207.

78. Ibid., 208.

79. Shilstone, *Monumental Inscriptions*, 146.

80. Pool, *Portraits Etched in Stone*, 225.

81. Barnett and Wright, *Jews of Jamaica*, 85.

82. Ibid., 9; Shilstone, *Monumental Inscriptions*, 110; *Publications of the American Jewish Historical Society* 21 (1913): 200.

CHAPTER 8

1. All these groups are more complex than the nomenclature in this chapter allows. More than half of "English" recruits were Scots and Irish. Stephen Brumwell, *Redcoats: The British Soldier and War in the Americas, 1755–1763* (Cambridge, 2002), 73–74. And many provincial companies had significant numbers of Indians in their ranks; in a few southeastern Connecticut companies over 20 percent of the men had "recognizably Indian names." Harold E. Selesky, *War and Society in Colonial Connecticut* (New Haven, Conn., 1990), 174. In this chapter, "Indians" refers not to these individuals who joined provincial companies but to members of autonomous groups allied with French or English forces.

2. Fred Anderson, *Crucible of War: The Seven Years' War and the Fate of Empire in British North America, 1754–1766* (New York, 2000), xx (quotation). See also Francis Jennings, *Empire of Fortune: Crowns, Colonies, and Tribes in the Seven Years' War in America* (New York, 1988); Peter Way, "The Cutting Edge of Culture: British Soldiers Encounter Native Americans in the French and Indian War," in *Empire and Others: British Encounters with Indigenous Peoples, 1600–1850*, ed. Martin Daunton and Rick Halpern (Philadelphia, 1999), 123–48; and James H. Merrell, *Into the American Woods: Negotiators on the Pennsylvania Frontier* (New York, 1999), esp. 225–301.

3. Ann M. Little highlights the similarities in the warrior culture of Indians, Englishmen, and Frenchmen in *Abraham in Arms: War and Gender in Colonial New England* (Philadelphia, 2007), esp. 2–3.

4. Daniel K. Richter, *The Ordeal of the Longhouse: The Peoples of the Iroquois League in the Era of European Colonization* (Chapel Hill, N.C., 1992), 37–38.

5. E. B. O'Callaghan, ed., *Documents Relative to the Colonial History of the State of New-York*, 11 vols. (Albany, N.Y., 1853–87), 7:135 (hereafter DCHNY). See also M. Pouchot, *Memoir upon the Late War in North America, Between the French and English, 1755–60*, trans. Franklin B. Hough, 2 vols. (Roxbury, Mass., 1866), 1:172; and Brumwell, *Redcoats*, 181.

6. Edward P. Hamilton, ed., *Adventure in the Wilderness: The American Journals of Louis Antoine de Bougainville, 1756–1760* (Norman, Okla., 1964), 333; DCHNY, 10:778. Although most often voiced by officers, the warrior ethic was also held by many common soldiers. See, for example, E. C. Dawes, ed., *Journal of Gen. Rufus Putnam* (Albany, N.Y., 1886), 54.

7. Little, *Abraham in Arms*, 194.

8. "The Journal of Dr. Caleb Rea, Written during the Expedition against Ticonderoga in 1758," *Essex Institute Historical Collections* 18 (1881): 113; Work Projects Administration, *Diary and Journal (1755–1807) of Seth Metcalf* (Boston, 1939), 8.

9. Peter P. Pratt, *Archaeology of the Oneida Iroquois*, vol. 1, Occasional Publications in Northeastern Anthropology, no. 1 (George's Mills, N.H., 1976), 137. This example is from the Marshall site, ca. 1630–50.

10. Alfred Procter James, ed., *Writings of General John Forbes relating to his Service in North America* (Menasha, Wisc., 1938), 236. See also "Journal of Sergeant Holden," *Massa-*

chusetts Historical Society Proceedings, 2d ser., 4 (1887–89): 392; Paul E. Kopperman, *Braddock at the Monongahela* (Pittsburgh, 1977), 271; and "Journal of Dr. Caleb Rea," 180.

11. Webster, ed., *Journal of Jeffrey Amherst*, 140; James, ed., *Writings of General John Forbes*, 233.

12. Captain John Knox, *An Historical Journal of the Campaigns in North America*, ed. Arthur G. Doughty, 3 vols. (Freeport, N.Y., 1970), 2:8; G. D. Scull, "The Montresor Journals," *Collections of the New York Historical Society* 14 (1881): 167. See also Webster, ed., *Journal of Jeffrey Amherst*, 64.

13. "Journal of Rev. John Cleaveland, June 14, 1758–October 25, 1758," *Bulletin of the Fort Ticonderoga Museum* 10 (1959): 215.

14. "Journal of Dr. Caleb Rea," 179.

15. See, for example, "Journal of Rev. John Cleaveland," 202; *Luke Gridley's Diary of 1757* (Hartford, Conn., 1907), 43; and "The Journal of the Rev. John Graham," *Magazine of American History* 8 (1882): 208, 210.

16. "Extracts from Gibson Clough's Journal," *Essex Institute Historical Collections* 3 (June 1861): 104. See also "Amos Richardson's Journal, 1758," *Bulletin of the Fort Ticonderoga Museum* 12 (1968): 278; "Journal of Col. Archelaus Fuller of Middleton, Mass., in the Expedition against Ticonderoga in 1758," *Essex Institute Historical Collections* 46 (April 1910): 216; Knox, *Historical Journal*, 1:258; Webster, ed., *Journal of Jeffrey Amherst*, 306; and Diary of Samuel Greenleaf, July 6 and September 19, 1756, Massachusetts Historical Society, Boston.

17. See especially Guy Frégault, *Canada: The War of the Conquest*, trans. Margaret M. Cameron (Toronto, 1969).

18. Louis Effingham de Forest, ed., *The Journals and Papers of Seth Pomeroy* (New York, 1926), 115. On plunder, see Fred Anderson, *A People's Army: Massachusetts Soldiers and Society in the Seven Years' War* (New York, 1984), 157–59.

19. Sylvester K. Stevens and Donald H. Kent, eds., *Journal of Chaussegros de Léry* (Harrisburg, Pa., 1940), 38. See also Little, *Abraham in Arms*, 15.

20. Hamilton, ed., *Adventure in the Wilderness*, 234. See also DCHNY, 10:304; and Joseph Nichols Military Journal, July 8, 1758, Huntington Library, San Marino, California.

21. T. H. Breen, *The Marketplace of Revolution: How Consumer Politics Shaped American Independence* (New York, 2004), 213–17.

22. Pouchot, *Memoir upon the Late War*, 1:112, n.1; "Amos Richardson's Journal," 275; and Hamilton, ed., *Adventure in the Wilderness*, 229.

23. James, ed., *Writings of General John Forbes*, 301–2. See also the elaborate funeral for Maj. Gen. James Wolfe, the romantic hero of the Battle of Quebec: *General Wolfe's Instructions to Young Officers* (London, 1768), iv–v.

24. Kopperman, *Braddock at the Monongahela*, 270; de Forest, ed., *Journals of Seth Pomeroy*, 119. See also, for example, "Extracts from Gibson Clough's Journal," 195; *Journals of the Hon. William Hervey, in North America and Europe, from 1755 to 1814* (Bury St. Edmunds, Eng., 1906), 170; Milton W. Hamilton, ed., "The Diary of the Reverend John Ogilvie, 1750–1759," *Bulletin of the Fort Ticonderoga Museum* 10 (February 1961): 364; and

Brian Leigh Dunnigan, *Siege—1759: The Campaign against Niagara* (Youngstown, N.Y., 1986), 59, 91.

25. Knox, *Historical Journal*, 1:139. On scarves, see Ralph Houlbrooke, *Death, Religion, and the Family in England, 1480–1750* (Oxford, 1998), 282–83; Gordon E. Geddes, *Welcome Joy: Death in Puritan New England* (Ann Arbor, Mich., 1981), 120–21.

26. Journal of Gideon Hawley, September 21, 1756, Gideon Hawley Papers, Congregational Library, Boston.

27. William A. Hunter, ed., "Thomas Barton and the Forbes Expedition," *Pennsylvania Magazine of History and Biography* 95 (October 1971): 452.

28. Pratt, *Archaeology of the Oneida*, 128–32; William A. Ritchie, *An Early Site in Cayuga County, New York: Type Component of the Frontenac Focus, Archaic Pattern* (Rochester, N.Y., 1945); Charles F. Wray et al., *The Adams and Culbertson Sites* (Rochester, N.Y., 1987), 255; and Charles F. Wray et al., *Tram and Cameron: Two Early Contact Era Seneca Sites* (Rochester, N.Y., 1991), 398.

29. Dean R. Snow, Charles T. Gehring, and William A. Starna, eds., *In Mohawk Country: Early Narratives about a Native People* (Syracuse, N.Y., 1996), 115.

30. Snow et al., eds., *In Mohawk Country*, 313. See also Daniel K. Richter, "War and Culture: The Iroquois Experience," *William and Mary Quarterly* 40 (October 1983): 529–30; Jon W. Parmenter, "La politique du deuil: Le factionalisme onontagué et la mort de Canasatego," *Recherches Amérindiennes au Québec* 29, no. 2 (1999): 23–35, esp. 31; and Helga Doblin and William A. Starna, eds., *The Journals of Christian Daniel Claus and Conrad Weiser: A Journey to Onondaga, 1750* (Philadelphia, 1994), 12–13, 17, 19.

31. Michael Cardy, ed., "The Iroquois in the Eighteenth Century: A Neglected Source," *Man in the Northeast* 38 (Fall 1989): 12. This anonymous source was likely written in the 1760s.

32. Ian K. Steele, *Betrayals: Fort William Henry and the "Massacre"* (New York, 1990), 149–85. See also David R. Starbuck, *Massacre at Fort William Henry* (Hanover, N.H., 2002).

33. Hal Langfur, "Moved by Terror: Frontier Violence as Cultural Exchange in Late-Colonial Brazil," *Ethnohistory* 52, no. 2 (Spring 2005): 258. See also Andrew Lipman, "'A meanes to knitt them togeather': The Exchange of Body Parts in the Pequot War," *William and Mary Quarterly* 65, no. 1 (January 2008): 3–28; and Richard White, *The Middle Ground: Indians, Empires, and Republics in the Great Lakes Region, 1650–1815* (New York, 1991), esp. 75–82.

34. Peter Silver, *Our Savage Neighbors: How Indian War Transformed Early America* (New York, 2008), 83 (sublime), 77 (barbarities).

35. *General Wolfe's Instructions*, 89; "Diaries Kept by Lemuel Wood, of Boxford," *Essex Institute Historical Collections* 19 (1882): 74. On brutal punishments, see Jennings, *Empire of Fortune*, 208–9; and Selesky, *War and Society*, 186–87.

36. DCHNY, 7:149.

37. Archives Nationals du Canada, Colonies, C11B, vol. 19, ff. 56v–57r. Bourville et LeNormand au Ministre, Louisbourg, 27 décembre 1737: "Le Chef des Sauvages de Lisle Royalle est mort ily a quelques jours il a ete enterré a Louisbourg, on luy a rendu

quelques bonneurs [honneurs?], M.r de Bourville ayant ordonné un detachment avec un Sergent pour Son Enterrement." Thanks to B. A. Balcom of Fortress Louisbourg for this citation.

38. Copy of George Croghan's report about Indian affairs from 1749 to 1755, Historical Society of Pennsylvania, Penn Manuscripts, Indian Affairs, vol. 1, p. 52 (viewed on microfilm, Francis Jennings et al., eds., *Iroquois Indians: A Documentary History of the Diplomacy of the Six Nations and their League*, July 10, 1755). Men and lads: *The Papers of Sir William Johnson*, 14 vols. (Albany, N.Y., 1921–65), 1:496, Croghan to Johnson, May 15, 1755 (hereafter PSWJ).

39. Charles Hamilton, ed., *Braddock's Deafeat: The Journal of Captain Robert Cholmley's Batman; The Journal of a British Officer; Halkett's Orderly Book* (Norman, Okla., 1959), 25, 47.

40. Ibid., 25.

41. W. W. Abbot, ed., *The Papers of George Washington*, Colonial Series (Charlottesville, Va., 1983), 1:121 (medals); 2:98, Washington to Andrew Montour, October 10, 1755 (brothers); 1:174, William Fairfax to Washington, July 5, 1754 (power and skill).

42. Hamilton, ed., *Braddock's Defeat*, 26, 47–48, 119.

43. Ibid., 48. Compare with the extraordinary burial of a sachem at Fort Hunter, February 23, 1761. Snow et al., eds., *In Mohawk Country*, 265.

44. For examples among non-Christians of eighteenth-century West Africa, see William Smith, *A New Voyage to Guinea* (London, 1744), 226; Ludwig Ferdinand Rømer, *A Reliable Account of the Coast of Guinea (1760)*, ed. Selena Axelrod Winsnes (Oxford, 2000), 184; and Selena Axelrod Winsnes, ed., *Letters on West Africa and the Slave Trade: Paul Erdmann Isert's Journey to Guinea and the Caribbean Islands in Columbia (1788)* (Oxford, 1992), 132.

45. I have not conclusively determined that Dinwiddie's godson was the same son of Scarouady who was killed on the Monongahela. But the circumstantial evidence is powerful: the godson, at age twelve, was one of only seven Indians who accompanied Washington on the Fort Necessity campaign. Abbot, ed., *Papers of George Washington*, 1:124, 125, n.10. It seems almost certain that this boy joined his father again the following year on Braddock's campaign.

46. Ibid., 1:123.

47. Hamilton, ed., *Braddock's Defeat*, 32, 51–52.

48. *Minutes of the Provincial Council of Pennsylvania* (Harrisburg, Pa., 1851), 6:589, August 22, 1755 (hereafter MPCP).

49. Paul A. W. Wallace, *Conrad Weiser: Friend of Colonist and Mohawk* (Philadelphia, 1945), 390–91.

50. MPCP, 6:524, August 15, 1755 (flesh and blood); PSWJ, 9:357 (Nica-anawa).

51. PSWJ, 9:80–81.

52. Ibid., 884.

53. Ibid., 10:254 (illustration on facing page).

54. "A Journal of an Expedition against Canaday by Moses Dorr Ensin of Capt Parkers Company," *New York History* 16 (1935): 457, 458, 459, 461.

55. PSWJ, 10:39 (fetching bark); "Journal of an Expedition against Canaday," 462–63 (alarm). All quotations about Kindaruntie's burial come from Dorr's journal.

56. William M. Beauchamp, ed., *Moravian Journals Relating to Central New York, 1745–66* (Syracuse, N.Y., 1916), 183. For archaeological evidence, see Charles F. Hayes III, *The Orringh Stone Tavern and Three Seneca Sites of the Late Historic Period* (Rochester, N.Y., 1965).

57. See, for example, Reuben Gold Thwaites, ed., *The Jesuit Relations and Allied Documents*, 73 vols. (Cleveland, 1896–1901), 8:259, 11:125, 24:173 (hereafter JR).

58. PSWJ, 10:69.

59. Online *Dictionary of Canadian Biography*, entry for Kak¢enthiony.

60. DCHNY, 10:233 (at Lachine); PSWJ, 9:117 (bear in tree); DCHNY, 6:967, 988 (support of English).

61. DCHNY, 7:133. For a thoughtful comparison between Iroquois condolence rituals and Anglo-American mourning practices, see Nicole Eustace, *Passion Is the Gale: Emotion, Power, and the Coming of the American Revolution* (Chapel Hill, N.C., 2008), 321–34.

62. Richter, *Ordeal of the Longhouse*, 32–33; Denis Foley, "The Iroquois Condolence Business," *Man in the Northeast* 5 (Spring 1973): 47–53, esp. 48; Matthew Dennis, *Cultivating a Landscape of Peace: Iroquois-European Encounters in Seventeenth-Century America* (Ithaca, N.Y., 1993), 79.

63. Jon W. Parmenter, *The Edge of the Woods: Iroquoia, 1534–1701* (East Lansing, Mich., 2010), introduction. The date when the Great League was founded is the subject of much dispute. Estimates range from roughly 1450 to 1600. An innovative and persuasive account puts the date at circa 1590 to 1605. Robert D. Kuhn and Martha L. Sempowski, "A New Approach to Dating the League of the Iroquois," *American Antiquity* 66, no. 2 (April 2001): 301–14, esp. 311.

64. The first condolence with the French is described in JR 27:247–67. On Delaware and Shawnee use of the condolence ritual, see William N. Fenton, *The Great Law and the Longhouse: A Political History of the Iroquois Confederacy* (Norman, Okla., 1998), 189. Ottawas likewise participated in condolences, including one at Michilimackinac in 1761. PSWJ, 3:538.

65. Fenton, *Great Law*; J. N. B. Hewitt, "The Requickening Address of the Iroquois Condolence Council," *Journal of the Washington Academy of Sciences* 34, no. 3 (March 1944): 65–85.

66. Parmenter, "La politique du deuil," 31.

67. PSWJ, 6:968.

68. Ibid., 2:442; Merrell, *Into the American Woods*, 265; Nancy L. Hagedorn, "'A Friend to Go Between Them': The Interpreter as Cultural Broker during Anglo-Iroquois Councils, 1740–1770," *Ethnohistory* 35, no. 1 (Winter 1988): 63. George Croghan participated in a condolence in Philadelphia in 1757, "which ceremony took up 3 days." MPCP, 7:466.

69. Fenton, *Great Law*, 449.

70. Ibid., 738–39.

71. DCHNY, 7:131. On the possible wampum shortage, see Fenton, *Great Law*, 738.

72. DCHNY, 7:133.

73. Fenton, *Great Law*, 736.

74. DCHNY, 7:133 (praying to god); SWJP, 12:305 (Peepy); JR, 53:215 (Pierron).

75. DCHNY, 7:134.

76. Fenton, *Great Law*, 739.

77. On Iroquois kinship, see Richter, *Ordeal of the Longhouse*, 19–22, esp. 21 on the relationship between kinship and mourning.

78. DCHNY, 7:134.

79. Ibid.

80. PSWJ, 2:127 (Mohawks); DCHNY, 7:151 (Oneidas).

CONCLUSION

1. David J. Silverman, *Faith and Boundaries: Colonists, Christianity, and Community among the Wampanoag Indians of Martha's Vineyard, 1600–1871* (New York, 2005), 236–45, quotations at 245; Daniel R. Mandell, *Tribe, Race, History: Native Americans in Southern New England, 1780–1880* (Baltimore, 2008), 80–85, 108–9; and Stephen C. Jett, "Cairn and Brush Travel Shrines in the United States Northeast and Southeast," *Northeast Anthropology* 48 (Fall 1994): 61–67.

2. Harald E. L. Prins, *The Mi'kmaq: Resistance, Accommodation, and Cultural Survival* (Fort Worth, Tex., 1996), 167–74.

3. Helen C. Rountree, *Pocahontas's People: The Powhatan Indians of Virginia through Four Centuries* (Norman, Okla., 1990), 175–76, 187–88.

4. Bruce G. Trigger, *The Children of Aataentsic: A History of the Huron People to 1660* (Montreal, 1976), 801–40.

5. Charles F. Hayes III, *The Orringh Stone Tavern and Three Seneca Sites of the Late Historic Period* (Rochester, N.Y., 1965), 5–7.

6. Ross W. Jamieson, "Material Culture and Social Death: African-American Burial Practices," *Historical Archaeology* 29, no. 4 (1995): 54. See also Albert J. Raboteau, *Slave Religion: The "Invisible Institution" in the Antebellum South* (New York, 1978), 230–31; Sylvia R. Frey and Betty Wood, *Come Shouting to Zion: African American Protestantism in the American South and British Caribbean to 1830* (Chapel Hill, N.C., 1998), 210–11.

7. Eli Faber, *A Time for Planting: The First Migration, 1654–1820* (Baltimore, 1992), 108–9 (Newport); Alan F. Benjamin, *Jews of the Dutch Caribbean: Exploring Ethnic Identity on Curaçao* (London, 2000), 102–3 (Curaçao).

8. Faber, *Time for Planting*, 122.

9. Philippe Ariès, *The Hour of Our Death*, trans. Helen Weaver (New York, 1981), chap. 10, quotation at 409 (emphasis added).

10. The best sources on these nineteenth-century changes are Gary Laderman, *The Sacred Remains: American Attitudes toward Death, 1799–1883* (New Haven, Conn., 1996); Martha V. Pike and Janice Gray Armstrong, eds., *A Time to Mourn: Expressions of Grief in*

Nineteenth-Century America (Stony Brook, N.Y., 1980); Robert V. Wells, *Facing the "King of Terrors": Death and Society in an American Community, 1750–1990* (New York, 2000), chaps. 3–6; and David Charles Sloane, *The Last Great Necessity: Cemeteries in American History* (Baltimore, 1991).

11. On the professionalization of death, see Laderman, *Sacred Remains*, chaps. 8 and 13; and James J. Farrell, *Inventing the American Way of Death, 1830–1920* (Philadelphia, 1980).

12. Charles Darwin, *The Voyage of the Beagle*, ed. H. Graham Cannon (London, 1959), 2. See also 161, 204, 211, 325, 354, 413, and 441.

13. Lewis H. Morgan, *League of the Ho-Dé-No-Sau-Nee or Iroquois*, ed. Herbert M. Lloyd, 2 vols. (1851; New York, 1966), 1:108–19, 166–70, 275–76 (Iroquois deathways); 166 (quotation). On Morgan's influence, see Adam Kuper, *The Reinvention of Primitive Society: Transformations of a Myth* (London, 2005), chap. 4.

14. Peter Metcalf and Richard Huntington, *Celebrations of Death: The Anthropology of Mortuary Ritual*, 2d ed. (New York, 1991), 30, 37.

15. Ariès, *Hour of Our Death*, chap. 12.

16. Amy Vanderbilt, *New Complete Book of Etiquette* (1952), quoted in Peter N. Stearns, *American Cool: Constructing a Twentieth-Century Emotional Style* (New York, 1994), 164. The classic analysis of death as a taboo subject in the mid-twentieth century is Geoffrey Gorer, *Death, Grief, and Mourning* (New York, 1965).

17. In 2007, the first full calendar year in which it was run by the National Park Service, the African Burial Ground received 68,085 visitors. The "large percentage" assertion is my own impressionistic observation. Park Ranger Douglas Massenburg, personal communication, August 14, 2008. See also the attention given to the African Burial Ground in countless black publications, for example, Eva M. Doyle, "The African Burial Ground," *Buffalo Criterion*, March 24–30, 2001, 2.

18. Elizabeth A. Fenn, "Honoring the Ancestors: Kongo-American Graves in the American South," *Southern Exposure* 13, no. 5 (September–October 1985): 42–47. See also Robert Farris Thompson, "Kongo Influences on African American Artistic Culture," in *Africanisms in American Culture*, ed. Joseph E. Holloway, 2d ed. (Bloomington, Ind., 2005), 283–325, esp. 305–18.

19. Karla F. C. Holloway, *Passed On: African American Mourning Stories* (Durham, N.C., 2002), 49–50.

20. Kathleen Fine-Dare, *Grave Injustice: The American Indian Repatriation Movement and NAGPRA* (Lincoln, Neb., 2002), 7.

21. http://www.nhpco.org/i4a/pages/index.cfm?pageid=5763, viewed March 10, 2009.

22. "Korea's Extraordinary Send-Offs for Ordinary People," *New York Times*, August 17, 2007; "In Japan, Buddhism May Be Dying Out," *New York Times*, July 14, 2008; "At Royal Balinese Funeral, Bodies Burn and Souls Fly," *New York Times*, July 16, 2008.

23. Adam Gopnik, "In the Mourning Store," *New Yorker*, January 21, 2008; James M. McPherson, "Dark Victory," *New York Review of Books*, April 17, 2008. See also Vincent Brown, *The Reaper's Garden: Death and Power in the World of Atlantic Slavery* (Cambridge, Mass., 2008).

INDEX

ACKNOWLEDGMENTS

DESPITE ITS GRIM subject, this book has been a pleasure to research and write, not least because its broad scope required me to rely on the expertise and generosity of countless friends and scholars. I am happy that I now have the opportunity to thank them properly.

More people than I can remember have offered copies of obscure primary sources, citations to unfamiliar secondary sources, and their own unpublished research. A partial list includes Howie Adelman, B. A. Balcom, Brandon Bayne, Nicholas Beasley, Aviva Ben-Ur, Kristen Block, Francis Bremer, Steve Bullock, Jose Buscaglia, Tom Chambers, Martina Will de Chaparro, Francis Rexford Cooley, Bob Cray, Natalie Davis, Jeff Donnelly, Rachel Frankel, Sylvia Frey, Marisa Fuentes, Chris Grasso, Jim Holstun, Mike Jarvis, Mima Kapches, Jason LaFountain, Jill Lepore, Mary Beth Norton, Bill Pencak, Miranda Spieler, Alan Taylor, and Karin Wulf. Rachel Wheeler and Doug Winiarski exceeded all requirements of friendship in the number and range of sources they sent me. When I was trying to track down hearts on coffin lids, I received valuable leads from Nick Bellantoni, Julian Litten, Adrian Miles, Elizabeth Peña, and Warwick Rodwell. Many people helped me obtain images and permissions, including Claude Ardouin, James Bellis, Jerry Handler, Elise Nienaber, John Spaulding, and John Warnock. At an early stage I profited from the skills of my crack research assistants, Michelle LaVoie, Chuck Lipp, and Gordon Marshall. Devon Reynolds translated a long Portuguese document into graceful English. Mike and Katie Vorenberg generously gave me a place to stay while I was researching gravestones in Newport. Thanks to all and to those I've unwittingly omitted.

This book has benefited immeasurably from the numerous people who have offered comments and suggestions for improvement. When the project was in an embryonic stage, probing questions after a talk at the University of California–Irvine decisively shaped the book's ultimate direction. Special thanks to Dave Bruce, Alice Fahs, and Karl Hufbauer. Soon thereafter I spent four weeks participating in a remarkable National Endowment for the Humanities summer seminar on death in America. Led by the inimitable David and Sheila Rothman, the seminar demonstrated the vibrancy of death studies. The endnotes in this book are stocked with sources I first encountered there. My fellow participants, a brilliant group of anthropologists, literary scholars, historians, and even clinicians, have become friends and co-conspirators in the field. I want to acknowledge the valuable intellectual exchanges I've had with, among others, Craig Friend, Jim Green, Gary Laderman, Steve Messer, Mark Schantz, Suzie Smith, and the late, lamented Gary Collison.

In subsequent years I presented my ideas at numerous conferences and seminars. At Indiana University's "Death in the Eighteenth Century" workshop I learned from a fascinating interdisciplinary group; many thanks to organizers Kon Dierks, Sarah Knott, and Dror Wahrman. I am grateful for the comments offered at conferences by Elsa Barkeley Brown, Jon Butler, Chuck Cohen, Nicole Eustace, Joyce Goodfriend, Karen Kupperman, Ben Mutschler, Robert Wells, and Mike Zuckerman. As I worked to publish my findings in journals, I received valuable suggestions from Scott Casper, Chuck Cohen, Denys Delâge, Jill Lepore, Joanne Meyerowitz, David Nord, Neal Salisbury, Gordon Sayre, Neil Schmitz, and Richard White.

Even more remarkable are those generous souls who have taken the time to read one or more (long) chapters and offer suggestions for improvement. If I have not always heeded their advice, it is due more to my stubbornness than to any deficiency in their comments. A special thanks to Kris Bross, Jim Green, Allan Greer, Mike Jarvis, Rich Newman, Alison Parker, Jon Parmenter, David Silverman, Holly Snyder, Kari Winter, Nancy Wolcott, and Joanne van der Woude. Cornell University's Americas Colloquium, led by Ed Baptist and Jon Parmenter, invited me at a crucial stage of my writing and gave me reams of suggestions. At the University of Pennsylania Press, Bob Lockhart has been an expert editor, reading chapters, suggesting revisions large and small, and instilling confidence. Kathy Brown and an anonymous reader took on the herculean task of reading the whole manuscript and offering detailed comments.

For the twelve years that I have worked on this book I have been fortunate to be a member of the University at Buffalo's history department. I cannot imagine a more collegial group of scholars. Almost everyone in the department has read portions of the book, but I have to single out the following former and present colleagues for their close readings of various chapters: Jorge

Cañizares-Esguerra, Roger Des Forges, Jon Dewald, David Gerber, Bruce Hall, Hal Langfur, Claire Schen, and Liana Vardi. The graduate students in my Fall 2004 and Spring 2008 seminars on the Atlantic world each read different chapters and bravely offered suggestions for improvements. In addition, UB's College of Arts and Sciences generously supported my research by granting me time off when I received external funding and by awarding me a Humanities Institute fellowship to help me complete the writing.

Other institutions have been generous with their financial support as well. The National Endowment for the Humanities underwrote a productive year of research and writing. Even more formative in my intellectual development, the Council for International Exchange of Scholars awarded me a teaching/research Fulbright fellowship in Barbados. For five months I taught U.S. history at the University of the West Indies in Cave Hill. I learned a great deal from my students, bright young Barbadians for whom an Atlantic perspective is second nature. I also learned a tremendous amount researching in several libraries and archives. Snorkeling in January wasn't bad either. Many thanks to Carol Robles at CIES for all her support. Among my many generous colleagues at UWI, I must thank John Mayo and Richard Goodridge for all their efforts to welcome me.

Four friends deserve special mention for the exchanges, intellectual and otherwise, that have helped make this a better book and me a happier person. Jorge Cañizares-Esguerra read a chapter with his characteristic incisiveness, but even more important, he has helped me expand my vision of the Atlantic world in years of memorable conversations. Hal Langfur has read several chapters and papers, always with his eye on the big picture. Every idea I serve up, he returns with intriguing spin. Rich Newman has been a true friend, reading everything I send his way, discussing ideas over a pint or two, and cheerleading for me when I need it. Jon Parmenter's fingerprints are all over this book. When I blindly ventured into his field at the very start of this project, he patiently answered questions and offered guidance. He has continued to read drafts and suggest sources for over a decade. I am deeply indebted to all.

My greatest debt, however, is to my family. My parents, Ray and Gail Seeman, taught me to love history and they continue to support me unquestioningly. My daughters, Nora and Maya Wolcott, have grown up with this book. Nora helped me research Newport gravestones, and Maya used her computer skills to help me format the book's images, but their real contributions have been as sources of joy and much laughter. Finally, my wife, Victoria Wolcott, to whom this book is dedicated. Not only does she read and critique everything I write with the acuity of a gifted historian but she has also maintained an enthusiasm for this project that has been inspiring. Who else would agree to spend a tenth-anniversary trip to Paris in Père Lachaise Cemetery? V, this is for you.

CPSIA information can be obtained
at www.ICGtesting.com
Printed in the USA
FSHW010121030122
87342FS